Complex Service Delivery Processes

Also available from ASQ Quality Press:

Outcomes, Performance, Structure: Three Keys to Organizational Excellence
Michael E. Gallery and Stephen C. Carey

Process Improvement Simplified: A How-to Book for Success in any Organization
James B. King, Francis G. King, and Michael W. R. Davis

Business Process Improvement Toolbox, Second Edition
Bjørn Andersen

Continuous Permanent Improvement
Arun Hariharan

The Quality Toolbox, Second Edition
Nancy R. Tague

Root Cause Analysis: Simplified Tools and Techniques, Second Edition
Bjørn Andersen and Tom Fagerhaug

The Certified Six Sigma Green Belt Handbook, Second Edition
Roderick A. Munro, Govindarajan Ramu, and Daniel J. Zrymiak

The Certified Manager of Quality/Organizational Excellence Handbook, Fourth Edition
Russell T. Westcott, editor

The Certified Six Sigma Black Belt Handbook, Second Edition
T.M. Kubiak and Donald W. Benbow

The ASQ Auditing Handbook, Fourth Edition
J.P. Russell, editor

The ASQ Quality Improvement Pocket Guide: Basic History, Concepts, Tools, and Relationships
Grace L. Duffy, editor

The ASQ Supply Chain Management Primer
ASQ's Customer-Supplier Division and J.P. Russell, editor

To request a complimentary catalog of ASQ Quality Press publications, call 800-248-1946, or visit our website at http://www.asq.org/quality-press.

Complex Service Delivery Processes

Strategy to Operations

Third Edition

Jean Harvey, PhD

ASQ Quality Press
Milwaukee, Wisconsin

American Society for Quality, Quality Press, Milwaukee 53203
© 2015 by ASQ
All rights reserved.
Printed in the United States of America
20 19 18 17 16 15   5 4 3 2 1

Library of Congress Cataloging-in-Publication Data
Harvey, Jean, 1950–
  Complex service delivery processes : strategy to operations / Jean Harvey. — Third
edition.
    pages cm
  Includes bibliographical references and index.
  ISBN 978-0-87389-916-1 (alk. paper)
  I. Service industries—Management. 2. Organizational effectiveness. 3. Industrial
efficiency. 4. Business planning. I. Title.
  HD9980.5.H375 2015
  658—dc23

                                                                2015020874

Publisher: Lynelle Korte
Acquisitions Editor: Matt Meinholz
Managing Editor: Paul Daniel O'Mara
Production Administrator: Randall Benson

ASQ Mission: The American Society for Quality advances individual, organizational, and
community excellence worldwide through learning, quality improvement, and knowledge
exchange.

Attention Bookstores, Wholesalers, Schools, and Corporations: ASQ Quality Press books, video,
audio, and software are available at quantity discounts with bulk purchases for business,
educational, or instructional use. For information, please contact ASQ Quality Press at
800-248-1946, or write to ASQ Quality Press, P.O. Box 3005, Milwaukee, WI 53201–3005.

To place orders or to request a free copy of the ASQ Quality Press Publications Catalog, visit our
website at http://www.asq.org/quality-press.

∞ Printed on acid-free paper

Quality Press
600 N. Plankinton Ave.
Milwaukee, WI 53203-2914
E-mail: authors@asq.org
ASQ **The Global Voice of Quality**™

To my wife and lifetime companion Carole, to my daughters Eve Julie and Marie-Claude, and to my grandchildren Charlotte, Malcom, Arthur, Nellie, Rosie, and Sofia, listed here in their order of appearance in my life, which they have incrementally transformed from a black-and-white feature into a multicolored, high-definition, 4-D, emotionally rich, and deeply satisfying one.

Table of Contents

List of Figures and Tables

List of Videos*

*All videos available for free viewing at http://videos.asq.org/complex-service-delivery-processes.

Major Abbreviations

CTC	Critical to cost
CTD	Critical to delivery
CTP	Critical to process
CTQ	Critical to quality
CTS	Critical to satisfaction
DCDV	Define, characterize, design, and verify
DMAIC	Define, measure, analyze, improve, and control
FAST	Functional analysis system technique
FMEA	Failure mode and effects analysis
IT	Information technology
PFD	Process flow diagram
PSDP	Professional service delivery process
PSO	Professional service organization
QFD	Quality function deployment
SDP	Service delivery process
SITOC	Supplier, input, transformation, output, customer
SMART	Specific, measurable, achievable, relevant, and time-bound
VAA	Value-added analysis
V2P	Value to processes. Refers to the model shown in Figures 4.8 and 4.9.

Foreword

The release of the third edition of *Complex Service Delivery Processes: Strategy to Operations* is great to see.

With the development of the Internet of Things, big data, cloud computing, and mobile internet, the whole world is moving toward intellectualization and a globalized network. In this new environment, the requirement for services is increasing, and people and organizations need more and more assistance and services, especially complex services. Many people and organizations lack the knowledge or skills that will lead them to reach their goals/targets; lack the proper tools, instruments, or facilities; or cannot get the proper network. Complex services offer the kinds of services that provide the proper methods to help them reach their goals/targets. This can be achieved through providing information and suggestions, developing activities, or providing the matching operation solutions.

Professor Jean Harvey's book is well known in this industry and is used as a reference book in many business schools and MBA or EMBA programs. Its second edition was published in Chinese in 2013, translated by the Shanghai Association for Quality and Shanghai Academy of Quality Management. In the meantime, Professor Harvey was invited to the Shanghai International Quality Services Forum and conducted a seminar for his book in Shanghai. His presentation was welcomed and received many positive comments from the enterprises and the quality management field.

The third edition includes videos on operational strategies that address case studies and technical analysis that meets the requirements of today's challenges. A major change of the third edition involves the direct link between the book and these videos. The whole series is 12 hours in duration and includes many case analyses, graphs (diagrams), and explanations of technology. These videos aid the reader in understanding the content of the book and serve as practical references, allowing for a larger readership and making the book suitable for online study. This is a fantastic book and is highly recommended regarding complex service and quality management.

I believe that the third edition of *Complex Service Delivery Processes: Strategy to Operations* will benefit all readers. Thanks, Professor Harvey, for sharing this great theory and practical approach to complex services.

Tang XiaoFen
President of Shanghai Association for Quality

Preface to the Third Edition

Reading is one way to get exposed to new ideas and engage the mind. When the goal is change, however, it is not enough. Face-to-face interaction with a coach or teacher is clearly a great complement to a book, but it is not always possible. Failing that, a video presentation is the next best thing. Soon after the second edition of the book came out, I started experimenting with video presentations to address questions and requests for clarifications that were often raised by readers. I got some professional help in setting up a small studio and getting started in the producing, editing, and uploading of video clips. Being self-sufficient, from ideation to distribution, is the only way to go nowadays, unless you dispose of a vast budget. Even if you do, it can be argued that eliminating intermediaries, with the unavoidable dilution, biases, and delays that they introduce, is a superior process, just as typing your own messages became best practice 25 years ago. The results, of course, lack the refinements and finishing touch that only experts can produce. Users gain much in the trade-offs, however, as they are exposed to the unadulterated message and spontaneity of the author.

This edition thus comes with an augmented value proposition: as you read and try to understand and experiment with the material, you are invited at various points to view video clips, lasting between 15 and 25 minutes, that will clarify, complement, illustrate, or go further than what you are reading. Experience has shown that this method works very well indeed. There is an additional benefit: if you come across an explanation that enlightens you on an issue that your organization has been struggling with, you can immediately share it with your colleagues and thereby generate some discussion and movement on these issues.

While this edition also includes many corrections and improvements, the addition of the videos constitutes a radical change in the learning experience over the previous editions. In total, there are 31 such videos, representing about 12 hours of viewing, which you can view at your convenience, pause and rewind at leisure, and share. The videos can be accessed at http://videos.asq.org/complex-service-delivery-processes. Your feedback, critique, and suggestions (info@complexservice delivery.com) are essential for the continuous improvement of this admittedly very imperfect material.

Preface to the First Edition

Professionals are some of the most rigorous and structured people in our advanced economies. They are trained to understand the relationships in a system of complex notions (such as the human body, the legal system, or the laws of physics) and to use different techniques and procedures to intervene and effect desirable changes for the benefit of a client. Yet, a single individual, competent as he may be, cannot single-handedly bring about the solutions that people and organizations need. For all their strengths, and probably because of their training, professionals are staunch individualists and often do not function well in teams, especially multidisciplinary ones. This situation is largely attributable to their lack of understanding of how organizations work. Ironically, they are unable to transfer the systems notions that have become second nature to them in their discipline to the discipline of management. This book means to facilitate such a transfer.

A process is a system of activities (together with the associated resources) that takes an input and transforms it into an output of greater value for a customer, and it is processes, not individual departments (or centers of expertise), that create value in an organization. Functions contribute to value creation through the part they play (that is, the tasks they perform) in processes. Processes create the benefits customers want by delivering the service or by making this delivery possible in one way or another. Treating a cancer, for instance, is a process. The input is the patient with an active cancer. The desired output is the patient with a cancer in remission. The transformation (treating the cancer) involves many centers of expertise, such as family medicine, radiology, medical oncology, surgical oncology, and radiation oncology, and value comes from the synergistic interaction of all these departments. Antagonism, or simply a lack of coordination, denies that value, in whole or in part.

Processes embody the know-how of an organization. Understanding the DNA of processes is the key to becoming a learning organization. The classical image of an organization—conveyed by the ubiquitous organizational chart—as a set of functions linked at the top is very convenient for professionals, as it reinforces their paradigm. It does not, however, reflect the reality of value creation. The reader will come to view an organization as a complex system of processes, crisscrossing the organizational chart as if there were no boundaries between functions. Nevertheless, boundaries do exist and are sometimes very hard to cross, thus producing the interference that can be so detrimental to the smooth operation of processes, and thus to value creation.

The process view of organizations is far from prevalent in organizations today. Professional service organizations may be the ones experiencing the most difficulties in managing processes, as professional "bubbles" create a multitude of rigid boundaries: professionals focus on their body of knowledge and on accepted practices in their field. All too often they pay little or no attention to the way their actions mesh with those of others in the generation of an overall result for a client. Compounded by the substantial power wielded by professionals—individually and as a group—this narrow perspective results in poor performance.

SERVICES AND PROFESSIONAL SERVICES

People need help, either because they lack the knowledge or skills required to achieve, by themselves, the result they want or because they do not have the right tools, facilities, or equipment. Perhaps they do not have access to the required network, or they would simply rather have help than do it alone. Help may take the form of providing information or advice, performing some of the required actions on the customer's behalf, performing some actions jointly with the customer, or assuming full responsibility for delivering the desired results (that is, providing a "solution").

The book focuses on complex services, that is, services sought because of a lack of knowledge or skills. Complex services fall into three categories: professional services, quasi-professional services, and technical services. Strictly speaking, we use the word "professional" to designate a university graduate in an applied field such as law, engineering, or architecture (excluding theoretical fields such as mathematics or philosophy). Professionals often belong to a professional regulating body, such as the American Board of Medical Specialties or a state board of public accountancy. We need such bodies because these services address very important needs and because the knowledge gap between the client and the professional makes the former vulnerable to malpractice. A constantly evolving body of knowledge, generally requiring compulsory continuing education, and a code of ethics guide professionals in their practice. They are subject to sanctions by the regulating body for any malpractice, including suspension or the withdrawal of practice privileges.

Quasi-professional services are similar in many ways to professional services, except that the service providers receive less training. Insurance brokers, real estate agents, radiology technologists, and electricians, for example, do not need a college education. They do need a permit, however, which can be revoked if they are caught breaking important rules. Their training is typically not at university level and may last between six months and two years. The knowledge and skills they acquire, linked as they are to specific legislation, procedures, or technologies, are typically shorter-lived than that of professionals. While the consequences of mistakes may be equally dramatic, the capabilities required to avoid them are more procedural than intellectual.

Finally, technical services involve helping the customer to use complex products or technology-based services. Computers, telecommunications systems, software, camcorders, internet access, and satellite dishes are examples of such products, and they are all critical to self-service. We exclude from this category the direct repair of complex products such as cars, aircraft, or home appliances, which are quasi-manufacturing activities, but we do include customer support activities (such as training car dealership technicians to service a new model, for example). Technicians providing such services are generally not responsible to a regulating body, but solely to their employers. People use these services in order to be able to perform complex tasks themselves (such as using a computer or a camcorder). Even though the knowledge gap may be very substantial here as well, the consequences of the service are often more immediate and easier to verify than would be the case for professional and quasi-professional services.

Why do these three categories of service deserve special attention?

- *Professional services*[1] are centered on the most important human needs, and it is very hard for the client to assess their quality, and thus to make sure he is in competent hands. As mentioned earlier, the knowledge gap between provider and client gives the former power over the latter and, like any power, entails the potential for abuse.

- As a class of workers, professionals share a number of characteristics, such as autonomy and independence, that separate them from other categories of workers and require a different management approach.

- Professionals represent an increasingly high proportion of the workforce in industrialized countries, as machines perform many tasks that add less value (such as many manufacturing tasks), and the tasks that remain are rapidly moving to developing countries. Using these machines, however, requires assistance, a sector of the economy that is growing very fast (and, incidentally, one that is not immune to international outsourcing, as information technology [IT] increasingly facilitates delocation).

- Finally, the management literature has focused excessively on the process of, for example, making a hamburger, to the detriment of processes that create more value, such as the counseling of a dysfunctional couple or helping someone fend off a liability suit. Professional services in general, and professional service delivery processes in particular, remain to this day a blur in the literature—a shortfall that needs to be remedied.

This book is also concerned with the many organizations that provide services requiring a mixture of professional and other services to produce the results that customers or clients want. Hospitals and banks, for instance, cover the spectrum of types of services. These organizations face the added challenge of managing the often-turbulent interface between professional services, technical services, and other services. We include internal services as well, such as those offered by the legal or engineering department within an organization.

TARGET AUDIENCE

We have written this book for professionals, quasi-professionals, and technical workers laboring in all spheres of human endeavor, from law to medicine, from accounting to engineering, who are involved or are interested in taking part in managing their businesses. Most professionals, even those who do not care about management, can benefit from the book. Indeed, most do assume some level of management responsibility through such activities as the following:

- Giving instructions to quasi-professionals, technicians, or clerical workers, or coordinating the activities of service providers of all kinds

- Assuming a responsibility for practice development, their take-home income depending on how good they are at it

- Managing their own one-person business

- Managing what customers do (customers are very much a part of the service delivery process)

Processes play a vital role in all these activities. The notions, methods, and tools presented in this book offer the reader a perspective on her work that she most likely never envisaged and that could be a source of insights and a lever for innovation.

STYLE

For the professional or manager interested in learning more about how the process view applies to his own environment, we provide hands-on end-of-chapter exercises. One's own organization and environment constitute the proving ground for the material presented in each chapter. The exercises are structured in such a way that the new theory added by each chapter can be immediately applied to work done in earlier chapters, giving the reader an opportunity to apply the theories she has just learned, and so transform knowledge into know-how. Thus, a global picture gradually emerges, as early chapters paint a broad-brush picture of the connection between strategy and processes and later chapters delve into the specifics of designing and improving processes in a professional service environment.

We do not shy away from theory, but illustrate it abundantly with examples. The case studies presented in the book fall into three categories: actual businesses (in those cases, the company is identified), personal situations to which the author was a party, and generic (thus fictitious) situations built from a composite of the author's general experience. While we broadly assume throughout the book the context of a for-profit organization, much of the discussion is readily transferable to nonprofit organizations. Indeed, the latter also have customers to satisfy, employees to keep happy, and shareholders looking for the "biggest bang for the buck," whatever the socially desirable "bang" (healthy population, low crime rate, socially healthy families, safe kids, and so on) may be. Such organizations, as illustrated by the health and social services examples used extensively in this book, are also competing for funds with other service providers, and achieving superior performance is just as important to them as it is for private sector organizations.

We also draw on a broad spectrum of complex services such as legal, financial planning and management, consulting, and real estate services. We first illustrate complex notions with simple examples—often drawn from the personal sphere (processes occur in the home as well) or simple services (such as restaurants or airports)—before adapting them to the more intricate reality of professional services.

Professionals evolving in organizations of all sizes—ranging from the one-person firm to the huge professional bureaucracies that constitute large hospitals—will discover that the process view of the organization is universal, and they can all benefit from it.

Senior executives who want to explore the potential of a process-based strategic initiative in their organization will find it worthwhile to share the book with their associates and compare notes on the end-of-chapter exercises. While this is not a "cookbook," it is detailed enough and specific enough to allow experimentation to take place, as well as vetting of the principles and tools of process-based management in one's own environment, and shaping of an operational change initiative. Of course, large organizations should use a consultant to guide them through such an undertaking. Having experienced the book, however, they will be in a better position to select suitable consultants and stay in the driver's seat throughout the initiative.

NOTE

1. A term used loosely throughout the book to refer to the three categories of complex services, unless otherwise specified.

Acknowledgments

The author has tested all the methodologies and techniques presented in this book. He cannot, however, claim them all to be his own. The content of this book has evolved over more than three decades of research, teaching, and consulting after obtaining a PhD in management science. It has been influenced—one way or another—by every business with which he interacted during those years as a consultant or researcher, by every executive that has attended an in-house seminar or executive MBA program (thousands, in more than 10 countries around the globe), and by every book and article that he has read during those years of practice. This is what we generally call *experience*. He cannot possibly give credit to all of them, nor name them all. However, he does most sincerely thank them all. The result is the author's own paradigm, and any limitations or errors that it may contain are his alone.

Part I

The Conceptual Framework Linking Strategy and Operations

In this part of the book we define many notions such as process, value, and strategy. We illustrate these notions with many examples, relate them to one another, and weave them together. Chapter 1 brings out the nature and importance of rigorous execution. Chapter 2 discusses value for customers, employees, and shareholders. The discussion leads to decisions about quality and positioning. Chapter 3 explores all aspects of processes from conceptual, operational, and organizational points of view. The key role of processes in learning, and thus in the creation of sustainable competitive advantage, is highlighted. Chapters 4 and 5 put together the preceding elements, using coherence, profit leverage, and dual positioning as adjustment variables, to ensure the viability of the business model.

1

Toward Value and Strategic Advantage through Rigorous Execution

If you keep hearing (or worse, repeating) "I want results, no matter how" in your organization, you work in an organization that does not learn. Focusing on the "how" is the key to learning.

In the learning organization, the basics of rigor, logical validity, evidence-based actions, and discipline combine with creativity and innovation to make things work the first time and to continuously find and implement better ways to compete.

After presenting the execution challenge, we illustrate it by comparing three situations related to transportation. In section 1.3, we present various features that distinguish organizations that learn from those that suffer from a learning disability. After discussing process management issues in complex services, we conclude the chapter by presenting the organization of the material in this book.

1.1 THE EXECUTION CHALLENGE AND THE NEED FOR RIGOR

In *From Poverty to Prosperity* (Kling and Schulz 2009), the authors argue that the major factor that separates fast-developing countries from the one that stagnates is "software." In economics 1.0—as they call traditional economic analysis—labor, land, and equipment (capital) are the factors of production that determine productivity and growth. Call that the hardware. In economics 2.0, the software—or operating system, to use a computer analogy—is the real discriminating factor. It is the "recipe" for how to use these resources, or "protocols." Some authors call them "routines." In this book, we prefer the word "process." This includes shared ways of doing things based on customs, technology, shared mental models, shared values, social norms, laws, and regulations. Some of these protocols are written and explicit, while others, no less important, are implicit and deeply ingrained in the social fabric of society itself.

The discriminating factor between fast-growing and merely surviving organizations is of a similar nature. Protocols smooth out and speed up interactions between individual and organizational units while leaving the necessary elbow room where it is required. Some interactions merely require discipline, such as

3

showing up on time for the game when you play basketball, while others, like the timely pass or the successful fake, require a combination of experience, practice, intuition, judgment, strategic thinking, opportunism, team spirit, and flawless execution.

Larry Bossidy (General Electric, Honeywell, Allied Signal) and Ram Charan make the point that many organizations fail not because they had a bad strategy, but because they executed poorly (Bossidy and Charan 2002). Execution, they say, is a discipline in its own right. Its practice is neither glamorous nor spectacular. It is not rocket science, either, but it does involve science and rigor. Interpreting facts, planning experiments, measuring results, and managing feedback, control, and learning loops are all predicated on rigor. This does not preclude intuition, spontaneity, and even improvisation at times. The scientific method, however, is one of the roots of the foundations of learning. Leadership and "people processes," as Bossidy and Charan call them, are complementary roots. In a study, 11 companies that crossed the chasm from being merely good to becoming great companies (tripling their already good stock return and sustaining this for 15 years) were matched to comparable companies that had failed to become great companies, and key differences were isolated (Collins 2001). Collins found that companies that became great stood out for the disciplined people they hired, the disciplined thought process they nurtured, and the disciplined actions they undertook. He defines discipline in this context as "freedom (and responsibility) within a framework."

In a sequel, Collins (2009) looks at how some great companies lost their grip and fell into irrelevance, while others, even after facing major turbulence, recovered and found a path out of their predicament. Arrogance, he finds, is often a factor that triggers wrongheaded decisions or lack of response to ominous events. Organizations that previously excelled at facing hard facts become complacent in their interpretation of unpleasant data, as they take their dominance for granted. Their perception of reality becomes warped by their unwavering belief that they are unbeatable. When the evidence becomes overwhelming, they return to reality with a shock. But it is often too late in the game. They then lose sight of their core strength, succumb to panic, change leadership, and go for the "Hail Mary" pass, grasping at any straw. In short, success can breed arrogance and loss of the very discipline that lies at its root.

During the last two centuries, science has triggered a great leap forward for humanity. During this period, our knowledge has grown incalculably, and with it the complexity of what professionals and technical workers do. This in turn has triggered specialization, as it is not humanly possible for anyone to single-handedly achieve the theoretical and practical mastery (knowledge and know-how) of the various disciplines required to deliver solutions at the level of quality and reliability clients have come to expect. Therefore, fully addressing clients' needs requires the coordinated intervention of many such specialists, each with a deep knowledge of his or her narrow field and a very limited understanding of what the other specialties do. This is often a source of contempt for the other, thus raising barriers between professionals on whose very cooperation rests the successful outcome sought by the client.

The challenges of coordination have thus grown exponentially. While technology has opportunely come to the rescue, it brings to the task its own flaws, challenges, complexity, and risks as well. Dr. Atul Gawande (2009) makes this vivid in his description of the tragic case of a three-year-old Austrian girl walking in a park with her parents. While the parents were momentarily distracted, the little girl ran onto a (barely) frozen pond and fell through the ice. Despite the parents' desperate efforts, she had spent 30 minutes underwater by the time she was rescued. The process of trying to save her life involved the coordinated work of a host of specialists (rescue personnel, emergency technicians, surgical team, perfusionists, and various medical specialists) using a battery of complex equipment (heart-lung bypass machine, artificial lung system, mechanical ventilator, and CT scan to name but a few). The story ends well: the little girl was resuscitated (that's not an exaggeration) and fully recovered.

What's remarkable in this story is that, even though the hospital had acquired all this equipment two years earlier with such cases in mind, until that case it had always failed at saving any victim's life, essentially because of the challenges involved in managing such extreme complexity. To improve the flow of the process and avoid errors (two notions that will be explored in this book), it had learned from its previous failures and finally devised a simple mechanism (part of a protocol, routine, or process) that made it possible to save the little girl's life, and others thereafter: a checklist. For all the years of study and research, as well as millions of dollars in investment, it was the simple device of ensuring that all the required steps are performed, in the right sequence, in the right way that "debugged the software" and made the difference between life and death. The reader, however, should not underestimate the challenges involved in developing, implementing, and sustaining the use of such checklists. The hard stuff is the soft stuff.

This book is about the development, implementation, maintenance, and continuous improvement of the "software" that seamlessly glues together individual human action in nimble value chains.

1.2 WHETHER YOU ARE ROLLING, FLYING, OR SAILING, GOOD PROCESSES ARE REQUIRED FOR A SMOOTH RIDE

In this section we use three transportation-related events to illustrate how investment in process mastery can allow organizations to rise and respond successfully to apparently insurmountable challenges, and how failure to do so can go undetected for a long time and eventually lead to disaster. These episodes are in the public domain and thus well documented. Together they span a century and occur on land, in the air, and on the sea.

We first present two events taking place in the Southwest and the Northeast of the United States some 20 years apart. One was an unmitigated disaster, and the other one an unmitigated success. Let us first consider the specifics of each situation and then proceed to compare them to isolate lessons. Finally, to gain some further perspective, we go back in time to discuss an event that took place almost a century ago.

1.2.1 Southern Pacific's Extra 7551 East[1]

As Southern Pacific's Extra 7551 East train reached the crest of the pass at 7 a.m. on May 12, 1989, 24 miles away and 2000 feet up from San Bernardino, California, its speed was 25 mph and everything was fine for engineers Frank Holland, operating the four head-end locomotives, and Lawrence Hill, operating two locomotives at the back of the train hauling 69 cars loaded with a mineral. However, while neither of them had a complete picture of this, there had been a number of flaws in the upstream process that led them to that point. These flaws constituted an unknown liability (a "bubble") that would prove fatal in the downstream process as they reached the curve at the bottom of the long descent toward San Bernardino:

1. The two engineers had never worked together, had not planned the trip together, and had had very little communication during the trip.

2. The shipper had not entered the weight of the mineral, assuming that Southern Pacific would know it (it did not).

3. Holland was unable to reach the shipper to confirm the weight, so he used his best guess. He came up with a weight of 6150 tons for the convoy, well short of the actual weight of 9000 tons.

4. Holland could not start one of his four locomotives. Lacking clear instructions about what to do in this situation, he left it on the train.

5. Hill learned that one of his two locomotives had no dynamic braking capability, but he assumed that this had already been reported.

6. Unbeknownst to either man, another locomotive had only intermittent power.

7. The company's directions to engineers on downhill braking procedures were inadequate.

Taken individually, none of these events appears to be a fatal flaw. Taken together, however, they would create a downstream situation where critical processes that had always worked were now out of control. Upstream, they reflect a "good enough" or "so what" attitude in action that appears to have been endemic in the organization.

   As the train gathered speed, Holland gradually applied braking power. After a brief stabilization of its speed, the train started to accelerate again. He applied some more, with the same effect. He did not start to panic until the train reached 45 mph in a straightaway. By that time Hill was really worried. He applied all the pneumatic braking power he had, without talking to Holland. Coordination between the two engineers was nonexistent as they did not have a game plan (braking procedures were not clear), did not proceed from the same fact sheet, and had not established an operational working relationship. When the train reached 90 mph (the recorder does not register beyond that), there was no backup plan. Maydays were sent and the engineers braced for the inevitable disaster. The train derailed in the curve. Four people died in the crash, and houses in a nearby residential development were destroyed. The damage was estimated at $12 million. The two engineers miraculously survived. No act of God was involved here, only poorly executed steps of men acting with little forethought, rigor, and coordination. Most of the blame does not fall on the two operators, however. It lies with the leaders of the organization, their lack of vision, and their poor understanding of the discipline of execution. The bubble was waiting to burst, and, as is often the case, it did so in a situation where the organization's processes were under maximum stress.

1.2.2 US Airways Flight 1549

Just two minutes after taking off from La Guardia Airport at 3:27 p.m. on January 15, 2009, the Airbus A320-214, under Captain Chesley Sullenberger and flown by first officer Jeffrey Skiles, hit a flock of Canada geese. The aircraft, headed for Charlotte, North Carolina, with 155 people on board, was hit in the windshield, and both engines swallowed one or two birds and simultaneously shut off. The two very experienced pilots were flying together for the first time. They had become an operational team while going through the pre-takeoff checklist, allowing them to verify the interoperability of their skill sets and their ability to function as a team at the command of their aircraft. They kept their cool as they peered through the blood-stained windshield in the suddenly frighteningly silent cockpit.

Sullenberger immediately took over (from the cockpit voice recorder— Sullenberger: "my plane," Skiles: "your plane") from his copilot and started assessing the situation and his options as Skiles began to go through a three-page checklist to try to restart each engine in turn. Although they were still too low to reach any runway, they had enough height to clear George Washington Bridge. The Airbus's fly-by-wire technology somewhat facilitated the handling of the aircraft in these unusual circumstances. There is, however, no substitute for the cool-headed thinking and perfect execution that come only with repeated training, drills, and experience, even for a cockpit crew that had met just 30 minutes earlier.

The simple instructions—"Brace for impact"—given 90 seconds before ditching were enough for the flight attendants to go through a well-rehearsed lifesaving routine. Their familiarity with the procedure allowed them to perform quickly and calmly, thereby avoiding panic setting in among the untrained passengers. The captain's training led him to pick a location on the Hudson River close to operating boats, allowing for a quick rescue. Getting the flaps out at the right time and hitting the "ditching button" to close openings that would otherwise let the water in were critical actions that were performed "by the book."

Evacuating 155 very scared passengers is certainly not something that the three flight attendants could have improvised. Here, again, a well-designed protocol, drilled in through repeated training, kicked in when it was required. The plane was fully evacuated in three minutes—by the book again—in standard time. All passengers and crew survived, and there were only five serious injuries. This was one of the most successful ditchings of an airliner in history. Thank goodness for a good book—shared, trusted, and well understood by all—when it is time to act quickly and synchronously.

1.2.3 Comparing the Two Events

It does not take anything away from the skills and human qualities of Captain Sullenberger to observe that flight 1549 did not simply avoid disaster because of the lone heroic actions of a superman. It did so because of the disciplined actions of a team of well-trained, experienced, level-headed employees, acting responsibly according to procedures, using equipment designed and maintained with just such an event in mind, under able leadership. His decision to ditch in the Hudson was his to make and to assume. He did not wait for instructions to proceed. Indeed, this would most probably have meant disaster, as Sullenberger himself had the best information to assess the situation and, with his team, was in the best position to execute it. His actions were totally in line with his training and best flying practice. The coordination system with his teammates and the air traffic controllers never broke down. In fact, the "framework" responded perfectly to the full and appropriate exercise of his freedom. Nothing else could have produced such a positive outcome.

The single most important difference between the two situations is that much effort and resources have been dedicated over the years at US Airways, Airbus, the Federal Aviation Administration (FAA), and the National Transportation Safety Board (NTSB), among others, toward building and continuously improving a quality system, that is, a system to ensure that desired customer outcomes are delivered reliably and flawlessly, even in the face of rare events. This investment and the resulting quality culture allowed all the players involved to communicate clearly and economically, to act effectively, and to coordinate seamlessly, even though they had never worked together prior to that day. This was obviously not the case at Southern Pacific at the time. The NTSB's detailed investigation of the event, however, provided Southern Pacific with a wealth of information about how to avoid a recurrence. A failure from which you learn is a step forward toward becoming a better organization. However, this is learning the hard way, and it comes too late to do any good for the four victims.

Designing and operating a quality system requires a thorough understanding of the nature of the task, of what could go wrong (failure modes), and of the best way to deal with such emergencies. Again, this does not require a stroke of genius, but dedicated, rigorous efforts over time to think risks through, learn from variations and defects, and use these lessons to continuously improve processes. Taking resources away from daily operations—with the immediate pain that this inflicts on the organization—to dedicate them to this long-term task, with no immediately visible benefits, requires vision, wisdom, strength, and leadership. This is nothing new, as the next example illustrates.

1.2.4 Going Back Farther: The Trip of the *James Caird*[2]

On April 24, 1916, the *James Caird* left Elephant Island near the South Pole with a crew of six, leaving the remaining 22 members of the British expedition stranded on the island waiting for the relief that the *Caird* would hopefully send back when it reached the Norwegian whaling station on South Georgia Island, some 1300 kilometers away. The boat was skippered by E. H. Shackleton, who had organized and led the expedition that set out to perform the first land crossing of the Antarctic continent. Facing a particularly harsh winter, their ship, the *Endurance*, had been caught in the ice pack that had formed, and as Shackleton put it, "What the ice gets, the ice does not surrender." In the middle of the Antarctic winter, the boat had indeed been crushed by the ice, leaving the crew stranded on the ice pack, hundreds of miles from the nearest land.

Through wonderful execution allowed by well-honed reflexes and splendid resolve, the crew had succeeded in escaping the melting ice pack the following summer and reaching Elephant Island on three lifeboats, with no loss of life. Reaching South Georgia Island before the new winter set in was their only hope of survival. The success of the expedition hinged on the hardware (or infrastructure) and the software, including processes and the people factor.

One of the lifeboats was improvised by the team's carpenter as best he could with salvaged material: a combination of naval carpentry processes and improvisation upgraded the infrastructure to the level required for the task. Shackleton picked his crew carefully (people processes), making sure he had all the expertise on board that he would need (process mastery). The crew managed several vital processes, including:

- Navigation—taking a sight with the sextant, dead reckoning, and plotting a course

- Sailing—"reading" the sea, the ice, and the weather; steering the ship; and giving instructions to set sails, trim sales as required, assess progress, adjust to conditions, foresee what's coming, and correct course

- Bailing the water to keep the boat afloat

A flaw in any of these processes would mean certain death for the six men and their mates waiting for rescue on Elephant Island.

Consider navigation error. Because of the distance, a very small error when taking a sight or dead reckoning would mean missing South Georgia Island, sailing endlessly in the South Atlantic, and running short of drinking water within a few days. Calculating the angle of the sun with the horizon using a sextant requires some stability. In a seven-meter lifeboat navigating the most turbulent sea on earth under a cloudy sky, performing this with the required precision is an amazing feat. To reduce variation to a tolerable level when taking a sight, for instance, Captain Frank Worsley developed an approach whereby two fellow crew members bracing him on both sides, like bookends, would stabilize him at the hip. To further reduce measurement error, they took several readings until the mean reading stabilized. Such meticulous focus on reducing variation in critical processes is a distinctive feature of high-performance organizations.

Shackleton also paid careful attention to the people factor, that is, the human qualities and compatibility of character among the crew, as the men had already lived in proximity and depended on each other for survival for the last 14 months since they had left civilization. He monitored the crew's situation on board continuously and took appropriate measures, such as having hot drinks prepared for everyone, when he detected a human situation that needed to be dealt with.

They successfully landed the craft on South Georgia Island after a 16-day voyage that stretched the limits of human endurance. As they were on the wrong side of the island, they still had to cross unexplored Antarctic terrain by foot through crevasses, cliffs, glaciers, blinding snowstorms, and treacherous ice. They reached the whaling station totally exhausted on May 21, 1916. "Who the hell are you?" asked the incredulous Norwegian station chief as the men appeared out of nowhere. "My name is Shackleton" was the bearded man's simple reply to the at-first incredulous, then highly emotional reaction of the first witnesses of one of the most phenomenal feats of exploration and navigation in history.

While we may be better able nowadays to name the various phenomena involved in high-performance processes, they are nothing new. From Phoenician sailors to Roman engineers and medieval artisans, human history is about getting better at producing results. The path of improvement, obviously, has been anything but linear, with numerous regressions and forgetting, and plenty of superstition meshed with the growing knowledge and know-how. What is different today is the complexity of the world. With globalized markets, instantaneous communication and access to data, phenomenal computing capability, the need for quick response and nimbleness, and strong international competition, cooperation, and coopetition, managing the ingredients of high performance presents new challenges and requires more method.[3] The goal, however, is not to do better than Shackleton's *Endurance* crew did in its time. It is in fact to try to do as well as they did, but in a world that is infinitely more complex.

The three situations just described highlight the importance of having a good game plan that adapts as the game unfolds, good infrastructure, the right people, processes, teamwork, commitment, and rigor. Clearly, the new "hardware" available today makes it possible to deal with complexity. It is only a qualifier, however, since any organization can acquire it. The differentiator lies in the "software"—the way the infrastructure is used and deployed to systematically create more value for the organization's customers, that is, to become a learning organization. This is the subject of the next section.

1.3 THE DIMENSIONS OF THE LEARNING ORGANIZATION

The learning organization has strategic, organizational, and operational dimensions. We discuss these in turn.

1.3.1 Strategic Considerations: Leadership and a Good Game Plan Based on Capabilities

Reaching the South Pole involved raising the necessary funding; planning the expedition in detail; assembling the right people, the proper material, and provisions; transporting crew, equipment, and provisions by sea to Antarctica, as close as possible to the destination; crossing the continent to the pole; coming back to the boat; and sailing back home. Any flaw in the initial steps could prove fatal later on in the expedition. Thus, good planning is crucial. Being willing and able to adjust the plan as reality unfolds in unexpected ways is no less critical a skill. It requires getting the facts right, taking a hard look at them no matter how much they differ from what we expected to see (or wished we would see), exploring options creatively, and making choices soundly based on clear priorities and well-understood capabilities.

It is the task of leaders to elaborate such plans, frame them into a compelling vision, and get everyone to understand it, buy into it, and then contribute to making it happen. Robert Falcon Scott's death with his crew in 1912 while trying to make his way back from the South Pole was a source of moral inspiration for the Britons. It was not an example of good planning, however. While the expedition involved many unknowns and great challenges, it was clear that being adept at managing dog sleighs and skiing in difficult terrain were critical capabilities for the success of the expedition. Yet Scott failed either to see the importance of these capabilities or to appreciate the extent to which his team had (or lacked, as it were) the required skills and what it would require to acquire them. Yet, his plan assumed those capabilities. Unfortunately, there is no good way to execute a bad plan. Scott's rival Roald Amundsen laid out detailed plans based on his team's mastery of these core processes. He reached the South Pole on December 14, 1911, 35 days before Scott. Scott and his team never made it back.

The success of complex projects, like the success of ongoing organizations (see Box 1.1), value networks (see Box 1.2), and societies (see section 1.3.2.1) as a whole, is predicated on the mastery of a critical set of interrelated processes. "People processes" (Bossidy and Charan 2002, pp. 22–27) such as recruiting people with the right skill set and the right mind-set, sharing common mental frameworks, and keeping them motivated and working harmoniously together are among these. Processes are shared, clearly defined, and well-controlled ways of doing things together (see Chapter 3 for a detailed discussion). They are inseparable from the discipline required to carry them through, repeatedly. Daily operation of these processes requires close monitoring, early detection of defects, quick correction, learning, and improvement. The challenge for organizations is to design logical chains of commitment, feedback mechanisms, and process management structures that ensure such quick mutual adjustment, adaptation, and learning.

1.3.2 Organizational Considerations: Commitments

As a customer trying to resolve an issue with a service provider, you should first try to deal with someone who is really trying to resolve it. This is easy to ascertain. Is the person actually listening to me or is her mind somewhere else? Is she looking for solutions or merely protecting herself—telling me I am at fault or someone else is at fault—and trying to close the episode by sending me somewhere else so that she can get back to her work as soon as possible? The body language tells it all. This is equally true when you are trying to resolve an issue with an internal service provider or supplier. When you reach a conclusion about this, this is a moment of truth (see Chapter 2). Now you know whether you can depend on that provider. Organizations with a logical and solid chain of such commitments deliver value. Others create frustration and waste resources. We now turn to three examples of processes gone awry in society at large, in a small professional service organization (PSO), and in an international service network.

1.3.2.1 Aligning the Chain of Commitment and Incentives to the Value Creation Flow—A Societal Example

The so-called subprime crisis of 2008 was the end result of a self-destructing chain of counterproductive inducements and a commitment to get rich quick, at any cost to others.

The mortgage lender would try to find anyone willing to buy a ridiculously big house, with a ridiculously low down payment, a very low interest rate, and low payments that the borrower could afford . . . for a while. The narrative would go more or less as follows: "What have you got to lose? You move into this beautiful new house with your family. Don't you think you owe it to them? Don't you think they deserve it? Within 12 months, the house will have gone up at least 10% in value—and I am being very conservative right now, just to be on the safe side. And it will keep going up. There is such demand out there. No way is this ending soon. You can then borrow on the value of the house, sell it to cash in, whatever."

As unconscionable, unethical, and unsustainable as the loan was, the lender would then proceed with the loan, the credit department would approve it, and disbursement would proceed without a hitch. The bank would then sell the loan to an institution (such as Fannie Mae or Freddie Mac) that would buy a huge portfolio, pool the mortgages, and "securitize it," that is, create a derived financial product (derivative) that would be sold in unit shares, mostly to institutional investors.

At that point, institutions have lots of margin for creativity, with vehicles with arcane names such as collateralized debt obligation (CDO), credit default swap (CDS), and structured investment vehicle (SIV). A rating agency would assess the quality of the investment and set a rating to inform investors of the riskiness of the investment so that they could decide if the yield was appropriate. In this case, the rating agency somehow gave it its highest rating, and government oversight agencies trusted that all was well.

All was not well, of course. The chain of commitment that should have existed and that investors trusted existed—between the original investment decision and the data they were getting at the time of making their investment decision—was in fact an illusion. A system that was sound 10 years ago had slowly drifted, with no immediate visible consequence. "Process controls," as we will call them later in the book, that should have raised a red flag apparently found it more convenient not to. The consequences were hidden in a bubble that, pretty much like an aneurysm, slowly got bigger and bigger with no noticeable effect until it eventually ruptured. The changes were subtle, exploiting a wave of government deregulation applauded almost unanimously: bureaucracy decreased, entrepreneurship flourished, value was apparently being created as the economy and the stock market grew. It was all seen as a tribute to the prescience and vision of free marketeers.

The drift occurred through a series of little-noticed pairwise mutual adjustments between players, followed by upstream and downstream ripple effects, pretty much as a local power fluctuation in an electrical network will trigger waves of adjustments to bring back equilibrium. The beauty of these changes is that they all improved or at least maintained the benefit accruing to each local player in the system, that is, always preserving a local win–win change. The insidious aspect of it, of course, is that they were all achieved at the expense of institutional investors— and ultimately individual depositors whose money they were investing—who were unaware of it and actually happy to get what seemed to be very good value. Nobody was in charge of the process. There was no "process owner." The public that was bilked is still looking for the parties responsible for the mess, and legislators are still looking for the fix. Irrespective of convenient, cozy, mutually satisfactory local arrangements, ignorance, indifference, or denial of the fact that processes have been corrupted can only go on for a while. Eventually, it all comes back to bite you with a vengeance.

This macro process failure finds its equivalent within organizations. An illogical, unsustainable process can sometimes exist and prosper for years with everyone apparently happy with it, and an invisible, asymptomatic bubble building up somewhere. It could be growing customer dissatisfaction that has not yet translated into loss of market share, hidden design or execution defects that have not yet been dealt with (such as Toyota's failure to recognize the importance of the sudden acceleration problem on some models), inaccurate asset valuation, unqualified employees being hired, or incompetent management being promoted. Only rigorous process analysis and control can reveal such misalignments and dysfunctions in processes and allow corrective mechanisms to be put in place before the bubble bursts. For when it does, it is often with dramatic and potentially fatal consequences.

1.3.2.2 A Small PSO Becomes Sloppy

The situation described in Box 1.1 bears many similarities to the 1989 train wreck described earlier. Slowly drifting processes have a delayed cumulative effect that

---

Box 1.1 Dear Colleagues—We Need to Talk ASAP

Issue: *Months of accumulated process drift come home to roost in a pharmacy*

Memo to: All my colleagues

From: Michael Acker, Pharmacist

Subject: Urgent meeting on quality issues

I'm writing to you tonight because I had a tough shift last night. The events I have had to deal with are not isolated cases, and they reflect very badly on our collective practice.
    I would like us to find solutions together, as we are all involved in the problems.

A. I checked everywhere but could not find Mrs. Keeney's angina medication for the full week, but only for Monday. She told me spontaneously that she has had it up to here with us, since this is the third week in a row that something or other was missing or wrong in our delivery, and she has had to run around to get it.

B. Mrs. Atkins came to get her statin drug, but I could not find it. I called Nina (the afternoon shift manager at the pharmacy), and she said she never saw the prescription. I eventually found it in Kathy's pile, and we sent a messenger to deliver it. She was very upset anyway and made a fuss.

C. Mrs. Henry came in for her cortisone cream. She always gets a 500-gram jar, but all I had was 100 grams. She's afraid she will run short during her vacation. I called Nina again, and she said she had no idea why we were short, but that we should rush the rest of the prescription to her, hopefully before she leaves.

D. While Mrs. Henry was with me, Mrs. O'Keefe came in to see if I finally had her medication. I did. This did not prevent her from reminding me that she had been promised it would be delivered yesterday. She then went on to list all our recent mistakes, and that got Mrs. Henry going. Listening to this litany was no fun. I wish I had made a recording: it would do a much better job of letting you know how I feel right now than this memo will.

E. Mr. Aaron told me that he had to go two days without his antacid last week and that he had plenty of time to think about us during the sleepless nights that followed. He told me that we'd better get our act together or he would take his business elsewhere.

I don't expect my job to be all fun and joy. I became a pharmacist to help make people better. Right now I feel like I am part of a conspiracy to make people suffer, and I must spend my day apologizing for the mistakes of others. I remember a time not too long ago when clients had only praise for our services and our dedication to their well-being, wondering what they would do without us. What happened to us, my friends?
    By the way, let's count our blessings: so far our clients have only been inconvenienced by our problems and none has suffered significant health consequences.
    Please, let's get together at the earliest opportunity (I mean this week) to discuss this. I have some ideas to put on the table. I'm sure you'll have some of your own as well. Let's not forget why we got into this business, and take stock of what we have to do.

---

can remain invisible for a long time and then manifest itself with a bang at a time that is not of our choosing. Processes feed on one another. If the information given to a client by a pharmacy technician on the phone is inaccurate or poorly communicated, it is the blameless pharmacist who serves her at the counter who will have to deal with her well-founded frustration. When a technician who feels that he is shouldering an unfair proportion of the workload starts cutting corners and making mistakes, it is the pharmacist who gets blamed. If a tired pharmacist dismisses the request for assistance of a technician, and as a result a batch of prescription is not ready on time for the night delivery person to pick up, the technician and the pharmacist on the morning shift will have to deal with the resulting mess the following day.

Defects in any other process, such as inventory taking, ordering, or preparing the weekly work schedule, have delayed systemwide effects that are not easily traceable. The longer the situation has been allowed to deteriorate, the more difficult it becomes to disentangle. Unless the organization has a clear cross-functional perspective on the flow of work and the specific contribution (mission) of every process, and commitment and incentives are designed with these in mind, bubbles may build up and tension increase until the organization is suddenly faced with a crisis.

1.3.2.3 Customers Lost in the Global Value Network

Box 1.2 illustrates a minor incident taking place in a global value network, where the customer is left to fend for herself and ends up fighting back. This escalation could easily have been avoided in several ways to the mutual benefit of everyone, starting at the source and at every point along the escalation route:

- FDY should have charged only for the damaged rim and provided the customer with an itemized bill on the spot. Laura would have signed and obtained all the required documents to file her claim with the insurance company. Instead, someone at FDY was motivated to charge more (incentive?) and felt quite sure he would get away with it.

- CareFree could have called Easyrent directly and used its clout to get action. But it was easier (and quite legal) to send the client on a wild goose chase in the hope that she would give up and move on to other things.

- Easyrent could have taken ownership of the case, followed through, and kept the customer informed of its progress. Company policy, however, was not to call back customers, presumably to reduce cost, and maybe in the hope that they would tire of the hassle and give up.

- FDY could easily have adjusted the unfair charge immediately and provided the required documents at the first request from Easyrent. For reasons unknown, it did not.

The incentive system built into the chain, however, was not designed with a view to producing a positive customer experience. With globalization, specialization, and cheap instantaneous electronic communication, value networks are increasingly composed of many organizations, each with its own business model and culture. Managing the interfaces along such complex value networks requires a global understanding of how the network competes (against other value networks), how the partners relate to one another operationally (that is, the ripple effect of the ill-considered or short-sighted decisions), how they cooperate, and how to resolve zero-sum issues in the chain so that the customer is not caught up in a web of conflicting information and endless procedures. Such disgruntled customers become "terrorists." With the advent of social networks, they can fight back. The cumulative effect of their actions can be devastating to a company's reputation. Fair play is the only sustainable course.

Box 1.2 You Don't Know How Good Your Insurance Provider Is Until You Make a Claim

Issue: *The challenges of coordination in the global value chain*

During a business trip to Europe, Laura had a few days off to visit Corsica. She rented a car through an online intermediary (Easyrent) and picked up the car at Friendly Drive Yourself (FDY) upon arriving in Bastia. The scenery was so beautiful that she missed a turn and hit a road divider, denting the tire rim and causing a flat tire. She duly reported the incident upon returning the car at the airport. When she handed over her credit card, she was asked to sign for a charge of 300€ for a rim *and* a flat tire. "Either you sign that and we close the rental, giving you finalized paperwork, or we will simply take it on the credit card," the clerk said flatly. In other words, we will do it our way, and whatever you say will not change a thing. Indeed, the obvious fact that the rubber tire itself was untouched did not move the agent. Laura was now late for her flight, and there was no time left for arguing.

Car rental insurance was part of her premium credit card (Diamond Card) benefits. By the time she arrived home, the charge had already been applied to her credit card. Here's the (partial) sequence of events that took place as she tried to collect her insurance:

- Diamond Card referred her to the insurer, CareFree Travel.
- CareFree asked for a written request (by mail) including the originals of several documents.
- Laura received a written request from CareFree for a rental closure document and an itemized invoice, neither of which had been provided by FDY.
- She filled out FDY's online request form, but was eventually informed that she had to go through Easyrent.
- She called Easyrent. The call center receptionist promised quick action. The required documents would be sent by e-mail.
- Laura never received the documents and had to call several times. The call center did not return her calls, and so she could not talk to the supervisor or fax in additional documents.
- Meanwhile, CareFree had sent Laura a third and final request for the missing documents. Failure to immediately provide the documents would result in final denial of her claim.
- A call to Diamond Card failed to resolve anything.
- Laura then asked Diamond Card to stop the payment, because of the failure of FDY to provide the required documents.
- She was asked to put all this in writing.
- By return mail, she was asked for proof that FDY had been requested to supply the documents and failed to respond.
- Et cetera.

The rest of the story is much too long and depressing to be told here. Cutting to the chase: in a four-way international conference call, the charges were reduced to 100€. Unfortunately, because of Laura's request, Diamond Card had denied the whole charge, an operation that could not be undone. FDY did not get any payment and probably gave up to cut its losses. The episode lasted six months. It's impossible to put an actual amount on the transaction cost, but it is undoubtedly substantial. This is the tip of the iceberg, however. Below the water line loom the wasted energy, the resulting distrust, frustration, and cynicism, along with the future defensive behavior triggered among all the players. The bubble just got a little bigger.

The "software" of high-performance organizations involves coherent networks of commitments where each player can rely on his providers to deliver on their promises and thus find himself in a position to confidently promise to deliver the results customers expect. This requires giving careful thought to the architecture of the organization and patiently nurturing a culture where everyone strives to deliver on their commitment and cares about the end result.

1.3.3 Operational Excellence

Creating value for customers in every transaction requires rigor. This consists of a combination of three things: logical validity, rule of evidence, and discipline. Lack of rigor denies value and fosters superstition rather than learning. Superstitious beliefs can be very sticky, resulting in wasted resources and loss of effectiveness. They also undermine a culture of learning.

1.3.3.1 *How Obstetrics Improved—Quick and Accurate Feedback Allows for Learning and Improvement*

In 1953, while a professor at Columbia School of Medicine, Virginia Apgar proposed the Apgar scale to measure the health of newborn babies. It is a 10-point scale that consists of the sum of five individual scores, each of which is rated on a three-point scale (for example, *Activity* [muscle tone]: 0—absent, 1—arms and legs flexed, 2—active movement; *Appearance* [skin color]: 0—blue, pale, 1—body pink, extremities blue, 2—completely pink). The Apgar score is interpreted as follows: 0–3 severely depressed, 4–6 moderately depressed, 7–10 excellent condition. The notion has caught on and is still used today as the best indicator of a newborn baby's health. It is typically calculated twice, one minute after birth and then again four minutes later. In problem cases, the scores can be taken again every five minutes as required to monitor progress and help adjust the interventions (Gawande 2007).

This innovation may seem innocuous enough, especially compared with such wonders as medical imaging devices of all kinds, new surgical techniques (laparoscopy), and new drugs. It did, however, have a huge impact on the evolution of the field by providing it with a way to immediately assess performance and link it with process "variables." Few medical fields, even today, can assess their performance with any precision in a timely fashion. When criteria are ill-defined and subject to different interpretation at different times, in different places, by different people, influenced by their own biases and limitations, the results are at best useless and more often than not misleading. Indeed, intentionally or unconsciously manipulated scores only reinforce preconceptions and serve the vested interests of those who design the system. The development of the Apgar score gave neonatology an edge that launched it on the path to individual and collective continuous improvement.

Of course, judgment is always involved in assessing the outcome of any complex service. This is indeed the case for the Apgar. Those who have never seen a newborn baby would be hard-pressed to come up with a score, and the odds are that a number of untrained watchers would come up with quite a bit of variation. Thus, a number of conditions apply for an indicator to be a valid guide to continuous improvement. First, it must be such that the same (trained) person, observing the same phenomenon twice, will come up with scores that are not significantly different (repeatability). Also, different observers of the same phenomenon must systematically come up with similar numbers (reproducibility). Further, the indicator must be shown to be measuring the right thing (validity). How can we know that? Through rigorous studies correlating the score with the actual phenomenon that we are trying to measure. For instance, does a higher Apgar score mean a higher three-month survival rate of a newborn baby?

Once you start getting a valid score for an outcome, you can start correlating variation in outcome to variation in input, process, and environmental variables. You can also manipulate some variables as a result of feedback received and move through a series of short learning cycles to process characterization, and through it to improvement. Discipline is an important ingredient in this pursuit. It involves the motivation and strength to stay focused on the task at hand, to stick to agreed protocols, and to relentlessly pursue further improvement, even as it diverts resources that could be used to relieve the pressure for immediate results.

We are poor data processors, a limitation compounded by our *belief* that we are actually really good at it. Our needs, motivations, emotions, and state of mind at any time affect the way we process information. Our thinking mind is all of a sudden hijacked by a rush of emotion, adversely and unconsciously impacting ongoing analytical processes. We forget things. Time pressure for short-term results discourages us from dedicating the required effort and resources to get the measurement system right. As a result, we all too often work with inadequate data and reach the wrong conclusion about what works and what does not. This fosters superstitious organizations that believe they are learning organizations. Eventually, of course, reality catches up with such organizations. If they are lucky, they can take stock and amend their ways before it is too late. These ways, however, are deeply ingrained in culture, and managing a quick change in culture is a feat that few organizations have achieved.

The field of obstetrics was transformed by someone who had never delivered a baby—not through the development of new technology or the discovery of a miracle molecule, but by the development of a simple way to calculate a quick-feedback performance indicator.

A valid real-time metric keeps us honest by confronting us with evidence. It protects us from the tendency to be complacent, from wishful thinking and self-delusion. Without it, there can be no learning or continuous improvement. Getting the right metrics and getting the metrics right are critical to sustainable strategic advantage.

1.3.3.2 *What Are These Data Really Telling Me?*

A defect or failure in a repetitive process, from which we do not learn, is one that we are condemned to repeat from time to time. As Box 1.3 shows, a defect from which we draw the wrong conclusion (superstition) is one that we are condemned to relive for a long time. One is reminded of the movie *Groundhog Day*, where a character played by Bill Murray has many chances to get a personal process just right, as he always wakes up on the same day until (if ever) he succeeds in learning it. Conversely, letting an unexpectedly good outcome go by without trying to understand its causes is missing out on the most immediately available source of continuous improvement.

Box 1.3 A Consultant "Improves" His Performance

Issue: *Knowledge versus superstition—take 1: a professional service*

Many years ago, as a young consultant with one of the then "big eight" consulting firms, I was going through my first experience with international executive training. It was a two-week course, with the first week taking place in France and the second week in the United States a month later. The first week went very well. On the last day, I asked the participants to fill out an anonymous feedback form. On the flight back, while enjoying what I thought was a well-deserved glass of French wine (you can't go wrong with that), I started reading the forms.

"They liked it," I thought to myself as the flight attendant was kindly offering to refill my glass. "Yes ma'am, I deserve it today," I replied. In the section on suggestions for improvement, most of the respondents had made minor points or had left it blank. That is, until I got to an executive who had filled it out completely—and continued on the other side of the page. Her comments (she had signed the form) were very incisive. The course was OK, she said, but many improvements were required. She had obviously given this considerable thought. I read it thoroughly several times over. I put aside the other 20-odd forms and kept that one on my table as I took out my notepad to start planning how I would go about reengineering my course.

I will cut to the chase. The second week was a total flop. One feedback form was laudatory, however, praising me on my openness and willingness to change. Most of the other forms, though, showed that the class was wondering what happened to me in that month since we had last met in France.

To say that one topic I was addressing in that course was statistical process control goes a long way in showing how in my mind—and in those of most quality professionals and academics at the time—this whole thing about processes applied only to manufacturing. I had about 20 data points (feedback forms). I "selected" one and disregarded the others. I wanted to improve the course and was looking for ways to do it. One person had taken the trouble to give me pointers. It did not occur to me that the fact that she was motivated to do so while the others were not made her an outlier (that is, different in some way from the rest of the class) and that I should deal with her feedback as such. I thought her comments made sense and accepted them as truth, without further validation. In fact, I disregarded the remaining evidence I had in my hands at the time.

Drawing the wrong conclusion from the evidence at hand is obviously much worse than not drawing any and keeping an open mind. Once you believe you *know,* it takes much evidence—and cost, time, and pain—to convince you to revisit your original conclusion. I drew the wrong conclusion, and all the energy and efforts I expended, with the best of intentions, in improving my courses resulted in destroying a very good process (the "training process" through which I was putting the participants).

As the example shows, learning and processes are intimately linked at a personal level. This link is even stronger for multi-person processes. Individual learning is one thing, organizational learning is another. An organization has not learned anything until it changes a shared way of doing things, that is, a process, and improves its capabilities as a result. Individual members of the organization may learn something and change the way they perform some activity as a result. However, unless other members adapt their own activities accordingly, the overall result may not improve. They will not do so unless they understand and share the reasons for the change and are willing to try something new. Thus, organizations need shared learning mechanisms to build, disseminate, and integrate knowledge.

Obviously, an organization cannot improve a process that it does not know. Organizations that do not know their processes may get a great result one day, but they are incapable of isolating the factor that made the difference. Thus, they are unable to exploit opportunities for improvement.

We classify the data we are faced with into mental pigeonholes: invalid data, known fact (that is, fits with and reinforces existing knowledge), irrelevant piece of information (discarded), and valid data that contradict existing knowledge. To the learning organization, the latter are considered gold prospects. Members of such organizations share a common method of ascertaining what is true, what is not, what is uncertain, what reinforces shared beliefs, what challenges them. Such organizations value inquisitiveness and the quest for validated facts more than blind faith or obedience. They have a huge advantage over those that do not. The latter have to proceed by arbitrary decree, creating cynicism among employees and cutting themselves off from a vast reservoir of learning opportunities.

The continuous improvement mind-set is one that pushes you to always be on the lookout for a better way of doing things. That means that you should not use 100% of your resources to complete a process successfully, but that you should dedicate some resources to analyzing and understanding the current process and trying to improve on it. Alexander Fleming's discovery of penicillin in 1928 was triggered by the chance observation (that is, a defect, just like the one discussed in Box 1.2) of a culture dish that had been inadvertently contaminated by airborne molds. The *Staphylococci* bacteria he was studying had spread to the area immediately surrounding an invading mold growth. He realized that something in the mold was inhibiting growth of the surrounding bacteria. He analyzed the mold, and this ultimately led him to isolate penicillin. Someone merely intent on completing the experiment would have cleaned up the plate, griped about laboratory assistants, maybe gone through a little bout of depression, and started over. Fortunately, Fleming had an inquisitive mind, a part of which was on the lookout for anything to learn, including from apparently disappointing process variations.

Process variations make every repetition of a process an opportunity for learning, and thus a potential source of seeds for improvement. The curious mind will always be alert and wonder "Why is this happening?" or "Why not?" In an environment where ideas get turned down, experimentation is discouraged, and only blind obedience is rewarded, continuous process improvement is not likely to flourish.

1.3.3.3 *Jumping to Conclusions—Lack of Logical Validity about Causality Leads to Superstition*

The example in Box 1.4 illustrates how superstition still drives much of what we do. Helen is disciplined and proud of her cooking skills. She probably has much success with her ham. She may attribute part of that success to cutting the tips of the ham. She may even keep it a secret that she only tells her best friends. This is called *attribution error.* The cutting of the tips does not cause her success. Her success stems from other things that she does (or other *variables,* as we will refer to process features in later chapters).

Box 1.4 Why Do You Do It That Way?

Issue: *Knowledge versus superstition—take 2: the secret to the perfect ham recipe is revealed*

A few months into their marriage, a man watches his wife Helen prepare a ham for dinner. She unwraps the football-sized piece of meat, places it on a butcher block, carefully cuts both ends of the ham, throws away the tips, and places the ham in a slow cooker.

"Why do you do that, honey? Ham is very expensive; why throw away the tips?" asks the man.

"You're not going to question the way I cook, dear, are you? I've been doing that for years. Daddy taught me. As you know, when it comes to cooking, he is world class."

"Yeah, I know; he says that a lot. . . . No, no, I'm not questioning, just curious. Still, I don't understand, why is it better to do it that way?"

"I think it has something to do with all the fat ending up there, or was it that this part is really tough? Honestly, I'm not sure. You know, there are so many things you have to do carefully in cooking, you can't remember the reason for every single one."

"But why would the fat end up at the tips? Or why would the tips be harder? It does not make sense to me."

"You ask too many questions. Why don't you prepare the salad and set up the table, or we'll never be ready on time."

"Sure, I was just about to do that."

The following weekend, "Daddy" is having the "kids" over for a barbecue. As the man watches Daddy perform his "world-class" culinary feats, the man thinks back on the ham discussion.

"Dad, Helen and I had this discussion the other day . . .," and he goes on to tell the story. "So why is it better to cut the tips of the ham?"

"Oh, that! Well, I learned cooking the hard way. My mother was so busy, she did not have time to teach me anything. But I have a keen eye. Everybody said she was the best, so I did not have to look any further. I watched carefully as my mother performed this procedure. You know, son, I've learned it from the best; that's why I'm the best now. But if you want to know why, you'd have to ask her. Me, I don't know, and if truth be known, I don't care."

"Ignorance, indifference, and mindless repetition," the man thought, "the key to world-class cooking! Now, here's a lesson I'd better keep to myself." Soon after, during a family reunion to celebrate Granny's 80th birthday, the man takes the opportunity to pursue his inquiry.

"Granny, why is it that you have to cut the tips of a ham before cooking?"

"What are you talking about, son? Why, I have not done that for 40 years! Funny you'd know this. We were very poor, you see, and I only had one small cooking pot. On those rare occasions when we bought a ham, I had to cut the tips so that it would fit!"

Because of this attribution error, Helen puts much effort into perpetuating a wasteful action (or non-value-added action) while the truly critical aspects of what she does are repeated mindlessly and may be lost one day, much to her dismay, because she is not aware of their importance.

The origin of this superstition is her blind faith in her father's cooking skills and in what he taught her. When it comes to understanding how and why things work the way they do in this world, blind faith is a fatal learning disability.

Implicit transmission of knowledge, such as the father observing his mother, and explicit transmission, such as the father teaching Helen how to cook a ham, are a double-edged sword. They can perpetuate and reinforce knowledge or superstition. In other words, when it comes to training: garbage in, gospel out. The father created the superstition and reinforced it by building a rationale around it after the fact and teaching it to his daughter. Then it became part of the family culture (albeit a tiny part): "That's the way we do things around here." It is easy to lose touch with the "why" of things when processes are mindlessly repeated. Whether we find ourselves in a family or business setting, we are the same person, subject to the same limitations. Businesses, like families, are social organizations. Once a belief is ingrained in the culture, it is very hard to change.

How are beliefs created? Through a mixture of faith (learning it, explicitly or implicitly, from someone you trust), logic, and experience. Science is a self-correcting process of discovery. The world has improved markedly since Descartes, Sir Francis Bacon, and others gave us a way to debunk superstitions (and we admittedly still have a long way to go as a society). You observe a phenomenon, correlate what you saw with what you know (your knowledge base), formulate a hypothesis, test it rigorously, and learn something. If the experiment fails, you reject the hypothesis and formulate a new one. Science progresses toward the truth from one failure to the next. There is no sustainable success that is not predicated on a number of failures. A failure or defect indeed carries the seed of worthwhile knowledge. Benefiting from it requires the disciplined pursuit of a number of practices: inquisitive observation with intent to learn, thorough understanding and analysis of the facts and current knowledge base in order to formulate a hypothesis, and careful design of experiments, analysis, and interpretation of results. Lack of rigor denies the progress and lets a failure be just a depressing failure rather than a step forward on a continuous improvement path.

1.4 MANAGING PROCESSES IN COMPLEX SERVICES

As illustrated by the pharmacy (Box 1.1) and the car rental insurance (Box 1.2) examples, complex services share a number of features from a process point of view:

- The output is intangible, and much subjectivity is involved in evaluating the quality of the outcome.

- The transformation involves information selection, human judgment, and joint processing of soft data.

- There often is no process to speak of. As the players are professionals, they feel they should be guided by their judgment alone and not be encumbered by rules that, they feel, only serve to keep clerical workers in line.

Such internal processes as evaluating new service ideas, managing the mix of service offerings, exploring new markets, supporting customers, introducing a new customer into the organization, and many more management and professional service delivery processes share these characteristics. These business processes can be vitally important, and in many organizations they still constitute a largely untapped reservoir of improvement opportunities.

Process improvement in organizations requires a concerted effort. An individual may get an improvement idea that she can implement on her own. She may also sometimes be able to convince an internal customer or supplier to go along with the idea. However, many improvements require resources, concomitant changes in several parts of the process, and even adjustment in adjacent processes. Organizations learn through project cycles. We discuss these learning cycles in Chapter 8. There are many types of process problems and opportunities. They require different methodologies, different tools, and different approaches to change management. Making this happen is the topic of this book.

There are processes that are well designed but that we do not follow because they were poorly implemented, or simply because we lack the discipline to stick with it. Take the simple example of driving a car. Before changing lanes, one should not only glance at the side mirror but also check the blind spot by turning the head. Yet, despite the potential dire consequences of not doing so, how many people check the blind spot all the time? Tired, careless, poorly trained, mind on something else—whatever the cause, the process simply needs discipline. Better information, education, and training can contribute greatly to better compliance through heightened awareness. Enforcement can go a long way as well. There is little value in designing new processes in organizations that lack the discipline to enforce any processes, let alone implement new ones. Such organizations must first take stock of the state of their management. This all too often comes with a wake-up call, through a culture-changing event such as a major setback.

When a process exists and displays poor capabilities, a question arises: Does this process have potential? If we can confidently answer that it does, then we should try to fix it. We present the process improvement methodology in Chapter 9. If the answer is no, it is better to start from scratch. Sometimes an organization has to develop a process starting from a clean sheet because the activity is totally new. In either case, we need the process design methodology, which we present in Chapter 10.

When it comes to leading the change, the two major approaches available are the *kaizen event* or *kaizen workshop* and the (improvement or design) *project*. The former typically consists of one week during which a dedicated team of process workers or managers is assembled and coached, with the express purpose of generating a quantum leap in the performance of an existing process. The latter takes place over a longer period, typically three to six months. A full-time expert, working with a part-time team of process workers and managers, leads it. We discuss the characteristics of these two different types of vehicles for change in Chapter 8.

Here is a typical reaction we get when the idea of a kaizen event is first suggested in an organization: "You can't be serious! We're all up to our eyeballs as it is. How do you think we can spare a team of workers for a full week?" I typically reply with the toaster analogy. Imagine a restaurant whose toaster is not functioning properly, burning most of the toast. Things are so bad that employees spend much time scraping the toast before it can be served to customers. When it is proposed to the owner to take some "scrapers" away from their task to devote time to adjusting the toaster, he replies, "Free up someone to fix the toaster? Are you crazy? They're far too busy scraping burned toast!" Things will not get better until we take away some resources from the daily chores of minding the store to focus on improving the process. In fact, when we do, things are likely to get worse for a while. Those that remain on the front line will just have to scrape twice as fast for a while, and yes, some burned toast may slip through the cracks while we are busy fixing the toaster.

An organization is what it does, and it can choose to see this as a system of processes and make them better. Organizations that embark on such a journey have to cross "Death Valley." This is the difficult period when the reduction in operating resources and the pain involved in learning new ways hurts, but the promised benefits are still "in the pipeline" and thus strong leadership is required for the organization to stick with it. The pressure to revert to the old ways is such that the initiative is often dropped before the new process capabilities kick in.

The process view of things is like a pair of X-ray glasses that allow one to see the value connection binding apparently unrelated activities taking place in different departments. Understandably, the reader might feel that at this point we have shown him or her only the frame of the glasses. Hopefully, that will result in added motivation to read on.

If I may paraphrase Christiaan Huygens, a noted seventeenth-century Dutch scientist: nothing is more glorious than to give rules to phenomena that, lacking any fathomable structure, seem to obey no rule and thereby lie beyond the grasp of the human mind. Huygens was talking about statistics. I am talking about processes (though statistics play a central role in understanding them). At the risk of stretching the point, I might make a last analogy: just as the long-sought double-helix structure of DNA unlocks the door to engineering a living cell, understanding processes gives an organization the key to unlocking its value-creation potential. Process management and process engineering are indeed disciplines well worth mastering. This book is meant to provide the reader with the rudiments of the underlying art and science.

1.5 STRUCTURE OF THE BOOK

Several videos are available to clarify, simplify, illustrate, or otherwise complement the material presented in these pages (http://videos.asq.org/complex-service-delivery-processes). Overall, they represent some 12 hours of viewing, with the wonderful features provided by the pause and rewind buttons. In each chapter, you will find a list of videos and a short description of the content of each video. For a high-level overview of the book, view Video 1.1; for suggestions about how to use this book, view Video 1.2 (see Figure 1.1). The quest for value drives customer behavior in the service marketplace. The quest for personal value drives employee behavior in the labor marketplace (both topics are covered in Chapter 2). The quest for economic value drives investor behavior in the financial services marketplace. Companies are competing simultaneously in these three marketplaces. They seek to find better ways to do things (processes) that will profitably provide their customers of choice with more value than their competitors provide. The added financial resources made available to them by investors reward those organizations that succeed in generating more economic value added than their competitors generate. They can, in turn, use these resources to recruit and keep the best people. They do so by providing them with more personal value than their

Figure 2 – Snapshot of Model on Tuesday at 2:31pm

1.1 Deploying complex services for maximum value creation

A process is a system of activities (together with the associated resources) that takes an input and transforms it into an output of greater value for a customer. It is processes that create value.

The video focuses on complex services (CSs), that is, services sought because of a lack of knowledge or skills. Complex services fall into three categories: professional services, semi-professional services, and technical services. This video also deals with the many organizations, such as hospitals and banks, insurance and telecommunications companies, that provide services requiring a mixture of professional and other services to produce the results that customers or clients want.

Professionals, semi-professionals, and technical workers laboring in all spheres of human endeavor, from law to medicine, from accounting to engineering, who are involved or interested in taking part in managing their businesses will find this overview invaluable for achieving success.

Part 1: Introduction—Value and the customer experience
Quality in CSs involves leadership—this is not the fast-food business. Understanding who the customer is and what he or she does is even more important in CSs: he or she is coproducing the outcome. Whoever produces a customer experience lives an experience himself or herself: only positive experiences on both sides of the encounter are sustainable.

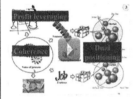

Part 2: Understanding processes, focus, and scope
The organization's knowledge is embedded in processes—shared ways of adding value that translate into a chain of commitments distributed logically in the organization. The only sustainable source of strategic advantage is the ability to learn (i.e., augment knowledge) faster than your competitors; understanding variation, thinking statistically, and managing processes are central to this endeavor. Any strategic move that you decide to make will only generate strategic advantage if you can translate it into the right change to the right processes, and execute it quickly and flawlessly.

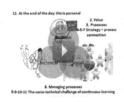

Part 3: Sustainable competitive advantage through faster learning
Fast and effective learning cycles require a solid connection to strategy, shared methodologies and tools, and an ability to mobilize people behind focused improvement efforts. Beware of management fads. Isolate and evaluate the new elements carefully, and make an enlightened decision about whether they fit your culture and can be a valuable addition to your learning strategy. Many organizations make it to "good enough." Few organizations cross the chasm from good to great. While the specific recipe required to do so may be debatable, rigor is definitely part of it. From business model to customer focus, from process management to team empowerment, from systems thinking to analysis of variation, no sustainable learning (i.e., no sustainable advantage) is possible without it.

1.2 How to use the book and website

A few suggestions by the author about the best way to use the videos and the book, depending on where you are coming from and what your goal and priorities are.

Figure 1.1 Videos associated with Chapter 1.

competitors can provide, and thus starts a positive cycle of reinforcement since better, more motivated employees will provide more value to customers.

Strategy is the company's evolving game plan for doing this. Operations strategy is that specific part of the plan that deals with how things will be done (Chapter 4). It is translated into specific goals, farmed out throughout the organization, triggering processes into action (Chapters 5 and 6). Companies must identify, design, manage, improve, and eventually redesign these processes in such a way that the game plan unfolds as intended. Except when a new business is created, organizations must decide on which processes to focus their limited improvement resources (Chapter 7) and how to mobilize the organization behind the change (Chapter 8). They must choose between trying to improve an existing process (Chapter 9) and designing a new one from scratch (Chapter 10). More difficult yet, they must ensure that the global coherence of their operations is not gradually lost through a series of such finely targeted changes (Chapter 4).

Understanding the inner workings of processes and the principles regulating sets of processes forming a business system is both a central underpinning of the book (Chapters 3 and 6) and a prerequisite to understanding the distinctiveness of professional service processes—a species of processes with unique features (Chapter 5). Finally, the book aims to present the reader with a broad framework for understanding how a set of shared fundamental beliefs drives the best professional service organizations in learning (process design and process improvement) faster than their competitors (current chapter along with Chapters 8 and 11). This is the only sustainable source of competitive advantage. Indeed, all other sources (such as new products, patents, or a brand name, for example) are readily copied, whereas learning faster than your competition cannot be. This is why this book is worth the reader's time and effort.

1.6 HOW TO USE THE BOOK

Figure 1.2 presents a simplified model of the learning organization. Processes must simultaneously create value for customers (market), employees (labor market), and shareholders (financial market). The organization's game plan to beat competitors in these three marketplaces is outlined in its strategy. Figuratively, the "learning pump" targets specific processes that need to be changed for the strategy to work, sends them to the "process workshop," fixes them or designs new ones, and puts them back into operation, improved. We classify the chapters of the book in Figure 1.2 according to which part of this value-creation framework they address. The first five chapters explore the relationship between strategy and processes. In Chapter 4 in particular, we revisit Figure 1.2 (see Figure 4.7), exploring its components in more depth and further specifying the roles of the remaining chapters. Chapter 6, dealing with process management, includes a mixture of theory and techniques aimed at providing the reader with a more detailed analytical framework to understand and manage processes. Chapters 7 (project scoping), 9 (improving), and 10 (designing) are the "technical" (how-to) chapters. Chapter 8 explains how and why the learning pump works. Chapter 11 presents and discusses the most widespread continuous improvement practices, and Chapter 12 brings it all to a personal level by exploring how the

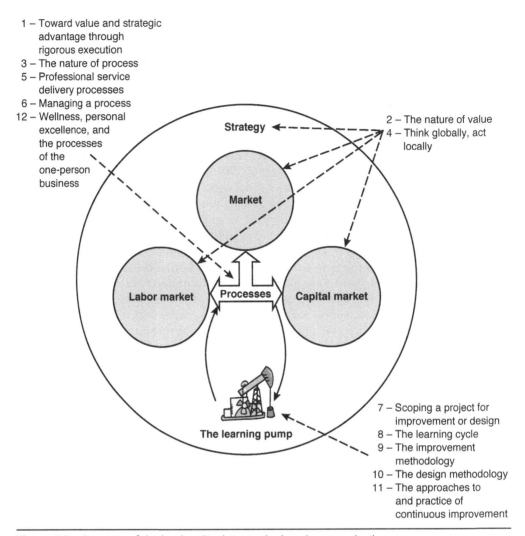

1 – Toward value and strategic advantage through rigorous execution
3 – The nature of process
5 – Professional service delivery processes
6 – Managing a process
12 – Wellness, personal excellence, and the processes of the one-person business

Strategy

2 – The nature of value
4 – Think globally, act locally

Market

Labor market

Processes

Capital market

The learning pump

7 – Scoping a project for improvement or design
8 – The learning cycle
9 – The improvement methodology
10 – The design methodology
11 – The approaches to and practice of continuous improvement

Figure 1.2 Structure of the book as it relates to the learning organization.

approaches presented in this book provide a useful framework for individual wellness and improvement as well.

The fact that you are reading this book indicates that you are dissatisfied with the way things are going in your organization and you would like to find out if there is a better way to run your business. Intelligent people first try to understand. When they do, and if it makes sense, they try it out, cautiously. Try the end-of-chapter exercises and let the concepts, methodology, and tools grow on you. Remember that the learning mind is like a parachute: more useful when open. Suspend disbelief for a while, and give it a try. It is the only way to benefit from this reading.

Many of the end-of-chapter exercises build on each other, that is, you need to do exercise 2.1 to be able to do exercise 2.2. Further, some exercises build on each other from one chapter to the next, leading you, one brick at a time, toward a holistic understanding of the connection of strategy to processes. These relationships are shown in Figure 1.3. While all the exercises will help you gain hands-on

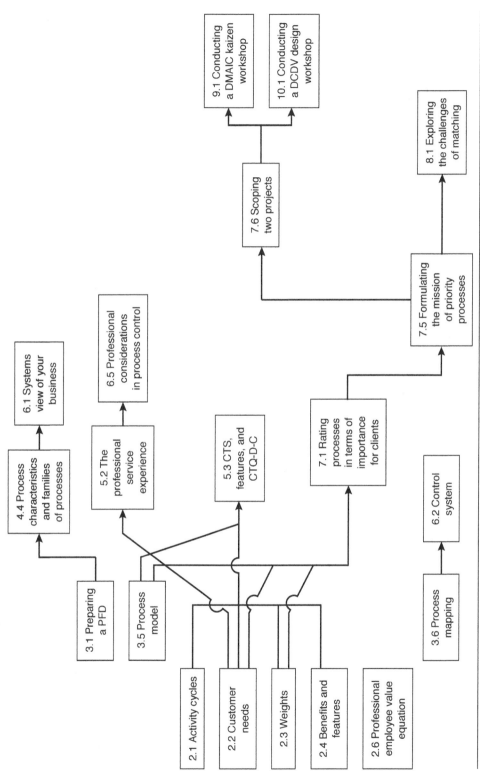

Figure 1.3   Logical flow and precedence relationship between some of the end-of-chapter exercises.

experience and appropriate the concepts and tools of the chapters, those that produce an intermediate result that you will need in future chapters (as shown in Figure 1.3) are particularly important.

1.7 SUMMARY

Any organization's strategy is worthless unless the organization is able to carry it out. Strategies are executed through an organization's processes. It is in the doing (that is, through processes) that value is created. It is in the doing as well that opportunities for learning lie. Finally, it is also in the doing that what has been learned (that is, newly acquired knowledge) is put to use, creating competitive advantage through superior capability. Value creation is best understood through the process perspective. It enables a focus on continuous improvement through a judicious combination of rigor and creativity.

EXERCISES

1.1 Changed Personal and Family Processes

Identify three personal or family processes that you have changed during the last year or so. This may include such activities as keeping in shape, eating, smoking, planning a vacation or a night out, or helping Tommy do his homework. You may have never thought about these activities as processes. For each one:

a. Describe the inputs and outputs.

b. What was the trigger that led you to change the process? How long did you wait before you decided to take action?

c. Describe how you went about the change. How successful were you?

d. What would you do differently if you had the chance to do it all over again?

e. Would a more rigorous approach have helped?

1.2 Personal and Family Processes to Change

Identify three personal or family processes that you want to change. For each one:

a. Identify the reasons behind the change.

b. Formulate a goal for the change. How important is it to you? How urgent is it?

c. Describe the inputs and outputs.

d. Who are the other "process players" (if any) who have to be involved in the project?

1.3 Rigor—Personal

a. Would you characterize yourself as a rigorous person? Why or why not?

b. What is the greatest result you have achieved because you were rigorous?

c. What greatest personal failure can you attribute to a lack of rigor?

1.4 Changed Business Processes

Identify three business processes that you have changed during the last year or so. For each one:

a. Did you consider the activities you changed to be a process?

b. Describe the inputs and outputs.

c. What was the trigger that led you to change the process? How long did you wait before you decided to take action?

d. Describe how you went about the change. How successful were you?

e. What would you do differently if you had the chance to do it all over again?

f. Would a more rigorous approach have helped?

1.5 Business Processes to Change

Identify three business processes that your organization has to change in the near future. For each one:

a. Identify the reasons behind the change.

b. Formulate a goal for the change. How important is it to the business? How urgent is it?

c. Describe the inputs and outputs.

d. Who are the other "process players" who have to be involved in the project?

1.6 Rigor—Business

Are there any rigorous organizations that you admire?

a. Would you characterize your organization as rigorous? Why or why not?

b. What is the greatest result the organization has achieved because it was rigorous?

c. What greatest business failure can you attribute to a lack of rigor?

1.7 Benchmarking

Are there any rigorous organizations (excluding direct competitors) that you admire and to which you could gain access (through friends and acquaintances)? If so, organize a visit with a few colleagues and ask them to explain how they manage processes. If not, the local American Society for Quality (ASQ) chapter can probably point you in the right direction.

NOTES

1. This example is narrated in great detail in Jeremy Main's 1994 book *Quality Wars*.
2. This is detailed in *The Endurance: Shackleton's Legendary Antarctic Expedition,* a fascinating book by Caroline Alexander (2001).
3. For a thorough discussion of these factors and their consequences, see Thomas L. Friedman (2006), *The World Is Flat: A Brief History of the Twenty-First Century.*

2

The Nature of Value

In complex services, you need to go beyond asking customers "What do you need?" This applies to employees as well.

To win at the business game, a company must master the art of simultaneously creating value for its customers, its employees, and its shareholders.

In this chapter, we introduce three critical notions that we will need throughout this book: quality of service, value, and positioning. Quality of service is about satisfying customers' needs, a key aspect of value. Value is "where the rubber meets the road," that is, the end point of business processes where the customer receives benefits in exchange for the time and money he has invested in the service. A good understanding of how and for whom a company creates value in the marketplace is the only possible starting point in designing, improving, and managing business processes. The journey toward this goal leads us to a discussion of positioning—both in the market[1] and in the labor market. In other words, without simultaneous value creation for customers and employees, no long-term value creation for an organization's shareholders is possible (Frei 2008). This is the topic of this chapter.

Figure 2.1 presents a map that guides the reader through the chapter. Customers' needs (top right) push them into action, triggering activities. These activities, in turn, drive customers to seek help whenever they choose not to, or cannot, perform them alone. They want this help—or service, as we shall call it here—to meet their needs; that is, they want quality (section 2.1). At the same time, they want the "biggest bang for the buck," which we will call *value* (section 2.2). There are many customers out there, with many competitors vying for their business; the company must target the right ones (positioning, section 2.3) and design a service concept (section 2.3.3) capable of delivering a superior value proposition. Service employees are the key players in this delivery (bottom half of Figure 2.1). Selecting the right ones, offering them a superior job concept (section 2.4.3), and keeping them happy (at least as happy as they think they can be working for another company) are equally important. This is what we call positioning in the labor market.

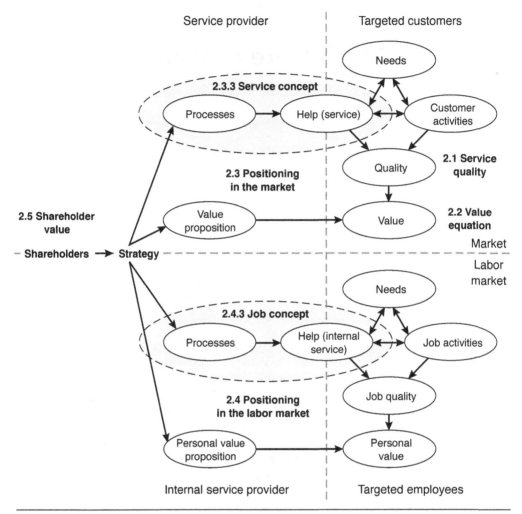

Figure 2.1 Value creation: the mirror image.

All of the above must happen as part of a concerted game plan (strategy) capable of keeping shareholders happy (section 2.5). These key concepts are summarized briefly in Table 2.1.

2.1 QUALITY OF SERVICE

A service episode consists of a sequence of events, activities, and encounters that take place between the moment a person becomes aware of a need and the time when the need is addressed, that is, when the person feels that no further action is required. For example, an eating service episode would start when a person thinks, "I've got to eat something" and ends with the thought, "OK, that's enough." Therefore, our discussion of service quality and service value goes

Table 2.1 Key concepts discussed in this chapter.

Customer activity cycle or customer corridor	Description of the activities of the customer from the origin of the need to the resolution of the service episode.
Needs	A person's or an organization's requirements for something essential or desirable that it lacks.
Segmentation	Action of grouping customers in categories that are significant for the organization.
Quality assurance	Systems and approaches aiming at defect avoidance.
Service episode (client perspective)	Sequence of events, activities, and encounters that take place between the moment a person becomes aware of a need and the time when the need is addressed.
Service	The act of helping a person or an organization.
Self-service	The act of helping oneself.
Result	The outcome of the service episode with regard to the goals of the customer.
Experience	The sequence of emotions and feelings that the customer feels throughout the service episode, and in particular, those that he will recall afterward.
Service concept	Service features (or offerings) together with the benefits (effects) they produce for the customer. Some of these features are inseparable from the processes that deliver them
Satisfaction	The state of being content with what happened during or after a service encounter.
Value	The ratio of what one received to what he gave up to obtain it. Perceived value is the customer's perception of such.
Service leadership	The critical responsibility of a professional service provider to create conditions conducive to the customer's understanding of the nature of his need and of what is required to address it.
Technical quality	The degree to which a professional service was provided in a state-of-the-art fashion.
Job concept	Job features together with the benefits (effects) they produce for the employee. Some job features are inseparable from the processes that deliver them.
CTS	Critical to satisfaction: key customer needs that must be adressed by the service provider to produce customer satisfaction.
Value proposition	A focused statement spelling out precisely the key differentiating benefits, and the associated value, created by a service for a specific market segment.
Positioning	The place that a company occupies in the customer's mind. "Desired positioning" is defined by the targeted segment, service concept, and value proposition.

beyond the restaurant service encounter per se to also include the decision to go to a restaurant, the reservation, the driving, the parking, and so on. Using such a broad definition makes it possible to compare alternate ways to satisfy the need, such as cooking a meal at home or having pizza delivered.

We divide our discussion of quality of service into two parts: customer satisfaction and technical quality. We first present each concept before turning to a discussion of how they are related. Customer satisfaction[2] consists of three components: results, service experience, and self-service experience. First, customers want results. We define *result* as the degree of fulfillment of the customer's need. Satisfaction with the results does not tell the complete story, however. It is modulated by satisfaction with what the customer had to do to get the result, that is, with the service experience (what the customer had to do in interaction with the service provider) and with the self-service experience (what the customer had to do on his own to achieve the results he wanted). For example, one may have enjoyed the meal that she had at a restaurant (that may be the result she wanted), as well as all aspects of her experience at the restaurant (service experience).[3] If, however, she found the driving time to be long and unpleasant (self-service experience), next time she may select an otherwise inferior restaurant that involves less driving. A bad interaction experience, on the other hand, can outweigh any positive feelings generated by great food. A lack of respect by a service provider, for example, may lead a customer to never come back, however good the food was.

We now discuss each of these elements in turn, to highlight their meaning for professional services. Viewing Video 2.1 at this point is a good place to start (see Figure 2.2).

2.1.1 Results

We decide to purchase a service because we want to address a need. One decides to buy a guaranteed investment certificate, for instance, because he needs to protect the value of his money over time. One may hire a real estate agent because she feels that it is the best way to sell her house. One may call a computer technician because he cannot get new software to operate correctly. Consequently, customer satisfaction with the result (or outcome) of the service is the customer's perception of the extent to which the initial need that prompted him to act was met. How one values a result is strictly subjective, and the extent of satisfaction depends, among other factors, on the expectations the person held at the outset. Past experience, the nature and importance of the need, word of mouth, and advertising are other factors that bear on customers' expectations.

2—THE NATURE OF VALUE
To win at the business game, a company must master the art of simultaneously creating value for its customers, employees, and shareholders.

FIGURE 1.1 Body and Mind Inc – Illustration of the links between the target segment, service concept, and selected processes

2.1 Value and dual positioning
This is a conceptual video presenting an overview of the connection between value creation and positioning with the service concept and service delivery processes. It is a good introduction to the material covered in this chapter.

Key concepts: value in use, value as a ratio, segmenting, service experience, work experience, value of service, value of work, value proposition, service concept, job concept, dual positioning.

Figure 2.2 Video associated with Chapter 2.

2.1.2 Service Experience

Empirical studies (Berry et al. 1988) of service quality in many industries have resulted in the isolation of four aspects of the service experience that bear on customer satisfaction:

- Responsiveness: The employees' willingness to help and provide prompt service

- Assurance: The knowledge and courtesy of employees and their ability to inspire trust and to reassure customers

- Empathy: Individualized attention that results in the customers feeling that the employees understand them

- Tangibles: The appearance of the personnel and of the physical setting, installations, equipment, premises, and signage

Again, customer satisfaction derives from a comparison of perceptions after the encounter with initial expectations held before. This may be misleading, however, as expectations are dynamic constructs that can be influenced by experience and by communication. Indeed, as one is induced—through some chance event—to reduce her expectations concerning a forthcoming service experience, an experience that merely exceeds these reduced expectations may leave her pleasantly surprised, but not satisfied.

2.1.3 Self-Service Experience

A service episode, as defined earlier, also requires the customer to perform some actions on his own, such as filling in an online form or following a doctor's prescription. Customer satisfaction with the self-service experience is therefore similar to the satisfaction one gets from performing any task, and may include any or all of the following aspects:

- Did it work the first time?
- Were instructions clear?
- Were the tools appropriate and available?
- Was my skill level appropriate?
- When I needed additional information, was I able to access it immediately, on my own?
- When I needed help from someone, was it immediately available?
- Was the work environment pleasant?
- Was the work itself interesting, enjoyable?
- Was it stressful in any way, or did it involve physical or psychological discomfort?
- Did I learn something that improved my personal capabilities, that is, something that I may use in the future?

The self-service experience can be broken down into four parts:

- Actions performed in the service provider's *physical service system* (that is, on the premises). Using a terminal to access a database on a real estate agent's premises or filling in a form (alone) in a bank falls into this category. We also include person-to-person phone calls in this category—even though physical presence is not involved—because they consist of synchronous human-to-human interactions (this is discussed in Chapter 4).

- Actions performed in the service provider's *virtual service system*. This refers to web-based services such as tracking one's portfolio in a financial portal or searching for comparable properties to estimate market value.

- Actions performed in *other providers' service systems* (physical or virtual). Carrying on with the portfolio example, this includes checking out a competitor's site or simulating the long-term effect of various investment strategies in yet another site. For the customer of a discount real estate broker, designing a classified ad online to sell a house would also fall into this category.

- Actions performed in the customer's own environment, that is, in one's *personal service system*. Using stand-alone financial planning software, capturing and editing photos electronically, or reading about investment strategy falls into this category.

Table 2.2 presents complete examples of the components of value for hypothetical customers of insurance and accounting services.

We conclude this section with three caveats. First, while understanding these distinct concepts is important, one should not forget that they are correlated. The separate and joint efforts of the provider and the customer are required to produce results. A poorly designed or poorly managed service encounter or self-service experience will not only produce an unsatisfactory experience but also deny the desired results. Witness the faulty diagnostic that can result from a patient's failure to mention an embarrassing symptom because he does not trust the doctor with that information. The same is true for a risk-averse investor leading his financial advisor to think he is risk-prone.

Second, in services—such as professional services—where the customer may not be able to evaluate the true result (because of her limited knowledge in the field—see section 2.1.5), her satisfaction with the experience has an important impact on her perception of results, even though the two may be totally unrelated. For example, an airline passenger may surmise from a well-run passenger cabin that the cockpit crew or the maintenance crew also run a tight ship—even though there is little, if any, relationship between the two. Clean bathrooms in a fast-food restaurant might lead customers to infer that the kitchen is equally clean. Hence, in many services, and particularly in complex services where results are difficult to evaluate, the immediate negative impact of an unsatisfactory service encounter on service quality is compounded by its delayed impact on the perception of results.

Third, there are services (tourism and entertainment, for example) where customers are essentially looking for an "experience" (Pine and Gilmore 1998). One watches a movie for his viewing pleasure or maybe to change his mood. One goes trekking in Tibet to experience new sensations, enlarge his perspective, or get in touch with his inner self. While the quality of such service still consists of the three

Table 2.2 Components of value—two examples.

Components of value	Providers	Insurance claim	Income tax preparation
		Insurance company (primary), car dealer (secondary)	Accountant
Results		Car is fixed	Accurate return is filed on time (legal obligation is fulfilled; I'm not paying a cent more than I have to)
Service experience		Phone conversation with adjuster. Personal encounters with service manager (at the dealer's)	Phone calls and meetings with head accountant and technicians
Self-service experience	In physical service system	Keeping busy reading a magazine in the waiting room	Filling out a couple of forms
	In virtual service system	Checking various addenda to the policy online	Consulting the checklist so I don't forget any form I may need
	In other providers' service systems	Checking regulations on the overseeing agency's site. Getting other expert opinion and cost estimates on my own	Checking the latest government budget. Getting some receipts I need (some face-to-face, some online, some by phone). Calling an online expert (on a per-minute fee basis) to verify a deduction the accountant thought would not be allowed
	In personal service system	Writing and sending a letter to the insurance company	Building an Excel spreadsheet to check the totals and compare with previous years
Price		Insurance premium	Accountant's fee
Total cost		Premium + deductible + charges for other cost estimates + mileage + allocated cost for computer and Internet access	Fee + online expert fee + some cell phone, computer, and Internet charges + mileage

elements presented earlier, results are particularly hard to distinguish from the experience itself.

2.1.4 Technical Quality and Leadership

One factor that complicates matters in understanding customer satisfaction and trying to improve it is that people (apparently) purchasing the same service may well be looking for very different results. One person buying real estate services to sell her house because she is in dire need of money to pay a debt may be mostly preoccupied with speed and much less with the actual sales price. Another seller's sole concern may be to generate enough money to buy the condominium she wants, with speed being merely a "nice to have" aspect of the service experience.

Further adding to this ambiguity is that customers do not always know what they want. Indeed, professional services are characterized by a knowledge gap between the professional and the client. We use the word "client" instead of "customer" to underline the fact that the relationship goes beyond the mere commercial relationship—implied by the word "customer"—between a buyer and a seller.[4] The knowledge gap means that the client is often unable to specify his true needs. He does, of course, know his symptoms and is able to express his wish that they go away. He also often goes further and attributes—often mistakenly—the symptoms to specific causes. Indeed, this may lead him to pick a professional whose specialty is—he believes—to fix these specific causes.

Hence, the customer's inability to formulate a diagnostic generally does not prevent him from attempting to do so instead of leaving that most complex part of the service to an expert ("I'm quite sure that my heartburn comes from a gastric ulcer"). Consequently, he may end up at the door of the wrong service provider or, if he gets that part right, reach the right specialist but ask for the wrong procedure. This is a common occurrence in all professional services, from the management consultant responding to a flawed request for proposal, to a patient asking his doctor to prescribe a specific medication or procedure, to the engineer realizing that the minor machine performance problem she is asked to fix is really a major design flaw.

Formulating a diagnostic is a distinctive feature of professional work (see Chapter 5). Since this diagnostic is often at odds with the client's own preconceived idea, the ability to lead him to abandon the latter for the former is an important professional skill. That same skill is also needed to lead him to understand and accept the prescription as well. These are not selling skills, but leadership skills. Professionals must lead their clients on the path to thinking differently about their problem, and thus of understanding what's good for them.

Be it the surgeon in the operating room, the notary public in his office, the financial planner at her computer, or the architect at the drawing board, when a professional makes a mistake, the client pays the price. The importance of the service to the client, coupled with the knowledge gap mentioned earlier, implies that the provider is in a position of power over the client during service delivery. Where there is power, there is potential for abuse. Therefore, society deems it essential to insulate the professional–client relationship from any undue influence the commercial dimension of the transaction may exert on professional judgment. This is achieved by removing some decisions from the realm of business authority and entrusting them to professional regulatory or self-regulatory bodies. This adds to the complexity of managing professionals in general, and professional service organizations (PSOs) in particular.

It would indeed be easy for a professional to use the power or influence achieved over a customer through the service encounter to slant her advice and prescription in such a way as to gain financial advantage. Professional ethics is about respect (Bitran and Hoech 1992)—that is, using the power of influence solely in the client's best interest. The potential for abuse is even greater in situations where the client would not be able to detect it—that is, in situations where the result of the service episode is very difficult to assess with any objectivity in the short to medium term, let alone trace to professional abuse. Professional service is indeed ambiguity intensive (Alvesson 2001).

Let us define client satisfaction (dissatisfaction) as the extent to which the customer's perception of benefits received after the service episode exceeds (falls short of) initial expectations. The foregoing discussion makes clear that, as important as it is, customer satisfaction cannot be a complete measure of the quality of professional services. That is why we characterize a professional service as having "technical quality" (to distinguish it from customer satisfaction) if it is performed in accordance with the state of the art in the field. Most of the time, clients are not good judges of this, at least in the short term. That does not hold them back, however. They interpret what they see and hear, however unrelated, and draw conclusions on important service aspects that they are in no position to assess. These conclusions, however misguided they may be, matter because they guide clients in current and future decisions, as well as in the word of mouth they spread around.

2.1.5 Customer Satisfaction and Technical Quality

Figure 2.3 shows four possible situations resulting from various combinations of technical quality and customer satisfaction (Harvey 1998). Quadrants 1 and 3 are particularly interesting (clinically speaking). In quadrant 1, professionals perform with a high degree of technical quality, but customers are not satisfied. This can occur in PSOs that value technical proficiency and ethics and pay no attention to customer expectations and perceptions. In other words, professionals are competent and propose appropriate courses of action. But, they fail to make customers understand the true nature of their need and to lead them to the right conclusion. In the absence of a trusting relationship between client and professional, no value

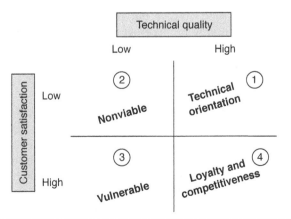

Figure 2.3 Customer satisfaction and technical quality.

is possible. This situation is often associated with professional arrogance and is not sustainable unless competition is somehow limited—otherwise the firm would soon be out of business.

Examples of this might include highly specialized medical services and notaries in underserved remote areas. This may also occur in internal professional services from the finance, engineering, or IT departments. Moving to quadrant 4 requires a change in the professional mind-set. They must become more inclined to listen to the feelings of their customers and explain what they are doing and why it is needed. This is essential in order to adjust and meet clients' expectations and perceptions, and to assume their leadership role fully.

In quadrant 3, the situation is reversed: aspects of the service delivery that influence client satisfaction are well managed, but the clients are essentially being cheated—that is, they are not getting the service they should get, but they are (as yet) unaware of it. Such a manipulative environment may prevail as long as the organization can get away with it. Some forms of alternative medicine fall into this category. Despite scientific evidence that some of these medicines do not produce any effect, some people will be duped, assuming that they are effective and never being able (or actually trying) to verify this assumption. Individual professionals in all fields can also "lead clients down the garden path" using their superior knowledge or intellect to conceal, interpret, or manipulate events, data, and facts to their advantage. Some use statistics as a drunkard uses a lamppost—for support, not for illumination (attributed to Mark Twain). Sometimes the behavior is clearly fraudulent. More often, it may simply involve complacency, lack of rigor, or convenient "little white lies" or omissions. These individuals and organizations are of course vulnerable. When clients learn the truth—helped in this, at times, by competitors—they are liable to feel cheated and become inexhaustible sources of negative word of mouth.

2.1.6 Before and After

Before the service encounter (ex-ante), we are dealing with expectations—after, with perceptions. Thus, the customer bases his purchase decision on experience with similar services, modulated by any factor such as brand name, publicity, word of mouth, and interaction with salespersons, which may lead him to expect the experience to be different. The actual service experience, including all the subtle clues that customers read from verbal and nonverbal aspects of service encounters, affects perceived quality (an ex-post concept). As well, while service failure may deny results to the customer, impeccable service recovery is an integral part of the service experience, and its impact on perceived quality may be a determinant. It can lead customers to expect high-quality results in the future, thereby enticing them to come back despite the failure.

Figure 2.4 illustrates the time relationship between customer satisfaction and technical quality. The gray funnel-shaped area shows the evolution of the breadth of expectations and perceptions about a service encounter. Initial expectations may vary widely. As the customer obtains more information about his need and the service provider, the breadth of expectations is somewhat reduced. The service encounter modulates initial expectations, transforming them into (ex-post) perceptions, which are less variable than expectations—that is, closer to technical quality. Technical quality does not exist before the service encounter. The gap

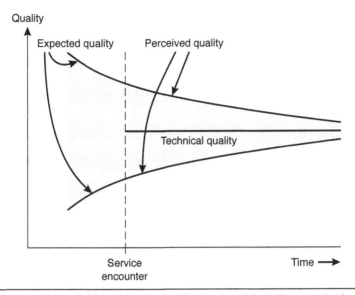

Figure 2.4   Time evolution of the relationship between expected quality, perceived quality, and technical quality in professional services.

between perception and technical quality, which can be substantial at the time of the encounter, tends to decrease over time, as customers learn (from experience and other sources), and as some delayed consequences start to appear. For example, design flaws in a house may show up over time, or the shortcomings of a financial plan may become more obvious as the economy goes through its multiple possible states.

2.2 THE CUSTOMER VALUE EQUATION

In this section we use the notions defined earlier to introduce one of the most important—and debated—notions in business today: value (see Figure 2.1). We first define it as a ratio before turning to a discussion of how to use it as a framework to better understand customer behavior, both in the case of the static single transaction and in the dynamics of an evolving relationship.

2.2.1 Value as a Ratio

In any commercial transaction, value is the ratio of what the customer obtained to what it cost her. Thus, in its simplest form, we can formulate the basic value equation as follows:

$$\text{Basic value} = \frac{\text{Results}}{\text{Price}}$$

No organization can survive without being competitive in basic value creation for its targeted customers. However, this equation does not tell the complete story: it does not take into account the customer's experience. Consequently, if we define the overall cost of a service to include (on top of the price) any additional expense incurred outside the service system, such as mileage cost to drive to a restaurant or internet access cost for online banking, we can formulate a more complete equation:

$$\text{Value} = \frac{\text{Results} + \text{Service experience} + \text{Self-service experience}}{\text{Overall cost}}$$

where each term stands as defined earlier. The additional terms (price and total cost) are illustrated in Table 2.2 for the cases of insurance claims and income tax preparation. Carrying on with the restaurant example (see Figure 2.5), on any given night one has a choice between preparing a meal at home and eating out. The decision hinges on such factors as:

- One's cooking skills (results)

- One's enjoyment of walking to the grocery store (self-service experience)

- The actual shopping (service experience)

- The pleasure one derives from preparing the meal (self-service experience)

- The meal at the restaurant may cost $75.00 (including the cost of a 30-minute drive) compared with $10 (including the cost of the ingredients, energy, and appliance amortization) for the home meal

If one is trying to lose weight, the very nature of the results one is seeking is different from that of a customer looking for a gastronomic experience. In that case, the value of the added control over calorie intake that one gets from preparing a home-cooked meal (self-service experience) may outweigh one's enjoyment of a five-star restaurant (service experience).

In the age of the internet, understanding the value equation is imperative. Technological advances and the coming of age of a new generation—one that,

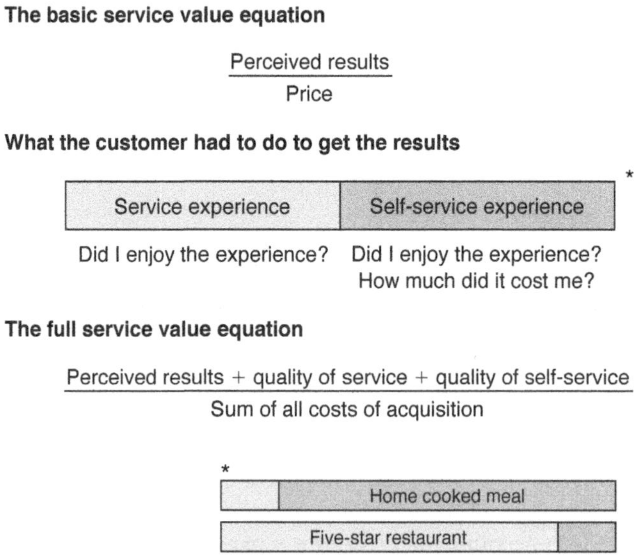

The basic service value equation

$$\frac{\text{Perceived results}}{\text{Price}}$$

What the customer had to do to get the results

Service experience	Self-service experience *
Did I enjoy the experience?	Did I enjoy the experience? How much did it cost me?

The full service value equation

$$\frac{\text{Perceived results} + \text{quality of service} + \text{quality of self-service}}{\text{Sum of all costs of acquisition}}$$

*
	Home cooked meal

Five-star restaurant	

Figure 2.5 The value equations.

having been raised in an environment where technology is omnipresent, enjoys the control and convenience that it provides—gradually and continually tip the balance of value in many service industries toward solutions that include an important dose of self-service.

Economic theory holds that a person spends her money in such a way as to maximize the satisfaction achieved per dollar spent. In most situations, however, customers are content with "satisficing"[5] rather than "optimizing," that is, stopping the search and settling as soon as they find a service that meets their minimal requirements. A person could, however, be expected to consider any new value proposition that appears likely to produce a "bigger bang for the buck," that is, have greater expected value than the perceived value received from the current provider.

Value is assigned to products and services through the lens of our beliefs. A system of shared beliefs is called a culture. The military, for instance, shares a set of beliefs. So do religious communities. As someone who has traveled to China, France, and Mexico, I can vouch for the fact that the same actions performed in each place can elicit very different reactions. A service employee in a national technical support center should be trained to "decode" and treat requests from a Midwest farm area differently than those from New York City.

2.2.2 Transactional and Relational Approaches

The very notion of value differs depending on whether one looks at it as a one-time transaction or as an ongoing relationship. In a one-time transaction, both parties are solely interested in getting the most out of the exchange at hand. In a relationship, since both parties expect to do business again in the future, they look at every interaction as both an immediate source of value and an opportunity to influence future value streams. As a result, either party may be willing to settle for less value than it would normally expect out of a transaction in exchange for expected future benefits. In other words, both parties may be willing to invest in the relationship.

The investment the customer is willing to make often has to do with quality of self-service. When learning how to use the provider's physical and virtual service systems, the customer may accept that it takes longer at first and that mistakes—even service failure—can occur. As the customer becomes more familiar with the system and adapts to it, however, and as the provider gets to know the customer better, both stand to benefit: the customer will get more value and become more adept at evaluating the result, and the provider will get a bigger "share of wallet," reduce costs, and benefit from well-targeted referrals.

2.2.3 How the Search for Superior Value Drives Customer Behavior

Expected value (ex-ante) and perceived value (ex-post) preside over people's decisions to come back for more, search for alternatives, respond to ads, respond to a friend's inquiry, or give advice to a friend. Perceived value lies at the root of business success or failure. Thus, it pays to understand the service value equation well.

Table 2.3 shows possible customer responses to five situations. A low basic value equation (1) will lead customers to actively search for an alternative, irrespective of the quality of the associated experiences. A high basic value equation, coupled with positive service and self-service experiences (2), leads to the development, maintenance, and growth of the relationship, with all the benefits that this entails.

Table 2.3 Customers' reactions to various satisfaction conditions.

#	Basic value equation	Satisfaction with service experience	Satisfaction with self-service experience	Action required
1	Low	*	*	Explore all options right away
2	High	High	High	Maintain or increase relationship
3	High	High	Low	Look for full-service supplier or improve your self-help process
4	High	Low	High	Look for alternate—especially with more self-service
5	High	Low	Low	Look for full-service provider and keep an eye open for breakthroughs in self-service technologies

In situation 3, results are good, service quality is high, but the self-service experience is unsatisfactory. To illustrate, imagine an investor who is gradually achieving her investment goals and enjoys the financial advice of and regular interaction with administrative personnel. However, she has to spend an inordinate amount of time in following up her investments, that is, putting all transactional and account statement information together to find out where she stands. One solution may be for the investor to improve her personal service system through building an electronic spreadsheet or buying specialized software. She could also ask her provider to improve his virtual service system—that is, develop a more user-friendly real-time statement of account. She could look for another provider for that virtual service or simply contract out the service to another provider, such as an accountant.

In case 4, the situation is inverted: the customer enjoys the self-service experience but dislikes the service experience itself. Imagine that an investor does all of his investing online in his provider's virtual service systems, and that he enjoys all the features of the system. However, he has to visit the provider's office to sign forms regularly, and some transactions are only performed on the phone—both of which he dislikes. He would then be tempted to look for an alternate provider whose virtual service system is more complete, thereby doing away with the unwanted interactions.

Finally, in case 5 the customer does not enjoy any aspect of what he has to do to get the good results he has been achieving. He is therefore on the lookout for a full-service (turnkey) provider or for a breakthrough in self-service technology (such as the quantum improvement we have seen in recent years in financial management websites) that would turn an unpleasant experience into an enjoyable one.

A number of factors may cause a customer's value equation to shift from one state to another in Table 2.3:

- The performance of the provider may change.

- The customer may be enticed—through word of mouth or publicity—to sample another provider's fare with higher expected value, with the outcome dependent on the perceived value (ex-post).

- A competitor may come up with a breakthrough service concept.

- Needs may change.

- Self-service technology may improve, for example, a user-friendly, voice-activated 24/7 answering machine.

- The customer may improve her capability for self-service through training or personal experience.

- The customer's values may change through a number of occurrences. For instance, he may suddenly have more time on his hands or need more face-to-face contact.

It pays to understand, monitor, and manage this dynamic well. Technical quality of service has a direct bearing on it. Customers may come out of a service encounter with high perceived value, only to find out later that they have been duped. On the other hand, they may have received fantastic value and never realize it (see discussion in section 2.1.4).

2.3 POSITIONING IN PROFESSIONAL SERVICES

Having defined quality and value, we can now discuss how companies can target specific customers and formulate a game plan (strategy) to create more value for them than competitors (see the upper part of Figure 2.1). To do so, we address a number of strategic concepts: customer activity cycle, segmentation, target market, value proposition, positioning in the customer market, and positioning in the labor market. We give a number of examples along the way to make these conceptual notions more concrete. Please view Video 2.2 before proceeding to the next section.

2.3.1 Understanding Where the Customer Is Coming From— An Illustration

Understanding where the customer is coming from and where she is going is essential to understanding her needs and preferences—that is, "wearing the customer's shoes." You may want to jump ahead momentarily to view Video 3.1 and read Box 3.1, as this information constitutes great preparation for what follows. You can come back here afterward, without loss of continuity. An example is best to explain this idea of taking the customer's view (see Box 2.1). We illustrate Jack and Linda's path in Figure 2.6. We can zoom in on any activity along this path to better understand the micro-activities involved. Figure 2.7, for example, shows the details of the activity "sell the house." At this level, for anyone who knows what kind of people Jack and Linda are, it becomes fairly easy to understand their needs (see the illustrative bubbles in Figure 2.7). Specifically, they can be obtained by grouping the elements (using an affinity diagram [see Figure 2.18]) shown in the bubbles in Figure 2.7 (see detailed instructions in the end-of-chapter exercises). For Linda and Jack, this is a once-in-a-lifetime project. If we consider the complete market segment, however, this is a cycle that is repeated, with individual variations, many times over.

The results Linda and Jack want can be stated as follows: getting the best possible net price, reaching a deal quickly, and being able to stay in their house till the new one is ready (for about six months). They would also like the process to be as smooth as possible—to have pleasant encounters and to minimize risks

Box 2.1 Jack and Linda Have a Vision

Issue: *Identifying customer needs, formulating a service concept, and positioning a service.*

The week before Jack turned 50, the younger of Jack and Linda's two daughters moved out of the house, turning it into the proverbial empty nest. After considering all their options, Jack and Linda decided to sell their suburban house and have a new one built in the countryside. They picked a nice village that would still allow Jack an easy commute to his office in town while affording the couple a better quality of life. Reaching that decision was not easy, as it involved hours of discussion to build a shared vision of the future they wanted. To turn the vision into a reality, however, they would need help, that is, services. Their plan of action started with the selection of a location and the purchase of a piece of land. They would design the new house while they were waiting for a buyer for the old one. Construction would start when they found a buyer, hopefully being completed by the time they moved out.

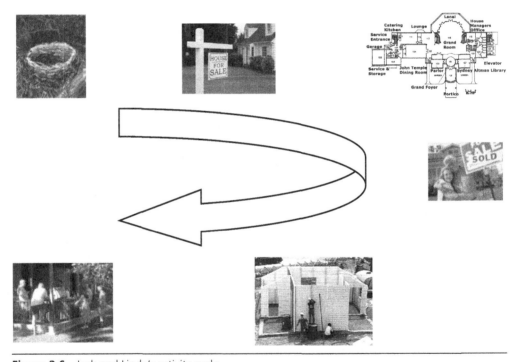

Figure 2.6   Jack and Linda's activity cycle.

(including "surprises"). To Linda and Jack, an encounter is pleasant when they deal with someone who is honest, competent, and trustworthy—someone with whom they could become friends—and when they do not feel any undue pressure. They would like to avoid such risks as fraud, delays, or NSF checks. We summarize Jack and Linda's requirements in Table 2.4, together with the relative importance they attach to each. We obtained the weights by asking them to spread 100 points among their requirements. We often call the most important requirements—the ones with the largest values in Table 2.4—*critical to satisfaction* (CTS) elements.

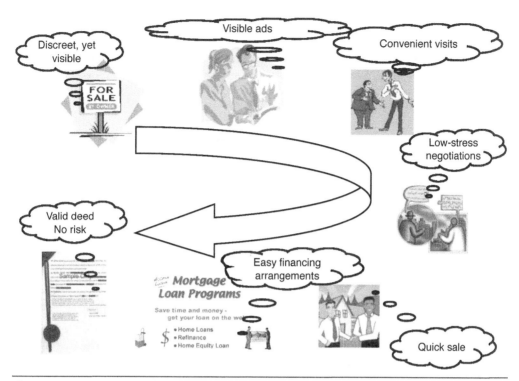

Figure 2.7   Zoom in: sell the house.

Table 2.4   Comparing needs of two couples selling their houses.

	CTS	Weight	
	Level 1	**Linda/Jack**	**Mike/Diane**
Results	1. Quick deal	15	0
	2. Maximum net price	30	80
	3. Occupancy in six months	15	0
Service and self-service	4. Low risk (fraud, technical glitch)	10	0
	5. Pleasant encounters	10	10
	6. Information (what's happening?)	5	0
	7. Control	10	0
	8. Ease	5	10

When Linda and Jack saw their longtime friends Mike and Diane, who had sold their house the previous year, they asked them what their weighting would have been at the time. They were amazed to see what they came up with (see Table 2.4). In the discussion that ensued, Mike and Diane said they were really just testing the market, having noticed a strong increase in property values in their neighborhood. They were ready to move out the next day if anyone met the asking price—and would even find the challenge of finding a place to live exciting. Mike and Diane are trusting people who think that all real estate agents and notaries are nice and honest people, and that you only see fraud on TV. Clearly, even though at first glance the two couples had the same needs, they were in fact looking for very different benefit packages.

2.3.2 Exploring How Customers May React to Various Service Offerings

The customer's capability and willingness to get involved in the satisfaction of his need is a critical determinant of the nature of the services that he requires, and therefore of the relative value that he places on alternate service options. This capability, in turn, is a function of the customer's knowledge of the subject area (medicine, finance, architecture, and so on) and of his ability to use information technology (IT) to access and use the information, advice, and capabilities that can help him solve the problem. If Jack feels comfortable with the real estate business and with navigating a website, he has many more options open to him than if he feels completely out of his depth in both fields. However, even in the former case, he may still opt for a full-service agency based on his evaluation of its cost-effectiveness. This has to take into account his own opportunity cost (that is, things that he will not be able to do if he undertakes this task by himself), whether or not he finds the task interesting and feels he may learn something by doing it himself.

To sell a house you need to advertise it, provide information to interested parties, negotiate with potential buyers, close the deal, formalize it in a binding agreement, sign the deeds, and finalize financial arrangements. This is represented in a FAST (functional analysis system technique).[6] (See Figure 2.8.) Three basic ways

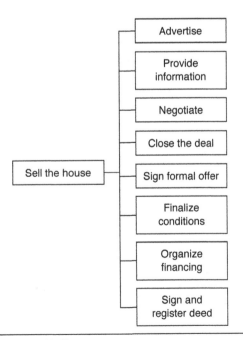

Figure 2.8   Selling the house: FAST diagram.

to sell the house are available to Jack and Linda: do it on your own, use a discount web-based real estate service, or use a traditional full-service real estate agent. Figure 2.9 shows, based on the FAST diagram, what each of these might involve for Linda and Jack. On the left-hand side we find the generic functionalities (or subprocesses) of the FAST diagram. Each of the three process concepts (a notion discussed further in Chapter 10) presented describes a specific way of performing the process.

Assuming that Jack is proficient with technology, he can place ads directly on many websites (some involving a fee), place ads directly in newspapers, design a for-sale sign on the printer's website that he can post in front of the house, and build his own web page to provide photos and information on the house, asking price, and conditions. Initial contact can be made through e-mails, through a messaging service, or by cell phone. Visits, negotiations, and the closing have to be face-to-face, without intermediary (we call these "contact modes"—discussed in

Function	Sell by myself	Discount agent	Full-service agent
Advertise	Hire help for the website software. Find printer for sign	Send electronic photos for posting on the agent's website. Takes care of sign	Takes care of everything
Provide information	E-mail, fax, phone messages	Mostly through agent's website	Agent, by phone, or face-to-face with buyer
Negotiate	Face-to-face	On a fee-for-service basis, if required	Agent acts as intermediary. Offers advice
Close the deal	Count on own interpersonal skills	As above	As above
Sign formal offer	Buy a standard form on the web	Agent supplies standard form and validates it	Takes care of everything
Finalize conditions	Face-to-face	Face-to-face	Agent acts as intermediary. Offers advice
Organize financing	Shop around for a good deal	On a fee-for-service basis, if required	Agent acts as intermediary with banker. Offers advice
Sign and register deed	Shop around for a notary	On a fee-for-service basis, if required	Takes care of everything

Figure 2.9   Selling the house: high-level customer process.

Chapter 4). Jack and Linda can use a notary, and a bank can finalize the transaction. Using a web-based real estate agent would make things easier on the technology side (at a price) and provide greater exposure through access to a widely advertised website. They could also contract additional help, as needed, in negotiation, formalization of an agreement, or any other legal and technical services.

Full-service brokerage, of course, provides the easiest route, but here again at a price. Because of the commission, Linda and Jack thought that this would probably not result in the best net price (criterion 2). However, they felt that the house would quickly get exposure to more potential buyers this way, thus beating the other two options on criteria 1 and 3. As for criteria 4 and 5, they depend on the choice of agent. We discuss the discount brokerage option later in this chapter.

From the little we know about Linda and Jack's preferences, we can surmise from an examination of Figure 2.9 that they will prefer the results proposed by the full-service agent. They should find the service and self-service experience offered by this agent generally more aligned to their expectations than that possible with the other two concepts. They would, of course, rather pay the price of the latter two concepts than that of the full-service agent. In deciding which course of action to choose, the couple's discussion is likely to focus on their appreciation of the relative importance of these service differences in view of the price differential. Thus, they will at some point decide which concept offers the best value prospect.

2.3.3 Positioning in the Market

Desired positioning is the way we would like our customers to perceive us. *Achieved positioning* is the way they actually perceive us. The gap between the two is the challenge we face in changing customers' perceptions. Advertising contributes to branding our services' performance in the mind of the customer. However, no matter how much and how well you advertise, subpar performance will never allow an organization to sustain the brand image it desires. Looking at the car market for illustration, one could say that Volvo is perceived as safe, BMW as high-performance, and Toyota as reliable. It took half a century for Toyota to achieve this superior positioning and become the number one car maker in the world in 2010. However, shortly after this impressive achievement, this positioning was badly shaken by Toyota's failure to respond in a timely and appropriate fashion to emerging safety issues. GM's image, often perceived in the United States as value for the money, was tarnished in 2014 by massive recalls, as well as by the leaks about a culture that discouraged reporting of bad news to top management.

Positioning involves segmenting, targeting, and formulating a value proposition. After explaining what these terms mean, we will illustrate them by pursuing the real estate example.

2.3.3.1 *Segmenting*

Just as it is in our personal life, wanting to be all things to all people is a sure-fire recipe for a business to fail. Positioning[7] is the art of selecting the right target market and gearing up to reach it. It can be broken down into three logical steps: segment the market, select the segments you want to target (while explicitly renouncing the others), and develop the value proposition and service concept.

Segmenting involves grouping customers into homogeneous clusters. There is no set way of doing this, and it is more art than science. Demographics, geography, and social condition are obvious criteria to consider. Frequency of use is another. However, this results in categories that can be very heterogeneous—far too much to be able to compete in many industries. Targeting an excessively broad market segment places a company in the uncomfortable position of choosing between a standard service that does not really please anyone and having to customize its offerings in a way that makes them prohibitively expensive to deliver.

Hence, including behavioral and psychological characteristics in segmentation criteria is essential. There are few guidelines available, and one needs to be creative. We can use such traits as enjoying technology, being social or reclusive, and being passive or active by nature. Financial planners, for example, target such segments as "get rich quick" and "retire by the book," reflecting fundamentally different attitudes and beliefs toward life and retirement. Some drugstore chains are targeting people who need personal attention and reassurance, while others are trying to appeal to those who want to walk out with their medication as quickly as possible without being bothered.

Understanding the path of people like Jack and Linda is a good starting point for segmentation, potentially leading to a segment that we might call "empty nest." "Broken nest" might represent another segment, grouping couples whose union has faltered and who are in a hurry to settle their accounts and get on with their lives. "Young nesters" may constitute yet another segment, grouping childless young working couples (which we can further segment by such criteria as income and proficiency with technology). The way an organization dissects market reality into individual bits, and groups them in discrete chunks, can be an asset or a liability. It becomes a pair of glasses through which the organization sees the market and may prevent it from seeing opportunities that are right under its nose but out of focus. Breaking the glasses occasionally and taking a fresh look can be a very profitable—if challenging—exercise.

2.3.3.2 *Targeting and Value Proposition*

Strategy is about how you are going to beat your competitors. *Targeting* is about picking your fights. This includes deciding which fights you are going to avoid, that is, which market segments you will renounce in order to better concentrate your resources where you stand a fighting chance. This requires a good analysis of your competitors' strengths and weaknesses as well as your own. One must evaluate each segment in terms of its size, growth, and satisfaction with current offerings. A package of benefits must then be developed that meets the needs of targeted customers better than competitors do, and the service itself must be designed in such a way that its features deliver these benefits. We will refer to the features–benefits pair as the *service concept*. It focuses on the numerator of the value equation and specifies it further, including the features of the service offerings designed to produce these benefits. Listing a number of benefits is easy. Specifying why these are the right benefits to win over and keep targeted customers and what service features are needed to produce these benefits is another matter.

A service provider's *value proposition* specifies the benefits offered to the customer in exchange for her money, that is, it is the expression of the service concept formulated as a promise made to the target market, clearly expressing how it is different from and superior to what competitors offer. In the competition for the heart, mind, and wallet of the customer, the best value proposition wins—but woe befalls the service provider that does not make good on this promise. A benefit is something that promotes or enhances well-being. More precisely here, it is the effect felt by the customer when a provider satisfies an implicit or explicit need. Therefore, the value proposition is the specific promise made to the customer about the value she will get (as defined by her value equation) if she uses the provider's services.

A web-based service—for example, one in which a customer can comparison shop for a car, access the dealer's cost, and buy a car—offers benefits such as convenience, speed, best price, assurance that you are not leaving any money on the table, and a low-pressure buying experience. The features of such a web portal could include links to the best sites for benchmarking technical data on cars, Blue Book prices, dealer discount programs, and so on. The customer sends a bid by e-mail to a participating local dealer, and if the dealer accepts it, the car is delivered to the customer's door. For the targeted market, this concept (that is, the benefits and features of the service) is vastly superior to that offered by a traditional dealership. The targeted market includes rational customers rather than impulse buyers—people with strong analytical capabilities who are comfortable using web-related technology and abhor the sales tactics used by dealers. By the same token, the web-based provider renounces the market segment made up of people who enjoy building a personal relationship with their neighborhood dealer, buying a new car there every other year, and enjoying the quality of service and clout that come from years of patronage and being on a first-name basis with their salesperson or the service manager.

2.3.3.3 Positioning—Pursuing the Real Estate Example

Returning to real estate now, imagine a small community where the real estate market can be broken down into the aforementioned segments (empty nest, broken nest, and young nesters). Imagine an additional market segment (see Figure 2.12) consisting of people like Mike and Diane (Table 2.4), to which we shall refer as the opportunists or "me too" market segment. Two full-service brokers dominate the market, each well established with a local office. Both are trying to serve all segments and are investing heavily in advertising to promote their brand name. They are essentially undifferentiated, offering the following value propositions:[8]

For sellers—"Using our services you will:

- Expose your house to the highest number of serious buyers

- Receive many serious offers, and only serious offers

- Receive the objective advice of seasoned experts who are well acquainted with your specific neighborhood

- Obtain the services of a trained negotiator who will ensure that you get the best possible price

- Be guided safely through the maze of legal and financial technicalities

- Find it much easier to move or find temporary storage or temporary accommodations you may need

- Deal with a single expert who will manage it all in your best interest"

For buyers—"Using our services you will:

- Have the widest possible choice of houses
- Receive advice from professionals who will help you find a house adapted to your needs
- Work with a trained negotiator who will ensure that you pay the best possible price
- Be guided safely through the maze of legal and financial technicalities
- Have help in facilitating your move, temporary storage, or temporary accommodations you may need
- Deal with a single expert who will manage it all in your best interest"

Figure 2.10 illustrates the corresponding service concept offered to the seller. It shows the benefits offered to the customer (the "what") with the feature or

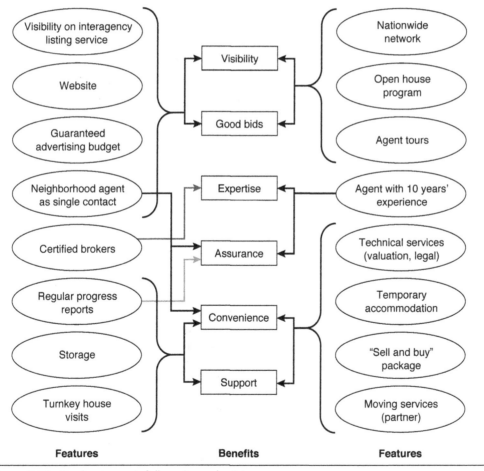

Figure 2.10   Service concept: full-service real estate agency.

characteristics of the service package itself (the "how"). The full-service broker can consequently be seen as an integrator, analyzing the specific needs of the customer (diagnostic) and custom designing a service package. Through a single point of contact, the broker manages the integrated delivery of multiple services in the best interest of the client.

Imagine now a new entrant in the market wishing to target people who are dissatisfied with the services offered by full-service brokers. For empty nesters and broken nesters (who have done this before) such dissatisfaction may stem from experience with brokers who, one way or another, did not deliver on their value proposition. They pass this on to "new nesters" through word of mouth ("What do you think of real estate agents, Dad?"). Understanding where the soft spots lie in your opponent's armor is as critical in business as it is in war. Full-service brokers, for instance, may be vulnerable to the following systemic delivery problems:

- Creating excessively high expectations on sales price and on a quick sale

- Underspending on specific advertising (as opposed to brand-name advertising)

- Putting excessive pressure on the seller to close the sale

Further, breakthroughs in the internet and IT make for potentially better results, a better self-service experience, and lower prices. The new entrant could focus on unsatisfied customers who have higher than average self-confidence and are technically literate ("techies" would be a subsegment), who are willing and able to take control of the sales process, and who are looking for access to the right network and for specialized support and advice. The value proposition for sellers could thus read as follows. "We will:

- Give your house as much visibility as you want

- Help you remain in control of the sales process from the day you decide to sell until you hand over the keys to the new owner

- Give you access on a fee-for-service basis to any specialized services or expert you may need (you will not pay for services you do not need)

- Assist you with any emergency that may occur throughout the sales process"

Figure 2.11 shows what a service concept for this new entrant might look like.

Figures 2.12 and 2.13 summarize the various notions related to positioning introduced in this section. In Figure 2.12, we fragment (figuratively) the market into segments—the circles represent the needs of a market segment (overlaps indicate common needs). Targeting (illustrated by arrows) is based on a market analysis and a competitive analysis, as well as on a strategic internal assessment of mission, capabilities, strengths, and weaknesses. Figure 2.13 illustrates how one's concept must represent superior value for your customers of choice—that is, for the targeted market segments stemming from Figure 2.12. The thermometers refer to customer value (see the equations discussed earlier). The provider must translate that concept into a value proposition that advertisers will find a way to communicate so that it reaches and has the right impact on the right people.

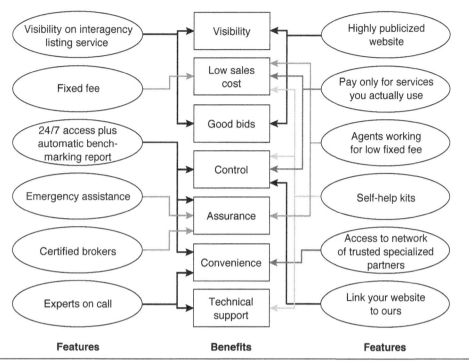

Figure 2.11   Service concept: discount real estate agency.

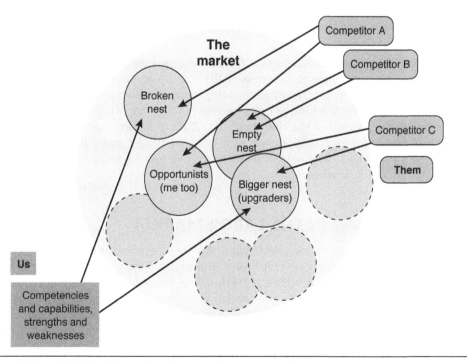

Figure 2.12   Positioning: illustration of segmenting and targeting.

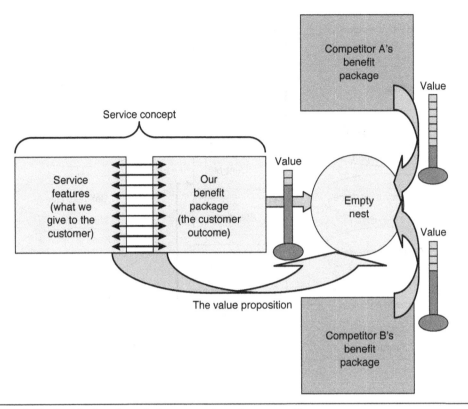

Figure 2.13 Positioning: formulating a superior value proposition.

The discussion in this section focused on consumers—that is, B2C (business to consumer). Business to business (B2B) is more complex in several ways. Several players are involved from various departments, often pursuing different goals and perhaps even working at cross-purposes. They are acting on behalf of a third party (the company or the shareholders). They may have access to sophisticated resources, and their buying power may be substantial. Finally, their activity cycles (processes, in this case), and thus the needs stemming from these activities, are generally much more complex.

2.4 POSITIONING IN THE LABOR MARKET

A company cannot create much value for its customers unless it is simultaneously creating value for its employees. Indeed, unhappy service employees tend to produce unhappy customers. Of course, an organization does not relate to its employees as it does to its customers. Conceptually, however, there are many similarities, as organizations are competing in the labor market for the services of the best employees. In this section we show that the notions presented earlier regarding positioning in the market can be used advantageously to understand the challenges involved in recruiting and keeping the right people (see Figure 2.1, where positioning in the labor market is presented as the mirror image of market positioning).

2.4.1 Personal Value Equation

Employees receive benefits from their employer, just as customers do. The latter buy these benefits with money, the former with their time and energy. Just as customers search the market for the best value, employees search the job market for the most benefits they can get for what they have to offer, that is, for the best personal value. Let us explore the components of the personal value equation:

- *Personal results.* People look for a job for various reasons: money, wanting to be useful, self-actualization and professional growth, learning, and so on.

- *Internal service.* Organizations use various means to help employees do their jobs—that is, produce the results the company needs—and through this achieve their own personal goals. These means include such activities as training, coaching, providing tools, placing the employees in situations where they can grow, and helping with personal problems.

- *Employee self-service.* The burden of getting the employee to perform on the job does not rest solely with the employer. The organization expects the employee to take an active role in acquiring the required capabilities, maintaining his knowledge, and keeping his skills up to date. He must look for situations where he can learn and grow, on and off the job, and make the most out of them. He must improvise and be creative when faced with unexpected situations or when internal service fails him.

The basic personal value equation (see Figure 2.14) is simply the ratio of results achieved to time spent on the job. A youth who has a job flipping hamburgers in a fast-food restaurant may summarize the personal value he gets from his job as follows: "I get seven dollars an hour, I've made new friends, and we generally have a lot of fun working together. The end-of-season party is always memorable."

The basic personal value equation

$$\frac{\text{Personal results}}{\text{Time spent on the job}}$$

What the employee had to do to get the result

Internal service experience	Self-service experience

Did I enjoy the experience?   Did I enjoy the experience?

The full personal value equation

$$\frac{\text{Personal results} + \text{quality of internal service} + \text{quality of employee self-service}}{\text{Opportunity cost}}$$

Figure 2.14 The personal value equations.

To get the full personal value equation (Figure 2.14), we first include the internal service and self-service experience in the numerator. Our youth, for instance, may appreciate (or not) the advice he gets from the supervisor (internal service) and may find it difficult to get up at 5 a.m. on Sunday morning and face the 6 p.m. rush on Friday nights, when two loaded buses pull into the parking lot at the same time (self-service). Consequently, we change the denominator from time spent on the job to opportunity cost, which we define as the sum of all benefits forgone to secure the benefits of the job.

The full value equation is the ratio of what the employee thinks he is getting from the job to what he feels he could get doing something else. When that ratio falls below 1, because of either a decrease in the numerator (salary reduction, more frustration on the job, and so on), an increase in the denominator, or both, the employee is driven to reconsider his present employment. Anything that may lead the employee to believe he could get better working conditions, more job satisfaction, or greater opportunities elsewhere will have that effect. Or, if leisure time becomes more valuable for any reason, such as the arrival of a new baby, an inheritance, or a close relative in dire need of assistance, the personal value equation of the job decreases.

The time aspect (ex-ante, ex-post) and the notion of technical quality discussed earlier also apply, mutatis mutandis, to the personal value equation. The reader should bear in mind that this equation and the customer value equations are strictly conceptual notions and are not meant to be quantified. They constitute interesting constructs to understand customers' and employees' choices.

2.4.2 Professional Service Workers

Advising a corporation on how to manage its financial affairs bears little resemblance to flipping hamburgers. Indeed, professionals, as a class of workers, share a number of characteristics that separate them from other categories of workers:

- They value their knowledge and skills. They want to use them to the fullest by having the best tools available and not waste any time on tasks that are best performed by less qualified workers. They want to improve on them.

- They understand the central role they play in the creation of value for customers and want to be compensated accordingly.

- They are experts in their field and do not tolerate intrusion—or anything they consider as such—in their professional realms.

- All of the above factors make them more independent. They can leave the company and take their expertise with them, and often some clients as well. They can strike out on their own or set up a competing business with a group of colleagues.

For all their specificity, however, the value equation presented earlier applies to them, mutatis mutandis (with some adaptation). The results they seek include much better compensation and an important professional growth component. The self-service component (keeping current and honing skills) tends to be more substantial. The opportunity cost is also higher because of the mobility their recognized (diploma and professional certification) skill set affords them in the labor market.

Here also, personal value is assigned to our work through the lens of our beliefs. The relationship and attitude vis-à-vis authority (in Spain, Germany, and the United States, say), the interpretation of instruction (based on context in China, but not in the United States), and the relationship to time (Middle East vs. UK, say) vary widely across national cultures. Yet, in this global world, the successful conclusion of a service episode often depends on the capacity of employees from a host of different cultures to perform their part of the process (see next chapter) in harmony and synchronism. Superior personal value propositions (that is, superior to competitors' propositions) are a basic requirement for this to happen day in and day out, and these can only be developed with a thorough understanding of the employees' value system.

2.4.3 Positioning in the Professional Labor Market

Just as the organization must position itself in its service market, it must position itself in the labor market. To become the employer of choice for the type of professionals it needs, it must:

- Have a clear idea of who they are and where they can be found (segmenting and targeting)

- Understand where they are coming from and where they are going, both in the short term and in the long term (activity cycle)

- Understand what they want from their job and how important each element is (affinity diagram and importance weighing)

- Develop an employee benefit package (job concept) that they will prefer to that of competitors (positioning)

- Find a way to translate the concept into a value proposition and communicate it in such a way that it will reach and be understood by the targeted individuals

- Find a way to translate the job concept into work processes and internal service processes that will truly generate the results and experience that they are looking for, and thus induce them to stay and prosper in the company, spreading the word to potential new recruits

Referring back to Figure 2.12, one can see that the notion of positioning it represents is conceptually analogous whether it refers to the market or the labor market. If one thinks of the labor market rather than the market in Figure 2.12, then the smaller circles represent groups of people with similar needs, skills, attitudes, or values, and the arrows illustrate how competitors (who may or may not be the same competitors we meet in the market) are targeting various labor market segments for employment. In this context, positioning in the labor market involves the elaboration of a superior benefit package for these employees of choice, and its translation into a personal value proposition to be communicated in its recruitment drives and to serve as a guide in the elaboration and management of relevant processes (see Figure 2.15).

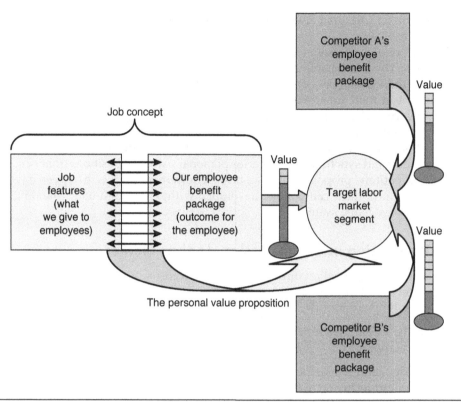

Figure 2.15 Positioning in the labor market: giving more value than the competition does to employees of choice.

Imagine, for instance, that we group real estate agents in the following categories:

- *Young techies*, who enjoy dealing with computers more than with people

- *Cruise control* ("earn my keep") agents, who make a living but are happy with what they have and do not wish to reduce their leisure time

- *Moonlighters*, who do this to supplement their regular income

- *High-rolling traditionalists*, who manage this as a business in an old-fashioned way (they sell and farm out some of the execution to assistants, *cruise control* agents, and *moonlighter* agents)

Figure 2.16 illustrates how companies must position themselves simultaneously in the market and in the labor market. Reaching and maintaining this positioning dynamically, as markets, competition, and technology change, is an essential component of the strategic challenge that any organization must address. It is compounded by the necessity to ensure a fit between service concept and job concept, so that win–win moments of truth are produced during service encounters, thus reinforcing the dual positioning.

We discuss this further in Chapter 4.

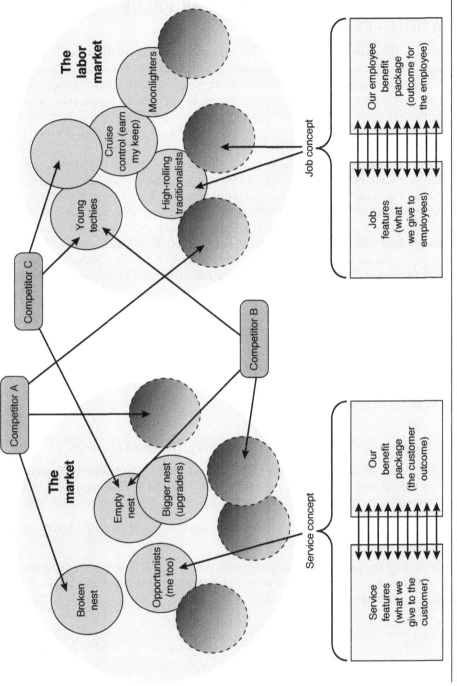

Figure 2.16 Dual positioning in the market and in the labor market.

2.5 MANAGING THE SHAREHOLDER VALUE EQUATION—EVA

Having discussed the dynamics of simultaneous value creation for customers and employees, we now turn to shareholders, whose money rides on the success of the venture (see Figure 2.1) and whose entrepreneurial spirit and willingness to take risks created the venture in the first place. In capitalism, businesses exist for the purpose of generating profits for their owners. They achieve this by beating their competition at value creation in the market and in the job market. Societal benefits derive from this competition and the survival of the fittest. *Economic value added* (EVA) consists of what remains when all resources (human, material, and financial) that have been used to generate income have been paid for. The sole purpose of creating value for customers and employees, as discussed in this chapter, is the maximization of EVA. Just as the search for value drives consumer behavior, and the search for personal value drives employee behavior, the search for EVA drives shareholder behavior. To avoid being sidetracked by the intricacies of EVA[9] calculation, financial leveraging, and the cost of capital (the interested reader should refer to Stewart 1999), we have chosen to use profit rate as a proxy. We define it by the following equation:

$$\text{Profit rate} = \frac{(\text{Number of clients} \times \text{Volume per client} \times \text{Profit margin}) - \text{Fixed costs}}{\text{Investment}}$$

The higher the percentage of clients who come out of the service encounter disappointed or for whom disillusionment follows initial delight, the lower the volume through:

- Loss of disappointed clients

- Dissuasion of potential clients through negative word of mouth

- Defection of clients (and potential clients) to the competition through word of mouth from these disappointed clients, who have now been delighted by competitors

- Initially lower frequency of purchase from the new clients that have to be attracted to compensate for the loss

The higher the percentage of clients who come out of the service encounter disappointed or for whom disillusionment follows initial delight, the lower the profit margin through:

- Increased advertising expense to attract new clients

- Initially lower margins for these new clients, as clients tend to become cheaper to service over time

Zero defection of targeted clients is therefore the only viable target for a firm that wishes to maximize its long-term profits. Technical quality and client satisfaction are crucial levers to moving profit in the right direction. Good positioning in the market[10] and in the labor market makes this possible. The former will make it possible to (nicely) turn away and refer to a competitor clients who are likely to defect because the firm cannot provide them—for some reason or another—with services of high technical quality that will produce durable customer satisfaction. The latter will make it possible to select and keep only those professionals who will find it to be in their overall best interest to give the best service they can to these customers. Single-minded focus on short-term profits clearly precludes any of this.

Ways (operations strategies) to increase the numerator while decreasing the denominator of both value equations—and thus run away from the pack—are discussed in Chapter 4.

Finally, we should keep in mind the organization's responsibilities to its partners and suppliers, as well as its responsibilities to society as a whole. Being a good corporate citizen, respecting the environment, and promoting the well-being of the communities where it operates are not merely niceties but distinct expectations society places on business. The social web provides organized and spontaneous communities that will emerge and quickly mobilize against companies that ignore their social accountability.

2.6 SUMMARY

Just as customers pick their providers, PSOs should pick the customers they want to serve and tailor-design a benefit package for them. Customers are looking for the best result they can get for the money they have to spend, and they want the process of obtaining it to be painless. Like heat-seeking missiles, they change targets when they feel that a hot deal—promising a "bigger bang for the buck"—is available elsewhere. Service providers must seek to understand and manage the implicit underlying value equations that preside over such switches in various market segments. Understanding the mind-set with which various market segments approach a service encounter is an essential first step to that end.

Value equations are particularly complex in professional services, where the joint effect of often hard-to-evaluate results and the presence of a knowledge gap between service providers and their clients allows for manipulation and abuse. Professionals must often lead their clients in directions different from where the latter's intuition would lead them. They must do so with sufficient tact that their customers will not defect to less scrupulous or complacent competitors. This introduces a layer of complexity to professional service delivery processes (PSDPs) not found in other services. We address this in the next two chapters.

Finding and keeping the professionals who can do all this requires the organization to pay as much attention to its positioning in the labor market as it does to its positioning in the market. Maintaining and adapting this dual positioning as markets and labor markets evolve, and competitors strive to preempt one's move and take advantage of one's mistakes, is the challenge facing PSOs. To the winners accrue the profits that will reward shareholders and thus draw the capital necessary to stay ahead of the pack.

EXERCISES

These exercises are an important building block in your learning process, a bridge to cross the chasm between theory and practice. A multifunctional team will get the most out of it. This is best achieved by pulling together a team from various departments and sharing the book with them. If the level you are at in the organization does not allow you to do that, you can still share the book with selected colleagues from other departments. Of course, you can do the exercises alone, which will produce the intended individual learning but preclude any organizational learning. This may be a valid strategy if your intent is to vet the book and first find out for yourself if and with whom you want to share it. The formulation of the exercises assumes that a multifunctional team does them. Consensus must be the modus operandi.

Most of these exercises require only a flip chart, stacks of sticky notes of various colors (stick to pastel colors and large format), and black markers.

2.1 Activity Cycles

Select two market segments from your current or prospective customer base and draw the respective customer activity cycles, such as those shown in Figure 2.6 and Figure 2.7. Make sure you start the cycle at the moment when the original need arises and end when the need has been addressed. In the case of a sports health clinic, for instance, one should start with "ouch" and end with "back in competition." Use sticky notes on a flip chart and draw arrows to connect them (see Figure 2.17 for an illustration). If the team finds it difficult to agree on what the customer does, several factors may explain this situation:

- Nobody really knows what the customer does.

  Action: Find out! Conduct interviews and organize focus groups, then come back to the exercise.

- Marketing knows, but has never shared this information with the rest of the organization.

  Action: Ask marketing to prepare a presentation for the rest of the team, then proceed to do the exercise.

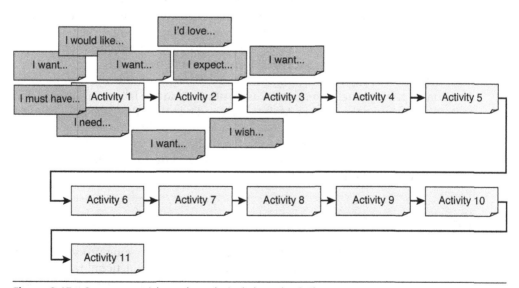

Figure 2.17 Customer activity cycle and needs (exercise 2.1).

- You are not thinking about the same people.

  Action: Review your segmentation or create one together if you have never done this explicitly.

If you find that the activities of the two market segments differ in only a few activities, draw a unique activity cycle and highlight the differences between market segments using sticky notes of different colors.

2.2 Customer Needs

"Put on the customer's shoes" and slowly "walk through" the customer's activity cycle as depicted earlier, thinking about what you may need or want or what you would simply enjoy as you go about performing that activity. The best way to do this is for team members to sit silently, write down on a separate sticky note each individual element (write in the first person, starting with "I need . . ." or "I want . . .") that comes to mind, and stick it at the right place along the cycle. Team members may look at the elements their colleagues are adding, thereby stimulating their own creativity.

When they are finished, members jointly eliminate duplications and clarify the meaning of each element. They then take these elements off the activity cycle and organize them in an affinity diagram to summarize them. This involves grouping them in homogeneous categories, that is, elements that reflect a common theme, and giving each category a name (see Figure 2.18). If you end up with upward of 15 categories, see if you can group them under a broader heading. Politeness, respect, and courtesy, for instance, might be grouped under a broader heading such as "treatment." If, on the other hand, you end up with four or five categories, see if you can split any of those into finer subcategories. We refer to the finer categories as "level 2 needs," as shown in Figure 2.19. Depending on the business

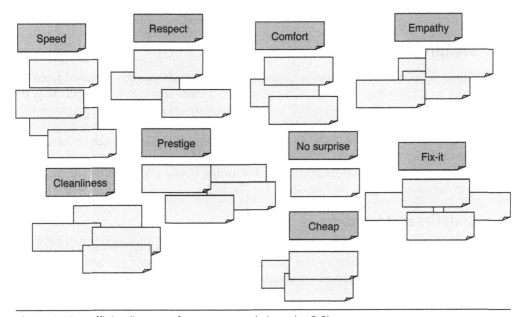

Figure 2.18   Affinity diagram of customer needs (exercise 2.2).

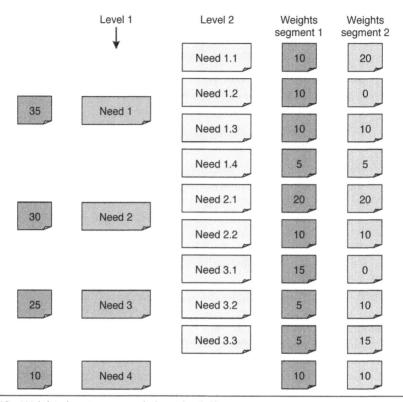

Figure 2.19   Weighted customer needs (exercise 2.3).

you are in, you should typically end up with 7–15 needs (at the lowest level—10 categories are shown in Figure 2.19). In complex services, it is sometimes required to split some level 2 needs into level 3 needs (yet finer categories).

2.3 Weights

Again wearing the customer's glasses, rank the needs you just defined from the most to the least important, and divide 100 points among them, reflecting the importance that customers attach to them. If the needs are divided into two levels, first rank the level 1 needs and divide 100 points among them, and then divide the points attributed to each level 1 need among the level 2 needs, as shown in Figure 2.19.

Translate your understanding of the differences between the two segments into different weights, such as shown in Table 2.4.

2.4 Benefits and Features

Identify the current features of the services you are offering to each of the market segments you identified earlier and link them to the needs of each segment, as identified earlier, producing a diagram similar to those shown in Figures 2.10 and 2.11.

2.5 Customer Value Equation

Build the value equation for these two market segments, as you perceive it, first explaining specifically what it includes (see Table 2.2 for an illustration) and then describing in one or two short sentences what you think is your customer's current appreciation of each element of the equation. Compare this result with what you believe to be the customer's experience delivered by your major competitor.

2.6 Professional Employee Value Equation

Repeat the four preceding exercises (2.2–2.5), this time thinking of your positioning in the professional labor market, rather than of customers. Select your major category of professionals—lawyers for a law firm, dentists for a dental clinic, and so on. If your major competitor is not your major source of competition in the job market, pick whoever is.

NOTES

1. Refers to the market for services, unless otherwise specified.
2. The expressions "service quality" and "customer satisfaction" are used interchangeably in this book. "Technical quality" of service, another aspect of service quality, is always referred to as such.
3. Depending on the customer's need, this may be, in whole or in part, the result she was seeking.
4. However, to reduce repetition, we use the words "customer" and "client" interchangeably throughout the book.
5. Finding a solution that meets basic requirements.
6. This is discussed in the next chapter. It is a decomposition of a process into its logical steps or functions.
7. What is being discussed here is *desired* positioning, not to be confused with *achieved* positioning. The first is a goal the company wants to reach, while the latter is *in the minds* of customers. In the car industry, for example, most customers readily associate Toyota with reliability, Volvo with security, and BMW with prestige, reflecting their respective *positions* in the minds of consumers.
8. Since brokers are intermediaries between buyers and sellers, depending on an agent's role in the transaction, she may have one or two clients: the buyer, the seller, or both. The discussion so far has focused only on the buyer.
9. "[EVA is] computed by taking the spread between the rate of return on capital r and the cost of capital and then multiplying by the economic book value of the capital committed to the business: $EVA = (r - c) \times capital$" (Stewart 1999, p. 136).
10. Unless otherwise stated, when used alone, the word "market" refers to the physical or virtual place where the services that a firm produces are traded.

3

The Nature of Processes

Civilization is not a collection of finished artefacts, it is the elaboration of processes.

—Jacob Bronowski, *The Ascent of Man*

Companies create value for their clients, employees, and shareholders through processes. They embody organizational know-how and are the key to strategic capabilities. Focusing on them is critical to learning and sustainable competitive advantage.

Having explored the notions of value and positioning in the previous chapter, we are now ready to take a more detailed look at how we do things in the organization, that is, at processes. Without a good understanding of our game plan for creating more value than our competitors for our customers and employees of choice, processes are meaningless. A quick glance at Figures 1.2 and 2.1 will remind the reader of the role of processes in business.

After explaining what processes are in the next section, we explore the various dimensions of the process space, which means that we look at various ways to classify and categorize processes. In the following section, we take a look at the nature of processes, viewing them as chains of commitment. We conclude the chapter with a discussion of the linkage between process and value and the importance of targeting the right process for improvement. Table 3.1 gives a short definition of the major concepts and techniques discussed in this chapter.

3.1 WHAT IS A PROCESS?

We begin with a very broad definition of a process, using examples drawn from everyday life, and introduce some basic process scoping tools. We then apply these tools to the business world and develop them further. The section closes with a list of requirements necessary for a process to exist (that is, to be "defined").

Table 3.1 Key concepts discussed in Chapter 3.

Service system	All the elements (human resources, machines, facilities, installations, software, roles, and relationships) standing ready to perform a service
Process	A system put into operation to transform some inputs into desired outputs
Project	A truly unique and complex endeavor that will not be repeated in any way in the future
Know-how	The capability to transform some inputs into desired outputs. It lies in processes
Organizational learning	The act of improving an organization's know-how
Functions	Center of expertise in the organization such as finance or marketing, around which most organizations are structured
Chain of commitments	Organizational view of a multiperson process, whereby responsibilities are distributed in a workable way throughout an organization, thus forming a chain linking inputs to outputs
SITOC	A process tool used to delimit the perimeter of a process
Interfacing processes	Processes that are adjacent to each other; in other words, processes that receive or provide deliverables (intermediate or final) to or from each other
Functionality	Some essential action that a process must be able to perform
FAST	A technique to decompose a process into functionalities
PFD	A graphic technique to bring out the (high-level) sequential flow of a process. It leads into a value stream map
CTP	One of the vital few variables that has a determinant impact on a dependent variable

3.1.1 Definition

Let's start with a definition that will be explained as the chapter unfolds: *A process is a shared and controlled way of doing things, involving a chain of commitments distributed logically in the organization, that operates a value-added transformation on inputs to meet customers' needs.* Let's now start with the basics.

Performing a process consists of taking an input and transforming it into a desired output. A simple example of a process would be "preparing breakfast" (note that here we have an action verb and a noun representing a sequence of activities that must be repeated frequently—this holds true for any process). "Making toast" is a subprocess or functionality of "preparing breakfast." You take a slice of bread (input) out of the refrigerator or bread box and put it in the toaster (transformation) to get toast (output). The supplier (the baker) provides the input, and the output goes to a customer (you). Consequently, we represent a process by the acronym SITOC (supplier, input, transformation, output, customer). The process starts when some input requirements are met (a slice of bread of the required type, size, and shape is available, and it is breakfast time) and finishes when some output requirements are met (toast of the required color and temperature).

Suppliers and customers of a process are often other processes. In the example, "bake bread" is a supplier process, and "eat breakfast" is a customer process. "Prepare financial statements," to cite a business example, may have "review company books" as a provider and "prepare income tax return" as a customer. In B2B situations, there can be many customers with different, often conflicting needs.

Video 3.1 illustrates this by presenting the dual perspectives of the passengers' experience and the airport authorities whose job it is to deliver the experience and manage the flow of thousands of inbound and outbound passengers every day (see Figure 3.1). Box 3.1 complements the narrative presented in the video.

3.1 An introduction to complex service delivery processes— The airport experience

The objective of this presentation is to provide a broad overview of the nature of complex service delivery processes. I use airports as illustration. While they typically include some of the simplest service jobs (such as bookstore clerk, parking attendant, and porter), they also include some of the most complex (pilot, air controller, and scheduler).

Key concepts: Servicescape, customer experience, service delivery processes, chain of value-adding processes, process breakdown

Techniques: SITOC, FAST

3.2 The process view

The notion of a process is fundamental to the systemic view of organizations as value-creating entities and the understanding of value streams flowing through the various departments and units. This video drives home the notion, bringing it to a personal level.

Key concepts: SITOC, customers of a process, chain of customers, outputs and outcomes, value stream, the mission of a process, transformation resources, zooming in and out

3.3 Processes and projects

The project notion has a good "branding," as it evokes new and unique ventures. The project notion is all too often associated with routine, repetition, bureaucracy, and control. The two notions are presented by some as clearly distinct. This video debunks some of these notions and presents a reality that is best described in shades of gray rather than black and white.

Key concepts: Project, process, temporary organization, improvement and learning, WBS vs. FAST. A host of examples are given to challenge popular paradigms and explore the relationships between the two concepts.

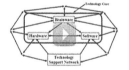

3.4 The nature of technology

All too often, an endeavor intent on process change ends up in technology implementation. Process improvement is about the brainware that should guide the choice, adaptation, and implementation of hardware, software, and the required support network. Technological capabilities and constraint are important factors to consider in process improvement and process design.

Key concepts: Technology, brainware, support network, organizational culture, created capability, technological change, process change vs. technology implementation

Examples: History (American war of independence), Pacific war (radar in the navy), the designer example. A simple model is proposed and the relationship between technological change and process improvement is clarified.

Figure 3.1   Videos associated with Chapter 3.

Box 3.1 An Introduction to Complex Service Delivery Processes—The Airport Experience

Key concepts: *Servicescape, customer experience, service delivery processes, chain of value-adding processes, process breakdown*

Techniques: *SITOC, FAST*

The objective of this presentation is to provide a broad overview of the nature of complex service delivery processes and customer experience, using airports as illustration. While they typically include some of the simplest service jobs (such as bookstore clerk, parking attendant, and porter), they also include some of the most complex (pilot, air traffic controller, and scheduler).

Airports are hubs and staging grounds where passengers, luggage, and crews are matched to an outbound aircraft, later disembarked from an inbound aircraft, and reinserted back into their respective activity cycles (figure shown in video). The respective dynamics and operating logic of these four elements are vastly different. The system exists to meet passengers' desire to go places, albeit for many different reasons. Wherever people go, they need to bring some belongings. Since luggage can be heavy, cumbersome, and potentially dangerous, people and their belongings fly in different parts of the aircraft, giving rise to handling and matching challenges. Crews have various costs, home bases, capabilities (for example, flying a Boeing 777-200LR), preferences, and constraints (for example, "Pilots must be given at least 8 hours of uninterrupted rest after a 10-hour flight," or "has 20 years of experience and thus first pick for her next affectation"). Aircraft are the most expensive resource of the system: their cycle and schedule drive the scheduling and handling of the other elements of the system.

An airport consists of various zones (figure shown in video), typically including a peripheral zone, an access zone, terminal zones, turf (the area between the terminal and the runways), and runways. The terminal itself consists of several areas, such as check-in, retail stores, duty-free shopping, food courts, VIP lounges, immigration, customs, luggage, gates, and aircraft access. Access between some of these zones and areas is strictly controlled, creating bottlenecks in the flows and making a timely and accurate four-way match more challenging. This can be quite intimidating to the uninitiated, and steering one's way to reach the right place at the right time can sometimes be a challenge.

Each area has its own mission, which determines its particular ambiance, modus operandi, and navigation rules, ranging from the quasi-military (immigration), to the functional (waiting room), to the strictly commercial (duty-free shopping). Sometimes different missions come into conflict with one another, and one gets the impression that the well-being of passengers ranks very low in the priorities of those who design and manage airports. In some airports, the distance that passengers have to walk makes one wonder if the airport was designed with only pilots and aircraft in mind (one is led to that conclusion by a process of elimination since, judging by current performance, luggage could not possibly have been the priority, either) or for maximum exposure to shop merchandise.

Let us now take a cursory overview of the air travel experience (figure shown in video). Travelers (right-hand corner, on the computer) first plan their trip and then purchase their ticket. They may use the services of a traditional travel agent, go directly to the airline's website, or use online travel agencies or meta-search engines such as Kayak. Competition in the distribution network is very intense, driven by competition among airlines and jockeying for position to take advantage of the new technology. Then comes packing, followed by traveling to the airport, where the traveler must go through a series of funnels: parking, check-in (self and luggage), security (in some places immigration as well), boarding, and seating. Each funnel has a different function, different filtering mechanisms and criteria, and different operators. Bottlenecks can occur in any of these funnels. These funnels are gateways that connect different environments and collectively regulate the flow through the process. They are critical to capacity management—which we will discuss shortly, after we take a look at travelers.

Market Segments

There are many ways to cut the air traveler "pie" into market segments. Segmentation criteria include, for instance, financial resources, purpose of trip, frequency of travel, who is paying for the trip, age, fitness, and propensity to self-serve. Here is a glimpse of how the needs and preferences of four illustrative market segments differ: backpackers, family with young children, "travel with my own money," and executives.

If you are a backpacker, you are likely healthy and strong enough to carry a backpack, and you probably do not need anyone to carry your luggage. Since you can serve yourself and may be short on resources (or tight with your money), you are not willing to pay any more than you have to to get where you want to go. Since you have more time than money, you are willing to go out of your way and spend a little more time at airports. You are also more willing than most to endure cramped spaces, lackluster service, and rigid change rules in order to have a few hundred dollars more to spend at your destination.

Let's now look at the customer's experience through the funnels mentioned earlier (in the following section, we look at it again, this time adopting a process view). At each funnel, various criteria are used to filter the unknown mass of arrivals, collect the required information, and admit only qualifying travelers to the next environment. The criteria may range from having a valid credit card (parking) to having a valid ID, "Gold" frequent flyer card, or boarding pass. The filtering may be automated (automated check-in), partially automated (fingerprints, X-ray machines), or done by a variety of people (parking attendants, customs agents, police officers, ticketing agents, cabin crew, and so on) and may be more or less rigorous depending on the consequence of a defect (lost revenue, lost luggage, security risk).

The environments in which this filtering takes place are quite different from one another. In the age of the internet and the electronic ticket, the comfort of one's home typically constitutes the pre-trip environment, except for some privileged executives.

The packing process is pretty much a funnel as well: assembling everything you are going to need and "funneling it" into a number of pieces of luggage.

The parking environment is vast and noisy. It smells of gasoline, requires caution (traffic, thieves), and may be exposed to the weather. The traveler's mind is focused on finding the closest parking spot, not forgetting anything, and making a mental note (or better, a written one) of where the car is parked.

The traveler entering the check-in environment at rush hour is first struck by the noise from the crowd and the loudspeakers. Endless lines appear melted into a shapeless crowd of people turning their backs on the newcomer. Infrequent travelers are overwhelmed and nonplussed by the electronic boards, direction signs, and backlit information signs.

While contact with the agent is short and the process is repetitive, the task is much more complex than that of serving hamburgers in a fast-food restaurant. The agent must learn many complex rules and regulations, and quickly use systems to resolve exceptions. Judgment and fairness are involved as well, since the agent, depending on his status, has some discretion in the application of the rules. Accuracy is very important as well, as mistakes can leave the passenger without luggage for days or stranded at the airport. Doing all this while remaining courteous with stressed—sometimes abusive—passengers is no easy feat, especially in situations where passengers feel (rightly or wrongly) that they have every right to be angry. The agent must have the required people skills to appease angry

(continued)

passengers (empathy is a great asset here) so they become receptive to the explanations and instructions the agent must give them.

While security clearance is more inconvenient than check-in, it is also a little less stressful environment. At that point, the traveler is concentrating on not forgetting anything metallic on his person, watching his belongings, and recuperating everything before leaving the area. While few and far apart, defects can have catastrophic consequences. Remaining vigilant toward the end of an eight-hour shift doing repetitive work can be a challenge for security personnel. While most security agents are courteous, some become arrogant and even aggressive at the end of a very busy day.

Travelers normally clear security with a sigh of relief, unless they are late for their flight and must run to their gate.

The gate area is a sitting-room environment that typically comes alive some 45 minutes before a scheduled departure, as the "conductor" steps behind the desk. The gate agent's task is to "process" a large group of passengers, guiding them courteously, rigorously, and quickly to the Jetway, while verifying (yet again) documentation and respecting priorities. Typical quality problems encountered in the gate area include a poor quality or defective PA system, absent or inaccurate flight information, insufficient seating space, broken or dirty seats, newspapers lying around, no lavatory or snack bar, and no electrical outlets for computers.

The Jetway is the tip of the last funnel that filters and routes the right passengers to the right plane at the right time. After the open space of the outdoors and the vast high-ceiling expanse of the terminal, the crowded Jetway queue feels cramped, the air is often stale, and the temperature is often too hot or too cold. Of course, the Jetway should never be full. Both the gate upstream and the plane downstream offer much more comfortable environments. The trick is to admit passengers to the Jetway at the rate at which they exit it, that is, the rate at which passengers take their seat and clear the aisle. Unfortunately, bottlenecks in the plane tend to occur suddenly, and the synchronization between the "taps" is not always what it should be. Thus, the Jetway often fills up and the heating/ventilation/air-conditioning system has difficulty coping.

The plane environment feels relatively open, compared with that of the Jetway, but that feeling quickly goes away as the passengers try to wedge their way toward their seat and store their carry-on luggage, without being hurt or hurting anyone. Much of that part of the process takes place among the passengers themselves, with cabin personnel gently prodding, offering assistance, ensuring compliance with the rules, clearing bottlenecks, and resolving conflicts. Again, an inadequate PA system is a frequent problem. When announcements have to be multilingual, poor command of a second language is a problem as well.

An experience is a sequence of emotions, created by activities, interactions with people (employees of all kinds and other passengers), machines, objects, the environment, and ambiance, that leaves a lingering feeling. Sometimes it does not linger very long. Sometimes it becomes a painful memory that we may recount to many others, and sometimes, thank goodness, it turns out to be a memorable service experience.

The Operator's Perspective

Passengers are "processed" through a series of funnels: parking, check-in, security check, boarding, and seating. Each funnel is meant to add value, that is, store the car safely, verify payment, dispatch to the right flight, and so on. Together, they constitute the airport's value stream. Of course, a lot of non-value-added or "noise" gets added to that in practice, so that the signal to noise ratio, or value-added to non-value-added, can become quite low, as waiting, errors, heated exchanges, and other aggravations occur. We focus on one of these processes to illustrate the use of two fundamental process tools: the

SITOC and the FAST diagrams. These are the first tools that an organization that wants to manage, improve, or design new processes must master. As simple as they may seem at first glance, using them correctly requires much practice.

For the five filters to work smoothly together and deliver a maximum output with a minimum of friction, quick information flow in the system, holistic understanding of the dynamics of the system, synchronized responses, and strategically located backup resources are required.

In travel, decisions do not end with the purchase of a ticket. The travelscape is dynamic and rich in events of all sorts, pregnant with risks and opportunities. The passive traveler will suffer the brunt of these risks and miss these opportunities. The attentive traveler, on the other hand, can surf the travelscape and be on the lookout for interesting waves and potential risks as they are shaping up, positioning himself to exploit the former and avoid the latter. For instance, any (and any combination) of the following events can take place in the course of a trip: the flight is overbooked, the flight is half empty, the aircraft arrives late, the gate/terminal has been changed, a severe weather system is affecting traffic in the Northeast, a technical problem has been detected, a major security alert has been issued, or the airport is overcrowded, for some reason or other. The airport-savvy traveler typically will be best able to mitigate the risk and get the best possible outcome.

A process is a system put into operation to transform some inputs into desired outputs. A system is "a group of interacting, of interrelated, or interdependent elements forming a complex whole" (TheFreeDictionary.com 2010). This definition is broad enough to include, for example, the solar system, the atomic system, the human body, or any ecosystem. More specifically, we are concerned with business systems, that is, systems standing ready to perform. The process puts it into operation. A service system, then, is a system standing ready to perform a service. At a fast-food restaurant, for instance, the service system would include the parking lot, the customer facilities, the cashier, the cash register and its software, the cooking facilities, the product design, the back-office personnel, the specified structure and distribution of authority, and so on. In this context, a process is the dynamic (intelligent) use of the system (and all of its needed elements or components) to transform input (such as hamburger patties and frozen french fries) into an output (a hot, tasty meal ready to go).

Many processes may take place in the same service system. Designing a service system requires thinking about all the processes that will take place within that system, such as taking an order, fulfilling an order, eating a meal, cleaning up the facilities, using the washroom, and so on. Designing a process to operate in an existing service system may involve modifying, improving, or redesigning the service system. As a rule, we use the word "process" in this book to mean the process and the relevant parts of the service delivery system. When we refer to an organization's processes, we include the complete service delivery system. As discussed in Chapter 1, the words "protocols" or "routines" are often used in the literature to refer to this same notion.

Both "assemble a car" and "brush my teeth" are processes (action verb and noun). In this sense, everything we have said about processes so far in this chapter applies equally well to both. The former, however, is a complex process that we can decompose into hundreds or even thousands of interrelated subprocesses, many of which we repeat many times over in the assembly of a single car. How can we identify these processes? By decomposing them layer by layer or level by level using a technique called the *functional analysis system technique*, abbreviated as FAST (already illustrated in Chapter 2).

A FAST diagram proceeds—left to right or top to bottom—from the highest-level process ("make a cup of coffee," say) to the lowest by asking the question *"make a cup of coffee: how?"* The answer is the list of level 2 subprocesses shown in Figure 3.2. Generally (but not always), these are listed sequentially from the top down (the "when" arrow). We could push the analysis further by asking the same question of each of the level 2 processes: *"buy beans: how?"* Hence, *choose a supplier* and *place the order* are level 3 subprocesses. Complex processes can easily consist of 10 such layers. We can perform a cursory coherence check by asking a series of directed questions (why?) from right to left, for example: *"placing an order: why?"* Answer: to buy beans. *"Buy beans: why?"* Answer: to make a cup of coffee, and so on. The purpose of a FAST diagram, however, is not to describe the way the process is currently performed (we use a technique called process mapping for that—see section 3.1.3), but solely to decompose it into subprocesses or identify the functionalities that are required of the process. Any process for making coffee must include the functionality *grind beans,* and there are many possible ways to do this. Thus, functionalities are generic, normative, and conceptual.

How far can we drill down (the way we often refer to decomposing the actions of a process)? Figure 3.2 illustrates this, admittedly to a ridiculous degree of detail in this case. Notice that, starting at level 3, the elements have lost generality: it is assumed that a funnel will be used, thus excluding many other possible ways (such as a piston) to filter water through coffee grounds. As shown in Figure 3.2, it is often possible and useful to organize the FAST diagram sequentially (When?).

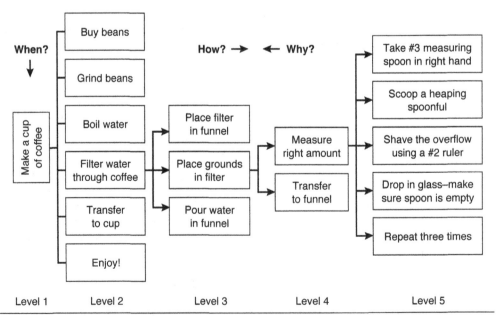

Figure 3.2 Functional analysis system technique (FAST) diagram for the process of making a cup of coffee—selective drill-down to level 5.

Let us consider now the process of brushing one's teeth. We may repeat this process over 70,000 times in our lifetime. Consider the effect of doing any of the following:

- Using a toothbrush that does not have rounded bristles (gum problems at 35; variable: shape of bristle tip—0 for flat, 1 for rounded)

- Using a toothpaste with excessively high abrasive content (receding gums and decay; variable: percent abrasive content by volume)

- Not brushing all the way to the last molar (extraction at 30; variable: gap in centimeters between reach of brush and extremity of last molar)

- Putting too much pressure on the gums (bleeding, sore, and receding gums; variable: pressure in kilopascals or PSI)

The devil is in the details! The outcome of any process rests on a few critical variables or aspects of a process. Identifying and controlling these is a complex but essential task (see Chapter 6). Doing things right requires that we zoom (Google Earth–style, that is, from 10,000 meters to street view) into processes (or selected subprocesses) down to the level where detailed process variables are visible. What is a *process variable*? It is a measurable aspect of a process, that is, one for which we can use a scale of measurement (see parenthetical illustrations in the teeth-brushing example). The measurement scale may be strictly nominal (a list of all the values that the variable may take), ordinal (ranking), interval (such as the Fahrenheit scale, where the zero value is arbitrary), or ratio (such as the Kelvin scale, where 20° represents twice as much heat as 10°). A crucial step in designing and improving processes is to differentiate the vital few (or critical-to-process [CTP]) variables from the many trivial variables. We cannot accomplish this unless we first identify all the variables, and that requires selectively drilling down into the process in detail.

There is one last notion we need to introduce to complete this section: process mission. Because processes consume time and resources, whoever decides to allocate these resources does so for a reason. The mission of the process is its purpose: a short statement about why we are doing it. Whoever is tasked with designing, improving, or managing a process must have a clear understanding of its mission or what part it plays in the scheme of things. This, in turn, requires a broader view of the overall value being created and the specific roles assigned to each process for that purpose. This brings us back to positioning (Chapter 2) and introduces the notion of strategy, discussed in Chapters 4 and 5.

The mission of a process can be deployed into specific missions for its subprocesses, or constituent parts. These appear at the second level of a FAST diagram. Refer back to Figure 3.2, showing the breakdown of the "make a cup of coffee" process. Imagine now that we are considering the specific process of a fast-food restaurant. Without knowing the specific competitive reality or strategy of the restaurant, an illustrative mission statement could read *Produce a hot and great-tasting cup of coffee without any delay in order assembly at the counter and with minimal waste of time on the part of the associate.* Since no specific mention is made of cost, smell, or quantity, this statement prioritizes "quality" (defined as here by temperature and taste), speed, and effort. Another restaurant, depending on its positioning, might prioritize the price and speed. The statement should not aim at being exhaustive, but rather focus on bringing out the essential. The mission of *filter water through coffee* could read *grind the beans quickly in a way that produces maximum flavor with the least effort*. The mission of the level 1 process is thus deployed to the subprocesses at level 2. This is discussed further in Chapter 7.

3.1.2 Viewing an Organization as a System of Processes

We can view an organization as a complex system of interconnected processes. An organization's process model is a high-level representation of these processes. Figure 3.3 shows a generic process model produced by the American Productivity & Quality Center (APQC).[1] Note that we still describe each process by an action verb and a noun (the "transformation" part of the SITOC).

Figure 3.4 shows a breakdown of one of these processes into subprocesses using a FAST diagram. We achieve this using the transformation performed by the process ("Deliver products and services") and asking the question *how?* The five level 2 subprocesses (4.1 to 4.5—called level 2 processes because they are identified by two digits) are the logical answer to that question. Each level 2 subprocess can be further exploded using the same technique: *"Plan and acquire necessary*

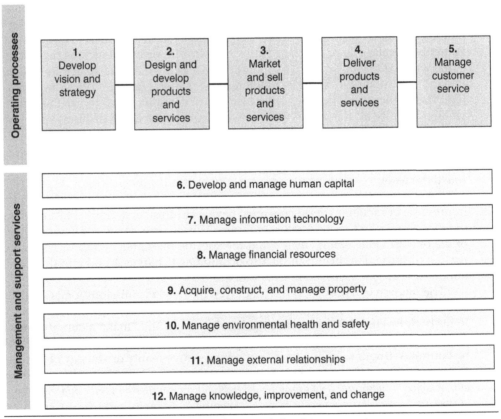

Figure 3.3 APQC's processes classification framework (level 1 processes).

Source: Developed by APQC's International Benchmarking Clearinghouse, in partnership with Arthur Andersen & Co., SC.

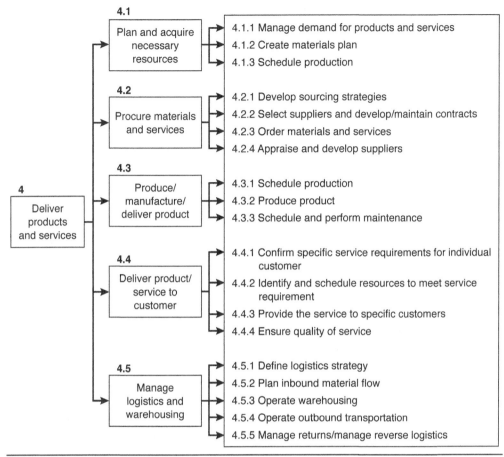

Figure 3.4   Breakdown of APQC's generic process #4 into subprocesses using a FAST diagram (level 2 and 3 processes).

Source: APQC.

resources: how?" The three level 3 processes (4.1.1–4.1.3) are the logical answer to that question.

Figures 3.3 and 3.4 are neatly organized and Cartesian. This provides a false sense of orderliness that begins to crumble when we look at Figure 3.5. This figure shows a selected subset of processes from the APQC model arranged in a flow pattern, that is, following the SITOC logic. Inspection reveals, for example, that process 6.2.1, "Define skill requirements," produces an output (skill requirements) that becomes the input for process 8.3.3, "Recruit, select, and hire employees." The latter, in turn, transforms this input into an output (an employee). The employee is a productive resource involved in process 4.4.3, "Provide the service to specific customers." This last process produces an output (information that the service has been provided as—or differently from—what was originally requested and accepted by the customer), which is in turn input to the 7.1 "Bill the customer" process. In a process system, processes can be suppliers to other processes or clients of other processes, and internal processes always play both roles. Processes in which the output goes directly to the end customer or client (these are said to

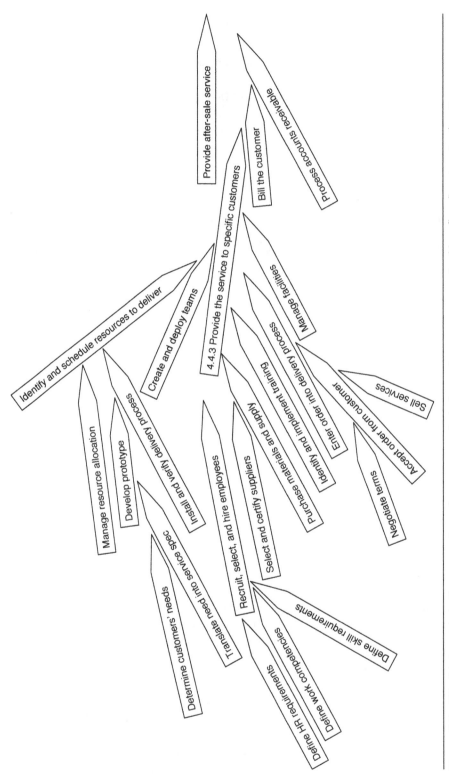

Figure 3.5 Viewing an organization as a system of processes—selected generic processes organized in a flow (input–output) pattern.

be "in contact") are the value-creating tip of the value chain (see the discussion on value connection in section 3.4.1). We suggest you view Video 3.2 at this time.

So far, our discussion has been strictly generic, that is, it applies to most organizations. To better understand processes, it is useful to work on a specific example. We have chosen to use the case of Medsol Clinic for that purpose. Medsol is a health center that includes a general hospital, an outpatient clinic, an emergency service, and a specialized cancer treatment unit. Let us focus on one of Medsol's processes, of the type 4.4.3, "Provide the service to specific customers." The SITOC diagram shown in Figure 3.6 defines the perimeter of that process. It shows the patient to be simultaneously the key supplier, the main input, the main output, and the customer, which is generally the case in health services.[2] Indeed, the process transforms the patient, hopefully making him healthier. Customers are those whose need the transformation is trying to meet. The "begins when" and "finishes when" boxes delimit the time boundaries of the process—much like bookends—by specifying the process start-up and ending conditions (input and output requirements).

The last element in the diagram relates to key interfaces. Because an organization is a system of processes, changing any process is bound to have an impact on other processes. If Medsol were to somehow modify the way it provides services to specific customers, it might have to adjust (see Figure 3.4) how it purchases material and supplies, or how it ensures quality of service, for example. Identifying the most important of these processes—in the specific organizational circumstances at hand—at the outset of any change initiative is critical to change management so that the right people are involved at the outset.

To dig further into the process of providing the service to specific customers (4.4.3) at the Medsol Clinic, we will use a different tool. A *process flow diagram* (PFD) goes one step further than a FAST diagram: it specifies and makes the high-level flow of the process more visual. Figure 3.7 shows the PFD we use for that process,

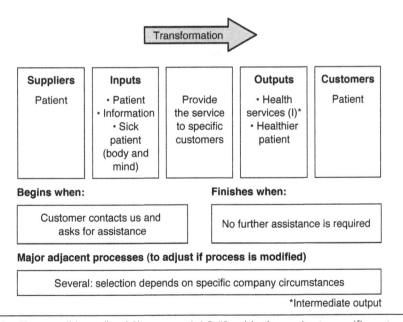

Figure 3.6   Circumscribing a (level 3) process: 4.4.3 "Provide the service to specific customers."

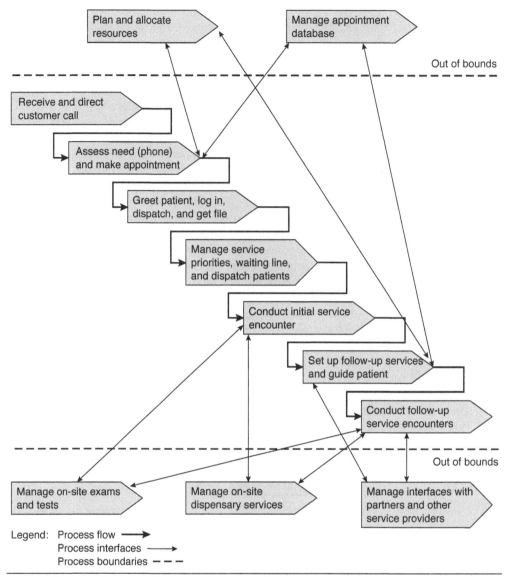

Figure 3.7 Exploding "provide the service to specific customers" (4.4.3) in a process flow diagram at Medsol Clinic (identifying level 4 processes).

with each arrow-shaped box representing a level 4 subprocess. We generate the list of subprocesses pretty much as we do in a FAST diagram, that is, by asking the question *"providing services: how?"* However, since answering that question yields 12 subprocesses, organizing them in a way that illustrates the general flow of the process becomes important to better understand its nature.

We do this in the PFD by representing the process (roughly) along a time line (horizontal axis) showing a logical sequence and spreading it along the vertical axis to show (approximate) subprocesses that can take place in parallel. The thick arrows show the process flow, and the thin ones show the most important interfaces with adjacent processes. Keep in mind that we have based this representation, like all the others used so far in this chapter, on logic and not on a detailed description of what actually goes on at the Medsol Clinic. Since all functionalities in the FAST diagram are value-adding steps, the PFD represents the process value stream. Adding data (such as time and resources required) for each step, we could produce a value-added map.

The process drill-down could be pursued further by selecting one of the level 4 processes—"conduct initial service encounter," say—and, using the same tools (see the SITOC, for example, in Figure 3.8) to establish its perimeter, exploding it into more detail. In Figure 3.8 "prepare customer file" and "perform tests" would be an alternate way to specify suppliers, and "fill prescription" and "organize follow-up" would be an alternate way to specify customers.

Figure 3.9 further illustrates the use of the PFD in the case of the real estate agent discussed in Chapter 2. The generic process depicted here is the same as that shown in Figure 3.7 for Medsol.

3.1.3 Describing a Process: Process Mapping

So far, we have used various techniques to describe processes (see Table 3.2): SITOC, FAST diagram, and PFDs. There are many others (Browning 2010). We now introduce the process mapping technique. A process map (or mapping) is a detailed description of the actual flow of a process. When you do a FAST diagram, you use your brain and logic. When you map a process, you are a camera. You do not map what you think it is or what it should be, but what you see. Mapping requires objectivity and thoroughness.

A process map is a step-by-step, sequential description of a process. It is more detailed than a PFD; it is specific and nonjudgmental about the way things are actually done, and further identifies the "players" (customer, department, job title, information system) that perform the activity. Each player has its own swim lane separated by lines, often given labels such as "line of visibility," "line of

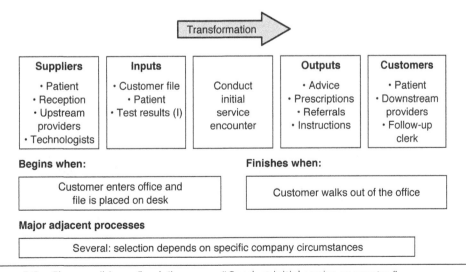

Figure 3.8 Circumscribing a (level 4) process: "Conduct initial service encounter."

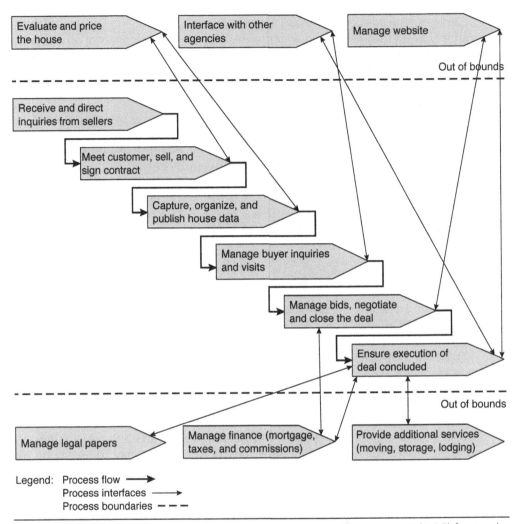

Figure 3.9   Process flow diagram for "provide the service to specific customers" (4.4.3) for a real estate agency.

interaction," "line of internal interaction," and so on. Time flows from left to right, and arrows connect the events sequentially. While each transaction may have its own quirks, it is best to start with the typical path common to most transactions and try to remain at the same level of detail (or granularity) throughout the map. If the process is complex, it is better to start with a high-level representation (or macro map) and proceed from there to do a detailed map.

Box 3.2 delineates a procedure that can be used to involve process workers (that is, the actors themselves) in the mapping exercise. This presents a number of advantages: they know what they do very well, they have never seen the complete picture and are often mistaken about what goes on in other parts of the process, and by working together, often for the first time, at building a shared representation of what they do, they start seeing opportunities for improvement, taking the first steps toward becoming a team.

Table 3.2 Description of major process representation tools, with their purpose and use.

Process tool	Description and use
SITOC	Supplier–Input–Transformation–Output–Customer. A form delimiting the perimeter of a process. The SITOC is generic: it is not a link to a specific way to perform the process. It defines a process and is therefore always the starting point of any discussion regarding a process.
FAST	Functional analysis system technique. A functional analysis (generic) identifying the functionalities that the process requires. It is used to analyze an existing process or as a starting point in designing a new one.
PFD	Process flow diagram. A generic diagram showing the general flow and sequence of the process, often starting from the functionalities identified in the FAST diagram. It is sometimes used in large processes to get a better understanding of a process than that afforded by the FAST diagram.
Process macro map	A diagram showing at a very high level how an actual (non-generic) process flows. Like a PFD (which is generic) it shows the flow, but adds the swim lanes, that is, shows how the process actually flows among the various players involved. In complex processes, it helps to have a macro map to plan the detailed mapping exercise and not lose sight of the forest. A PFD shows the logical flow of value-added steps or the value stream.
Process map	A detailed representation of an actual process, as is. It is used to document or improve a process.
Process blueprint	A detailed representation of the desired future state of a process (that is, to be). It is used as a guide in the construction of a new process.

Box 3.2 Building a Shared Image of Our Common Process

Issue: *How to facilitate process mapping by the process workers themselves*

Once the goal has been formulated (see Chapter 7 for "SMART" goal formulation) and the process to change has been identified (SITOC, FAST, process mission), a team of employees from all the departments involved is assembled. The goal and targeted process are explained to them. The mapping symbols shown in Figure 3.11 (page 88) are then explained, and they are given the following instructions:

1. Individually: Take a pack of sticky notes and write down on separate notes all the tasks that you perform in this process. Use a different color for each player, or otherwise identify the player. A task is described by an action verb and a noun. When the task involves a form, pick one as an illustration and cross-reference it with the corresponding sticky note by writing the same letter on both. If it is done online, take a screen shot and print it.

2. As a team, with a facilitator: Gather the team (with all their material) in a room with lots of wall space. Stick a wide and long strip of paper (a roll of butcher paper works well) to the longest wall. Write down the names of all the players in an equally spaced vertical column at the left-hand side of the strip. Draw long horizontal lines or use colored tape to separate the "swim lanes."

(continued)

3. Randomly place all the sticky notes on the right half of the strip. Each participant can then take 10 minutes to examine all the notes.

4. Go back to the SITOC form, and in particular to the "starts when" box. The team then locates the sticky note corresponding to the first action that takes place at that time and sticks it on the left of the appropriate swim lane, next to the name of the player. "What happens then?" asks the facilitator. The resulting discussion leads to the selection of the second activity in the process, which is placed in the appropriate column using the horizontal axis as a timeline. The process continues until the "ends when" point is reached.

5. Missing activities are added as the exercise proceeds, while others are merged or clarified. Whenever an activity involving a form is reached, the form is stuck above or below the sticky note on the wall.

6. Two flip chart pages, one labeled "Issues" and the other "Ideas," are stuck on another wall at the outset. Whenever an issue arises that cannot be resolved through a quick discussion, the issue is noted on a sticky note and stuck on the corresponding page. The idea page serves the same purpose: capturing important elements for later discussion, while avoiding being sidetracked or derailed by them.

Figure 3.10 depicts the basic process map for filling a new prescription at Golden Years Drugstore (GYD), as described in the last two paragraphs of Box 6.2 in Chapter 6. Figure 3.11 explains the symbols used for process mapping in Figure 3.10 and for the remainder of the book. Notice that we use the line of interaction (such as the dotted line separating the client from the contact person in Figure 3.10) to depict face-to-face contact only. We depict remote contact as double-headed arrows (such as the one connecting the pharmacist and doctor in Figure 3.10). Some further comments are required to better understand the diagram. Delays are indicated only when they are likely to affect total cycle time, that is, when they may lie on the critical path. Idle time for the doctor and for technician 1 is not specified. The diagram depicts the path of an order and the activities of the customer. The players themselves may be involved in other activities, that is, part of other processes not shown here. We use a special symbol (capital "Q") when customers are waiting in line. A range is included to represent the duration of each element. A mean and standard deviation may be used as well, if the data are available. The organizational line (the heavy black line at the bottom) separates GYD from its partners and suppliers. Sometimes it is useful to represent the computer, or various computer systems, as players in the process. We then place them beyond an imaginary "line of automation" (not shown here). Finally, we may use a layout diagram with dotted arrows to display the flow of things (prescription, medication) and the movements of people (employees and customers).

The mission of this process is to conveniently provide targeted patients with the prescribed medication, to give them the advice they need, and to promote compliance with the prescription. Its first priority is avoidance of errors. Making sure that the patients understand how to use the medication is a close second. Building a solid professional relationship, empathy, convenience, and speed (in that order) are its other objectives.

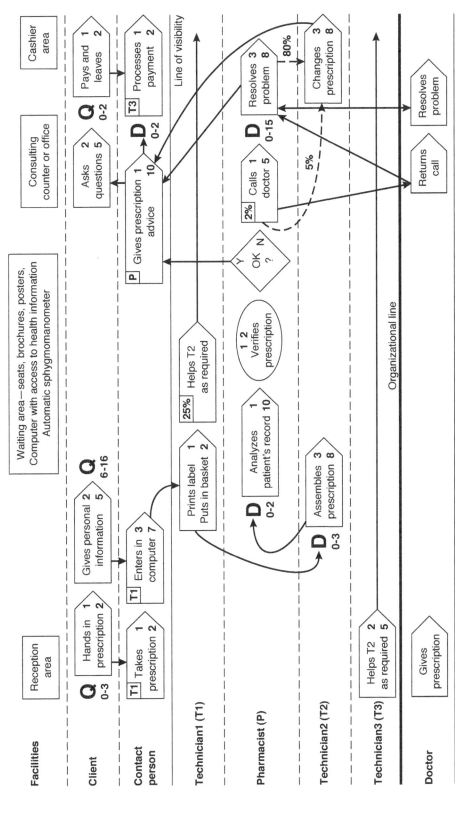

Figure 3.10 Process mapping: filling a new prescription for an existing customer at Golden Years Drugstore.

⟶	One-way flow.
⟵⟶	Two-way flows, interaction, back-and-forth.
▭	Document—use sparingly.
▽	Storage or filing.
◇ Y OK ? N 1 2	Decision. May lead to any number of branching points. The bold numbers indicate a range of duration—that is, from one to two minutes. A probability is attached to each outcome.
⇨ 1 2	Movement or transportation.
D 0-3	Delay—any time when nothing is happening other than waiting for the next operation. Used only for activities lying (or potentially lying) on the critical path.
T1 Enters in 3 computer 7	Task or activity. When the activity takes place in contact with the customer, the square identifies the player (swim lane) performing the action. A percentage indicates how frequently the task is required.
1 2 Verifies prescription	Inspection, that is, verifying the work done by someone else.
Reception area	Any element of the service delivery system, other than a human being, that comes into contact with the customer.
Ⓐ	Connector. Used to avoid long arrows that would interfere with legibility.
Q 0–3	Customer in queue. This is a special type of delay that has a direct impact on customer satisfaction.

Figure 3.11   Process mapping symbols used in this book.

3.1.4 When Is a Process Defined?

The word "process" is part of everyday language, and we use it in a variety of contexts to mean a host of different things. What does it take for a sequence of more or less repetitive activities to qualify as a defined process? While there are many

opinions on this, we propose to use the following criteria (or minimal requirements) to make this determination:

- We (the organization) know how well the process is performing and thus can
  validly say whether its performance is improving, stable, or getting worse

- Someone in the organization (a manager) is accountable for the performance
  of the process

- All the process workers[3] could, if it were explained to them, complete the SITOC
  of the process and specify the role they play in that process, that is, identify
  their internal providers, transformation, and customers and spell out what
  their internal customers' requirements are, as well as their own requirements
  of their internal suppliers

- The above knowledge would not be lost if one or two workers were to
  suddenly leave the organization; organizational memory goes beyond one
  or two individuals

- The workers are committed to meeting their internal customers' requirements
  (this is discussed in section 3.3)

Processes that meet these criteria may vary in their degree of formalism. However,
tacit knowledge does not constitute a process, as it cannot be communicated to or
shared with other employees; thus, it must be made explicit.

    To clarify these criteria further, Table 3.3 shows a number of situations illus-
trated by typical statements an organization may make about its process, as well
as their interpretation, that is, whether the process is defined.

Table 3.3 Evaluation of various situations with respect to the existence of a process.

Statement	Is the process defined?	Why
We have a process, but it is not followed.	No	Maybe we have a process design, but we don't have a process because commitments are not real.
The process produces much variation and the customer is threatening to leave.	Maybe	The process may not be capable, but it may still exist.
We're the best in the business, but nothing is documented.	Maybe	The process may be undocumented, but it may still exist.
The procedures are all charted and duly documented in our quality manual.	Maybe	The key is whether they are followed.
Paul never delivers; I often have to do it myself.	No	If Paul can get away with it, it's because his commitment is not real.
Only Joe can do this; if he leaves we're in big trouble.	Maybe	If Joe's departure would cause the company not to know what to do anymore, then we don't have a process. If the only problem is that Joe is the only one with the required skills, then we do have a process, but lack depth (or backup).

3.2 EXPLORING THE PROCESS SPACE

With such a broad definition, we need to classify processes into categories in order to understand them better. Being able to classify things, that is, to develop a typology, is the beginning of knowledge. In this section, we present some dimensions (see Figure 3.12) along which we can do this. We discuss them in turn in this section, except for the "nature of commitment" dimension, which is important enough to justify a section of its own (section 3.3).

3.2.1 Number of Players

Single-person processes are in a category of their own. We include in that category all processes wherein a single person is involved in the transformation from input to output. The distinguishing feature of single-person processes is that no human interaction is involved. Single-person processes fall into two subcategories: processes where the person is the customer, that is, something he does for himself (such as brushing his teeth or planning his day), and those directed at external customers, such as producing a painting, writing a book, or cleaning the house (the whole family being the customer in this case). We refer to these as *personal* and *one-worker* processes, respectively. Although the latter involves an external "judge" of the results, in both cases all the decisions about the way things are done involve a single player, which makes things much easier. Complexity increases exponentially with the number of players.

3.2.2 Reference Systems

Individuals, families, businesses, and societies are all systems within which processes take place. The relationship they bear to one another is much like that between Russian matryoshka dolls: the first fits within the framework of the

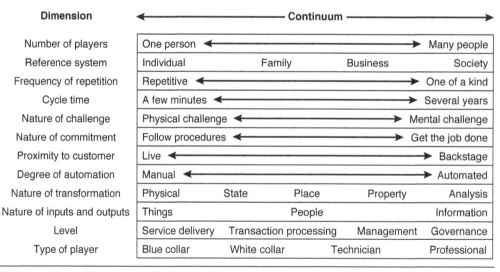

Dimension	Continuum			
Number of players	One person ⟵⟶			Many people
Reference system	Individual	Family	Business	Society
Frequency of repetition	Repetitive ⟵⟶			One of a kind
Cycle time	A few minutes ⟵⟶			Several years
Nature of challenge	Physical challenge ⟵⟶			Mental challenge
Nature of commitment	Follow procedures ⟵⟶			Get the job done
Proximity to customer	Live ⟵⟶			Backstage
Degree of automation	Manual ⟵⟶			Automated
Nature of transformation	Physical	State	Place	Property	Analysis
Nature of inputs and outputs	Things	People		Information
Level	Service delivery	Transaction processing	Management	Governance
Type of player	Blue collar	White collar	Technician	Professional

Figure 3.12 Various ways to classify processes.

second, the second within that of the third, and all three are included in a broad societal system. Let us explore these systems to see how individuals fit in.

Processes in the family unit, whatever its composition, are unique because of the strong emotional bond that unites its members. The family plays a central role in any society, and much of our well-being rests on it. Children raised in dysfunctional families face a long uphill battle in their quest for happiness. The roots of family problems are numerous, deep, and tightly interwoven, and addressing them goes far beyond the scope of this book or the competence of this writer. We do find, however, numerous processes in a family. Social workers and specialized educators direct much of their intervention effort toward fixing family processes that have broken down or designing and implementing new processes ("monitor Johnny's social activities," "help with homework," or "prepare meals for the kids"). Even families that function well devote much effort—implicitly or explicitly—to improving processes, from getting Junior to do his chores to decorating the house for Halloween.

The existence of a customer, paid employees, and a decision-making hierarchy characterize organizational processes. In a business—a special type of organization—processes are further characterized by paying customers, the profit motive, and the existence of competition. The goal of business processes is to profitably deliver a superior value proposition to customers and employees, as discussed in Chapter 2. Maintaining this superiority is vital to the survival and growth of the company. This continuous search for superiority and dominance accounts for the vitality of business processes in capitalist systems.

That brings us to processes in society involving the relationship between individuals, families, organizations, and communities. Capitalism is an economic system within a society. "Allocate capital," for example, is a process—albeit at an extremely high level—within the capitalist system. At the other end of the spectrum, transferring money from a savings account to a mutual fund is a minute subprocess within that macro process. Indeed, a FAST diagram linking the former to the latter would have many levels.

The democratic system is another critical societal system, and processes are at its core. The basic inputs are the individual opinions and preferences of a people about the way their society should be managed. The output is a set of elected representatives empowered to legitimately wield the levers of government. The notion is simple enough. Making it stick is another story, as the history of civilization amply demonstrates.

Where do governmental processes fit into this classification? The answer is, somewhere between business processes and societal processes. The relationship between governments and individuals falls into one of four categories according to the role played by the individual (Mintzberg 1996): consumer, client, citizen, or subject. The consumer buys services from the government on a commercial basis, such as electricity or garbage collection. The client receives professional services, such as educational services. The citizen utilizes services, such as public infrastructure, to which he has a right. The subject must perform the duties that follow directly from his rights as a citizen, such as abiding by the law or serving in the army. We can assimilate processes associated with the first two roles into business processes. Processes related to the role of citizen have characteristics of both business processes and societal processes in that both the user and society are customers of the process. Processes where the individual is compelled—by moral suasion or by force—to act in a predetermined fashion uniquely belong to societal processes.

Finally, processes that cross the boundaries of an organization are worth mentioning here. They face an added level of complexity. Crossing the boundaries of functions, as most processes do, has its challenges, but crossing different organizational cultures and structures is much more difficult. Buying a book on the internet, for instance, may involve several organizations for a single transaction, such as web service provider, online bookstore, online payment service provider, and express package delivery service.

The reader can see how we could generalize the preceding discussion to other systems such as ecosystems and international systems. Of course, this book focuses on business processes. However, many process notions apply to any reference system. Our discussion of personal, family, and societal processes thus serves the following purposes:

- Illustrates the material with simple examples to which anyone can relate and facilitates understanding by drawing examples from different reference systems

- Provides the reader with a convenient field of application to test the newly acquired knowledge

- Helps business to better understand and therefore interact more effectively with individuals (employees and customers) and society (regulations, community integration, social responsibility)

- Provides the reader with a valuable by-product: improve her personal processes and those of her family

3.2.3 Repetitiveness

Some processes take place only once. We call these *projects*. Video 3.3 explores the relationship between projects and processes. Examples of projects include learning to drive a car or to play the piano (individual), moving headquarters from Seattle to Chicago or going through bankruptcy (company), or replacing a tyrant with a democracy or revolting against a colonial power (society). This is in contrast to repetitive processes, such as preparing a cup of coffee, helping Diane do her homework, billing a customer, or collecting taxes. A major difference between projects and processes is the learning aspects. If you are going to do something only once, only the result matters. You are not concerned at all about being able to do it better next time. "Results, no matter how" may constitute a valid marching order at the outset of a project. However, if this order refers to a repetitive process, it is a counterproductive one. The importance of successfully concluding a repetitive process must always be balanced against the need to be able to do it better, cheaper, and faster the next time.

The distinction between projects and processes is not, however, as clear-cut as it may appear at first glance. Writing a book is a project: one is not going to write the same book twice. However, one may write several books, in which case the subprocesses of preparing a table of contents and of harmonizing writing styles are repetitive. Further, even within a single project, some subprocesses may be repeated, such as proofreading a chapter several times. Thus, there are very few pure projects where the "how" does not matter. Conversely, many repetitive projects involve changes from one cycle to the next. A company may repeat the strategic planning process, but it can make improvements every year, and also the company's circumstances may vary widely over time.

A company whose business it is to implement enterprise resource planning (ERP) systems in client organizations may frame its business as managing projects, or alternately see "implement ERP" as its core business process. Even though successive implementations are likely to vary considerably, the second option is much more conducive to learning and continuous improvement.

Improving a process is a project, and this project can be described using a SITOC. The key input will be a broken process, the key output a repaired process. The project will be conducted only once, but the process that will be fixed as a result will be repeated many times over—albeit differently from the way it had been run before it was fixed. If one pushes the reflexion one step further, though, a learning organization that continuously runs improvement projects can best frame "run an improvement project" as a process in its own right and seek to improve that process from one project to the next. This is called *double loop* learning. Every improvement project improves a process (first loop), and the organization finds ways to improve the next project (second loop).

3.2.4 Cycle Time

Related to the difference between a project and a repetitive process are the notions of cycle time, complexity, and frequency of repetition. Most people brush their teeth two or three times a day, which translates into roughly 70,000 repetitions over a lifetime. Cycle time is about five minutes (including two minutes of actual brushing), and the process is simple. Clearly, the process remains "frozen" for long periods of time during which one tries only, with more or less success, to repeat the same activity without variation.

Preparing monthly financial statements requires hundreds, if not thousands, of person-hours, depending on the size of the company. While it remains a repetitive process, the sheer complexity of the task makes it unlikely that it would ever be repeated in exactly the same manner—nor should it be. To carry the process through to a successful conclusion, some players have to continually find new ways to deal with unforeseen circumstances. We cannot fully program and blindly repeat complex processes: they require judgment and skills. If we repeat them often, and if a continuous improvement philosophy prevails, they will evolve toward a better and more complete definition of vital aspects, and the gray areas and ill-charted sections will be reduced.

Fixing short-cycle and long-cycle processes requires a different approach.

3.2.5 Nature of Challenge

Some processes involve a mostly physical challenge on the part of process workers, and others a mostly intellectual one. Even though no human action other than a reflex can take place without the conscious brain being involved, moving a piano up a flight of stairs is a mostly physical challenge. Making a decision, on the other hand, is a mostly intellectual task. Most processes fall somewhere between these two extremes. Whenever physical challenges are involved, so are the laws of physics and chemistry. Improving such a process requires at least an intuitive understanding of these laws. Characterizing and optimizing it requires an explicit one. In addition, since parts of the process do not talk to you (for example, objects and machines), designed experiments will be required to make it "talk," that is, to learn about it.[4]

When an intellectual task is involved, the process takes place more between one's two ears or between two people than between two hands. Thus, a substantial amount of subjective information has to be processed, requiring a different approach and different tools. Table 3.4 illustrates this dimension of processes, as well as the previous one (cycle time), with a number of personal examples.

Improving processes where physical flows dominate falls largely into the realm of industrial engineering and will not be discussed in any depth in this book.

3.2.6 Service and Customer Contact

Service processes are characterized mainly by the intangibility of the results they produce and by the contact between provider and customer (face-to-face or otherwise). Thus, an important difference between manufactured goods and services is that the former can be separated from the production process per se, but not the latter. Indeed, consumers are not present when the good is built and often will never find out (nor care) how it was built (though things may be different for business customers). In services, the customer witnesses part of the process (the "contact" part versus the "back office" part). In fact, the process itself is an important part of the service. The very fact that the name of a service often involves an action verb (for example, repairing cars, cleaning houses) reflects this linkage. Put another way, the service *is* the process (or an important part of it, depending on the industry). When making a phone call for technical assistance on a computer problem, for instance, the process of helping the customer solve the problem *is* the service. Hence, designing a service *is* designing the service delivery process—and that goes for internal services as well.

Table 3.4   Illustration of personal processes, their major challenge, approximate cycle times, and lifetime frequencies.

Physical challenge	Intellectual/mental challenge	Cycle time	Lifetime frequency
Brush teeth	Plan your day	10 min	60,000
Shop for groceries	Plan meals for next week	1 hour	1500
Prepare reception	Plan next year's vacation	4 hours	300
Winterize house	Annual home budgeting	1 week	40
Redo landscaping	Teach daughter how to drive	3 months	2
Learn how to play golf	Learn how to write	1 year	1

Service takes place "live." If you do something wrong when assembling a product, you can fix it before it is shipped. If you do or say something wrong in a face-to-face encounter, you cannot take it back: the damage is done (though you can, and should, apologize and try to make up for it). A service is a human experience. It is lived, not bought. The difference between good and bad service is well illustrated by the difference between seeing *The King and I* on Broadway and buying the DVD of the movie starring actress Jodie Foster. It is the same story, but both the actors and the audience will have quite a different experience. The processes involved are radically different as well. After all those years of the play being on Broadway, one would expect the process to be "optimized" to the finest level of detail. Still, professional actors will tell you that reproducing the same emotions performance after performance is always a challenge, even if the required level of adrenaline is there. The movie captured on DVD has been "optimized" scene by scene, some of which may have required as many as 30 takes, and assembled in a "bottled" experience that the customer can enjoy where and when he pleases, without any variation.

3.2.7 Inputs and Outputs

We can also classify processes in terms of the nature of their inputs, transformation, and outputs. Inputs and outputs may be people, things, information, or any combination of these. The transformation of things or people involves some sort of change: physical or chemical properties, personal state (sick, well, happy, and so on), ownership (retail, sales processes), or place (transportation processes). Data can be structured and organized to become information. Information can be analyzed to become knowledge and thus used to facilitate decisions. Designing, managing, or improving a process requires familiarity with the nature of the input. An industrial engineer, say, who excels at improving manufacturing processes would probably be at a loss when dealing with processes involving human emotions or information.

3.2.8 Technology and Automation

"Technology is created capability: it is manifested in artefacts the purpose of which is to augment human skills" (Van Wyk 1988, p. 342). This definition is discussed in Video 3.4. For a technology to operate, four components are required: hardware, software, brainware, and a support infrastructure. The latter is well illustrated by one of the challenges faced by electric cars: a complete and convenient network of charging stations. Traffic rules, driving schools, police network, driver permit control, points penalty system, and courts are some of the existing elements of the network that are readily transferable to electric cars.

Brainware is about processes. It consists of combining the technology with other productive resources to create value. When a new technology comes about, it is typically used as a replacement for the old technology without significant changes to the process. War offers many examples of this, as the introduction of new weapons over the ages, such as the crossbow, firearm, artillery, tanks, and aircraft, was dreadfully slow and ineffective until the process was redesigned from scratch (see Chapter 11) in order to use the new capabilities to the fullest. Culture is often an important impediment to such changes as it becomes tightly associated with various artifacts: crossbowmen were not knights, they should not bask in the glory of victory; the tank will never replace the horse, thus it should be used as backup for artillery; and "typing on a keyboard is a secretary's job, not the job of a high-flying manager or a talented professional." When it comes to technological change, the hard stuff is often the soft stuff.

Processes that can fully accomplish the transformation without human intervention differ from those that require it. Human intervention involves motivation, judgment, and skills. As much as we may try to standardize these through training, testing, and selection, the outcome will always remain unpredictable to some extent—witness the "human error" to which we often attribute plane crashes. Machines are generally much more predictable. As technology progresses, it offers new ways of doing things better, faster, and cheaper. Rather than replacing humankind outright, it complements it at first. Work-flow software, for example, nicely forwards work from one player to another, avoiding dispatching errors and delays, and providing tracking and expediting capabilities to boot. For a while, and sometimes for a very long time, the old and new processes coexist and compete in different market segments. For instance, the old-fashioned Shouldice technique for operating on hernias still competes effectively today with laparoscopic surgery (see Chapter 4). Hydromechanical flight control systems still coexist with fly-by-wire technology.

As customers get to share in the new technology, professional services must adapt their processes to deal with the better-equipped and better-informed client. A doctor has to deal with a patient who spends hours on the web getting (good and bad) information on the best possible therapy differently than she does with a patient who relies solely on her. A designer called in to help design and build a new kitchen also has to adapt his process for a client who has already made a 3-D model of the kitchen he would like (see Chapter 12). There used to be only one way for passengers to check in for their flight. Now there are many competing systems with different requirements, benefits, and costs for passengers, employees, and shareholders.

As technological advances make it possible to create value differently, they destroy old ways, forcing evolution and sometimes revolution—in the case of disruptive new technologies—on the service provider. As the game changes, new competitors enter with new skills and new business models (see Chapters 4 and 5) while some established providers succeed in adapting, and others fade away.

3.2.9 Level and Type of Worker

Delivering the service directly creates value for the customer. In order to perform the service, these processes need information about the service to perform (order) and they need to capture information about their performance in order for billing, collection, and accounting to function. The latter are transactional processes. These data are aggregated and processed in order to feed management processes (see process control in Chapter 6). At the strategic apex of the organization, governance processes aggregate this information further and use external information as well to steer the organization in the desired direction. As we go from blue collar and white collar workers to technicians and professionals, external knowledge and know-how, including very abstract knowledge systems (such as the laws of thermodynamics or the principles of common law) that are not under the control of the organization, are brought to bear on the action.

As seen in this section, the breadth of the process space is vast—as varied, in fact, as human endeavor itself. For all this variety and complexity, however, processes share the simple definition of being ways to transform some inputs into outputs that better meet some human requirement. In this book we exploit this commonality to show how we can manage processes better and develop superior ones. To show the wide range of applicability of the process framework, we will use examples drawn from all quadrants of the process space.

3.3 CHAIN OF COMMITMENT

Processes involve people making commitments to one another and trusting that commitments made will be fulfilled. In this section we first explore the nature of commitment and then present a number of examples. We subsequently look at the difficulties large functional organizations encounter with processes.

3.3.1 Commitment to the Task or to the Result

When our understanding of a process is poor, or when it operates in turbulent environments,[5] the ability to innovate and make adjustments on the fly is at a premium. Without a team fully committed to end results, failure is virtually guaranteed. Think of the early start-ups in the field of e-commerce, such as Yahoo! and eBay, facing new technology, new markets, and new business models. Only unflinching commitment and talent—driven by leadership and vision—allowed some of them to pull it off. This type of commitment translates into "push–pull" behavior (helping internal providers [pulling] or customers [pushing] when they are experiencing difficulties), creativity, and team problem solving.

In processes that are completely defined and programmed in the *most minute* detail, and where few chance events are involved (because of the stability of the environments), commitment to the task—its timing or the way it is performed—rather than to the end result may be the only thing that matters. This is typical of bureaucracies—not only of the governmental type but also of the corporate type. Getting a construction permit at city hall or borrowing a book from the library is a typical example. In these processes, woe typically befalls anyone who tries to be creative or asks for special treatment.

Nowadays, the rules of e-business are becoming clearer (for the survivors), and the processes required to ensure flawless execution are slowly emerging. Commitment to end results is still required, but commitment to performing the activities correctly is becoming increasingly important. Performing open-heart surgery or controlling air traffic at a busy airport, for example, requires both a strict adherence to procedure and great commitment to deal with unexpected situations.

In the process world, these three types of situations (commitment to end result, to the task, or both) have to be dealt with differently. However, they have something in common: without a real commitment by each player, the process fails miserably. We therefore turn now to a more detailed discussion of the link between commitments and processes.

3.3.2 Commitment—A Personal Example

Consider Box 3.3. The payment process flows in a linear fashion, without any adjustment or upstream feedback. Everyone is committed to (eventually) performing a task based on the information received from an upstream source and passing it on to another player downstream. If the information Marie gets is inappropriate in any way, she cannot perform her task: tough luck, "It's not my fault if somebody messed up." If something goes wrong in the downstream process: "It's not my fault—I did what I could with what I had." Nobody is committed to producing a result. In fact, nobody even sees, understands, or cares about the complete process, the result, or the customer. This is typical of a bureaucratic process. The players spend much energy to protect their backs, sparing no effort to maintain credible deniability of responsibility in case of a problem and getting no personal satisfaction out of a successful conclusion.

Consider now a surgical team performing routine surgery, such as gall bladder removal, an appendectomy, or a caesarean section. The surgeon, anesthesiologist, scrub nurse, and circulating nurse are a team performing a repetitive, well-rehearsed process. Each player's role is well defined in the "no surprises" scenario, and the most common contingencies are scripted as well. Each team member must commit to playing his or her part. If excessive bleeding occurs as a result of an inappropriate cut, the surgeon has to stop the bleeding, the scrub nurse has to quickly provide the required instruments and supplies, the circulating nurse has to quickly fetch and provide any missing element, and the anesthesiologist must inform the surgeon of any consequence on the patient's metabolism. Failure to respond quickly, accurately, and synchronously can have dire consequences. Communication must be fluent, and any emotion that can interfere with this must be controlled. Information flows back and forth between team members. As requests are made, either they are acted on immediately or more information is requested and provided. Mutual adjustment follows, and the team's response is adjusted as required by a dynamically evolving situation.

A commitment is a promise to deliver. It is real when the person who makes it is responsible, which means accepting the personal consequences of not delivering on the promise. If there is no personal consequence, then there is no commitment, and therefore there is no process. A commitment does not have to be written or formal. Eye contact may be enough (see Box 3.4). The consequences can be of any nature as long as they are meaningful enough to the person making the commitment to motivate him to do what he is expected to do.

3.3.3 Commitment—A Multiagency Process Example

Process notions are just as relevant in business. Processes involving many players only work if everyone who has a role to play—providing some intermediate output to one of the other players—is willing and able to play his part. Designing such a process thus involves decomposing the result desired into a set of intermediate results. The responsibility for each of these is then farmed out to the various players,[6] who must accept this responsibility, that is, commit to it. They will not do so unless they are motivated (positively or negatively). They should not do so

Box 3.3 Nimble Payment System

Issue: *Bureaucratic processes flow like a stream, albeit a very calm one, and never look back*

Nick Chisholm is a specialist in program evaluation in the public sector. Every year, he is called in to evaluate different programs administered by a large French para-governmental organization. He submits his invoice when he completes his evaluation. He is paid through a direct money transfer to his US account. It takes forever—three or even four months is not unusual. Considering that his work takes place over a four-month period and that he cannot submit his bill until the work is complete, he feels that he is making a direct contribution to the working capital of the French government. Those are the rules of the game, however, and he had agreed to play by them. And hey, this is Paris.

This year, however, the process was proving to be particularly lengthy. Five months had passed since he submitted his invoice. It was now time to buy his airline ticket for next year's assignment, and he still had not heard from them. Since his bill included reimbursement for a substantial out-of-pocket sum for travel and expenses, he was becoming irritated. Here are excerpts from the resulting exchange of e-mails:

Nick: "I think it would be reasonable to settle accounts dating back 12 months, since I spent the first dollar on this assignment, before I go on and invest more. Yet, if I don't book now, it will only become more expensive to do so in the future."

Marie (administrative assistant in Paris): "You mean you have not been paid?"

Nick: "Indeed. You mean you don't know?"

Marie: "No, I don't. I never hear back from the bank. Let me check."

Two weeks pass.

Marie: "Nick, I just heard back from my query to the bank. They did process the payment a month ago, but it was rejected by your bank. Something about a nonexistent account, a wrong address, or something to that effect. Please send a new invoice with the correct coordinates for money transfer. Regards, Marie."

As it turns out, the payment instructions were exactly the same (cut and paste) as those used successfully the year before. After a phone call to the director and a threat from Nick to stop doing business with them, the matter was resolved within two weeks. On his next trip to Paris, Marie explained the payment process to Nick over a cup of coffee at a sidewalk café in the beautiful surroundings of Saint-Germain-des-Prés in June.

Marie: "When I get your invoice, I check the contract. If everything is in order, I fill out the payment form and put everything in a folder and leave it on the director's desk. Unfortunately, he's very busy and travels quite a bit. Eventually, he signs it and sends it to the president through internal mail. The president is even busier, but he eventually signs it too and sends it to accounting. I don't really know what happens in accounting, but when they are through with it, it goes to the bank. They somehow consolidate payments from various branches and manage cash flow, balancing payments with incoming budget installments from the Ministry of Finance. The money is eventually wired to your account. Voilà."

Nick: "What if it is rejected?"

Marie: "Well, it should not be."

Nick: "Apparently it can be. What then?"

Marie: "Then they will file the proof of refusal and move on to the next payment in the stack. They have a lot to do, you know."

Nick: "They don't bother to let you know?"

Marie: "No. We asked them to transfer money. They have. Their job is done. If it does not go through, someone must have messed up. It is not their problem."

Nick: "What if they are the ones who messed up?"

Marie: "Well, it certainly was not intentional. Besides, they don't know that they have; otherwise I'm sure they would correct it."

Box 3.4 Eye Contact

Issue: *Conventions are unwritten rules that allow many social processes to work smoothly. They are, however, culture-specific.*

Even though drivers are more courteous in some parts of the country than in others, you can safely count on some unwritten rules in any part of North America. The pedestrian that reaches an intersection at about the same time a car does will instinctively look at the driver. Once they make eye contact, the pedestrian knows that she can safely cross the street without risking her life. You do not realize the important role that such conventions play until you travel to countries with a different culture.

On his first trip to South America, a jogger was reminded of this as he set out for his early morning jog around his downtown hotel. He was mentally going over his agenda for the day when he reached the first intersection, marked by four-way stop signs. As he slowed down, he glanced at a blue 4×4 SUV that was also slowing down before reaching the stop sign. He made eye contact with the nice lady driving the car and thus proceeded to jump (the height of the sidewalk was anything but standard) into the street to cross to the other side. Unexpectedly, however, rather than coming to a full stop as expected, the nice lady stepped on the gas and the SUV roared ahead. Both the jogger and the driver were totally surprised by this situation, and the jogger owed his life to his quick reflexes. The angry expression on his face only confirmed to the nice lady that she had been very fortunate not to run this "loco" over. The "loco" himself noticed the angry expression on the driver's face and realized that he had made a tacit, culture-based assumption that could have cost him his life. In South America, as our jogger would soon find out, eye contact between pedestrian and driver means that the pedestrian stops. Why? ¡Porque sí!

unless they feel that they are able to meet their commitment—that is, they have the resources, tools, and skills required—as well as any required upstream commitments from other players.

In this context, we view a process as a logically distributed chain of commitments. Since a chain is only as strong as its weakest link, processes are vulnerable to a lack of commitment on the part of any player. To illustrate how these notions apply in complex processes, let us focus for a moment on the processes involved in airline security. The mission of these processes is to prevent anyone or anything that might constitute a security risk from boarding or being brought onboard the aircraft and taking control of the plane. It starts when security officials begin boarding and loading. It ends when the doors are closed and the captain asks the tower for clearance. How many distinct units are "responsible" for the passengers' security throughout this process? If local airport police, federal agencies, private agencies, and airline personnel are included, as well as the different divisions of these same agencies (in airlines, for example, there are ground crews, ticket agents, luggage handlers, gate crews, flight crews, and security), the number would be frightening.

Let us look at the interfaces and commitments along the chain as a passenger boards the plane. A security agent first searches her before she checks in at the airline's counter. The agent checks her papers and puts an "Inspected" seal on her luggage, thus communicating to downstream players that he has fulfilled his commitment to search the bag thoroughly. When the counter agent and baggage inspectors downstream see that seal, they trust that the job has been done. Later, as the luggage comes out of the X-ray machine and the official waves the passenger through, he trusts his colleagues and the X-ray machine that the luggage does not represent a threat to security. As the pilot gives a thumbs-up for pushback, he trusts that the baggage control personnel, and those in charge of the computers and databases they are using, have made sure that each piece of luggage loaded belongs to a passenger. He also trusts that everyone involved has delivered on his or her respective commitment.

How effective is the process? The answer to that depends on a host of factors, including process design, people selection, training, and technology, as well as on the effectiveness of the processes intent on impairing it, that is, the processes used by terrorists. Failure can occur equally well within an individual task or at the interface between two or more players.

Any one player who is not committed to producing the intermediate result that was imparted to him by process designers will simply "go through the motions" in order to "protect his back," an approach typical of a bureaucracy. An agent inspecting a bag, for example, might look to an observer as if he were totally immersed in his task, but in fact his mind may be largely caught up with a fight he had with his wife the night before. Such lack of commitment often occurs when failure to do the job right is perceived as not having any personal consequence.

It is a critical part of the process designer's job to ensure that nothing falls through the cracks in terms of individual responsibilities, and that the connections or interfaces between various subprocesses allow for maximal verification of the quality of intermediate outputs. Placing a colored security seal on a bag is one way to avoid it being opened in the queue that forms between the search point and the counter. It also informs the counter agent that the bag has not been totally overlooked. If the seal bears an identification code that allows traceability (that is, identifying who has done the inspection), however, the commitment becomes much stronger.

3.3.4 Process Commitment and the Functional Organization

Clearly, the creation of team spirit and the sharing of a common understanding of the global process, as well as its individual components, are great contributors to the maintenance of the integrity of a process under various conditions, that is to say, they are critical to the *adaptability* (see Chapter 4) of the process. Without the right incentives and training, individuals will focus on their own tasks and lose sight of the purpose of the process. The 400-meter women's relay in the Sydney Summer Olympic Games (see Box 3.5) makes this abundantly clear: individually, American runners were the fastest—collectively, they were the third-best team. Each runner focused on her 100-meter leg, obviously with little thought or preparation for the transition. They apparently listened to their individual ("functional") coaches much more than they listened to the relay race coach ("process owner"). The narrow-minded pursuit of excellence in the task does not make for excellence in the process as a whole. Without commitment to team results, the value gets destroyed in the transition.

Box 3.5 Lost in Transition

Issue: *Individual versus team excellence*

On September 29, 2000, the women's 4 × 100-meter race took place at the Sydney Olympics. The United States had the fastest runners and was the favorite to win gold. Chryste Gaines bolted out of the starting blocks and ran very well. She reached the transition zone first. She got out of it second, however, as about one meter was lost in the transition. Torri Edwards also ran very well and just about caught up with the Bahamian runner. Unfortunately, the transition to Nanceen Perry did not go smoothly, and about three meters were lost. Nanceen Perry ran a fast 100 meters, but the transition to Marion Jones cost the US team another three meters. Marion Jones's 100-meter dash was spectacular. She caught up with a couple of other teams, and the United States won bronze. Apparently, excellent individual performers do not necessarily make an excellent team. Incidentally, both the US men's and women's teams dropped the baton in the 2008 Beijing Olympics. The bronze medal was also retroactively withdrawn from the Sydney US women's team, as Marion Jones was found guilty of using unauthorized substances, but that is another story.

Large functional organizations—famous for their lack of adaptability in an environment that increasingly requires it—are particularly challenged as they try to adopt a process orientation. A functional organization is one in which people with similar expertise are grouped together under a functional leader, for example, vice presidents for finance, human resources, strategic planning, and marketing. Most processes, however, do not respect these functional boundaries (or "silos," as they are frequently called) and flow back and forth between functions. An invoicing process, for example, may require people from sales, pricing, inventory, production, shipping, customer service, and finance. Producing a mortgage loan in a bank involves people from account management, credit, collateral, legal, and the back office.

While the employees of such organizations may pay lip service to the concept of the next function in the sequence being their internal customer, their only true commitment is generally to their functional boss. That makes processes very rigid and slow to adapt. Even requests for minute changes often have to go up the hierarchy and come back down, involving long and disruptive delays every step of the way. Hence, there are no processes to speak of in such organizations, only a disjointed, loosely related, and static set of activities, much like that of the US women's relay team in Sydney, with each runner centered on running her part of the race and not willing to adjust her own individual contribution to the process for the common good. The reader interested in digging deeper into this area should read Pall (1999).

Box 3.6 illustrates a related issue. The cashier is part of two processes. As he punches in the order, he is both collecting money due to the owners and sending the inventory manager important data to ensure appropriate and timely replenishment of the bins. If he does not collect the right amount of money, he will likely be in trouble. However, if the data entered for inventory management purposes are inaccurate, nothing happens to him. There is no traceability and no accountability, a major process design flaw. So, rather than face the wrath of an impatient

> ### Box 3.6 Process Confusion at the Checkout Counter
>
> Issue: *If you do not even know it exists, you are certainly not committed to it.*
>
> Harry and Liz have reached the checkout counter at the supermarket. At the grocery store, October marks the arrival of a crop of squash of all shapes and colors, many of which you see only once a year. As Harry was placing a multicolored selection of the vegetables on the counter, the cashier seemed puzzled.
>
> Cashier: "Are these buttercup or butternut squash?"
>
> Harry: "I am clueless, but they sure are beautiful, aren't they?"
>
> Cashier: "They sure are. But I need to punch the right key here. Let me go and find Maureen; she always knows everything."
>
> Liz: "Oh, don't bother, we're in a hurry here. It does not matter anyway. We took them all from the same bin and they are all $1.25 a pound."
>
> Cashier: "OK. That's true. Let's assume that they are buttercup, then."
>
> He then proceeded to place the produce on the scale and process the payment. As Harry and Liz were navigating their grocery cart through the parking lot, Harry commented to Liz, "Well, they did not lose any money on this. Some poor inventory manager, however, might be in for a surprise when he places his next order for squash. Let's hope he is not a trusting person and takes a walk by the fruit and vegetable section before going ahead."

customer (not fun), he would rather enter erroneous information (what's it to him?). Clearly, if there is a process owner here, she's doing a poor job of training process workers (they probably do not work for her), or the evaluation system is biased. In later chapters, we discuss the notion of process owner as a countermeasure to this problem.

3.4 PROCESSES: AT THE HEART OF VALUE CREATION AND LEARNING

This last section should help the reader who is wondering what any of the material presented in this chapter has to do with the notion of value discussed in the previous one. We also highlight here the need for continuous improvement and the challenges involved in selecting the right process for improvement. Finally, we present an additional typology to facilitate this improvement.

3.4.1 The Value Connection

Processes, not *functions* (marketing, operations, finance, and so on), create value. Functions contribute to value creation through the part they play (that is, the tasks they perform) in processes. Processes create the benefits customers want by delivering the service or by making this delivery possible in one way or another. We illustrate this point by referring back to the discount real estate broker example discussed in Chapter 2. Figure 3.13 builds on Figure 2.11 to show the three-way connection between selected processes of a real estate broker, the features of the service (the delivery of which they affect), and the benefits thus created for the customer. While in manufacturing the output of a process is clearly distinct from the

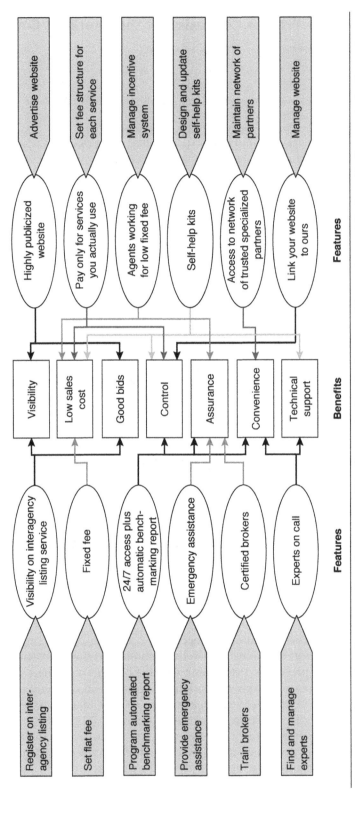

Figure 3.13 Connections between selected processes of a real estate broker, the features of the service, and the benefits they create for the customer.

process itself (that is, a car is distinct from the assembly line that put it together), this is often not the case in services. For instance, the output of the training process, that is, training, cannot be separated from the training process itself. Thus, while one can design a car first and then the assembly line to build it, it is often impossible to distinguish service design from service process design. Hence, there is a wide gray area where marketing and operations in services overlap. The price that the service organization will pay for a poor connection between marketing and operations is even higher than that paid by a manufacturing organization.

As much as we like to think that our processes create value for the customers, even a cursory analysis of most processes reveals a host of non-value-added activities (see Chapter 9). They are full of wastes of all kinds, such as waiting time; excessive, obsolete, or mismatched inventory; idle resources; too much or poor inspection; rejects (rework); and excessive movement. Poorly designed, implemented, and controlled processes result in excessive variations (see Chapter 6), which in turn produce low quality, delays, and bottlenecks, with dire consequences for customers, employees, and shareholders alike. In short, the process–value connection is all too often a very poor one.

3.4.2 Why Should We Improve Processes?

The International Space Station orbits the earth at an altitude of about 390 kilometers. However, this altitude decays at a rate of about 40 cm per revolution. Consequently, unless some action is taken to lift it up, the station will eventually reenter earth's atmosphere and burn up. Processes decay over time as well, and tend to stray farther and farther away from their initial state (this is analogous to the principle of entropy in thermodynamics). Now, humans are a great source of variation. We become tired, we forget, we grow careless, we make mistakes, and our priorities shift. Feelings may interfere, and coworkers under pressure may blame one another or become angry with one another. As anyone using a computer knows, machines are not exempt from variations, either. Moreover, human–machine interaction and environmental factors are further sources of variation. Thus, processes have to be improved just to maintain current performance.

However, fixing processes because they show signs of problems is only half the answer. The world is a dynamic place. Technology changes and creates new opportunities. Markets change as well, also creating new opportunities. In business, every opportunity comes with a concomitant threat: if you do not seize it, your competitor will. At an individual level, your body and mind change. All social organizations, such as families and companies, are subject to dynamic influences. Process improvement skills are vital to survival and prosperity in such an environment.

Finally, and perhaps most importantly, as discussed in Chapter 1, processes lie at the core of organizational learning, the key to becoming a world-class organization.

Data are digits. When we build relationships into the data, they become information. When decision rules link the information, it becomes knowledge. Knowledge is static. While it can and should evolve dynamically, it does not produce anything by itself. Know-how refers to the organization's ability to produce a given result, repeatedly and with minimal variation, that is, processes. Processes, however, need to access information, data, and knowledge bases. When we refer to the learning organization in this book (see Chapters 5, 9, and 12), we mean the organization that dynamically improves its know-how.

3.4.3 Which Process Should We Improve?

Processes are many, and time and resources limited. Which ones should we pick for improvement? It is worthwhile for a person or organization trying to answer this question to classify its processes into three categories:

* *Value-adding processes,* which are those that are directly involved in the achievement of our goals. For an individual, this may involve obtaining a degree or reaching some other personal goal such as completing a marathon or getting a book published. For a family, it may mean spending more time together or getting the kids to stop fighting all the time. A company may want to reduce its time-to-market or increase the turnover of its inventory. At a societal level, ending child abuse and ensuring airline safety are good examples. Table 3.5 shows illustrative value-creating processes associated with these and other goals. Corresponding enabling and support processes are shown as well. "Provide the service to specific customers," for instance, including all the subprocesses shown between the boundaries in Figures 3.7 (Medsol) and 3.9 (real estate), is a value-adding process. In business, value-adding processes

Table 3.5 Illustration of classification for personal, family, business, and societal processes.

Goal	Value-adding process	Enabling process	Support process
Personal			
Book published	Write a book	Improve writing style	Proofread
Marathon completed	Train for endurance	Eat the right foods	Renew track club membership
Family			
No fights between kids	Identify causes of fight	Monitor the kids' activities	Transport to Little League
Quality time together	Synchronize our schedules	Develop common tastes	Get good seats at the theater
Business			
Quick to reach market	Develop new product	Train design engineer	Build common parts database
Fast inventory turnover	Eliminate low-turnover items	Train people in just-in-time	Manage in-plant traffic
Society			
No child abuse	Protect endangered children	Raise awareness in population	Type reports
Safe airline	Spot terrorists trying to board	Select the right technology	Manage telecommunications

include transactional processes (involved in creating value for specific customers) and developmental processes (involved in the development of new services and new markets).

- *Enabling processes,* which are those that enable value-adding processes to work well. Whereas the impact of value-adding processes on goals is direct, that of enabling processes is indirect. Therefore, they are no less important than value-adding processes; they simply play a different role. They are often about the acquisition or development of basic competencies and capabilities. After a team of design engineers underwent training for a week, for example (see Table 3.5), time-to-market has not been shortened by one second—in fact, it is probably longer because the engineers were away for a week—but training may be a prerequisite (enabler) for the product design process to reach the desired capability. Recruiting doctors at Medsol or recruiting agents in the real estate business would be enabling processes as well. Governance processes, such as capital budgeting, strategic planning, and succession management, belong in this category. Some management processes may fall into this category.

- *Support processes,* which are related to building or maintaining the required infrastructure for value-creating and enabling processes to work. Some management processes fall into this category. Failure of support processes may well impair the functioning of other processes and thereby have a negative impact on value creation. These processes, however, are quite remote from the core of the business and thus require vastly different expertise. Therefore, they are often good candidates for outsourcing. Indeed, why not delegate some of these processes to organizations whose core business it is to perform them (potentially resulting in higher quality and lower cost)?

Unlike the typologies presented in section 3.2, this classification is based on the goals currently pursued. Clearly, as the goals change, so does this classification. Once an individual has completed a marathon, he may well decide that his knees hurt too much, and so he quits sports altogether and decides to write a book. The process of training for endurance then ceases to exist, and a writing process has to be designed from scratch. On another level, since the events of 9/11, the salience of processes such as immigration and ensuring the safety of airlines has increased dramatically.

Setting the right goal and finding the most important subprocesses require one to take a global view of things, starting from a strategic (business) or philosophical (personal, family, or society) approach. It requires clarity of purpose, sound macroanalysis of environments, and rigor in priority setting and process identification. Such an analysis (discussed in Chapter 7) could, for example, lead the discount real estate broker discussed in Chapter 2 to scope a process such as "write up property description for website" in response to a problem statement such as "while the *click-through*[7] rate is about 2% for our properties, it should be 5%." Improving this specific process is then *the right thing to do,* and we can now move on to *doing things right,* which takes us into a very different realm (discussed in Chapters 9 and 10).

Doing things right involves digging into the process to characterize it, that is, to understand in detail its dynamics and critical variables. The mind-set, skills, and tools required at the two levels—which we can figuratively refer to as the 10,000-meter versus the ground-level view—are vastly different. Failure at either task is fatal. Failure to identify *the right thing to do* results in investing time and effort *doing the wrong thing right* (that is, things that are not important), which adds little value and distracts us from the important issue we should be addressing. Failure to *do things right* results in *doing the right thing wrong*—also a recipe for disaster.

One last thought on selecting which process to improve: salience cannot be the only criterion. Current performance is also very important. Among value-adding processes, those that display the worst performance (relative to what it could or should be) are prime candidates. We discuss this in Chapter 7.

3.5 SUMMARY

Performing a process consists of taking an input and transforming it into a desired output. This notion applies equally well at a very high level (making a car) and at a very detailed one (snapping on the bumper). SITOC, FAST, and PFDs are essential tools for understanding and delimiting the perimeter of a discrete process functioning within a system (such as an organization). Process mapping zooms in on how things are actually done, in detail. These tools help us on our path from the macro view to the vital few variables within.

For a process to be defined, a loosely related sequence of ill-defined activities is not sufficient. A number of conditions are presented.

Several different ways to classify processes are presented in the chapter, ranging from the number of players, repetitiveness, and cycle time to degree of automation. They are helpful in coming to grips with this very broad concept. Classification is the beginning of knowledge. One additional classification—of particular importance to organizations—relates to the nature and degree of commitment the players in the process make to each other. Without commitment, there is no process.

Processes create value, as shown in Chapter 2. Understanding the nature of value for our customers of choice is a prerequisite to the design and management of processes. The ability to identify the most important processes to focus on at any point (doing the right thing) and the ability to improve, design, or redesign them (doing things right) are vital components of an organization's learning ability.

EXERCISES

3.1 Preparing a PFD

a. Prepare a SITOC (see Figures 3.6 and 3.8 for illustrations) for the two following processes drawn from the APQC model (see Figure 3.3): *4.1.7, "Sell products and services"* and *7.1.2, "Invoice the customer."* Use the form shown in Figure 3.14.

b. For these same two processes, prepare a PFD using the approach outlined in section 3.1.2 (see Figures 3.7 and 3.9).

c. In each of the PFDs you have just prepared, check off the processes that are defined in your organization (as defined in section 3.1.4).

d. From these same PFDs, pick two processes: one that is checked off and one that is not. Prepare a SITOC for each of these four processes.

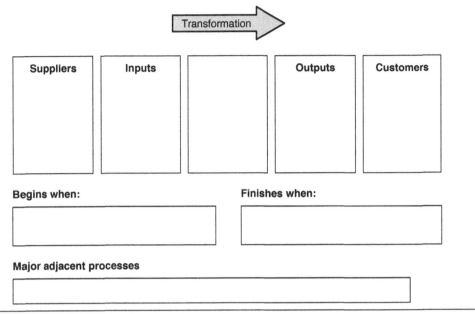

Figure 3.14 The SITOC form used to circumscribe a process (exercise 3.1).

3.2 Commitment

Explore the nature and strength of the commitments associated with the two processes you identified with a check in step c in exercise 3.1 and those for which you prepared a SITOC in step d. Talk to each of the players and discuss with them who their providers and customers are and what happens when they do not deliver.

3.3 Experience with Cross-Functional Processes

Identify a cross-functional process that has been modified recently or that is currently being implemented. Find out about inter-functional issues that arose and how they were resolved—if they were resolved. Draw a conclusion from this and from the previous exercises about your organization's "process-friendliness" and about the challenges that await it as it embarks on a process-oriented style of management.

3.4 Processes–Features–Benefits

Prepare a diagram similar to that shown in Figure 3.13, connecting benefits, features, and processes. Start from your answer to exercise 2.4 in Chapter 2.

3.5 Process Model

Before doing this exercise, review section 3.1.2, dealing with viewing the organization as a set of interconnected processes, and section 3.4.3, classifying processes into three major roles.

a. Prepare a process model for your company. Refer to the APQC process classification framework presented in Figures 3.3 and 3.4 (you can download the full model for free at http://www.apqc.org). This model is generic and is applicable to any industry. Make it specific. A medical clinic, for instance, might replace "produce and deliver for service organization" with "diagnose and treat patients," and "manage external relationships" with "manage relationship with laboratories" and "manage relationship with hospitals." Only include processes that currently exist in your organization (do not add processes that you think should exist). You should get between 8 and 15 processes.

b. Prepare a FAST diagram for all value-adding processes, such as the ones shown in Figures 3.2 and 3.4. Keep them at a high level, generating three to five subprocesses for each of the typically three to six value-adding processes. This should yield 15–25 processes. Bear in mind that designing the service and service delivery process, reaching the right customers, delivering the service, and managing customer data are all value-adding processes.

c. Prepare a FAST diagram for each remaining process. From the resulting list of level processes (you should have between 20 and 40, depending on the industry you are in), identify the ones you consider to be value enablers and the ones you consider to be support processes.

d. Identify the major processes performed by partners and suppliers. For a pharmacy, for example, this may include "manage inventory" (in the case of a supplier-managed inventory) or "provide online drug interaction information."

3.6 Process Mapping

For one of the two processes you discussed in exercise 3.2, formulate the mission of that process. Next, prepare a process map such as the one shown in Figure 3.10. If specific computer systems are involved, which is probable, include them as players with their own swim lane. Use the symbols presented in Figure 3.11. You may select another process. If you do, you will find it useful to prepare a PFD and macro map before mapping the process. The best way to do this is to assemble a team of process workers and to use sticky notes on a flip chart as described in Box 3.2. Physically taking a walk along the process path can be useful preparation for this exercise.

NOTES

1. This model was developed as a facilitating tool for benchmarking, that is, a reference to help compare apples to apples.

2. Productive resources, such as process worker, machinery, and IS/IT, are not inputs. They are not transformed by the process: they perform the transformation. Thus, they belong conceptually in the "T" of the SITOC model.

3. The term used in this book to describe people who work in processes.

4. This is called the "voice of the process" in Chapter 6.

5. Including the political, economic, social, technological, and ecological environments.

6. The word "player" is used in this specific context to refer to a function (for example, marketing), department (for example, publicity), or section (for example, graphic design) with a role to play.

7. The rate at which browsers exposed to the ad will click on it.

4

Think Globally, Act Locally

If you fail to plan, you are planning to fail.

—Benjamin Franklin

Processes come in many varieties. Operations strategy states how processes turn the organization's game plan into a reality. The design, improvement, and management of processes must ensure that they all work in harmony toward that end.

In Chapter 2 we discussed value creation, without which no business can exist for very long. In Chapter 3 we discussed the processes that create this value. This has laid the groundwork necessary to present the big picture. Thus, in this chapter, we turn to the connection between processes and value. To do this we must first discuss three unifying notions in business: business model, business strategy, and operations strategy. We are then able to present the logic connecting positioning, operations strategy, and processes. After that, we explore that connection in the specific case of professional services before turning to an exploration of the major families of processes and their fit with various strategies. Table 4.1 presents a short definition of the major concepts discussed in Chapters 4 and 5. Chapter 5 indeed pursues the application of the notions presented in this chapter to the specific context of professional services. Video 4.1 uses a historical situation to highlight the importance of execution, no matter how good the strategy (see Figure 4.1).

4.1 BUSINESS MODEL AND STRATEGY IN PROFESSIONAL SERVICES

Capitalism is predicated on competition. Business has borrowed the notion of strategy from another competitive field: war. Rather than destruction of the enemy, however, business model and strategy deal with creating more value than competitors, capturing the largest market share, and reaping maximum benefits for stakeholders. We explore these notions before investigating in more detail one component that is closely related to processes: operations strategy.

Table 4.1 Major concepts discussed in Chapters 4 and 5.

Business narrative	A story (sequence of unfolding events) featuring well-depicted character, performing in a compelling plot, narrated to make the logical case to support a value proposition.
Business model	A narrative of how the business will work, simultaneously creating value for customers, shareholders, partners, suppliers, and employees, together with the corresponding credible financial scenarios.
Value network	The respective complementary roles of the major players involved directly or indirectly in the creation of the customer experience, meshing into a sustainable self-supporting system.
Intended customer	A narrative of what the customer goes through, together with its experience associated emotions, that clarifies where the value lies and identifies the critical ingredients in the moments of truth that punctuate the encounter.
Value proposition	A focused statement spelling out precisely the key differentiating benefits, and the associated value, created by a service for a specific market segment.
Strategy	The company's game plan to beat competitors. Positioning decisions are made in the context of strategy formulation. Differentiation, niche, or low cost are typical competitive strategies.
Service strategy	The extent to which the service is customized to specific customers (custom vs. standard service) and the degree of customer involvement in the production of the service (service vs. self-service).
Customization	The extent to which the service, and therefore the SDP, lends itself to adjustments to meet the specific needs of various customers, or various market segments.
Operations strategy	Statement of how the company's operations will contribute to beating the competition through higher value and lower costs.
Operations policy	Important modality of execution of the operations strategy. It provides guidelines for the design, improvement, and management of processes.
Service standards	Performance levels, derived from the service concept, at which value-adding processes must perform. Performance standards for value-enabling and support processes are derived from the requirements of value-adding processes.
Coherence	The quality of SDPs that implements operations strategy and policies cohesively (in a complementary and mutually reinforcing manner).
Families of processes	Major kinds of processes (fully automated, line flow, job shop, and craftsman are discussed here) sharing a flow pattern and different characteristics.
Process characteristics	Desirable features of a process (effectiveness, efficiency, productivity, capacity, flexibility, and reliability are discussed here). Designing a process involves trade-offs between these features: you cannot have it all. We use operations strategy and policies as guiding principles in making these trade-offs.
Learning organization	An organization that is capable of improving its know-how faster than its competitors can.
Learning cycle (pump)	The "unit" of learning: selecting a process, designing or fixing it, and putting it into action with a new level of capability.

4.1.1 Overview and Illustration

Flawless execution cannot make up for a poor business model and strategy: it will merely lead to failure faster. In this section we present an introduction to the essential building blocks of a winning business plan and service strategy. It

4.1 So you have a good strategy, but you have not won yet
This 7-minute video provides a quick overview of the importance and challenges of rigorous execution.

4.2 V2P model—A technical note
This video explains how to use two templates to correlate positioning in the market, positioning in the labor market, shareholder value, operations strategy, value propositions, service concepts, job concepts, service standards, value-adding processes, enabling processes, and support processes into a high-level business model. It is technical in the sense that it gives detailed instructions about how to use these templates.

4.3 Business process outsourcing (BPO)—The evolving challenges and opportunities
Part 1: Exploring the process space
Trends in outsourcing are anything but linear. The political, economic, social, environmental, and infrastructural landscape of developing countries is changing very quickly. The pace of change in technological capabilities does not show any sign of slowing down, either. Thus, the decision-making process for outsourcing and offshoring business and knowledge processes must be reviewed regularly: what made sense five years ago may not make sense today. This video takes a fresh look at the question and, based on a review of recent research, proposes conceptual models that can guide and support enlightened decisions.

Outsourcing a process that you do not understand is abdicating. Outsourcing without strong process management capabilities is risky business. Enterprise architecture maturity is a critical determinant of this capability. The process space is presented here along two important axes: knowledge embedded in the process and extent of customer contact involved.

Part 2: Understanding the sourcing space
How far is it desirable to place each process? Distance here refers to ownership distance, physical distance, and cultural distance. Different risks grow with distance. While cost reductions may be immediately visible on the bottom line, risk is not, especially long-term risk such as loss of strategic nimbleness. We present here a global picture of these complex issues.

Figure 4.1   Videos associated with Chapter 4.

is beyond the scope of this book, however, to enter into a detailed discussion of how an organization should go about performing a strategic analysis and preparing a business plan.

Competition is inherent to capitalism, and a key source of its effectiveness at resource allocation. When the legal and regulatory environment allows for its smooth functioning, the company with the best value proposition gains the most market share. As discussed in Chapter 2, the company must also set itself up in such a way that it reaps the economic benefits of the value it creates. Once a company has clearly defined what value it is creating and for whom, and how this value meshes with that created by its suppliers and partners in the value chain, it must identify the points of greatest leverage in generating revenue and negotiate trading conditions conducive to a sustainable business relationship. We will refer to this mutually supportive set of arrangements to create more economic value than competitors and share it in a mutually profitable way as a *business model.* This value-creation scheme would not be complete if it did not specify how value will be created for key employees. In this context, the business strategy is the specific game plan to develop and maintain competitive advantage based on available market facts and intelligence about competitors' own game plans and actions. The business model is the broader concept within which a strategy is formulated, and reformulated as the situation changes on the chessboard.

The reader should resist the tempting simplification of reducing the strategic challenge to that facing the chess player. Consider, as someone once said, that since the pawns and other pieces (the professionals and managers) have a mind and will of their own, they are often striving to pursue their own purposes and follow their own path. The challenge of strategic planning is not limited to that of dynamically charting a winning course, but includes that of leading the organization along a path rich in unexpected opportunities and challenges.

An example will best illustrate the strategic notions discussed in this chapter. Box 4.1 presents the BMI case. The mission statement specifies why the entrepreneurs are investing their time, money, and energy in this venture. The short statements about competitive weaknesses and BMI's strengths and weaknesses are the result of competitive analysis. The strategy statement is the overall game plan, and the service concept (see Figure 4.2) outlines the major benefits and service features. Operations strategy and policy are discussed in the next section.

Box 4.1 Body and Mind Inc. (BMI)—Elements of a Business Model and Strategy

Issue: *A start-up reflects on its positioning*

Background and context. BMI is launching an innovative concept in the field of training. Mike Gross, a former sports club manager and globe-trotter, has noticed that moderately vigorous training stimulates the mind. When he was pressed for time to learn the rudiments of Spanish before a planned trip to Spain, he bought a training DVD and studied while doing his daily workout, with the stationary bike placed in front of the TV. It struck him that the unusual combination of physical activity and mental activity had saved him much time and resulted in both activities being easier, less tedious, and more productive (he felt his retention rate had been higher and his training more intense than usual). Discussion with a friend who teaches foreign languages had led to their original service concept and to the incorporation of BMI.

Company mission. Create stimulating individual and social experiences through the synergistic combination of intellectual and physical challenges for busy people wishing to learn new intellectual skills while they train.

Business opportunity. Competitors serve a broad, indiscriminate spectrum of customers. They sell as many yearly memberships as they can to anyone who can pay. Once customers have signed up, the companies leave them to their own devices, knowing that there will be an 80% abandon rate. Some companies often leave the most frequently used equipment in a state of disrepair. There is an important pool of unsatisfied customers and ex-customers who would be receptive to a low-risk proposition that addresses their frustrations.

BMI's strengths and weaknesses. The founders live what they preach. They have the required expertise and network to find the right people. They have firsthand knowledge of the systemic weaknesses of the competition. *Their access to capital is limited, however, forcing a small-scale start-up to reduce the initial risk to investors, but risking quick copy-catting by already established and better financially backed competitors.*

Market segments. Professionals and qualified technical workers who travel for their work and value wellness in general and fitness in particular. These world-wise individuals value language skills, for both cultural and professional purposes, but are too busy to dedicate much time to them. Specific segments include recent graduates from professional programs (for example, lawyers, MBAs, doctors); professionals nearing retirement age or recently retired, either singles or couples; and immigrant professionals. Segment sizes, yearly availability cycle, and natural affinities have to be considered in group makeup.

Value proposition. Stay fit and learn a new language with the least possible time investment, combining two activities that, alone, can be boring into a stimulating physical, mental, and social experience, as you interact with a group of like-minded professionals. We make this possible for you while letting you achieve superior results in half the time, make friends, and develop a mutually reinforcing group of activities.

Strategy.* A professional who wants to take both language and fitness training sessions has to find two service providers (a gym and a language institute) with schedules compatible with his own—an often impossible feat and a costly and time-consuming proposition in the best of cases. We will beat competitors who keep mental and physical activities separate on cost, quality (performance and ease in both physical and mental activities), and time by exploiting innovative combinations of "body and mind" learning activities. These activities are adapted to the lifestyles of busy, stressed, ambitious, active, and well-off professionals (target segment). We will exploit the social synergism created by these activities to become a magnet (and broker) for all industries offering related services to this prized market segment, such as travel agencies, training equipment dealers, and developers of websites and CDs dedicated to developing language skills. To get a quick start, we will invest substantially in branding the concept and lease the required space and equipment, upgrading it as required to meet the high standards we are setting.

Operations strategy, cost structure, and profit potential. For such superior value, we can charge customers somewhat more than they would pay both suppliers (gym and language school) together. However, since we combine the two sessions into one, our cost will be lower (the gym and the classroom are combined). That is how we will make money. We will perform ourselves only the high-value tasks that are vital to our concept and outsource the rest, while nurturing and protecting the critical knowledge and skill required to successfully create and capture the value of these experiences. By creating maximum interaction between participants within a stimulating learning and training environment, they will essentially create their own value, at a minimum cost for BMI.

Operations policy, value chain, and value network. Language instruction will be given by an instructor, who is on a bike, to a group of 12 executives working out on training bikes laid out in a half-circle around her. The course will be very interactive and personalized. We will provide clients with headsets to facilitate communication with the instructor and with other class members. We will also provide them with interactive DVDs to train and learn at home, in between gym sessions, and thus speed up their learning. The

(continued)

gym owner will rent us space and equipment at first. Distributors of language teaching and learning ware will be our suppliers. We will partner with tour operators and bar and restaurant owners to organize events where our clients can socialize, train, and practice language skills outside the gym environment.

Our strategy will generate enough cash to provide first-class service in the type of superior environment (including the training rooms, lobby, service area, and locker rooms) that is customary for the clients, and to recruit and retain as instructors the type of professional with whom they feel comfortable. The clients themselves will be involved in supervising the composition of the classes and in organizing special activities, such as action trips ("use your language skills while biking along the Rhine") or viewing the Tour de France on a giant screen while they train. We will favor word-of-mouth advertising and require referrals from existing members. Partners' sales activities will be seamlessly integrated with our own in a relaxed, low-pressure environment, and they will pay us a commission.

Job concept. Fitness trainers and language instructors will work in partnership. They will initially have day jobs with regular 9–5 hours, leaving them much time and physical energy to spend on their favorite sport. They will be able to stay fit all the time. As individuals, they will share an important value with their clients ("mens sana in corpore sano") and naturally enjoy the interaction with their groups. They will be encouraged to get involved as much as they can in the other dimension of the class and in other class activities. Whenever possible, we will allow them, as part of their benefit package, to learn other languages as well and accompany their clients on organized trips at reduced rates. Hence, they will get many of the benefits that their clients are getting, and financial compensation will not be the key motivator, and should not be prohibitive. Young retirees and graduate students are also potentially interesting labor market segments.

---

* Since the book deals exclusively with services, the words "strategy" and "service strategy" are used interchangeably. Because the case is hypothetical, specific facts about markets and competition are lacking, thus the broad terms in which this strategy is formulated.

The overall strategy branches out into the financial, operations (more details follow), marketing, and human resource strategies. These respectively specify in more detail how BMI will get and use money, how it will operate profitably, how it will build and manage relationships with customers, and how it will get and keep the people it needs to do all this. The job concept is a summary portrait of who the major players are and how BMI plans to create personal value for them (refer to the personal value equation in Figure 2.14). We focus here on operations strategy. While we do not discuss the other strategies in any detail, the reader should bear in mind how important it is that all these strategies fit together well.

Figure 4.3 (page 121) presents a first representation of the strategy-to-process connection. Most elements of the model were introduced separately in Chapters 2 and 3. The service concept, that is, the benefits and features of the service, is central to the model. The concept is delivered through processes (the large circle to the left) to the target market segment (the small circle to its right). Figure 4.2 is a zoomed-in view of a part of the model applied to the BMI situation. The service features are what it actually gives the client to produce the benefits. In other words, the

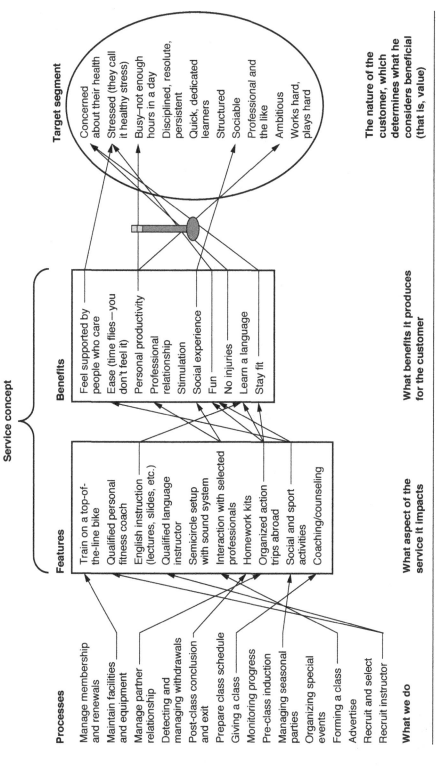

Figure 4.2 Body and Mind Inc.: illustration of the links between the target segment, service concept, and selected processes.

features are the "how" of the benefits. The connection between features and benefits, however, is not one to one. For example, the answer to the question "how do we produce the social experience benefit?" is "through interaction with selected professional, organized trip, and social activities." Hence, we could use a diagram like those shown in Figures 2.10 and 2.11 to represent the service concept.

Of course, the benefit package only makes sense if we know who the clients are (see the target segment column in Figure 4.2), as we did in the case of Jack and Linda in Chapter 2 after having described their personal activity cycle (Figures 2.6 and 2.7). Having identified the major competitors, the segment they target, and the benefits they offer, we could represent BMI's positioning with diagrams such as those shown in Figures 2.12 and 2.16. The first column of Figure 4.2 lists some of the processes that BMI must develop. They are identified by action verbs and nouns, following the rule presented in Chapter 3. The process–concept connection shown here parallels that of Figure 3.13. The arrows illustrate some (by no means all) of the logical connections between these elements. The process of forming a class, for instance, will ensure that the right interaction takes place between the professionals (feature), thereby contributing to the social experience (benefit) sought by these sociable (segment) individuals.

The global model of service profitability involving positioning, operations strategy, and coherence was initially proposed by Heskett et al. (1997) in their seminal book *The Service Profit Chain*. Even though the many examples and illustrations they use are now somewhat dated, it is still an excellent complementary read to this chapter. The book generated much empirical research, generally validating the model (Yee et al. 2010).

4.1.2 Operations Strategy and Profit Leverage

Positioning is about designing a service concept that is superior to those offered by competitors to targeted market segments. Good positioning, however, is not sufficient for business success. Operations strategies and policies are needed to deliver this concept to clients profitably. To generate profits, a business must be able to produce superior value with minimal costs. To dominate the market, it needs to produce more benefits than its competitors at the lowest cost. The spread between benefits provided to the customer and the cost to the provider affords the service provider leverage to charge a price that will leave customers, employees, and shareholders with enough value to secure their ongoing association with the company (that is, a win–win–win proposition). Thus, the service provider needs operating strategies that will maximize profit leverage.

An operations strategy is a defining aspect of how the company plans to deliver the benefit package. Put another way, it is a statement of how the company's operations contribute to beating the competition. BMI's operations strategy clearly states how the proposed concept creates more value for the client while generating a relative cost advantage at the same time.

If we refer back to the real estate example discussed in Chapter 2, appropriate use of the internet, for example, may deliver great value to buyers and sellers alike by providing virtual guided tours on a 24/7 basis. In addition, because it requires little human intervention on the part of the provider, it can give the seller a huge cost advantage over a competitor making extensive (and indiscriminate) use of costly face-to-face contact. Giving the customer control over service delivery through user-friendly technology is a great feeling (that is, value) for some people and relieves the provider of the burden and cost of doing so. Creating seamless (both on the website and in actual delivery) links to trusted specialized partners is very valuable to customers and does not cost the provider a penny. It may even generate additional revenues. Those are all operations strategies that can create leverage. The devil, of course, is in the details, but we are getting there.

Full-service providers, on the other hand, can elect to maximize their visibility in selected neighborhoods, initially "buying" market share through heavy advertising, discount pricing, and extensive house-to-house solicitation. This visibility then becomes a self-fulfilling prophecy: sellers and buyers alike are more likely to take their business to the broker with the most signs in their neighborhoods, thus producing more sales and word of mouth. Intensive local penetration is a marketing–operations–human resource strategy (it very much involves delivering personal value to agents actively involved in their community) that delivers superior benefits to customers while reducing the cost to the provider through economies of scale (reaching a critical mass that becomes self-sustaining).

The real estate market is also characterized by wide cyclical fluctuations. In such an environment, an operating system that can expand its capacity rapidly to meet peak demand and then contract to minimize costs—without losing the key productive resources it will require to face the next expansion—is a great advantage. Full-service brokers pay their agents on a commission basis to match their cost and revenue curves. However, if they do not keep their agent on at least a survival income during market troughs, they lose a vital linchpin in the delivery of their value proposition. Our new entrant could potentially be very resilient to market cycles. However, considerable initial investment is required for creating brand awareness and systems development, resulting in substantial financial charges, a situation that may be hard to withstand during extended periods of low revenues.

An operations policy is a modality of execution of the operations strategy. It is tactical in nature and subject to more frequent changes. BMI's operations policies (see Box 4.1) are really spelling out the operations strategy in more detail, making it clearer and pinpointing how it materializes in specific aspects of the operations. In the real estate business, developing self-help kits may be an operations policy that goes together with the strategy of empowering the customer: it can be of great help to the customer and does not cost much to produce and distribute. Another operations policy that would create leverage involves the production and automatic e-mailing of a weekly benchmarking report. A software agent could easily be programmed to compare the number of hits on the house, average stay, number of requests for additional information, number of new houses sold in that price range, and so on, impressing the customer with the wealth of information it provides in a timely manner.

4.2 SERVICE STRATEGY: THE PROCESS CONNECTION

Viewing Video 4.2 at this time would facilitate understanding of this section. Having defined strategy, and operations strategy in particular, we can now see how processes relate to these notions. In this section we first discuss the link between positioning and processes in the market (4.2.1) and in the job market (4.2.2). We then discuss the implications of some distinguishing characteristics of professional services (4.2.3) and conclude with a generic way to classify professional services, illustrated by a legal services example.

4.2.1 Delivering the Service Concept

The notion of operations strategy we just introduced sheds new light on positioning. Indeed, it does not appear anymore as stemming only from customer needs and market opportunities ("outside in") but also from internal considerations about the possibility to exploit these opportunities profitably. We can now see the service concept as the hinge between strategy and operations. Figure 4.3 builds on Figure 2.13 to show a more complete picture. Strategy is formed as discussed earlier (and illustrated in Figure 2.12) and deployed into operations, finance, marketing, and human resources. The search for the right formula (benefits–features) for the right market segment involves simultaneous prospection and introspection.

As shown in Figure 4.3, the value proposition (see the examples in section 2.3.3.3), or promise to clients, stems from the service concept and defines marketing's job. The same service concept is also the source, together with the operations strategy, of service standards. Since service features (or service offerings) are the output of the provider's value-adding processes (see process classification in Chapter 3), the service standards set the performance levels at which these processes must perform. Performance standards for value-enabling and support processes are derived from the requirements of value-adding processes.

Notice that even though both the promise to the market and service standards stem from the service concept, they are formulated in very different languages. The promise to the market is the translation that marketing and advertising creative staff make of the service concept so that it reaches the target market segment. It may take such forms as 30-second TV spots, magazine pages, or web spam. Service standards, on the other hand, have to lend themselves to measurement in a repeatable and reproducible manner (see Chapter 6) so that they can be used as the basis for process design, management, and improvement. The promise creates or adjusts clients' expectations. Processes managed in the light of appropriate service standards allow the provider to meet these expectations at the moment of truth (see Chapter 5). One condition for this to happen is that marketing and operations—both fluent in their respective languages, but generally largely illiterate in the other—see eye to eye on the service concept. Such communality of views allows "desired" or "intended" positioning to become "achieved" position, that is, in the mind of customers.

Figure 4.3 also highlights the role of operations strategy and processes in the value chain. In Chapter 3, we introduced processes as the sequences of activities transforming inputs provided by suppliers into outputs needed by the customer (or SITOC—refer back to Figure 3.6). Retracing the value chain backward, we can see in Figure 4.3 that the service features are the output of value-adding processes. They are the transformation of inputs received from upstream processes, including enabling, support, and suppliers' processes (and customers' processes as well—not shown in the figure). These inputs to value-adding processes are, of course, the outputs of the aforementioned processes. Value-enabling processes in turn produce these outputs from inputs received from support and suppliers' processes (as well as value-adding and customers' processes—not shown in the figure).

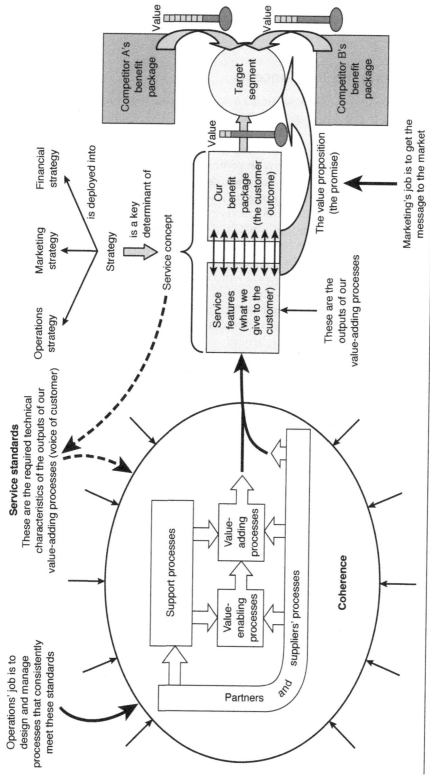

Figure 4.3   The service concept and standards as the linchpin between strategy and operations.

Just as service standards define the targets, operations strategy is the source of the vision and guiding principles required to ensure coherence in all aspects of service delivery.

4.2.2 Delivering the Job Concept

The reader will recall from section 2.4 (and Figure 2.15 in particular) that there is a dual aspect to the positioning challenge. Indeed, the organization is continuously competing to recruit the right employees, keep them appropriately challenged, support them in their jobs, and compensate them adequately. This is particularly difficult when we are dealing with professionals, since they are a workforce with unique characteristics: they value their skills and want to improve on them, they are mobile, they value their autonomy, and they are demanding of themselves and others. Hence, they have unique needs and requirements, requiring an appropriate benefit package. Their jobs must be designed in such a way (job features) that they reliably deliver these benefits (benefits and requirements together constitute the job concept, as shown in Figure 2.15).

Imagine that BMI has targeted a niche of energetic young educators working in public schools who value fitness and are disillusioned with their jobs. BMI's benefit package for this labor market segment could include such benefits as a social experience, stimulation, additional income, fitness, and travel. The job features that would deliver these benefits could include working only at night and on weekends, doing part of the teaching while working out on a stationary bike, learning other languages for free while training, accompanying groups on action trips abroad, participating in social events, and so on.

Of course, the job concept is delivered jointly by the organization's processes, which must simultaneously deliver the service concept. Figure 4.4 illustrates this dual value-creation role of processes. It also shows the pivotal role of operations strategy as a set of guiding principles that ensure coherence (discussed in the next section) in the company's actions (that is, in the company's processes) in such a way that positioning in the market and in the job market can be achieved and maintained. We refer to this representation as the "value-to-process" or V2P model. Figure 3.5 gives a somewhat more realistic perspective on the complexity of processes in the organization, using a subset of level 3 processes drawn from the APQC model.

Of course, processes relating directly to human resources development and management play a central role in delivering internal services to employees. Referring back to the APQC process model (Figure 3.3), these would all be included under process #6. The explosion of this process into level 2 and 3 subprocesses is shown in Figure 4.5. Well-designed and well-managed processes—6.2.5, "Manage new hire/rehire," and 6.3.1, "Manage employee orientation and deployment," for instance—ensure that new additions to work teams keep getting mutual stimulation and support from each other, and that conflicts are minimized and manageable when they do occur. Indeed, interaction with colleagues is an intrinsic part of the benefits that one derives from one's job. These same processes, however, are also very important for delivering the service concept, as a team's dysfunctions inevitably disrupt service delivery, reducing quality and even denying the client results. Disgruntled customers, in turn, are liable to provide negative feedback to

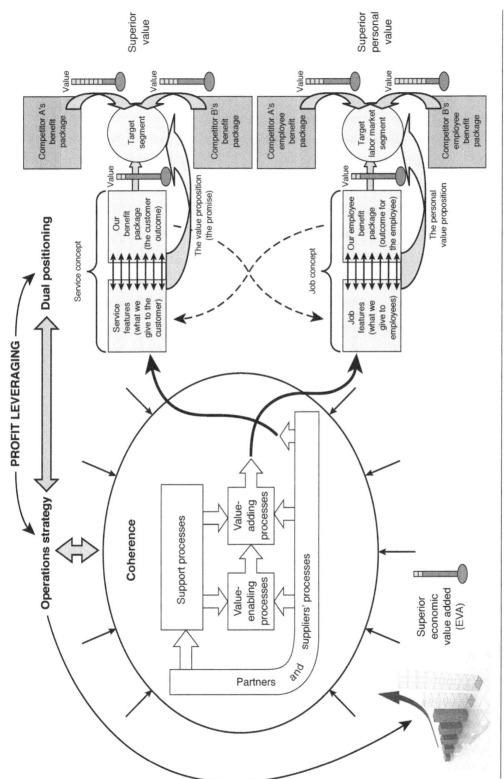

Figure 4.4 The three-way fit between operations strategy, positioning, and coherence ("value-to-process" or V2P model).

6.1 Create and manage human resources (HR) planning, policies, and strategies	6.4 Reward and retain employees
6.1.1 Manage/align/deliver human resources strategy	6.4.1 Develop and manage reward, recognition, and motivation programs
6.1.2 Develop and implement HR plans	6.4.2 Manage and administer benefits
6.1.3 Monitor and update plans	6.4.3 Manage employee assistance and retention
6.2 Recruit, source, and select employees	6.4.4 Payroll administration
6.2.1 Create and develop employee requisitions	**6.5 Redeploy and retire employees**
6.2.2 Recruit candidates	6.5.1 Manage promotion and demotion process
6.2.2.1 Determine recruitment methods	6.5.2 Manage separation
6.2.2.2 Perform recruiting activities/events	6.5.3 Manage retirement
6.2.2.3 Manage recruitment vendors	6.5.4 Manage leave of absence
6.2.3 Screen and select candidates	6.5.5 Develop and implement employee outplacement
6.2.4 Manage preplacement verification	6.5.6 Manage deployment of personnel
6.2.5 Manage new hire/rehire	6.5.7 Relocate employees and manage assignments
6.2.6 Track candidates	6.5.8 Manage employment reduction and retirement
6.3 Develop and counsel employees	6.5.9 Manage expatriates
6.3.1 Manage employee orientation and deployment	6.5.10 Manage employee relocation process
6.3.2 Manage employee performance	**6.6 Manage employee information**
6.3.3 Manage employee relations	6.6.1 Manage reporting processes
6.3.4 Manage employee development	6.6.2 Manage employee inquiry process
6.3.5 Develop and train employees	6.6.3 Manage and maintain employee data
6.3.6 Manage employee talent	6.6.4 Manage human resource information systems (HRIS)
	6.6.5 Develop and manage employee metrics
	6.6.6 Develop and manage employee time and attendance
	6.6.7 Manage employee communication

Figure 4.5 Develop and manage human capital: process list (down to level 3, based on APQC).

service providers, thus fueling a downward value-creation spiral triggered by the path shown by the dotted arrows in Figure 4.4.

Other processes, such as 6.3.5, "Develop and train employees," that are directly supportive of service delivery (4. Deliver products and services, in Figure 3.3) also have important bearing on the job concept. Even an operational process such as 4.4.3, "Provide the service to specific customers" (shown in Figure 3.5 and illustrated in more detail in the case of Medsol [Figure 3.7] and real estate [Figure 3.9]), is just as important to the professionals as it is to the clients, even more so, in fact, because professionals repeat it much more often than clients. Recall that this process involves face-to-face contact and is therefore important, albeit in different ways, to both interlocutors. All of the other processes involve many interactions with other professionals, managers, partners, suppliers, and so on. Such interactions are important sources of satisfaction and learning when they work well, and of stress and frustration when they do not.

Quick inspection of Figure 4.2, which displays a selection of specific processes for BMI, makes it clear that many of these processes, such as forming a class, giving a class, and managing seasonal parties, must be designed with both the client and the instructor in mind. For further discussion of how to use this model, see Video 4.2 and Exercise 4.6.

4.2.3 Positioning in the Fog of Professional Services

The challenge that positioning poses should now be clearer: simultaneously offering and delivering superior benefit packages to selected customers and professionals in such a way that much money is left for profits and growth. The knowledge gap, discussed in Chapter 2, between client and service provider in professional services makes positioning professional services particularly challenging.

Consider the plight of a patient who suffers from whiplash.[1] He can use a medical book or search the web to find treatment advice. He can also consult any of the following service providers: physiotherapist, orthopedist, general practitioner, osteopath, physiatrist, acupuncturist, or massotherapist. To make things more complex, some physiotherapists are free practitioners, while others work for orthopedists or physiatrists. The treatments offered by each vary widely, involving various mixes of service and self-service. Others double up as massotherapists, while some osteopaths are also trained as acupuncturists, and so on. Each of them will claim incontrovertible evidence that her angle is best, and after a 20-week treatment the poor patient may well be left wondering what percentage improvement he really feels, and whether that's attributable to the $2000 treatment he received or to the mere passage of time.

As discussed in Chapter 2, the gap in knowledge between the service provider and the client and the latter's difficulties in ascertaining the effect of the service make selection of a professional very difficult. The decision as to which provider to select is generally based on beliefs, which in turn are induced by experience and word of mouth. Hence, reputation and branding are even more important here than they are in other sectors.

Because all professionals are well aware of that, much competition takes place in the media. Clearly, the professional who provides the best value has an advantage, but she is not sheltered from competition from less scrupulous competitors who manage advertising, perception, and public image better. Newspapers are full of stories about highly reputable professionals who have been caught red-handed and whose professional practice turned out to be very different from best practice (witness the Enron debacle and the subsequent demise of the audit practice of Arthur Andersen). Thus, the best professional service will not make it and prosper in the marketplace on its own. The perception and branding war must also be won.

4.2.4 Customization and Customer Involvement— An Illustration in Legal Services

Consider the case of someone who wants to prepare a will. He is faced with two decisions concerning how to go about it: To what extent am I able and willing to get involved in the process? To what extent do I want it customized to my own specific needs? The first question relates to the issue of service versus self-service discussed in Chapter 2 (see Figure 2.5, for instance) and to the importance of the knowledge gap discussed earlier. The second question raises a fundamental issue, not discussed so far, about service and service delivery processes, that is, that of standard versus customized services. It has an important effect on all three stakeholders. Figure 4.6 illustrates the four basic possibilities resulting from the two decisions. The two axes involve a continuum along which many possibilities exist, even though we present only two in the body of the diagram. The bars on the degree of service axis refer to those used in Figure 2.5.

While we present the four possibilities from the customer's perspective, they clearly imply positioning opportunities for service providers as well. A different operations strategy, and different processes, underlies each opportunity. Each also implies a different job concept. Let us assume that four providers (labeled 1 to 4 in

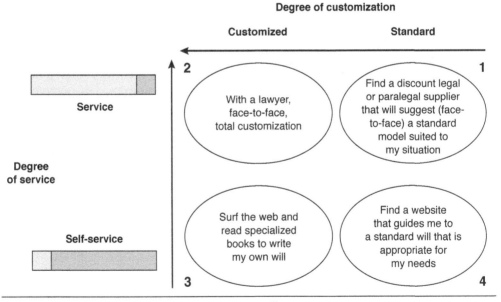

Figure 4.6   Four generic ways for one to prepare a will.

Figure 4.6) are competing with each other in a given market. Provider 1 delivers a result that is quite close (for clients with simple needs) to that offered by provider 2, with the difference that it is faster and cheaper. His operations strategy might involve using personable legal technicians to leverage lawyers. Technicians are the primary service providers. He selects them for their people skills and professionalism. The contact mode is face-to-face (tightly or loosely scripted), but because of the technicians' people skills and availability, customers do not feel this limitation. A few lawyers work in second line, mostly developing service offerings and acting as backup and support to technicians. Clients in the target market are delighted by the availability and human qualities of the technicians, who in turn enjoy the positive feedback they are getting (refer to the dotted lines in Figure 4.4). He selects lawyers for their preference for work that is more intense in professional content than in client contact. As it is much easier to manage technicians than lawyers, customer requirements weigh much more in the design of delivery processes, including selection of modes of contact, than in those of lawyers. This is an important advantage over provider 2.

Provider 4 offers clients who have some technical knowledge and who are willing to get involved in the process the same result that provider 1 offers, except that she does so faster, more conveniently, and cheaper. Her operations strategy involves a substantial investment in automated service delivery, essential to providing the aforementioned benefits, that becomes profitable as extremely low variable cost allows setting a price that is attractive to a mass market. There are very few lawyers on staff and many IT professionals. She uses specialized technical expertise on a contractual or consulting basis, with in-house lawyers acting as the interface with IT experts. The interfacing between these different professionals is vital to the success of the business, and much management attention is directed at ensuring smooth contact between them and early detection of conflicts. Provider 3 is in a different business altogether, acting as a content assembler, integrator, and distributor. However, emerging expert systems are gradually blurring the line between providers 3 and 4. As technology evolves, customer knowledge increases, and the market matures, many synergistic merger and strategic alliance opportunities will emerge.

This example shows that the existence of a viable operations strategy is indissociable from the positioning exercise. The customer value equation reminds us that value is a function not only of the benefits produced but also of the price paid by the client. Price, however, is a function of cost, and the latter is, in turn, a function of the resources used. Since experienced professionals are generally the scarcest and most expensive resource in a PSO, it is advantageous to use their time with parsimony, allocating it to tasks that technicians, trained personnel, or machines cannot perform. The number of ways to combine professionals, technicians, customer service representatives, and IT into service delivery processes is virtually infinite. The number of viable ways to do so for a PSO, at any point in time, is much more limited. It is the purpose of the operations strategy to find, formulate, and act as implementation guide and bulwark for the "right way of doing things" in the organization.

It is also impossible to dissociate the formulation of the service concept from that of the job concept. The different mixes of resources that are possible not only offer different value propositions to the customers but also imply different job concepts as well. To understand this better, it is worthwhile to further explore some important aspects of professional work, professional workers, and PSOs. We pursue our discussion of this example in section 5.4.4.

4.3 BETTER UNDERSTANDING PROCESSES TO ENSURE STRATEGIC FIT

In this section, we further explore processes and their characteristics with a view to illustrating the required fit with positioning and operations strategy. After presenting the major process characteristics, we show how these are unevenly distributed among the various families of processes, thus forcing difficult trade-offs. After a short discussion of waste avoidance (staying lean) we conclude with the required coherence among processes and the difficulties involved in maintaining it as processes change over time.

4.3.1 Process Characteristics

There are many ways to achieve a desired result. In preparing a cup of coffee, for example, one may boil water in an electric kettle, on a range, or in the microwave oven. Beans may be ground with an electric blade grinder, ground with a stone grinder, bought pre-ground, or ground in an industrial-quality machine at the supermarket. Water may be filtered through the grounds through a funnel, under pressure (espresso), or using a piston (Turkish style). Are these all equivalent? Of course not. The taste, smell, effect, temperature, and texture of coffee will vary. So will the cost, the cost structure (fixed versus variable), the tasks of the employee and skill requirement, input requirements, suppliers, and so on. How can we compare these processes and select the best one? In order to do that, we have to understand a little more about processes and their characteristics. In this section, we describe and illustrate a number of such characteristics: *effectiveness, efficiency, productivity, capacity, flexibility,* and *reliability.*

A process is *effective* if it produces the desired effect (or result). If one is preparing a cup of coffee because one feels sleepy, effectiveness is directly proportional to the amount of stimulation one gets from the coffee. Consider the case of Midtown Child Protective Services (see Box 4.2). Process effectiveness is related to the security it provides to the children. In both these cases (the cup of coffee and CPS) it is a question of degree. Sometimes, however, effectiveness is either 0 or 1—it worked or it did not—such as fixing a broken computer or transporting a letter from point A to point B by 10 a.m. the next day.

A process is *efficient* if it uses the most economical means possible to achieve the desired results. If I buy Jamaica Blue Mountain coffee beans at $60 a pound for the sole purpose of ingesting 120 mg of caffeine, that's inefficient, even though the inefficiency comes from the choice of inputs and not from the brewing process per se. If I brew a full six-cup percolator and throw away the rest, that is inefficient as well. At Midtown CPS, if Sam sends the police and a special intervention team to place the children in a reception center for a week, when a good night's sleep at the neighbors' and a simple visit by a social worker the next day would have been sufficient, that's inefficient (not to speak of the potential side effects of the first approach). While the definition of efficiency is quite clear, how to measure it raises

Box 4.2 Midtown Child Protective Services

Issue: *A complex public professional service dealing with a sensitive societal issue*

Sam Alonzo looked worried as he cut the line by flipping off the switch with his thumb. A glance at the clock told him it was almost midnight. A flashing red light on the console indicated that Mark, his colleague at Midtown Child Protective Services (CPS), was busy taking another report. The caller was obviously concerned:

> "The poor little things are three and five," the man had said. "They've been playing outside all evening wearing T-shirts, and it's freezing out there. They had been banging at the door of their parents' house for half an hour when my wife decided to invite them in. They're downstairs having a hot chocolate now. The parents must be having a really good time in there. I knocked at the door and rang. No answer. The music is so loud in there! Besides, we could distinctly smell that they're not smoking the normal kind of tobacco, if you know what I mean."

The caller was worried, and so was Sam now. CPS's mission is to enforce the state's child protection legislation. Sam, a trained social worker, was working in the emergency service department. On a 24/7 basis, the department received reports from professionals (doctors, nurses, teachers, social workers) and concerned citizens about children in need of protection. They had to assess these reports and decide, sometimes on the spot, on an appropriate course of action.

Sam was mentally reviewing his options. He could have the police department send a patrol car right away to pick up the children and drop them at the city's reception center or at the home of a specially trained family willing to handle this situation. A team of specialists would then take over the case first thing the next morning as they came to work. That, of course, could trigger a chain of events, including legal procedures, that would be very consequential for the family, and thus for the children. Also, he had to consider that the team's resources were already spread very thin. Instead, he could ask a special intervention team composed of a family therapist and a specialized educator to make it their next stop. However, it would be a couple of hours before the team could get there, and then they would not be available if something more urgent came up elsewhere in the city. Finally, he could ask the caller if he was willing to keep the children overnight and slip a note under the door for the parents. However, could the caller and his wife be trusted? What would be the parents' reaction as they read the note? At this point in his thought process, the red light on the console turned off.

"Oh good," he thought as he got up, grabbing his empty mug. "I need a sounding board on this one . . . and a good cup of coffee!"

---

many issues. For instance, should one focus on the transformation per se, excluding the cost of the inputs? In many instances, it is convenient to use unit cost of output as a good proxy for efficiency (that is, including the cost of the inputs). This is impossible, however, if one wants to analyze the efficiency of several interconnected subprocesses or in situations where one is trying to track efficiency over time, excluding the influence of market price variations.

Productivity is traditionally defined as the ratio of outputs to inputs—that is, the quantity of output per unit of input. Since that leaves out quality entirely, a better definition would be the quantity of good output per unit of input. However, one can see the difficulties that would arise in trying to define, let alone count, "good output" at Midtown CPS. The best measure—though measuring it remains a challenge—is the ratio of effectiveness to efficiency, commonly referred to as *cost-effectiveness.* CPS being a public service, its mandate is to provide maximum protection to the children at risk in their community, given the budget it has. Thus, cost-effectiveness plays an important role in every resource allocation decision the agency makes.

The *capacity* of a process is a measure of the volume of work it can perform. The security check process at a given airport gate may be able to handle 500 people an hour. A Boeing 767-200 accommodates 224 passengers—206 six abreast and 18 first-class passengers six abreast. Sam and Mark at Midtown CPS may be able to investigate an average of four calls an hour during their shift. A fast-food drive-through service may be able to process 50 cars an hour. Often, however, capacity is not a fixed number. A full plane means less personal attention and a longer wait at the bathroom. Sam and Mark could handle six calls an hour for a while, but if that rate was to be sustained for a whole night, they might become tired, and the risk of a bad decision would increase. Short-term response to an unforeseen increase in demand, as the process approaches maximum rated capacity, often means loss of effectiveness and/or efficiency. If the increase in demand is sustained, the process can generally be modified to adapt to the new level. With an all-coach configuration, a Boeing 767-200 can seat 290 people eight abreast. However, one had better make sure that the increase is not just a short-term blip before incurring the changeover cost. Thus, a good volume forecast is a precious tool for both process designers and process managers.

A process is *flexible* if it can deal with much variety with a minimal penalty. The penalty to which we refer is the higher cost, lower quality, or longer cycle time that afflicts processes that do many different things compared with processes that do only one thing. The latter benefit from a high level of standardization, special-purpose tools, lower cost employees, and an optimized layout and flow. Anyone who gets a hepatitis shot at a traveler's clinic and compares the procedure with that used in a general practitioner's office knows the difference. The time penalty is even more obvious if one compares one's personal process for changing a flat tire with that used by the pit crew of a Formula One car. Hence, while variety always entails a penalty, a process that minimizes the penalty is said to be the most flexible. A five-star restaurant, for instance, offers a vast selection of coffee. However, if one asks for a Turkish coffee—which the restaurant brews only once a month when it has a special request—the customer may have to wait a while (time penalty) for a coffee that is not to his taste (quality penalty) and pay a hefty price for it (cost penalty). Midtown's emergency service process is very flexible. It can deal with any type of emergency on a 24/7 basis. To achieve this, it must often pay an expensive professional (university trained, 10 years' experience, working a night shift) for hours to wait for that truly urgent call, and pay a premium to other specialists to remain on 30-minute call all night.

A *reliable* process is one on which one can depend. An unreliable process is one that generates an excessive number of failures. No process is infallible, but some are pretty close to being so, with defect rates (see Chapter 6) under one per million. What is acceptable and what is not depend on the customer's needs. A cleaning process that we would consider unreliable in a surgery room, for instance, may be perfectly acceptable in a hotel. We discuss this notion further in Chapter 6. Other process characteristics, such as capability, stability, predictability, reproducibility, and repeatability, are discussed in later chapters.

Designing a process involves making trade-offs between the characteristics presented earlier. Let us go back to the coffee example presented in the opening paragraph of this section. Buying the beans pre-ground saves time in preparing coffee, but the coffee does not smell or taste the same (ineffective). Preparing a filter-coffee one cup at a time allows you to personalize bean selection and grinding (flexible), but it takes much time (inefficient) and would be impractical for a large party. It may also introduce much variation in taste, caffeine content, or temperature from one cup to the next, and may thus be unreliable. Espresso tastes great (effective, if you like that) but may require a long lead time and a substantial investment. It also utilizes much counter space and has the highest cost per cup (inefficient). Further, it is very rigid, producing a unique taste that will not please all guests. Its capacity is much lower than that of a percolator, and the labor content per cup is much higher.

Such trade-offs must be made with a clear understanding of the mission of the process (that is, what contribution do we want it to make to the execution of our strategy? [as discussed in Chapter 3]) and also based on a realistic look at the constraints of every nature that limit our choices: financial, technical, and circumstantial. Understanding the major families of processes and their characteristics somewhat simplifies that choice.

4.3.2 Major Process Families

We consider four major families of processes: artisan, job shop, line flow, and continuous (or fully automated). In any service, we process three different elements: people, things, and information. Things may include food, medication, the client's property (pool, house, or dog), and hard documents (deeds, drawings, certificates). We first illustrate job-shop and line-flow processes with a simple example.

Compare two types of cafeterias. One is a line-flow process where everybody follows the same sequence directed by the guiding rails supporting the trays: trays, dishes and utensils, cold drinks, salads, cold sandwiches, soup, hot plates, desserts, hot drinks (placed last to improve the odds that it will not be too cold by the time one drinks it), and cashier. The other one is a job shop organized as a set of islands (hot drinks, cold drinks, salad bar, soup bar, hot plates, sandwiches, desserts, and so on). Each customer decides where to go and in what sequence.

For a homogeneous set of customers wanting a complete meal with salad, soup, dessert, and drinks, the line flow will tend to be the fastest, most reliable, and efficient process, provided it is well balanced. Line balancing is about making sure that each station along the line requires about the same amount of time. Since the longest station determines the pace of the line, total process time is equal to the processing time at the longest station multiplied by the number of stations. If the group is heterogeneous, many people who do not want soup will end up waiting this station out or trying to jump the line, with all the disruptions and friction that this may entail. The same will happen when someone is coming back for seconds. Thus, the line is quite rigid and becomes inefficient (from the customer's point of view) as the group becomes more heterogeneous. In this context, reliability might involve delivering each plate with little variation in the quantity of food, temperature, and cycle time. Reliability and capacity (measured in number of customers served per hour) will tend to be superior to the job shop.

Assuming again a homogeneous group of people, a job shop would result in unpredictable and unmanageable bottlenecks surfacing here and there because of random customer decisions. More staff would be required, running around to replenish the food supply as shortage randomly occurs in various spots and trying to alleviate bottlenecks as they occur. To do so, employees should be cross-trained to be able to perform at any workstation where they may be required (there is a cost associated with that), and more variation would be introduced by frequent switchovers. For a heterogeneous group, however, the job shop would be the fastest and most efficient process. Customers wanting only a sandwich and coffee and customers wanting soup and a hot plate would not be in each other's way because they would use different parts of the service delivery facilities. The job shop is also more flexible for such a group, involving a lesser time penalty to customers than a line flow would.

Employees working in both environments receive different benefit packages. The task is very repetitive on the assembly line, which may be boring for some people, and workers have to work in close synchronization with each other. Job shop workers receive much more training and are called upon to use their initiative much more often, which some people may like and others may not.

Of course, there are many intermediate options between the two processes presented here. Depending on customer needs, operational problems encountered, and layout constraints, one may create a sandwich counter to relieve some pressure from a regularly congested line. The job shop may add an express one-stop meal (including payment) for customers willing to sacrifice choice for speed (provided there are not too many). Having such a mix of job requirements may allow employees with different preferences to find something suited to their taste.

An artisan type of process involves a single worker working alone to produce most of the process's deliverables. Continuing with the meal preparation example, a person preparing a meal at home uses such a process: planning the meal himself, buying what he needs, preparing, and cooking (and in this case, consuming the output as well). Compared with the line flow and the job shop, it is generally less efficient and less reliable. It is, however, more flexible and may, depending on the customer and the provider, be considered very high quality. Japanese steak houses, where the grill is on your table and the chef cooks your meal in front of you, come close to being an artisan process (the host serves the salad, soup, rice, and drinks, but the cook does the rest). To make this economically viable, however, the menu has to be reduced considerably (grilled chicken, shrimp, or steak, typically), thereby limiting the process's flexibility.

Strictly speaking, a continuous process involves the continuous flow of a product (generally in liquid or semi-liquid form such as molten steel, crude oil, or paper paste). Electric utilities provide a continuous flow of electrical services along wires. Radio and TV stations provide a continuous flow of information carried by electromagnetic waves. Food, obviously, cannot be served this way. Information, however, can be digitized and flow along wires, electronic components, and electromagnetic waves. Such processes involve a continuous flow of data. They can be fast, efficient, and reliable. They can, however, be very costly to build, requiring an important investment in infrastructure, and are rigid, though this last limitation is receding as IT keeps on pushing the frontier.

Table 4.2 summarizes the foregoing discussion of the four major types of processes and their characteristics. The four types of processes really represent

Table 4.2 Major families of processes and their characteristics.

Fixed cost ↑ / Variable cost ↓	Family/ characteristics	Cost-effectiveness*	Flexibility	Reliability	Capacity
↑	Artisan	− −	+ +	− −	− −
	Job shop	−	+	−	−
	Line flow	+	−	+	+
↓	Fully automated	+ +	− −	+ +	+ +

Legend: + + Very good
+ Good
− Bad
− − Very bad
* At a high volume

discrete points along a continuum. Artisan processes are not very structured, leaving much leeway to the (typically highly qualified and thus highly paid) worker. They are neither very efficient nor reliable and have a low capacity. They compensate for these weaknesses with a high level of flexibility. As we go from an artisan to a continuous-flow process (when this is possible), we introduce more structure and standardize the process. We also limit the variety of services it can render and we increase cost-effectiveness, reliability, and capacity at the expense of flexibility. Hence, the general trade-off implied by the table is clear. An organization's positioning and operations strategy guide it in the selection of the appropriate family of processes. Organizations whose expertise lies in managing a particular type of process must also take this capability (and the corresponding limitations it implies) into consideration in its positioning decisions.

As we go from artisan to line flow, work is increasingly divided, workers perform increasingly limited tasks, and less qualification and training are required. Workers, however, become more closely interdependent, and more coordination is required. A continuous or—more to the point in our case—fully automated information process is a different animal altogether. Much of the cost of such a process comes from its design, maintenance, and updating, as transactions themselves are extremely cheap. A few very specialized, highly trained, and costly resources (mostly analysts and programmers) do this work. Obviously, management's job varies considerably from one process to the next.

Our discussion of cafeterias essentially focused on the flow of people through the process. Thinking about customers first is certainly the right approach. However, we have to simultaneously consider the movement of food as well. The design of processes that ensure that no workstation ever runs out of food is based on both the needs of the customer and those of employees in contact, and thus on the process selected to serve customers. The shape, weight, and accessibility of food containers from which the customer's plates are prepared (as well as the ordering and refilling procedure), for instance, are unimportant for the customer but are very important to the contact employee. The flow of people and the flow of food jointly determine information requirements. This forms the basis for the design of information systems. The three flows (people, things, and information) must stem from a unique vision that ensures coherence in the implementation of the operations strategy.

Process choices regarding the flow of things and people have implications for layout, as the cafeteria example should make clear. The line flow requires sequential stations to be aligned and in proximity. The job shop requires enough space to allow a free circulation lane between each functional island and to accommodate waiting lines wherever they form. An artisan process requires organizing all the tools and equipment around the artisan and ensuring the flow of all required material to each artisan; that is, since the artisan does not move, the material must come to the artisan.

One last consideration is required before coming back to professional services: the location of the line of visibility (see section 3.1.3) is an important process design decision. Rather than have the customer go to the food, we could have the food come to the customer. In hospitals, for instance, where patient mobility is limited, food trays are assembled on a full-fledged assembly line connected by a moving conveyor. In a five-star restaurant, customers select from a vast array, and the meal is prepared and assembled in a back-office job shop. The modes of contact are face-to-face, "tight spec," and total customization, respectively.

As this chapter makes clear, the choice between one process and another depends on positioning and strategy, including operations strategy.

4.3.3 Avoiding Waste

The ideal process is one that uses the least amount of resources to produce a result that exactly meets the client's needs, at the right time and place, while making her experience as pleasant as possible, even memorable. It is not wasteful of the customer's or the employee's time. It uses the most economically effective technology—not necessarily the latest. It flows evenly without bottlenecks, which cut throughput and result in wasted capacity upstream and downstream. It does not build up inventories "just in case," but rather operates "just in time." It's been organized to minimize the number of players, their movements, and handovers. Coordination and adjustment decisions are made by whoever has all the required information and knowledge to do so, most of the time by process workers themselves. It takes place through the simplest possible means, using visual clues whenever possible, through pre-agreed mechanisms.

The ideal process is simple, and simple is very difficult to achieve. Simplicity and frugality have historically been the cornerstones of Japanese culture. In the 1960s and '70s, the best Japanese companies revolutionized the way processes are designed, managed, and improved. This is called the *lean* philosophy of operation. We discuss it further in Chapter 11.

4.3.4 Outsourcing, Value Chain, and Value Network

Should we perform our legal work internally or use specialized firms as required? Should we manage our own call center or let an outside firm do it? Whether we own it or not, should it be located in India, Atlanta, or Mexico? Should radiologists in India analyze CT scans at night so that reports can be available the next morning in New York? Critical decisions all, replete with factors to weigh, risk and uncertainty to ponder and assess, and trade-offs to make. The reader should view Video 4.3 for a discussion of the issues involved.

A value chain[2] is a sequence of processes taking inputs from an upstream process, adding value, and delivering their output as an input to a downstream process. To illustrate, imagine that an insurance agent gathers information about a request for insurance from a chemical processing plant. The information is sent to an industry specialist who in turn receives data about industry risks. The data are processed by a risk analyst and sent to an underwriter, who proposes to hedge that risk. Legal experts are then consulted and the resulting policy is prepared by a specialized firm. The agent then meets the client to present the proposal.

A value network is a set of related processes or value chains that deliver related outputs to meet the various complementary needs for assistance of a customer during a live event episode (for example, taking a family vacation, addressing financial problems, or finding a job) or a business event episode (for example, responding to a suit, building a new plant, or developing a new distribution network). Responding to an employee suit following an industrial accident may require a number of related services: industrial risk assessment, event analysis, legal analysis, insurance liability analysis, labor relation, and so on. The value network is the set of processes or value streams that provide these services. Whether these processes are provided by the same organization or not, the customer would like them to be coherent. This notion is discussed in the next section.

4.3.5 Coherence

A service delivery process (SDP) is coherent if:

- Its design reflects a clear understanding of the needs and preferences of the market segment and of the employees, of the benefit package to be delivered to each, and of what it is that must be done right to beat the competition while maintaining and growing the skills and motivation of the workforce

- All its components are complementary and mutually reinforcing

- It exploits operations strategies and policies to their fullest potential

The notion of coherence is best understood by looking at examples of incoherence. Indeed, a coherent service delivery goes so smoothly that it is seamless and effortless for the customer. Delivery is incoherent when the way things are done systematically works against the fulfillment of the promise made to any of the company's stakeholders.

Here are some examples of incoherence in different types of SDPs:

- A fast-food restaurant with a menu from which the customer will require more than 30 seconds to make a decision

- A five-star airport hotel where the only food available after 11 p.m. is whatever is available in the minibar

- An airline with slower check-in for first class than for economy

- A gourmet coffee shop that serves coffee in a cardboard cup

- A telephone banking service that asks the customer to key in a host of information about her account number, transaction, and PIN and then asks her to repeat it all verbally

Anyone who is minimally attentive as a service customer can, unfortunately, recall many more observations of the same flavor.

Back to the real estate example, a full-service agent (see Figure 2.10) subtly putting pressure on a customer to accept an offer he is inclined to reject is being incoherent if the benefit package includes "assurance," that is, "you are in the competent hands of a professional whose only interest is that you get the best possible price for your house." Other possible examples of incoherence for the full-service agency include:

- Agents are switched around regularly from one sector to another (local expertise is lost)

- It takes two weeks for the photographer to come take pictures of the house (speed of sale)

- The agent can never be reached on the phone after hours (easy access)

The new entrant's (see Figure 2.11) SDP would also be incoherent if its website is only listed on the second page of a Google search for "house for sale." Other examples of potential incoherences for the discount real estate agency include:

- The automated report is impossible to understand (assurance, convenience, and control)

- Agents act like bureaucrats, not really motivated to help the customer sell his property (assurance)

- Partners are not really integrated with the brokerage firm, and the customer has to reach an agreement with them from scratch, as if she were an anonymous individual who just walked in off the street (convenience)

Notice that all the examples of incoherence given so far are related to the delivery of the service concept to the customer. The notion of coherence, however, is broader than that: it also includes employees and shareholders. Therefore, incoherences include delivery system dysfunctions that result in denial of benefits to any of the three stakeholders or that pit one stakeholder against another. Table 4.3 shows various potential process dysfunctions at BMI, along with the reasons why they are incoherent and which stakeholder or combination of stakeholders they would affect.

The foregoing discussion does not go very far in helping the reader design coherent service delivery processes. This is a complex issue that will require much of the rest of this book.

Table 4.3   Potential process dysfunctions at BMI, explanation, and stakeholders affected.

Incoherent element of service delivery process	Why it is incoherent	Stakeholders affected
Noisy or worn-out equipment with frequent breakage and adjustments	The noise and frequent interruptions will make learning impossible	Client and trainer
Recruiting a language instructor who does not care much about fitness	He will not fit in and will not be able to accompany the group on action trips abroad. He will stick out like a sore thumb at parties.	Client
Setting fees too low—less than the cost of the alternative	The alternative is taking two separate courses, with the time and inconvenience that this entails Charging less than that will result in cheating the shareholders or in a self-defeating decrease in service standards	Shareholders
Not detecting an excessive dropout rate early on and taking immediate steps to correct it		Client and shareholder
Assigning trainers daily according to who is available	Convenient for trainers, but denies the clients continuity in learning and social interaction	Client versus trainer

4.4 THE LEARNING ORGANIZATION

In earlier chapters we explained that processes lie at the heart of value creation and learning. More specifically, the company, through its processes, must create more value than its competition in the respective markets for its three stakeholders: customers, employees, and shareholders. The foregoing discussion shows that the strategy–process connection is central to this global purpose. Figure 4.7 illustrates this graphically. The organization's strategy simultaneously addresses positioning in the market and in the labor market (as illustrated previously in Figure 4.4). The unfavorable "value gap" shown in the "market" squares must be bridged to increase competitiveness. At the same time, it must deliver a job concept of superior personal value to its employees of choice (competitors vying to obtain the services of these employees may be totally unrelated to those we face in the market). The dotted line across Figure 4.7 illustrates that if the organization fails to deliver to either stakeholder, the other one suffers as a result, thus triggering a spiral of failure. Over the long haul, they have to be win–win value propositions. Win–lose is not an option.

As discussed in Chapter 3, the organization must decide how many resources it can afford to devote to improvement at any point in time, given that in the short term these resources are withdrawn from those available for daily operation.

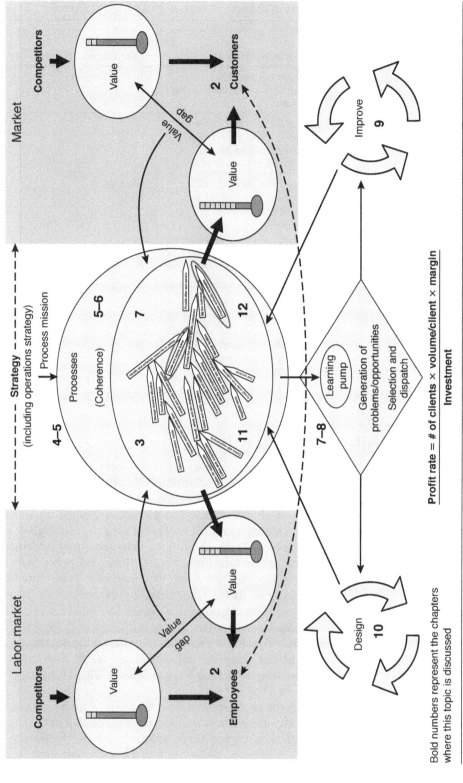

Figure 4.7 The learning organization: doing the right thing (picking the right process) right (designing or improving that process) as a key organizational routine.

Thus, processes that need attention are many, and resources to attend to them are limited. Selecting the processes that will contribute most to the enhancement of the organization's competitiveness at that point in time (that is, "the right thing to do") is crucial. Fixing that process (using improvement resources efficiently) so that it performs at the level required by the organization (that is, "doing things right") is just as important.

There are four basic inputs to process selection: strategy, process performance, value gap in the market, and value gap in the labor market. When an organization reviews its strategy, it explores opportunities and threats of all kinds facing it and diagnoses its strengths and weaknesses. Out of this exercise key strategic issues emerge. Addressing these issues requires first finding the processes that have to be modified or designed. This exercise often results in the formulation of new missions for processes to achieve. It also highlights the competitive value gaps, which in turn point to different processes. Daily operations and entropy (the natural deterioration of processes over time—see Chapter 3) also create many more problems and opportunities so that we must manage processes continuously (Chapter 6).

Figure 4.7 revisits Figure 1.2 with a higher definition. The bottom part illustrates the process that the organization uses to generate, select, and exploit improvement opportunities ("the learning pump"—Chapters 7 and 8) to generate more profits. One of its important functions is to decide whether the process should be improved (Chapter 9) or designed (Chapter 10) and what change "vehicle" (Chapter 8) should be used to do it. This is the organizational learning loop. It is the subject of Chapter 8. The better and the faster it works, the faster the organization learns and adapts to its changing environment, and the more competitive it gets. This is the most sustainable form of strategic advantage, as it is virtually impossible to copy. Maintaining coherence through such a continuous series of local changes, however, poses a particular challenge. Bold numbers in Figure 4.7 indicate the chapters where this topic is covered. The reader interested in delving further into the relation between processes and learning should see Garvin (2000).

4.5 SUMMARY

Strategy is the organization's game plan to beat the competition. In that sense, positioning is about picking one's fight, that is, selecting the market segment where one wants to compete, and differentiating one's services. Operations strategy is that part of the game plan that deals with how one will provide the service in such a way that it will make money and keep employees happy doing so. Formulating an operations strategy requires simultaneously considering market opportunities, internal capabilities and competencies, and the need to find a viable positioning in the labor market.

It is in the light of such an "umbrella" orientation that processes must be considered. Processes are where "the rubber meets the road," that is, where these abstract notions are concretized. From artisan to continuous flow, processes have different characteristics (effectiveness, efficiency, productivity, capacity, flexibility, and reliability) that can facilitate or hinder the creation of the strategic advantage sketched out in the game plan. An assembly line reliably produces high volume at low cost, but it is rigid. A job shop is flexible and responsive, but results in high costs. Designing processes is about making trade-offs—you cannot have it all. Strategy is the umbrella that guides the organization in making these difficult choices coherently.

An organization is a complex web of interrelated processes. These processes must work together, complementing and reinforcing each other in the delivery of the benefit package to the customers, to the employees, and to the shareholders. In other words, they must be coherent. They each have a specific contribution to make (or mission) to the execution of the game plan. Whoever designs, improves, manages, or partakes in any process must be well aware of its mission.

EXERCISES

4.1 Strategic Overview

Write up a short case study of a new service that you would consider launching, including (refer to Box 4.1 for an illustration):

a. Mission

b. Business opportunity

c. Target market segment

d. Competitors' weaknesses (opportunity)

e. Your strengths and weaknesses

f. Strategy

g. Service concept

h. Operations strategy

i. Operations policies, supply chain, and value network

j. Job concept (if there are several categories of employees, write a concept for the major categories: professional and technician)

4.2 Positioning and Processes

a. Identify your major competitors and position them in a diagram such as that shown in Figure 4.6, based on the degree of customization and the degree of service. Then, position your new service in it.

b. List the major processes that you will need to deliver this service concept, in a fashion similar to that shown in Figure 4.2.

4.3 Human Resources—Processes

a. If the job concept you described in exercise 4.1j is different from the one you currently deliver to your employees, specify the differences and identify the processes you would have to change to be able to deliver the new benefit package.

  b. Is the new concept compatible with the existing one from a cultural point of view? How will the new employees (assuming you would have to hire them) fit with existing employees?

  c. Does this involve minor changes or, on the contrary, would you have to design new processes from scratch?

4.4 Process Characteristics and Families of Processes

  a. Review your answers to exercise 3.1. Characterize your sales process and your invoicing process, writing a short statement for each of the following characteristics: effectiveness, efficiency, productivity, capacity, and reliability.

  b. For each process: what are the most important and least important characteristics in view of what you believe to be the mission of the process? Does the current process reflect the competitive priorities of each process?

  c. Select two of the processes that you listed in your answer to exercise 4.2b. What are the two most important characteristics required of each process in view of the positioning and strategy you spelled out in your answer to exercise 4.1?

  d. For each of these two processes, prepare a rough-cut design using a PFD of what an artisan process and an assembly line process look like. Which one seems to be better (refer to your answer to the previous question [4.4c] to answer this question)?

4.5 Coherence

  Continuing with the same example, give two examples of incoherence (as defined in this chapter) that could happen if the designers and managers of these processes are unaware of the organization's strategy.

4.6 Positioning to Processes: Visual Representation of the Value Stream

  a. Use your answers to all preceding exercises to complete the forms provided in Figures 4.8 and 4.9, inspired by Figure 4.4. Refer back to Figure 4.4 to better understand what goes in each box. We call the forms "value to processes," or V2P for short. The first form provides an overview, while the second one allows you to specify some aspects in more detail. Their purpose is to allow you to produce a visual representation of the (simplified) value stream of your company. The profit rate equation has been added as a reminder of the purpose of the venture. Since the "Competitor" boxes in Figure 4.8 are very small, specify only the major benefit that differentiates each competitor's offerings from your own. Competitors in the labor market may or may not be the same as the one you picked for the market itself. For the job concept, select a category of professionals. Service standards must be quantitative and specify target values (for example, customers should never wait more

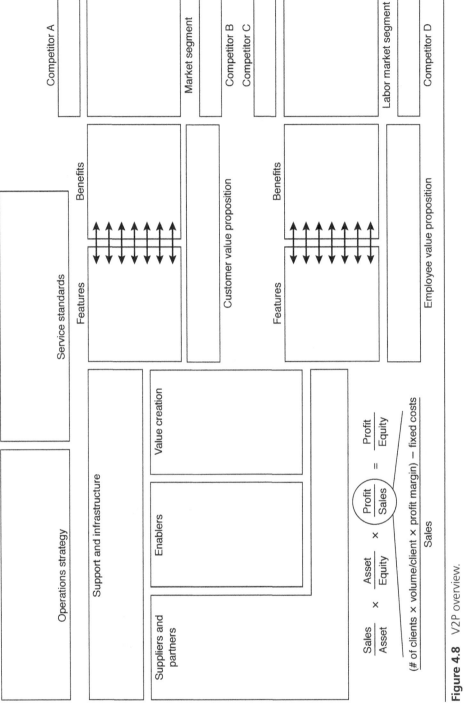

Figure 4.8 V2P overview.

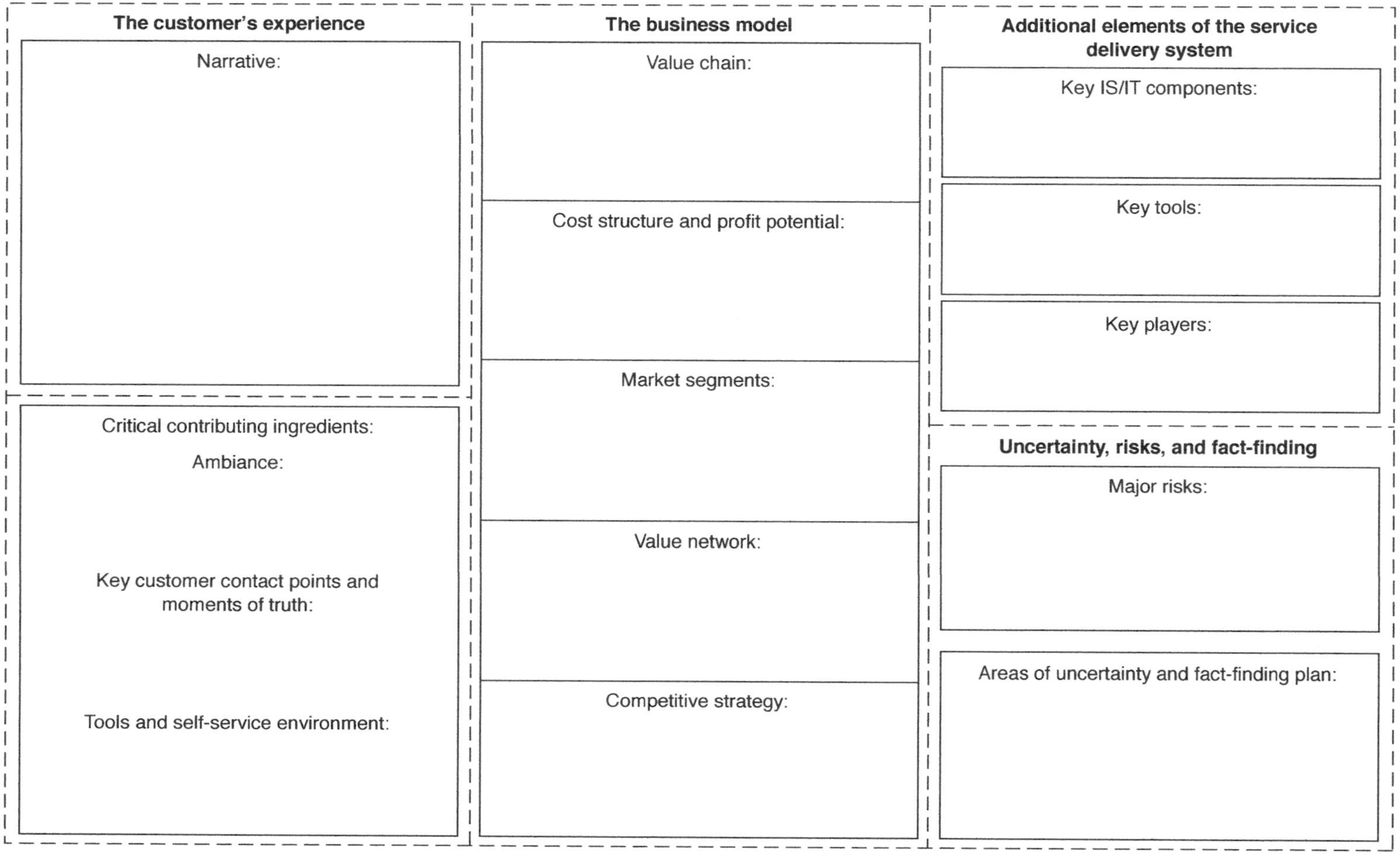

The customer's experience

Narrative:

Critical contributing ingredients:

Ambiance:

Key customer contact points and moments of truth:

Tools and self-service environment:

The business model

Value chain:

Cost structure and profit potential:

Market segments:

Value network:

Competitive strategy:

Additional elements of the service delivery system

Key IS/IT components:

Key tools:

Key players:

Uncertainty, risks, and fact-finding

Major risks:

Areas of uncertainty and fact-finding plan:

Figure 4.9 V2P clarifications.

than 10 minutes). You cannot possibly write down all processes in that form, so select the most important. In Figure 4.9, called the clarification form, depending on the context, some aspects (boxes) are more relevant than others to understand the value stream. For critical aspects, don't hesitate to add additional pages. Video 4.2 provides an illustration of this exercise.

b. When you have completed the forms, pick one key value-adding process that you would like to design or improve. Use arrows pointing toward that process to connect upstream processes to it. Use arrows pointing away from it to connect it to offerings, elements of the value propositions, and service standards. Use one-direction or bidirectional arrows to connect the process to elements of the operations strategy, as appropriate.

c. Use the resulting diagram as a basis for discussion at a management committee meeting. Try to reach a consensus on it, that is, build a common vision of the value stream. This is an important document for communicating management's vision to the team involved in the development of the new service.

NOTES

1. Neck pain that typically occurs after being hit in the rear by a car after coming to a sudden stop.
2. We reserve the expression "supply chain" to refer to situations where "things" are being moved, such as the chain of processes from a rare earth deposit in China to an eventual smartphone in Mexico.

5

Professional Service Delivery Processes

The tasks of professions are human problems amenable to expert service. They may be problems for individuals, like sickness and salvation, or for groups, like fundraising and auditing. They may be disturbing problems to be cured, like vandalism or neurosis, or they may be creative problems to be solved, like a building design or a legislative program. (Abbott 1988, p. 35)

Professional services exist in different types of organizations and contexts. The professional service encounter is an experience for both clients and provider where the latter is expected to demonstrate leadership and respect. Professional SDPs share a common nature but take a variety of shapes and forms depending on the type of business in which they operate.

We first propose a classification of professional services before revisiting the professional service experience. This leads into a discussion of professional leadership and use of power (section 5.3). We then turn to processes and positioning in professional services using the example of a consulting firm and further pursue the legal services example discussed in Chapter 4. The last section includes a broad-brush application of the V2P model in three industries: journalism, health, and financial services. Figure 5.1 discusses the videos associated with this chapter's content.

5.1 CLASSIFYING PROFESSIONAL SERVICES

Following the discussion in the preface to the first edition of this book, we defined a professional as a person whose mastery of a practical field of human know-how requiring strong intellectual capabilities has been certified by a recognized body. We thus exclude theoretical fields such as pure mathematics and philosophy, and crafts that require mostly manual and artistic abilities, such as masonry or carpentry. Medicine is one of the oldest professions. Financial planners and management consultants are among the most recent ones. The know-how of quasi-professionals and technical workers (technologists and technicians) is typically more procedural and linked to specific technologies. While it is readily usable, it is also more short-lived than that of professionals.

5 — PROFESSIONAL SERVICES

This three-part video explores the dimensions of complex services, such as banking, health, legal, accounting, engineering, insurance, or education. This is vastly different from making fast food or driving a cab. It involves power—the power of knowledge—and it can be used to create superior value in crucial human or business needs, or it can be abused by the provider (individual or organization) for its own benefit. Built around nine examples and metaphors, the video isolates the major dimensions of complex services, highlights the risks, opportunities, and pitfalls involved, and suggests ways to manage these unique services.

5.1 The power of complex services: Foster, use, and abuse

Part 1: Balancing creativity, judgment, and discipline

The contrast between two transportation accidents (Southern Pacific 7551 and US Airways 1549) provides the background required to understand what a quality culture means in complex services. Rigorous training and enforcement of well-thought-out and shared rules combine with freedom to act to produce the best outcome when experts are faced with unforeseen circumstances. On the other hand, a "good enough" quality culture slowly takes hold as sloppy work without immediate consequence is tolerated. The silo mind-set hides the potentially devastating systemic effect of these defects.

Part 2: On diagnosis, leadership, operational focus, and the power of a good metric

Examples discussed here include the doctor's office, the surgical block at Shouldice Hospital, the Apgar score to immediately measure the health of a newborn baby, and the social emergency team intervening when children are at risk. "First do no harm" is an oath that all complex service providers should make their own. Largely determined by history, inertia, and drift, our operating units often mix together incompatible activities and are thus unmanageable. Deconstructing these jumbled flows and rebuilding focused units makes management (appropriate balance between autonomy and control) possible. Quick response to emerging needs, by a multifunctional "commando" unit, can trigger a paradigm-changing breakthrough.

Part 3: Some ingredients in the recipe for the memorable customer experience

Without a profound shared understanding of the nature of value in our business and of the different demands it makes on our experts, our processes and performance will evolve randomly, as a result of actions made on the spur of the moment by a host of uncoordinated experts. CEO should stand for Chief Emotions Owner—meaning the emotions of the customer and those of the employee. Nevertheless, as client, we must always assume the primary responsibility for results, that is, we are managing our way through the information flows and branching points of the service maze.

Figure 5.1   Videos associated with Chapter 5.

It is useful to classify professional services into the following six categories:

1. *Professional service firm (PSF).* An organization consisting essentially of professionals working largely independently of one another for different customers, with the assistance of clerical staff. The customers may be businesses or individuals. Law firms and psychology clinics are examples.

2. *Professional bureaucracy.* A large public or para-governmental organization providing services based on the diagnostic formulated by a professional.

Transactional or technical services are then rendered on the basis of the professional's "prescription," after the client has agreed. They may involve complex and expensive machines or installations operated by technicians or quasi-professionals. Clerical and nonqualified workers are required as well. A hospital or university falls into this category.

3. *Technology-based services with customer contact.* An organization involved in whole or in part with assisting customers (businesses or individuals) in the use of complex technological products and services. Technical support companies for hardware and software fall into this category.

4. *Technology-based services without direct customer contact.* Here the professionals work in a back office to resolve complex technical issues for the ultimate benefit of customers. While contact personnel are required, they are typically less technically qualified and focus on sales, services, and perception management and generally serve as a buffer for the back office. In air transportation, for example, passengers do not come into contact with pilots, air traffic controllers, or maintenance engineers. They do come into contact with clerical and technical personnel (onboard personnel and gate agents). This is also the case with actuaries in insurance organizations. The absence of customer contact allows professionals to create a work environment that allows them to focus on technical challenges and not on the management of customer perceptions and emotions.

5. *Quasi-manufacturing services.* An organization providing a service product that reaches the customer without direct contact with employees (clerical, professional, or otherwise). This is the case with public utilities, for instance, or news organizations. Customers "interact" with the service product (such as an article posted on the web or electricity being directed to various appliances in the home) but not with service workers, unless a problem occurs. In this case they only deal with customer service. While this is not a professional service organization, many professionals are involved in the design, production, and delivery of the service.

6. *Internal professional services.* An individual or organizational unit providing professional services to other employees or organizational units in any public or private organization. Depending on the nature of the organization, this may include the full range of professional services, from engineering to medical expertise, from IT support to legal opinion, from tax advice to ergonomics. The specificity of such services lies in their being internal. Internal customers and service providers are partners. They have distinct areas of expertise and play different roles in the organization's value chain. Ultimately, however, they work for the same shareholders and participate jointly in the delivery of superior value to targeted market segments.

Any classification is a simplification of a complex reality and thus has limitations. There is always more than one way to cut it. Some services do not fit neatly into any single category. A pharmacy, for instance, is a small PSO, but there is an important sales and distribution function associated with it. Operators (captains, pilots, navigators, engineers, drivers, and air traffic controllers) of people transportation vehicles require training and certification. In many decisions of great consequence they have the ultimate say. They are professionals as defined in this book and would seem to be providing an internal professional service. However, they are but a small part of a complex organization whose profitability rests on the effective use of these vehicles. They are not focused on their customers, but on their vehicle, which they operate in the best interest of their passengers and of the company. These services are in a category of their own.

In spite of these limitations, the typology helps us better understand the nature of the organization, its business, its operating reality, its unique challenges, and its core processes. Before reading on, the reader is encouraged to view Video 5.1 (see Figure 5.1).

5.2 THE PROFESSIONAL SERVICE EXPERIENCE

Whatever the customer hears and sees during service encounters, that is, what takes place within her "line of visibility," may have an impact on her perception of the provider and the organization. In the case of QKM (a PSF according to the typology given earlier), before the contract agreement, it influences her decision to do business with the organization—after, her decision to keep doing business with it (see Box 5.1). Process maps (such as the macro map shown in Figure 5.2) represent these activities above the line of visibility, spread on both sides of an imaginary line of interaction. We refer to whoever in the organization is interacting with the customer as a *server*. The same person may at times work as a server (that is, "onstage") and at other times in the back office (that is, beyond the line of visibility, or "backstage"). The theater analogy is a vivid way to highlight the direct impact of every aspect of a provider's "performance" on the client. In Figure 5.2, we identify the "player" involved in each task that appears in the "server" swim lane by a letter.

Box 5.1 Quality Knowledge Management

Issue: A consulting firm develops proposals in response to an open call for tenders

Quality Knowledge Management (QKM) is a small consulting firm involved in helping a variety of organizations improve their quality systems, which includes such assignments as auditing existing systems, training, quality improvement consulting, and building integrated quality information systems. Long established and having a good reputation, the firm employs about 30 professionals, drawn mostly from the fields of engineering, quality, and management. QKM also employs a number of technicians, all graduates of technical colleges, in such fields as quality, metrology, and programming.

In its line of business, QKM is asked by potential customers to submit proposals for contracts that are awarded competitively. Business customers approach this from the standpoint of designing and managing a competitive bidding process to acquire services. Service providers view it as designing and managing a selling process to beat the competition in securing contracts. The two processes obviously overlap, with the bidders designing their process to meet the parameters (or ground rules) set forth by the customer.

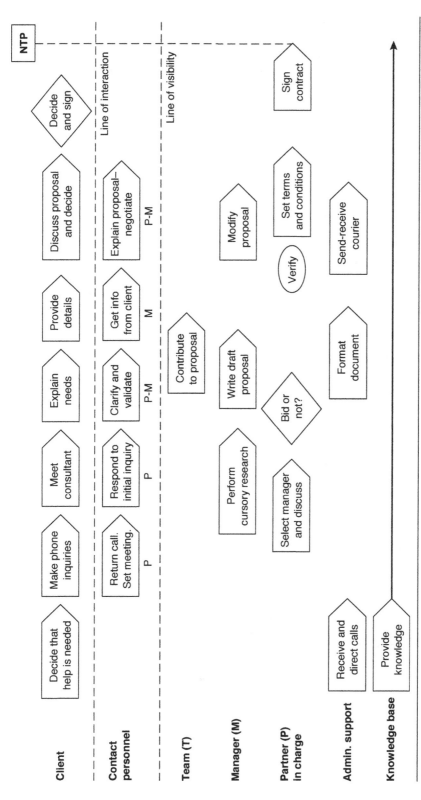

Figure 5.2 Macro-mapping of the "sell services" process at Quality Knowledge Management.

Service delivery starts when the customer agrees to the (explicit or implicit) terms and conditions set forth by the provider (that is, gives notice to proceed, or NTP). The form that such consent may take ranges from a simple nod to a formal signature, and may include verbal acknowledgment ("OK") and a handshake. Whatever means is used to communicate it, the agreement must be clear to both parties. When it is, the parties are thus mutually committed to perform their part of the agreement. From that point on, any contact between the customer and the organization (SAS's Jan Carlzon called these encounters "moments of truth") is an opportunity for the former to verify that the latter's behavior is compatible with its commitment and form an opinion about whether this is a good place to do business. This monitoring may be active or passive, overt or covert, explicit or implicit depending on the stakes riding on the outcome and on the customer's trust in his provider. Bear in mind that because of the client's possible inability to assess technical quality (see Chapter 2), the "moment of truth" may be a "moment of lie"; that is, the potential for manipulation exists.

In any encounter, emotions are critical determinants of outcome. In a service encounter with a professional, a client goes through a sequence of such emotions, more or less intense depending on the nature of the need, context, and the specific individuals involved. The right sequence of emotions makes effective coproduction possible. Anxiety, contempt, or anger, for instance, interferes with it. Figure 5.3 illustrates various aspects of the professional service encounter. Starting from the center, the professional interacts with the client (relation) and processes the data she obtains about him and his situation (analysis). The influence of many other players is felt during the service episode: external influencers of all kinds (such as family, friends, and trusted sources), other professionals, and other PSO personnel.

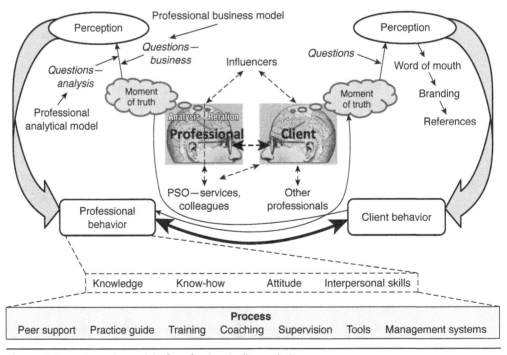

Figure 5.3　A dynamic model of professional–client relation.

Successive moments of truth shape the customer's perception of the professional, of the service he is getting, and of the organization that provides it. This perception in turn drives word of mouth, and through it the branding of the organization, which is the source of referrals. No amount of advertising can substitute for a job well done. The client's perception also affects his behavior as coproducer of the service, and thus the nature of the relationship.

Whoever creates an experience for a client lives an experience of her own. Indeed, the professional does not remain cool, analytical, and detached throughout the encounter (even though she may try to project this image), nor is she expected to. Emotional intelligence is required to effectively put analytical skills to work. The professional's own sequence of moments of truth shapes her perception of the client and his problem. As the encounter unfolds, different questions arise in her mind to clarify, probe, and orient the exchanges in the right direction. These questions are inspired by her "professional paradigm" or model (including professional ethics) on the one hand and by the PSO's business model on the other. Thus, there is mutual adjustment between the professional and her client as the service episode proceeds.

Many other factors bear on the professional's behavior and reactions to various situations, as shown in the lower part of Figure 5.3. They have been grouped in the shaded "process" box. There is much that the organization can do to shape the customer's experience (Meyer and Schwager 2007). Designing, managing, or improving a process in professional services requires a good understanding of this complex dynamic. It should be clear that no matter what the rigor that goes into this, all that can be done by the organization is to create the conditions for success: the outcome ultimately rests on the skills of the professional.

It is useful at this point to highlight the difference between complex and merely complicated services. Getting a passport is complicated: it involves many steps and hand-offs, many clerical players, and many approvals and verifications, and the applicant must provide several inputs. However, the overall process can be broken down into a series of simple processes connected to each other. Each subprocess can be analyzed and standardized, thus improving the whole process and making it more predictable.

In the design of a chemical plant, however, several experts operating in vastly different fields, such as architecture, chemistry, chemical engineering, mechanical engineering, law, insurance, and accounting, must intervene and interact with each other to produce the required design. There is no standardizing the way lawyers or architects think. There is no imposing on an engineer that she should approve a plan that she believes, based on her training and experience, is faulty. There is no predicting the discussions between actuary A and accountant B. This complex process is laced with irreducible uncertainty. Putting more pressure on the experts to work in a "standard" way is bound to backfire. Of course, complex processes are also often complicated, and professional processes are connected and interlaced with complicated administrative and clerical processes, thus compounding the management challenges.

5.3 LEADERSHIP AND RESPECT AT THE MOMENT OF TRUTH

The attendant in a fast-food restaurant is not expected to lead, but to serve. The professional must lead. It is the nature of the job. This leadership includes service, not subservience. The line between the two is sometimes very fine, and a professional whose vision is blurred by the prospect of short-term profits may easily cross it unwittingly. Hence, the critical role played by a well-thought-out and widely shared business model. Since clients are often vulnerable, professionals must use their authority with respect. This means complying with the needs of the customer in a nonjudgmental, accepting fashion (see discussion on the potential for abuse in section 2.1.4).

The result the client gets depends on, among other factors, how he performs his part of the process. An inaccurate statement of need or lack of follow-through on recommended courses of action, for instance, will deny results. It is the professional's responsibility to lead the client in this co-performance. Compare, for instance, the following two financial planners. The first one asks all the questions she must legally ask her client, reads him a prepared text on the risks involved in investing, and asks him to fill out and sign a form stating his attitude toward risk—all said and done in 10 minutes—so she can move on to the next customer. The second one takes an hour to interact with his client, asking him about his past investment experience, his feelings about it, lessons learned, and his plans. Imagine that he succeeds through several such meetings (over a period of a year or two) in making his customer truly understand such fundamental notions as one's own attitude toward risk and the costs involved when one compromises a long-term strategy through impulsive decisions based on momentary greed or fear. Through such a process, he may lead the customer to an investment strategy that is radically different from what he had asked for when he originally walked into the planner's office.

The first planner has protected herself. Her client is none the wiser for it. He does not really know what to expect and may be very upset with the outcome of his investment. He may end up doing much damage to the provider's business through negative word of mouth. While the planner may feel she is very productive (four clients an hour, 30 clients a day), she is not creating value for her customer, her shareholder, or herself. The second planner has exerted professional leadership. He has shown his client that he cares, that he is competent and trustworthy. This led the client to put his initial beliefs on hold, listen, and gradually open up. A win–win–win (customer–professional–shareholder) relationship may ensue.

A professional must lead her customers of choice in doing their part correctly. Professionals should give their clients the services they need, not necessarily the service they ask for. They should give them the advice they need to hear, not necessarily what they want to hear. Thus, professionals serve through leadership rather than subservience. Doing what is right for the client (see the notion of technical quality in section 2.1.4) may result in short-term dissatisfaction on the part of the customer. The skilled professional should, however, be able to make her case convincingly enough to get the customer to do the right thing and to trust her enough to wait for results. In some fields of professional endeavor—such as health, insurance brokerage, and financial planning—this may take years. Once results are achieved, however, the bond between the professional and her customer will be very strong and hard to break.

When two persons work together, as the professional and her client do, they must decide who does what. Therefore, an important service design decision involves how to divide work between the customer and the service provider. The professional leadership role includes getting the client to understand that failure on his part to play his role correctly will deny him the result he seeks. As discussed in Chapter 2, customers are very different in terms of their capability and willingness to get involved in the satisfaction of their needs. Doing more for the customer does not necessarily create more value. Indeed, one is never better served than by oneself. Some customers prize the added control over execution and the speed that self-service provides—witness the fact that many customers prefer a cafeteria to a restaurant, or a self-service gas station over a full-service one. Further, advances in IT, expert systems, and social networks create more opportunities for clients with less knowledge and know-how to be more involved. Depending on which tasks we would like the customer to perform, he may need tools, training, and coaching. Physiotherapists, for instance, train their patients to perform some exercises through demonstration, asking the patients to reproduce the exercise and correcting them until they get it right. Together with a complex prescription, pharmacists give patients a medication organizer as well as an instruction sheet. Lawyers often prepare their clients for testimony in court through role playing. Therefore, PSOs should carefully design the tasks they want their customers to perform, assess their current knowledge level (which may differ from segment to segment), develop the required instructions and tools, and develop and manage a training process. At times the provider–client relationship seems to invert itself. For instance, a cabin crew giving instructions to passengers—"*I need you to* place your seatback in a vertical position"—and verifying compliance leaves little doubt about who has to comply with whose requirements. Prefacing this sentence with "If you want to arrive safely" makes the reason for this inversion of roles clear.

This section may leave the reader with the impression that in some respect we treat the customer as an employee. Indeed, leading, empowering, giving tools, training, and coaching are all key management roles vis-à-vis employees. However, the fact that, unlike employees, the customer is paying us, and not the converse, fundamentally changes the nature of the relationship. The professional has no formal authority over the customer. His sole source of authority is that which the customer grants him. It stems at first from the professional's status (degrees and professional certificates) and reputation. However, it quickly moves on to leadership. Failing that, the relationship deteriorates and eventually peters out.

5.4 DELIVERING THE PROFESSIONAL SERVICE EXPERIENCE

In this section we illustrate a generic view of professional service delivery processes (PSDPs) with the example of a small consulting firm. We then pay particular attention to the dispatch phase of that process (5.4.2) and to the flows in SDPs (5.4.3). Lastly, we pursue the legal example started in the previous chapter to further illustrate the relationship between positioning and process selection.

5.4.1 Generic View of PSDPs

Most PSDPs can be broken down into four generic stages. For clarity, they are presented here and illustrated in the case of a PSF.

- *Matching.* As discussed in Chapter 2 (quality of service), because of the knowledge gap between the professional and his client, the latter often does not know which professional is best qualified to solve his problem. The first generic stage in the process is therefore to get the customer to meet with the right professional. A mistake at this stage results in a waste of time for the customer (that is, delayed solution) and in wasted resources for the organization. Matching takes place in one of two ways: dispatch or competitive bidding. In the former, the potential customer calls on the organization and the organization dispatches him to a professional. In the latter—more commonly used by business customers—the customer invites a selected (or prequalified) number of firms to submit a proposal to supply the desired services. In both cases, the customer must first conclude that he needs help, identify potential providers, and evaluate them.

- *Diagnostic.* This stage and the next stage (prescription) are the defining functions of professional work. Professionals first interact with the client to obtain information. They then take the required actions to validate this information. Finally, they apply a number of decision rules, learned during their training and honed through experience, to reach a conclusion about the nature and origins of the client's problem. A diagnostic generally emerges gradually throughout this stage through a series of iterations involving the formulation and testing of hypotheses. Validation is required before moving on to the next stage.

- *Prescription.* This is the professional's statement of the course of action required to solve the problem. Again, it results from the application of professional judgment and decision rules. Of course, any prescription founded on an inaccurate diagnostic will not solve the client's problem and may do more harm than good. Without a diagnostic and a prescription, the other productive resources of the organization (technicians and technologies of all types) are incapable of helping the customer.

- *Treatment.* This is the execution or fulfillment of the prescription. The actions spelled out in the prescription generally involve the professional and his clients themselves, separately and together, and may involve a number of other players, including other professionals, technicians, and other categories of workers. The professional is normally responsible for ensuring the correct execution of prescribed actions, in the required sequence, and their continuous monitoring and adjustment as needed throughout the treatment.

Hypothesis testing and formulation in the diagnostic and prescription stages often require engaging adjacent processes that will return information to the professional. A real estate agent, for instance, may ask a clerk for a web search of comparable houses for sale, and an engineer may ask a technician to test the properties of some material. The reader may want to peek at Figure 5.5 to see what this might look like in a hospital. PSDPs are also surrounded by a host of other processes (the latest version of the APQC model can be downloaded at http://www.apqc.org/process-classification-framework), such as 3.3.4, "Develop and manage pricing" (upstream), 8.2.3, "Process accounts receivables" (downstream), and 6.6.7, "Manage employee communication" (throughout).

The next two sections explore the short but critical matching stage in more detail. We then turn to some implications of this particular process structure.

5.4.2 Dispatch

As the need for professional services gradually takes shape in the mind of the customer, she starts searching for information. She needs to make up her mind on three basic questions:

- Can I fix this myself?

- What kind of professional do I need?

- Whom should I choose?

There are many sources of information to help her in her search for answers: experience; discussions with friends, relatives, and associates; advertising (newspaper, television, websites); and literature (articles, books, and electronic and web sources), as well as information brokers of all kinds. While there is no shortage of valid information on just about any topic, telling it apart from the rest and understanding it may be a challenge. People vary widely in terms of their ability to access, validate, and process this information. As a result, the self-diagnostic (for example, "I need to see a physiotherapist") may very well miss the mark.

The first contact with a PSO is very important for both the customer and the organization. As the aphorism goes, "You never get a second chance to make a good first impression." Imagine a potential patient calling a sports medicine clinic. He talks to a receptionist whose job it is to manage the appointment books, greet customers as they arrive, process payments, and give receipts. This one-minute conversation with that busy receptionist will determine whether the customer comes to the clinic and whom he sees if he decides to come.

The best outcome, of course, is that the patient comes to the clinic and sees the right professional. The second-best outcome is that he sees the wrong professional and is redirected to the right one. This involves a loss of time (and maybe money, if he is charged for the time of the professional) for the customer. It also involves a loss of professional time for the organization, as well as a potential loss of goodwill and negative word of mouth. A PSO creates value for the right customers by first matching them with the right professional at the right time. A good match from the organization's perspective is one that maximizes the organization's long-term earning potential. This involves the judicious application of a number of dynamically evolving criteria, such as available skill mix, workloads, complexity, urgency, and long-term potential income from a customer, as well as the personalities involved.

The patient could also hang up and call another clinic, but even that would not be the worst outcome. The worst outcome would be that a misdirected customer gets worse because of an inappropriate treatment and starts spreading negative word of mouth.

There are several ways to handle the dispatch phase. We will limit our discussion to two examples: a simple dispatch process (through a receptionist) and a more elaborate one (through a series of filters).

The simplest solution, as described earlier, is to have the receptionist greet the caller or visitor, inquire about his needs, interact briefly—according to a programmed script—with the potential customer, and either direct him to an available professional or make an appointment, using agreed-upon decision rules. A receptionist in a law firm, for instance, may try to find out if the caller needs a tax expert, a criminal lawyer, or a specialist in immigration law. He may then assess the urgency of the need, see who is available, and use dispatch criteria established by the firm. What qualifications are required to perform that function (receptionist)? Interpersonal skills are obviously very important. Given the stakes, however, and the challenges involved in reaching the right decisions quickly, substantial knowledge, judgment, and experience are required to do it well.

Organizations that leave this job to junior personnel may pay dearly for that mistake. Some do so because they do not realize the critical importance of the job. Internal considerations, however—such as the inability to draw the right people to the job (or keep them there), or failure to adjust career paths, incentive systems, or organizational culture to reflect that importance—also play a big role in the neglect of that function.

Hospitals need a more elaborate dispatch process. All emergency rooms, for instance, use some form of triage. Some patients roll in (on a gurney) directly to the reanimation room or intensive care unit, where an urgentologist takes care of them. Most, however, are identified and checked, for ability to pay or admissibility under a health regime, before being directed to sit in a waiting room and wait for a triage nurse to call them. After a short examination, the nurse assigns a priority code (for example, a code 2 should not wait more than five minutes, but a code 5 can wait all day) and the case is placed into a dynamic queuing system. The system factors in the urgency of the situation as well as arrival time (and maybe ability to pay). The system is dynamic in that later arrivals may jump the line if they are attributed a more urgent code, thereby increasing the remaining waiting time for patients attributed a less urgent code.

Figure 5.4 provides a generic illustration of such complex dispatch processes used to match customers and professionals. The process shown here involves three filters: a receptionist (unqualified, applying simple rules), a dispatcher (a senior technician such as an experienced dental assistant in a dental clinic), and a generalist professional (such as a general practitioner in a medical clinic). In the case of Medsol emergency clinic, the dispatcher would be a triage nurse, the generalist a general practitioner, and the specialist a resident medical specialist—and there would be an additional level involving his supervisor. The receptionist sends the customers with an easily identifiable need directly to the right professional while informing the dispatcher, who keeps tabs on resource utilization. The dispatcher himself evaluates the needs and dispatches remaining cases, except for those that require a professional judgment. The latter are sent to the generalist on duty, who makes the dispatch decision (and informs the dispatcher, who keeps track of customers). The rationale behind the process is to try to use qualified resources only when their expertise is required, that is, after a less qualified resource has concluded that this is the case. For instance, the receptionist may dispatch 50% of the customers, and the dispatcher may dispose of 80% of the remaining cases, leaving the generalist to assess the 10% of the customers who require her expertise. The process would therefore result in a lower cost per customer dispatched and in fewer dispatch errors.

The weakness of the process is that it makes customers, especially those with the most complex cases, pay the price (through delays, intermediaries, repetition) of the added efficiency. It is used extensively when resources are rationed—such as they are in public systems—or when the resources are extremely costly, and

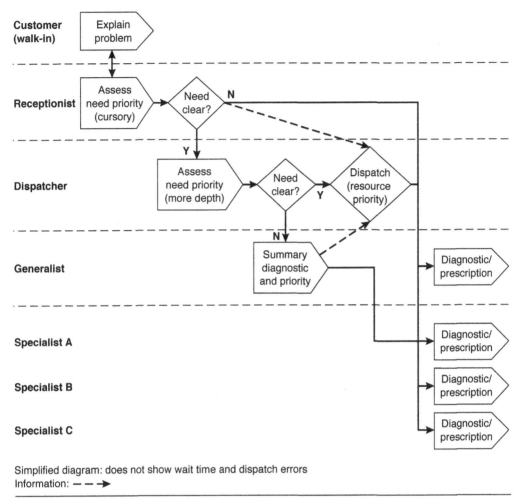

Simplified diagram: does not show wait time and dispatch errors
Information: — — ➤

Figure 5.4 Generic illustration of complex dispatch processes to match customers and professionals.

customers would rather put up with the process than pay more to gain direct access to the resources they want (but may not need).

PSOs must decide how much "filtering" of customers they want to do and how they want to do it. Questionnaires—of the physical or electronic sort—may be used, even tests. PSOs should measure the performance of the dispatch process and improve or redesign it (see Chapters 9 and 10) as needed.

In a B2B context, dispatch takes the form of a request for quotes and competitive bidding.

5.4.3 Flows in PSDPs

The flows within a PSO generally consist of a flow of information and decisions around the professional core of the service. Decisions flow out of that core to peripheral processes (technical, administrative, and support) and information flows back into it (this is shown in Figure 5.5, illustrating a cancer service episode)

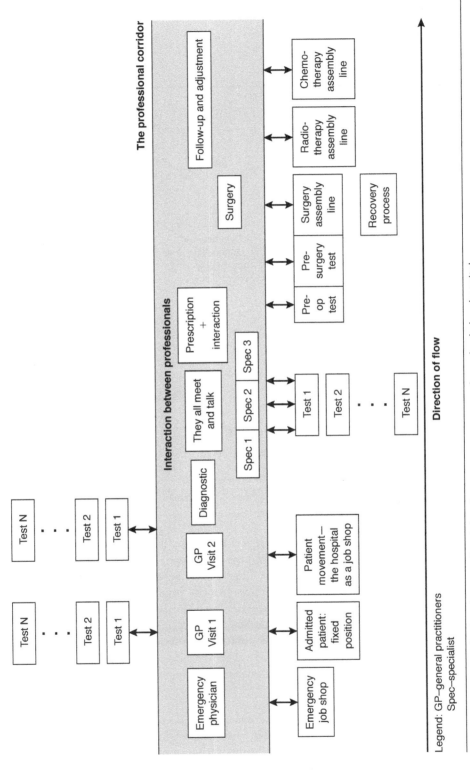

Figure 5.5 The professional core and peripheral processes: cancer service episode in a hospital.

as these processes report back after acting on the instructions they received. This information, in turn, triggers further interactions between professionals and with the client and, eventually, new decisions. In the professional core we find generalists and specialists. Generalists normally act as case managers, dispatching customers to specialists or interfacing directly with them as required. They integrate all the technical information flowing back to them, interpret it, and translate it into a form that is understandable by the customer. They communicate this, together with recommended courses of action, to the client for him to digest and make decisions. Technicians work in the immediate periphery of the core as owners or operators of various technical subprocesses. Support and administrative processes take care of logistical, informational, relational, financial, and other functions.

Interfaces between professionals are a major source of tension and risk in the system. As Vertosick (2008, p. 146) puts it: "There is a constant tension between internists and surgeons, the internist viewing the surgeons as brainless technicians, the surgeons viewing the internists as medical Neros fiddling as patients burn." It is easy to imagine what kind of turbulence this may create in the process, disrupting the complex process and leaving the patient stuck in the middle, with nurses and technicians as powerless spectators.

PSDPs are meant to manage the flow of people, things, and information throughout the service encounter. In health services, the body itself is processed, that is, it is a key input and output of the process. Thus, the flow of people takes on a very central place in process and facilities design. Most other professional services are very information-intensive, and the flow of people is limited to the area defined by the line of visibility. This is not to say that human contact and emotions are not important, since information flows between the emotional persons that we all are. As discussed in the previous section, information can be captured in images, word of mouth, paper, or digits, and it can be transformed from one form to another.

Digits are particularly convenient, as they allow for massive and cheap storage and retrieval of information, as well as instantaneous and cheap flows of rich (multimedia) information between the various players in a process, including the client, irrespective of layout or distance. Workflow, for instance, is a family of software applications whose purpose it is to ensure the semiautomatic flow of information along predefined process steps, irrespective of location, as long as each player is connected to the system or to the internet. Such a process shares many of the characteristics of a continuous-flow process (speed, low cost, reliability)—even though we can view it as a connected line because it requires human input along the way—without the rigidity associated with this type of process in the physical world (where people or things have to be processed).

Some information (such as land titles and contracts) still has to be kept on a paper support because of legal requirements. In addition, many customers do not have easy or convenient access to the technology required to digitize their instructions, requests, and responses. These are transmitted either on a paper support or by human voice (phone or face-to-face). The extent to which information can be digitized and the point in the process where it is (customer, reception, dispatch, generalist) have a direct effect on the choice of contact modes. The nature of professionals and their work also introduces many constraints on these choices. One does not simply tell a professional to digitize information (such as entering her instructions in a system). The professional must be involved in the decision process as part of a carefully planned change strategy (see Chapter 8). The same goes for deciding to provide a professional with a digital input rather than a paper one. It is not enough to install the "plumbing" of the process to change the flow of information and work. Somehow, one must secure the commitment of the various players. Securing the commitment of professionals is particularly important, as they generally have the power to kill any process change initiative they do not like.

5.4.4 Pursuing the Legal Services Example

There are many ways to combine professionals (generalists and specialists of all kinds), technicians, support workers, and technology in the design of a PSDP. An example will make this clear. Refer back to the will preparation example discussed in Chapter 4 (see Figure 4.6). Provider 4's process is fully automated (from the provider's point of view). Her marginal cost is virtually zero, but her process can be very rigid: adding new services or adapting existing services to changes in legislation can be very costly. Provider 2 could use an artisan process, where each lawyer, with the help of a clerk performing whatever clerical task the lawyer delegates to him (such as word processing, filing, making appointments, and billing), is in charge of the complete service, from input to output. That process is the most flexible, but it is very costly. Several alternate designs are possible involving the use of technology to replace the clerk or use of a mix of generalists and specialist lawyers. Management has to consider whatever takes place in the lawyer's office (the artisan) as a black box, essentially beyond its control. An assembly line or even a loosely connected sequence of tasks involving different lawyers is not an option because of professional resistance triggered by their fear of loss of autonomy. In this environment, professional leadership, teams, and peer groups are central ingredients in building and maintaining cohesion in service delivery.

To understand provider 1's processes, we must first recognize that the market for will preparation may not be large enough to sustain such a business. The firm would have to offer a number of similar legal services as well—such as simple contracts, proposals to buy a property, and leases—that technicians can perform under the supervision of a professional. Technicians can be specialized in specific services, or even specific steps of service (work flow works wonders in this environment), and the tasks and procedures can be optimized, standardized, and controlled. Customers call for an appointment and, depending on their needs (advertising only brings in targeted customers), are routed through a programmed sequence. Tight design of the task allows for minimal variation in execution time (see Chapter 6) and thus optimal use of resources, limited waiting time for the client, and mostly on-time delivery.

Those are typical benefits of line-flow processes, and it may sound like paradise. In any context, however, such processes have their limitations, and even more so in professional services. First, they are inflexible. Technicians can perform only the tasks that they have learned. If demand shifts toward more leases and fewer wills, the firm may have to support the cost of idle resources and may not be able to meet the added demand. Cross-training its technicians to provide several different services, such as changing from face-to-face "tight spec" to "open spec," would alleviate this problem. However, it would also increase cost (training), increase variation in duration, and reduce reliability. A second and related limitation, obviously, is that we are trying to address a complex need using an employee who is not a professional and thus has not been fully trained to perform clinical work (diagnostic and prescription) in that field. Since the technician does not fully understand the ramifications and implications of his work, he is liable to make mistakes, and in professional services such mistakes can be very costly.

Because of their respective strategies and operations strategies, providers 1, 2, and 4 have very different processes and cost structures (see Figure 5.6). Provider 1 has a lower cost than provider 2 as soon as the required volume is achieved. A larger part of his cost consists of allocated fixed costs stemming from process design, implementation (including technology), and training (technicians). Provider 1's high variable cost stems from the intensity of its processes in costly professional time. Provider 4 has an even lower cost (volume allowing) consisting of an essentially fixed cost resulting from the full automation (from the provider's point of view) of the process.

This cost structure results from process choices by providers that are consistent with their respective positioning. It has obvious strategic implications for each provider, creating different opportunities and vulnerabilities. The implications for management cannot be missed, either. The challenge of managing a loosely connected collection of artisans is vastly different from that involved in controlling the line flow or making sure that the automated process stays online, that customers flock to it, and that they come back for more.

Turning to the labor market now, provider 1 could target people-oriented legal secretaries or legal assistants with 10 years' experience who, even though they like legal work, have reached a ceiling in their current position, in terms of both job richness and pay, and who would welcome a change and new challenges. Such persons are most likely to be found in firms like that of provider 2. The job concept would include benefits such as prestige, independence (not being at the disposal of an exclusive boss), job satisfaction (providing a service to a grateful customer), and personal growth (gradually learning new skills as the firm offers new services). Hence, training and incentive processes would be particularly important for provider 1. Lawyers, on the other hand, would be selected for their relative dislike of traditional law practice (typified by the artisan process) because they do not

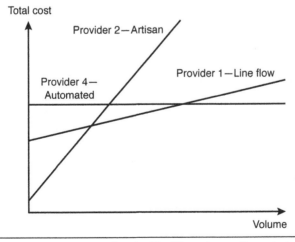

Figure 5.6 Different cost structures associated with different operations strategies.

enjoy direct customer contact or court appearances, or for some other reason. They could be offered a salary equivalent to or higher than that of the artisans because of the extent to which technicians would leverage them, allowing for a larger customer base per lawyer on staff. Because lawyers by training are naturally more at ease with artisan work, processes related to recruiting and keeping these lawyers happy are particularly important for provider 1. A similar positioning analysis (on the labor market) could be carried out for providers 2 and 4.

We have shown in this section that operations strategy, including process selection, does not flow linearly or sequentially from market positioning decisions. Indeed, it is in and by itself a key consideration in the simultaneous exploration of alternate positioning opportunities in the market and in the labor market, as shown in Figure 4.4.

5.5 THREE SHORT CASES

In this section we present three short cases meant to illustrate the notions discussed in this chapter and the previous one. The first two cases are actual businesses. The third one is a fictitious composite that will allow us to illustrate the methodological and technical elements presented in this book in more detail. Indeed, this latter example will be pursued in later chapters. It is thus treated in more detail.

5.5.1 A Quasi-Manufacturing Professional Service: Demand Media (a Low-Contact, High-Tech, Quasi-Manufacturing Professional Service)

As professionals, journalists may suggest topics on which to write, or more often are assigned topics to write about. They typically do background research using secondary sources prior to contacting the actors or key witness in the story itself. This may involve phone conversations, face-to-face interviews, travel, and direct observation. Demand Media, involved in the content-production and social media industries, developed a different business model from that of its competitors. The need is to cheaply and quickly produce articles on topics that people want to read about. Readers' interest is indeed fickle, but good journalists are expensive and like to take the time required to do a good job. What Richard Rosenblatt (founder of MySpace) realized is that by browsing the web one can readily identify what's in and what's out. Further, there is no shortage of content on the web itself, except that self-professed writers do not necessarily match what readers are looking for. If one were to systematically match this pent-up demand with this inexhaustible supply, post the resulting articles on appropriate websites, and generate advertising revenues, it could constitute a viable business model.

The core business process is article production. Seven thousand freelancers have been recruited. The recruitment process is critical since turnover is likely to be substantial, and the availability of a sufficient number of good writers is critical to sustained readership. Topics are generated through a sophisticated search algorithm elected and targeted (length, readership) by a second editor and offered to writers, who pick them up from a database. The article is then quickly written using web sources, for which the writer is paid between $3.50 and $15.00 depending on length. An editor then gets $3.50 to review the work, which is either sent for rework or passed on to the appropriate webmaster or traditional media. This whole process often takes less than a day, at an average cost of $10–$15.

While they need appropriate qualifications, the writers do not typically have day jobs at the *New York Times* or the *Atlantic*. They may be retired, beginners, in-between jobs, or simply moonlighting. A productive writer apparently can make $60 an hour without leaving the comforts of home. Admittedly, this is not the most satisfying work for a writer, but it is proving to be a viable job concept in the labor market. It is not directed at readers looking for depth, insight, originality, or wisdom, but who will be satisfied with basic information on a hot or practical topic (for example, how to remove a wine stain from a tablecloth).

Since the process is a "flow shop," with an automated work flow, it is fairly easy to measure performance and use the resulting information to improve the process, reward the most productive writers and editors, coach those who have potential, and quickly get rid of the others. Copy editors use a five-point scale to rate the quality of what they read, paying particular attention to grammar and research. The readership attracted by articles (hit rate and time spent reading) is also readily available, as well as the revenue generated, providing tremendous leverage for continuous improvement and learning.

There is an abundant global source of workers. They do not require a contract, an office, company-provided equipment, or training. They produce demand-driven basic-quality content in a timely fashion. The operations strategy consists of using a largely automated process to ensure speed, quality control, low cost, and continuous improvement, thereby providing more benefits (speed, relevance) to the targeted market segment at a lower cost than the competition.

5.5.2 A Professional Bureaucracy: Shouldice Hospital (a Focused Medical Process)

Located north of Toronto, in Thornhill, Ontario, Shouldice Hospital performs surgery to fix inguinal hernias, a common ailment in older people. That's all it does, but it does it well. In fact, it is the best: its recurrence rate is about 0.5% compared with 5% to 10% for other hospitals. The surgery is performed under local anesthesia using a very old but very robust technique. Patients' stay is three or four days. Most hospitals perform the procedure on an outpatient basis using laparoscopy. Yet the overall cost is still 30% lower at Shouldice. The hospital looks like a country club, and that is in line with the nature of the hospital experience. There are pool tables inside and putting greens outside. Patients are active throughout their stay. Some come back to Shouldice not for surgery but for the annual meeting of "graduates." One caveat: not everybody gets in. You have to be generally healthy so that you can safely perform your part in the process without complications.

5.5.2.1 *Market Segment and Value Proposition*

You are a healthy senior who just happened to discover a hernia. You are a bit scared of the knife and do not like hospitals. You are willing to take the time to do this right. We will fix your hernia once and for all, at the lowest possible cost and risk. Your experience will in many ways resemble that of a country club more than that of a hospital. You will remain active and entertained throughout. You may even make friends and want to come back for our annual reunion. You'll be ready to go back to work quickly and will not face any limitation in what you can do.

5.5.2.2 Customer Experience

You will do everything but the actual surgery by yourself. You will diagnose your own hernia, set yourself up in your room, shave the area to be operated on, eat in the cafeteria, perform (light) group aerobics exercise, get up from the operating table, walk around and talk with people going through the same experience, and participate in the "induction" of new arrivals. You will be mostly free of discomfort and feel reassured by people-oriented and experienced nurses and through sharing your experience with like-minded people.

5.5.2.3 Elements of a Business Model

Some patients will contact Shouldice directly, while others will go through their family doctor. By selecting "healthy patients" we can leverage a much more effective process while delighting our patients with an experience that they do not expect. The "processing of a standardized input" will allow us to use a unique, well-adapted process, with extensive patient involvement, and optimize it. We will thus produce a superior result and patient experience at a lower cost than our competitors. Word of mouth will create the branding of this experience and ensure a constant stream of new patients.

5.5.2.4 Operations Strategy

Involve the customer (make the customer work, really) in all aspects of the process. This way he gets better quickly, does not feel anxiety as much, and goes through a social experience as well. It also reduces our costs—managing ambulatory patients is much cheaper than taking care of them in bed. Use of local anesthesia makes this possible while reducing patients' discomfort and reducing our costs. Using a standardized surgery technique in an assembly-line process ensures the highest possible reliability (benefit) and productivity (low cost).

5.5.2.5 Labor Market Segment and Personal Value Proposition for Surgeons

As a surgeon, you do not like the complexity and stress of the emergency ward or the impersonal work environment of the large hospital. You are OK with limiting yourself to a single operation, performed in a stable environment, with few surprises or calls in the middle of the night. Though you enjoy your job, there are other things you want to do with your life. As a Shouldice surgeon you will be part of a team producing world-class results for patients suffering from hernias. You will not have to worry about the cost and trouble of renting and managing an office, or building a patient base. You will have regular hours, five days a week with weekends off, with surgery in the morning and exams in the afternoon. You will make as much money as other surgeons. No need to retrain every time a new technology comes about. You will have close contact with your patients and be part of the all-star team.

5.5.2.6 Key Processes

Select patients (or exclude patients who do not have the required health profile). Examine patients. Prepare patients for surgery. Get the operating team ready to operate. Operate on patients using the Shouldice technique. Train and coach patients to do their part in the process. Select surgeons. Select nurses. Manage surgery rooms. Monitor patient recovery. Prepare work schedule. Manage patient relations. Manage annual meeting.

5.5.2.7 *Voice of Customer*

Recurrence rate. Complication rate. Number of letters from delighted patients. Attendance at annual reunion. Patient satisfaction with their experience (exit surveys). Number of requests for information. Number of admission requests. Number of patients turned away after traveling to Thornhill. Number of operations that have to be rescheduled. Doctors' and nurses' turnover rates. Doctors' satisfaction with their work (composite rating made up of such indicators as absenteeism rate, overtime worked, and surveys).

Many hospitals are stuck in a business model that is appropriate only for complex cases requiring evaluation and treatment that are uncertain at the outset and that will evolve as test results come in, closing avenues and opening new ones dynamically. Processing patients that require a known treatment through such a job shop is terribly wasteful and contributes to the sorry state of our health system today. Because there is little specialization and much variety and variation (CTQ), they are plagued with bottlenecks and long cycle times (CTD) and have high costs (CTC). Focused shops such as Shouldice are much more effective at this. Sending more patients to such "value-added process shops" (Christensen et al. 2009) would free up costly hospital job-shop capacity for those cases that truly require it: both types of patients would gain, and the overall system cost would be much lower. It does, however, require a culture change in the health system, and this is particularly challenging when it comes to doctors.

5.5.3 A Professional Service Firm: Financial Planning Associates

> *Issue:* Following a merger, a PSO wants to identify the key processes on which it should focus its improvement efforts

Personal relationships and trust lie at the heart of financial planning. A financial planner (FP) must know and understand his client very well. He also must be able to explain to the client all relevant options and their implications, design a financial plan tailored to the customer's needs, and explain all its implications, to the point where the client clearly understands what he is getting into. Technology also plays a crucial role in facilitating interaction with customers and suppliers— the latter consisting mostly of brokers, mutual fund companies, traders, insurance companies, trusts, banks, and notaries.

Financial Planning Associates (FPA) is a small firm dispensing professional services in the area of financial planning to a customer base of wealthy individuals. Created by the recent merger of three independent companies, it now has a staff of 200, including 70 certified FPs as well as a number of specialists in tax, insurance, and investment. One of the companies involved in the merger had a strong IT group that had been involved in the development of investment decision support systems and portals for large players in the industry.

Following the merger, the partners (all FPs own at least some company stock) had expected profits to grow because of economies of scale and synergism, but this did not happen. On the contrary, back-office costs had soared and response time had decreased, prompting some clients to complain. The company set out to review its business model, strategy, and operations.

5.5.3.1 Segmenting and Targeting

Though the company serves various market segments, its core market consists of busy professionals and managers with assets under management of at least $500,000. An increasingly sophisticated and very busy customer base now demands online access to their FPs and their accounts, as well as to user-friendly analytical and simulation capabilities. Following a market study and a strategic planning session, FPA decided to target an affluent market segment, which the market research firm's report characterizes as follows:

> They are professionals and executives between 40 and 55 with portfolios of half a million dollars or more. They are busy individuals with a clear focus on ensuring that they are financially independent by the time they reach their planned retirement date. They are generally knowledgeable about financial matters—without being experts. They are users (with varying levels of sophistication) of laptop computers and the internet, to which they have access. They tend to be analytical and systematic. They have iPhones, BlackBerries, and iPads, and most of them travel widely. They are well educated and cultivated, and are generally good judges of character. They need time and solid evidence before they trust someone, especially after the well-publicized fraud cases recently exposed. They tend be active and controlling, and will typically interrupt salespeople with directed questions. They are demanding of themselves and of others, particularly of their service providers. Since they are very busy, they expect to get service at their convenient time and location.

The market research firm points out as well that there is another larger and growing market segment quite similar to this one except for a lack of sophistication in financial matters. FPA's partners decide to keep this attractive segment in the back of their mind as they proceed with this strategic exercise.

5.5.3.2 Customer Experience

The customer explains his financial situation, perspective, and goals. He answers the FP's questions and asks his own, in a comfortable, relaxed atmosphere. He reacts to the FP's ideas and explores them on his own on the web and by talking to banks and other providers of financial services. An expert guides him on how to use the web and on the best software for making investment decisions and tracking the evolution of the situation. He does so at his own pace, whenever he has free time. If he experiences technical problems of any kind, a technician is available to help him solve the problem. When major changes occur in the markets or economic outlook, or there are discontinuities of any sort, he calls or can quickly meet with his FP. He gets regular, short, and targeted messages from his FP regarding changes in outlook or specific actions that are recommended. They also meet at prearranged regular intervals to do a financial health checkup.

5.5.3.3 Value Proposition

We will develop, maintain, and assist you in the implementation of a personal financial plan reflecting your specific financial goals, assets, earning potential, family situation, and attitude toward risk. We will provide all the assistance you require (training, hardware, software, coaching) to be as involved as you wish to be in any part of the process, and help you become better at it. We will apply the gold standard to continuously demonstrate our integrity and transparency.

5.5.3.4 Elements of a Business Model

FPA also wants to take advantage of major fault lines in its competitors' strategies. Indeed, many banks, trusts, and other financial institutions claim to provide independent financial planning services to their wealthy customers while the planners are in fact pushing the institutions' own financial products. A truly independent FP can help her client achieve better performance than that through selection of the best products and through bargaining power with various providers. Further, many full-service providers of financial services have a stake in their clients remaining dependent on their services. By developing a fee structure based on a percentage of assets, adjusted by a performance factor, it will be in FPA's own interest to make the client as autonomous as he wants to be, as quickly as possible. The risk for FPA in doing so is that autonomous investors might migrate to discount brokers. Thus, it is critical that FPA use the close relationship it will enjoy with the client during training to build trust and sufficient value-added services for the client to perceive the value he is getting, and to decide not to "mess with a winning formula." A trusting, open relationship will be FPA's key asset. FPA will focus its resources on high-value-added activities. Whenever outsourcing or partnering is sensible, the best outside provider/partner will be found, and FPA will ensure that it delivers as promised.

5.5.3.5 Operations Strategy

FPA's operations strategy is predicated on using technology, and helping clients use technology better, to leverage the client's knowledge and desire for convenience and control. Teaching, coaching, and technical support are required for this to happen. Suppliers will be selected and held on a tight leash. Competitors will be split into two groups: those offering high-tech contact with little, if any, high-touch expertise, and those offering (pricey) "tender loving care." This leaves the target segment stuck in the middle. While these investors enjoy the control and access offered by the former, they also need the guidance and reassurance provided by the latter. FPA plans to deliver a value proposition that is just right for these clients through high-touch initiation of the relationship, including a strong dose of training and education meant to build trust and make the client autonomous for day-to-day operation. Afterward, high-touch contacts with FPs would gradually spread out, to eventually be limited to periodic face-to-face encounters or special events. FPA wants to use the hedge it holds in IT to develop an investment portal that is second to none. It feels that its resulting costs would be lower than those of "strictly high-touch" competitors while offering a superior value proposition to this market segment.

5.5.3.6 Labor Market Segment and Personal Value Proposition for Financial Planners

The first market segment consists of experienced FPs used to dealing with wealthy clients. Their performance-based (including customer feedback) compensation will be at par with the top tier of the industry. A substantial part of it will be directly linked to ownership shares. Much professional satisfaction will come from the total liberty and empowerment to do whatever is best for the customer and play their leadership role to the fullest. Their intervention in training sessions will provide public recognition. The second segment consists of FPs with strong technical skills, or "financial planning engineers." Their teamwork with the former segment and with technicians will create a stimulating social experience and allow them to focus on what they like best: being on the leading edge of financial technology. They will fully share financially in the value-added they generate. As they assist clients in becoming more autonomous, they will build satisfying, lasting relationships.

5.5.3.7 Key Processes

Select suppliers. Monitor suppliers' performance. Evaluate new software. Integrate IT suppliers' offerings. Prepare seminar. Prepare financial plan. Review and analyze portfolio. Review economic outlook. Prepare financial newsletter. Train customer. Evaluate and benchmark performance. Prepare performance report. Manage compliance, audit, and public reporting process.

5.5.3.8 Voice of Customer

Benchmarked financial results, by client profile. Degree of autonomy achieved by client. Cost per client. Client turnover. Referred customers. Assets under direct or indirect management. Quality of supplier performance. Response time.

At that point FPA set out to do four things: (1) better understand clients' needs (critical to satisfaction [CTS]), (2) formulate value proposition, (3) define rough-cut service package, and (4) further specify the key metrics (voice of customer—critical to quality [CTQ], critical to delivery [CTD], critical to cost [CTC]).

1. FPA hires a market research company. Focus groups are then held with selected investors to establish their needs and their expectations of their FP. To put it succinctly, FPA finds that clients are looking for a professional service provider to help them achieve peace of mind about their financial future. However, we need much more detail than that to design the services and delivery processes. Achieving peace of mind is the clients' overarching goal. It can be broken down into specific needs, grouped under two general headings: results and customer experience (the reader may wish to review our earlier discussion of the service and self-service experiences in section 2.1). The latter includes quality of service (that is, what the customer does in interaction with a service provider) and quality of self-service (that is, what the customer does on his own or with technology).

Using the information from the focus groups, FPA draws a customer activity cycle, such as those shown in Figures 2.6 and 2.7, to place the needs in context, to better understand how they arise, and to make them visual. With the help of the market research firm, FPA develops from the available data a weighting scheme (such as that shown in Table 2.4) that accurately reflects the importance that these clients attach to their various needs. Table 5.1 presents a summary of customer needs and wants in these two categories. Note that we write all the statements in this table in the first person, as if the client were addressing the organization directly.

Results include performance, price, trustworthiness, and knowledge. The client's experience includes treatment, access, relationship, ease, information, and communication. Service and self-service experiences are not distinguished

Table 5.1 Weighted clients' needs for target market segment.

	Result	Weight	Service and self-service		Weight
Performance	Help me develop and maintain the best possible financial strategy and plan. Help me keep it constantly aligned with my evolving personal needs, income and tax patterns, risk profile, and evolving market conditions	30	Treatment	Treat me like a VIP	10
			Access	Be reachable at all times through my medium of choice	2
			Relationship	Assign me a top-notch, personable professional that will remain my single contact over the long term	10
Price	Charge me a fair price with no hidden or invisible costs	4			
			Ease	Make the process simple and painless	4
Trustworthiness	Ensure that your financial interest is in line with mine at all times (no conflict)	8	Information	Give me all the information I need to make enlightened choices while ensuring that I do not suffer from information overflow	4
	Always represent my best interest in our dealings with financial institutions	4			
Knowledge	Help me understand my true needs and attitude toward risk taking	9		Keep me informed of the evolution of my financial situation	4
	Facilitate my understanding of the major choices I am facing and their implications	8	Communication	Communicate in plain English	3
	Subtotal: 63			Subtotal: 37	

yet because neither FPA nor the client knows what the client should do with the assistance of a service provider and what he should do alone. In determining the respective weight of each need, FPA initially feels that results should be assigned two-thirds of the weight and customer experience one-third. A finer analysis of the data leads to the final 63/37 split shown in Table 5.1.

We refer to the most important needs in this table as CTS elements. "Develop and maintain [a] financial strategy and plan . . . constantly aligned with my evolving personal needs, income and tax patterns, risk profile, and evolving market conditions," for instance, is a CTS, or one of the vital needs. The four most important needs account for almost 60% of the weight, while the bottom four represent only 13%. Thus, process selection decisions (and later, process design or improvement decisions) must be strongly slanted toward the former.

2. In this case, it is felt that the customer experience constitutes mostly "hygiene" factors or qualifiers, while the most important needs under "results" are order-winners and differentiators. As discussed in Chapter 2, however, the two are closely interrelated so that a poor relationship, for instance, may have a negative

impact on trust and eventually on performance, as the client may not heed the advice of the financial planner. Therefore, FPA should not disregard any client need.

As discussed in Chapter 2, before moving on, FPA must assess competitive offerings, position its customer benefits package vis-à-vis that of competitors, specify how it will differentiate itself, and explicitly formulate value propositions such as:

> We will never hold back any knowledge, training, or information that could bring you closer to the level of autonomy you wish to achieve.

> We will always make sure that our interests are fully aligned with yours, and thus will only succeed as a business if we are better than competitors at helping you reach your financial objectives.

Such propositions go beyond customers' stated and implicit needs to specify the basis selected by FPA on which to compete, thus emphasizing the satisfaction of some needs over others. Formulating value propositions, however, would require a strategic analysis of external opportunities and threats, and of internal strengths and weaknesses, which is done in the context of a strategic planning exercise and lies beyond the scope of this book. The reader interested in learning more about understanding customer requirements and measuring customer satisfaction should read Fisher and Schutta (2003) and Hayes (1992).

3. The next step is to define the service package, that is, the offerings (including contact personnel behavior) that FPA will supply to its customers to meet their needs. Every offering should contribute to the satisfaction of one or more needs, and the service package must address all the needs. With this goal in mind, FPA comes up, through brainstorming, with an initial list of services required. Through further focus groups, it establishes the relative importance of each feature to the customer. This is shown in Figure 5.7.

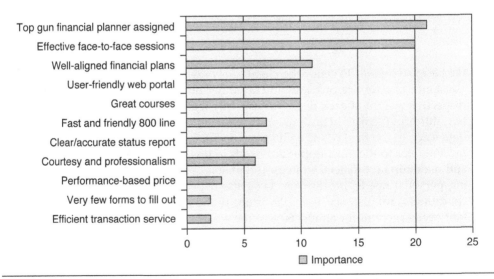

Figure 5.7 Most important service features for the client: weighted using focus groups.

4. What you measure is what you get. What are the key metrics that FPA should use to design and manage its services and processes? Measuring customer satisfaction is essential, but one cannot wait for the results of surveys to manage the business. The firm needs *metrics*, to which we shall refer as *technical characteristics*, that can provide useful and timely feedback about the performance of processes. Each service offering that is part of the service package is the output of one or more processes. We need processes to deliver these outputs with the right quality, at the right time, and at the right cost. Hence, we need metrics for each of these aspects to ensure early detection of process shift or drift (discussed in Chapter 6). These metrics, together with the target values we set for them, will guide us in the identification and design of key processes (Chapter 7).

Looking at each service feature, FPA partners now ask themselves how they can measure it. How do we know, for instance, if our courses are great, besides asking the participants if they enjoyed them, which FPA will certainly do? They come up with the idea of developing their own course "fog index," that is, a metric based on various indicators such as the number of complex words, quality of slides, use of examples, and so on. They will conduct an internal "dry run" of each course and calculate the index beforehand, thus allowing for changing the course before it does any "damage." They think that the index is related to other important offerings, such as having financial plans that are well aligned with the client's goals (hard to achieve if the client does not understand some important financial notion) and a user-friendly web portal (for the same reason). The result of their completed work is shown in Figure 5.8. Such a figure can also be generated using a matrix, such as the one shown in Figure 7.3, as explained in Chapter 7.

We will carry on with this example in Chapter 7, with process selection and scoping, and later in Chapter 10, with the process design methodology. The reader who wishes to seize the moment and go directly to Chapter 7 and then to Chapter 10 can do so without loss of continuity and come back to this point afterward.

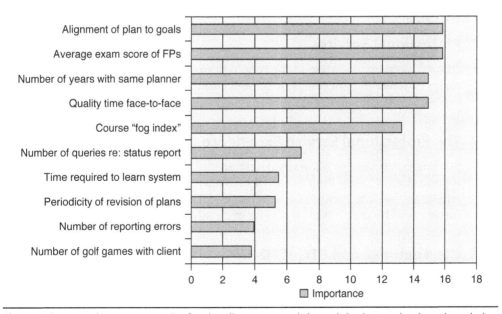

Figure 5.8 Most important metrics for the client, assessed through brainstorming based on their correlation with the various service features.

5.6 SUMMARY

Professionals evolve in a variety of organizations, ranging from the lone architect with her secretary to the university hospital. The new graduate in accounting can decide to set up his own office, join a large accounting firm, or provide internal accounting services for a large organization or government department.

Society invests in the training of these professionals. They are relatively well compensated. In return, professionals address important customer needs and contribute to the nation's competitiveness. In this pursuit, society and organizations give them power, which they must use with rigor, judgment, creativity, and respect. As they create the customer's experience, they themselves live an experience of their own, of a very different nature.

They do not provide the service alone. They must interface with other professionals, managers, and employees, using the service delivery system to maximum effect. Their joint actions have systemwide implications: they are a major cost and value driver, and thus directly impact the performance and competitiveness of the organization. It is essential to view these actions within the process framework we have presented. These processes in turn must be viewed within the strategic framework presented in Chapter 4. This allows one to think globally about the contribution of each process to the organization's scheme of value creation and the systemic effects to consider when making changes.

The other side of the coin is that a detailed understanding of execution is required to take effective action where and when it is required. A precise understanding of the critical elements of the service experience and of the processes that allow it to unfold without a hitch is required. Particular attention must be paid to professional interfaces, which can be very turbulent, with devastating effect for all stakeholders.

EXERCISES

5.1 Professional Services

Classify your organization in the typology presented in section 5.1. What are the major differences between your organization and (1) organizations in the other types of professional service, and (2) other organizations in the same type?

5.2 The Professional Service Experience

Starting from exercise 2.2, write a narrative of a typical client experience in your organization. Do not limit yourself to what the customer does, but specify the emotions that the customer experiences at different moments. What are the moments of truth in a typical service encounter?

5.3 CTs, Features, and CTQ–CTD–CTC

Starting from your answers to all exercises in Chapter 2, prepare diagrams similar to those shown in Figures 5.7 and 5.8, specifying and weighing service features and metrics.

Part II

Methodologies and Techniques to Achieve Operational Excellence

Intellectual understanding (knowledge) is necessary but insufficient to achieve significant changes. The how-to (know-how) is also required. How do you understand, bring under control, and manage a process (Chapter 6)? How does the organization decide on which processes it should focus its attention, and how do you scope a process change project (Chapter 7)? How do you mobilize an already overburdened organization behind the change initiative (Chapter 8)? How do you improve an underperforming process that has potential (Chapter 9) or design a new one (Chapter 10)? In answering these questions, many techniques are involved. They fit within methodologies. The methodologies fit within the philosophy and logical framework presented in Part I. The reader needs to get into action mode. It is impossible to go very far without starting to apply the toolkit provided.

6
Managing a Process

If you're not keeping score, it's just practice.

—R. D. Snee (2006)

Variation is the voice of a process. It is the enemy of value, but the friend of anyone who wants to characterize a process and learn how it works. Statistics is the language of variation. Adopting a systems view of the organization potentiates the process approach.

In the previous chapters we explained the importance of identifying and focusing on the right processes, and we proposed a methodology and tools to help the organization do this. These important processes must be managed. In this chapter we present some basic notions about managing a process. We first explain the critical role that variation plays in process control and present a systems view of process control. We then discuss the distinctive features of process control in professional services using the examples of a drugstore, social services, and consulting. Much of the rigor discussed in Chapter 1 is rooted in the approaches and tools presented here. Figure 6.1 discusses the videos associated with this chapter's content. Table 6.1 gives short definitions of the major concepts discussed in this chapter.

6.1 VARIATION AND PROCESS CONTROL

To introduce basic notions about variation and process control, we use a simple example (see Box 6.1). It is critical to Judy's satisfaction (CTS) to live in a comfortable home environment. Comfort can be defined by two technical characteristics, or CTQ criteria: room temperature and relative humidity. Let us say that Judy is comfortable when room temperature is within the 68°F–72°F range and relative humidity within the 35%–45% range. While the average daily temperature and humidity provide useful information, this is not enough to evaluate Judy's comfort level. Indeed, half a day at 60°F and the other half at 80°F, while very uncomfortable, yield an average temperature of 70°F—which is right on target. Hence, we also need a measure of variation in temperature and humidity.

6.1 Understanding and managing processes

This is a conceptual video. It explains and illustrates the systems view of processes, value creation, process control, and the all-important learning loops using a few simple examples. Consider driving a car as a system. The driver gets feedback from the internal and external components. He processes this information and decides to make adjustments such as braking, accelerating, deactivating the cruise control, turning up the air conditioner, and switching gears. The feedback he gets may lag the actual event that he is now noticing (the following car is really close), and it may take a while for the corrective action to take place (such as decision time—i.e., change lanes—and the time required to make it happen). He may also be getting leading information of a traffic jam five kilometers down the highway and take appropriate steps to adjust for it. These notions, as well as the voice of the customer and learning loops, are also presented using climate control in a house (see section 6.2 and Figure 6.6). The video then shows how these notions can be transferred to a business context using the example of a pharmacy, previously presented in Figure 3.10 and Box 6.2. This last example allows for further discussion of the linkages between strategy and process, presented in Chapter 5.

Key concepts: External environment, internal environment, feedback and control, feedforward control, voice of customer, lead and lag, learning loop, strategy-process connection

6.2 Measuring and learning

"If you can't measure it, you don't know anything about it," W. Edwards Deming used to say. "If it matters, it has to be observable and detectable. If it is detectable, it can be detected as a range of amounts," adds D. W. Hubbard. Let's not find what is easily measured; let's explore in depth the phenomenon of interest (e.g., assurance, empathy, satisfaction) and find a way to measure it.

Key concepts: Validity, repeatability, reproducibility, variation, precision, accuracy, interlinking, voice of the customer, voice of process, measuring the right thing right. Examples include the history of the measurement of longitude, toast color, taste, courtesy on the phone, and a Japanese sushi restaurant.

6.3 Supply chain—Complex service version

Consider the following service episode: a person suffering from knee pain consults a physiotherapist at a nearby clinic. Dissatisfied with results after several sessions, he decides to seek the counsel of a general practitioner at a medical clinic, who injects cortizone to no avail. The general practitioner therefore refers him to an orthopedist at a local hospital. The orthopedist requests situation-specific images produced under the direction of a radiologist at another clinic. At the time of the next visit with the orthopedist, the person and the physician agree to surgery, which is later performed at a specialized hospital by a resident under the supervision of another orthopedist. Physiotherapy treatments are subsequently prescribed and performed at the hospital. Home exercises are also prescribed but never carried out. After a certain time, still dissatisfied with the results, the patient is treated successively by a chiropractor, physiatrist, physiotherapy technician (as opposed to professional), and acupuncturist before concluding that the situation is unlikely to improve and giving up. The above sequence includes eight different processes ranging from physiotherapy at a local clinic to examination by a general practitioner and subsequent action. The sequence of services is shaped by a combination of patient decisions, professional advice received, intra- and interorganizational connections, and rules governing the transfer from one professional to another. Another patient with the exact same symptoms may well follow a totally different sequence and obtain radically different results. The "supply chain" is quite a different notion in complex services.

Key concepts: Server episode, client system, professional system, complex service delivery system, complexity science, power, irreducible uncertainty, control, and emergence. Several examples used in other videos are revisited here to highlight the specificity of supply chains in complex services.

Figure 6.1 Videos associated with Chapter 6.

Table 6.1 Short definitions of major concepts discussed in this chapter.

Concept	Definition
Systems view	A way of thinking—often supported by a visual representation—about a group of elements as a dynamically interacting set of variables taking inputs and providing outputs to one another within an environment.
Variations	Changes in the value of a dependent or independent variable.
Interaction	Reciprocal action between two or more variables, which makes it essential to consider the value of the other variables when setting the value of one of them.
Statistics	The science of variations and risks. As complexity increases, statistics quickly become essential to make up for our limited unaided capacity to analyze variations, and thus understand processes.
Standard deviation	The most common statistical measure of dispersion of values around the mean. The smaller the standard deviation, the tighter the values cluster around the mean.
Normal distribution	A statistical distribution that describes well many naturally occurring phenomena.
Voice of the process	The range of values (typically three standard deviations on either side of the mean) within which the results of a stable process fall most (99.7%) of the time.
Voice of the customer	A translation of customer requirements into a quantitative specification that the process must meet.
Process capability	A quantitative assessment of a stable process's ability to consistently produce results that meet the client's specifications. It involves a (statistical) comparison of the variations produced by the process to the client's specifications. The ratio of the voice of the customer to the voice of the process is a commonly used metric for this.
Special causes	A factor or variable interfering with the normal operation of a process, thereby modifying the patterns of variation and making predictions of future behavior unreliable.
Shift	A special cause that produces a sudden change in a process's performance, leaving it stable at different operating parameters (that is, different distribution of results).
Drift	A special cause that produces a gradual change in process performance.
Stable process	A process whose performance is not subject to the effect of any special cause, and whose performance thus lends itself to statistical prediction.
Process control	A process designed to monitor another one and keep it stable. A control system receives information from the other process, processes it (assesses stability), and sends control instructions as required to correct it.
SPC	Statistical process control. A rigorous control system based on statistics.
Capacity management	A management process whose task it is to control operating processes in such a way that capacity and demand are continuously matched in the most profitable way possible.

Box 6.1 Judy's Environment Control

Issue: *Basic notions on variation and process control*

Judy has just moved from Jacksonville, Florida, to Edmonton, Alberta, Canada, where she had a new house built. In early December she discovers the wonders and challenges associated with her first winter at a northern latitude. One of these unexpected "pleasures" is the difficulties she faces in maintaining a comfortable home environment, that is, the temperature and humidity in various rooms of her three-bedroom cottage. Upon handing her the keys to the house, the contractor had indicated that there were three simple controls at her disposal to make adjustments as outside conditions changed:

- A thermostat (controlling a central electrical furnace)
- A knob (with settings labeled 1 to 7) to set the lower humidity level at which a humidifier would turn on and start circulating the air through a humid filter to reduce dryness
- Another knob to set the upper humidity limit beyond which an air exchanger would start, expelling hot (pollutant-charged), humid air and taking in dry, cold air, thus avoiding excessive humidity

For all this "simplicity," after three weeks of a Canadian winter, there were very few times when Judy felt comfortable in the house. Unless set correctly, the humidifier might well work against the air exchanger (injecting humidity while the exchanger expels it): a costly situation, since the furnace would be functioning most of the time because of the cold air coming in. When she felt cold, she would raise the temperature setting on the thermostat. Soon after, however, her throat would feel dry and she would raise the humidifier setting. As the outside temperature mellowed, however, the furnace would function less often and humidity would rise, eventually triggering the air exchanger and reducing both temperature and humidity. She was well aware that the more the exchanger functioned, the higher her heating bill would be, and was thus tempted to set the humidity level at which it would start rather high. Thus, she would lower the humidifier setting, only to find the dryness problem coming back when the outside temperature dropped again, and then the humidity would never rise high enough to trigger the air exchanger, so the quality of the air she breathes would go down. . . .

The most commonly used measure for this purpose is the standard deviation, often represented by the Greek letter σ (sigma). It measures how far away from the mean each observation lies, on average. The farther the observations lie from the average—that is, the higher the standard deviation—the more variation there is and thus the lower Judy's comfort level. Suppose that Judy decides to use some rigor to solve her problem. She goes to the hardware store and buys a thermometer and a hygroscope. Every day, at a convenient time, she jots down on a piece of paper the readings on both instruments. The results are shown in Table 6.2. Also shown are the mean and standard deviation of each sample. The *standard deviation* is the square root of the average squared deviation from the mean. That is not as complex at it sounds. The standard deviation of the humidity data, for example, is calculated as follows:

$$\sqrt{\frac{(37.9 - 38.7)^2 + (40.4 - 38.7)^2 + (49.2 - 38.7)^2 + \ldots}{29}} = 7.6$$

Table 6.2 Temperature and humidity data for 30 days in Judy's home, compared with comfort levels.

Day	Humidity	Temperature	68°–72° Temperature OK	35%–45% Humidity OK	Both OK
1	37.9	68.6	X	X	X
2	40.4	64.3		X	
3	49.2	69.7	X		
4	19.9	69.0	X		
5	46.3	66.2			
6	32.4	67.4			
7	36.6	70.7	X	X	X
8	29.9	78.8			
9	38.3	68.1	X	X	X
10	39.1	73.6		X	
11	47.6	74.7			
12	42.0	75.4		X	
13	35.0	69.2	X	X	X
14	49.5	73.5			
15	45.1	65.9			
16	30.0	68.4	X		
17	51.2	67.3			
18	36.3	69.3	X	X	X
19	37.9	75.0		X	
20	30.0	67.2			
21	33.6	73.8			
22	40.7	73.4		X	
23	30.1	68.3	X		
24	44.3	72.2		X	
25	34.1	69.0	X		
26	30.9	71.2	X		
27	49.2	72.3			
28	39.2	72.5		X	
29	51.4	73.7			
30	34.2	69.1	X		
Total			12	12	5
Mean	38.7	70.6			
SD (σ)	7.6	3.3			
VC	20%	5%			
%			40%	40%	17%

SD: Standard deviation
VC: Variation coefficient

The division by 29, that is, the sample size minus one, rather than by 30 is a correction factor required because this is really an estimate of the unknown value of the standard deviation of a much broader reference set (referred to as "the population" in statistics) of temperature values. We could obtain the real standard deviation only by continuously monitoring the house. We generally consider a sample size of 30 to be sufficient to produce a valid estimate.

With a standard deviation of 3.3, temperature appears more constant than humidity, at least in absolute terms. Percentage variation, however, would be much more useful. We call this the *variation coefficient* (VC) and calculate it by dividing the standard deviation by the mean. It shows (Table 6.2) that humidity displays four times the variability of temperature. A more useful measure yet would be to compare the actual variation with what Judy considers acceptable. This is illustrated in Figures 6.2 and 6.3.

The comfort zone reflects the voice of the customer, that is, the translation of the intangible and subjective feeling of comfort (CTS) into specific values of two measurable variables (technical characteristics or CTQ). The connected dots reflect the voice of the process, that is, the actual values produced by the underlying processes. Comparing the voice of the process with the voice of the customer shows (as a time series in Figure 6.2 and a histogram in Figure 6.3) the capability of the

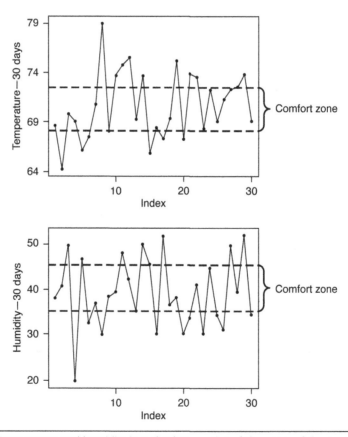

Figure 6.2 Temperature and humidity in Judy's house: plot of the voice of the process against the voice of the customer.

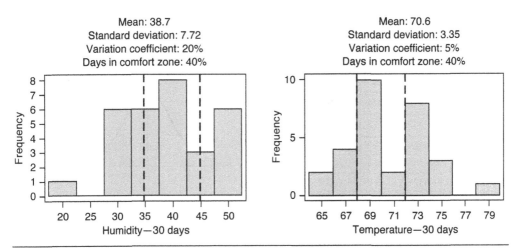

Figure 6.3 Temperature and humidity data in Judy's house: histogram with basic statistics, 30-day sample.

process to meet the customer's requirements. We could give a tentative quantitative value to this capability by calculating (see Table 6.3) the proportion of the sample that lies within the comfort zone. On this count, both CTQs seem comparable (40% for temperature, 40% for humidity). Indeed, while humidity displays much more variation, the comfort zone is also much broader for humidity than it is for temperature. A common measure of process capability is based on the ratio of the voice of the customer to the voice of the process. The target value here is often set at two.

One problem with the capability analysis is that we based the conclusions on a sample of 30 observations. Drawing another sample would certainly produce different numbers, and the difference could be very significant. For instance, the "hole" in the distribution of the temperature data (in the 70–72 range) is most likely not representative of the population but simply a random occurrence. An obvious solution is to increase the sample size. Let us assume that Judy goes on gathering data for 500 days. We show the resulting distributions in Figure 6.4. It turns out that the initial sample resulted in a substantial overestimation of the variability of humidity, resulting in an underestimation of the capability of the process to meet Judy's requirements.

Increasing sample size, however, is not always feasible or economical. In order to improve the estimation resulting from a small sample, statistical techniques are used. We limit our discussion here to the normal distribution. The area under a normal curve sums to one. The area over any range of values thus represents a probability (with a total of one [100%] for the entire range [minus infinity, plus infinity]). We show the normal curve as the bell-shaped lines in Figure 6.4. Figure 6.5 shows the probabilities associated with various intervals defined by the number of standard deviations on both sides of the mean. If we can assume, for instance, that variations in relative humidity in Judy's house are normally distributed with a mean of 40 and a standard deviation of 6, then we know that there is a 68.26% probability that the temperature falls in the range (34, 46), that is, in the range ([mean – sigma], [mean + sigma]). Hence, we can calculate the probability of being in the comfort zone (35, 45) at any point in time as the probability (found

Table 6.3 Areas under the standard normal curve for various values of x, the number of standard deviations away from the mean (prob $[X > \mu + x\sigma]$).

X	Probability	X	Probability
0.1	0.46017216	3.1	0.0009676
0.2	0.42074029	3.2	0.00068714
0.3	0.38208858	3.3	0.00048342
0.4	0.34457826	3.4	0.00033693
0.5	0.30853754	3.5	0.00023263
0.6	0.27425312	3.6	0.00015911
0.7	0.24196365	3.7	0.0001078
0.8	0.2118554	3.8	7.2348E-05
0.9	0.18406013	3.9	4.8096E-05
1	0.15865525	4	3.1671E-05
1.1	0.13566606	4.1	2.0658E-05
1.2	0.11506967	4.2	1.3346E-05
1.3	0.09680048	4.3	8.5399E-06
1.4	0.08075666	4.4	5.4125E-06
1.5	0.0668072	4.5	3.3977E-06
1.6	0.05479929	4.6	2.1125E-06
1.7	0.04456546	4.7	1.3008E-06
1.8	0.03593032	4.8	7.9333E-07
1.9	0.02871656	4.9	4.7918E-07
2	0.02275013	5	2.8665E-07
2.1	0.01786442	5.1	1.6983E-07
2.2	0.01390345	5.2	9.9644E-08
2.3	0.01072411	5.3	5.7901E-08
2.4	0.00819754	5.4	3.332E-08
2.5	0.00620967	5.5	1.899E-08
2.6	0.00466119	5.6	1.0718E-08
2.7	0.00346697	5.7	5.9904E-09
2.8	0.00255513	5.8	3.3157E-09
2.9	0.00186581	5.9	1.8175E-09
3	0.0013499	6	9.8659E-10

in Table 6.3) that a normal distribution lies within 5/6 sigma on either side of the mean, or about 58%.[1] With the relatively bad sample we had at first, the estimate would be 49%. The improvement in the estimate results from using the additional information we now have (or rather that we have assumed in this case) about the shape and the properties of the distribution of the population. Statistical tests are available to verify the normality hypothesis.

The normal distribution nicely describes many naturally occurring phenomena that are the sum of a host of independent individual actions and events. Other

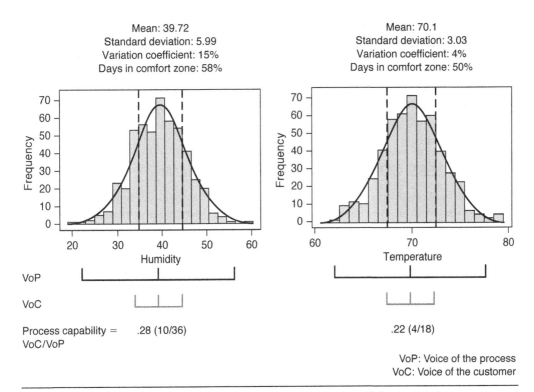

Figure 6.4 Temperature and humidity in Judy's house: histogram with basic statistics, 500-day sample.

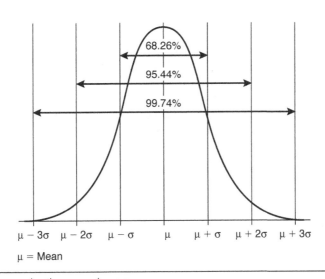

Figure 6.5 Areas under the normal curve.

distributions are known and available to approximate other phenomena and thus improve estimation accuracy.

A common way to calculate process capability is by dividing the voice of the customer by the voice of the process. In the case of relative humidity, we calculate the voice of the customer as the range of the comfort zone (45 − 35 = 10). We take the voice of the process to be three standard deviations on each side of the mean, that is, an interval spanning six standard deviations (see Figure 6.4), representing 99.74% (see Figure 6.5) of the area under the curve. This assumes that the voice of the process is centered on the central value of the voice of the customer. While this is the case in this example, it is obviously not always the case. When the process is off-center, this calculated capability will not be actualized until it has been centered.

6.2 PROCESS CONTROL—A SYSTEMS VIEW

Judy's actions to maintain and improve her comfort level fall within the realms of process control. We illustrate this in Figure 6.6. Judy is controlling three distinct processes: exchanging air, humidifying the air, and heating the air (Video 6.1; see Figure 6.1). The inputs, transformation, and outputs (ITO; that is, the center part of the SITOC, without specifying the supplier and the customer) are shown in

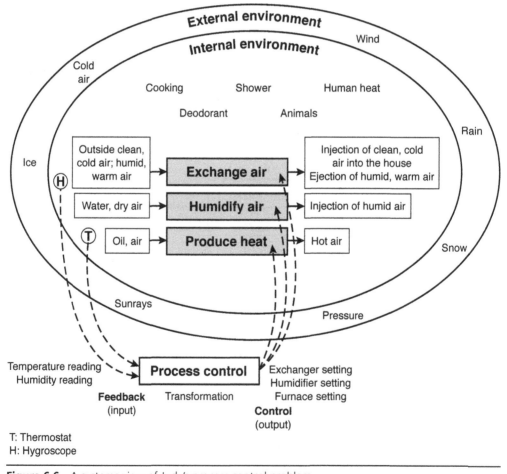

Figure 6.6   A systems view of Judy's process control problem.

Figure 6.6. These three processes are automated. The only human intervention required consists of setting dials. The processes are shown to function within the internal environment of the house, with all the other human, animal, chemical, and microbiological processes that take place within its confines. The house itself exists within an external environment influenced by several environmental factors. All these processes interact with each other, either in a synergistic or antagonistic fashion, thereby conditioning the air that Judy feels and breathes. Some of these processes are controllable (taking a hot shower), others are partially controllable (such as the quantity of pollutants introduced into the house environment by the cat), and yet others lie totally beyond her control (such as physical [condensation] or chemical [rust] reactions).

Judy measures two characteristics of that air: temperature and humidity. She places her thermometer and hygroscope conveniently on the kitchen counter, where she spends much of her time, and glances at them when she feels something is wrong. Thus, this feeling, together with the data she reads on the instruments, provides feedback on the joint effect of all these processes on the climate (the input arrows to the process control box in Figure 6.6). Judy processes this information mentally. She first assesses the extent to which her feeling of warmth and dampness has strayed from her comfort zones. Then she tries to understand why this has happened and what she should do to correct the situation. This is the transformation (the T of the SITOC) that the control process operates. The outputs are decisions on the settings for the three knobs (or variables) she controls (the output arrows, transmitting operating instructions to the three automated processes). She then goes on with her business until a feeling of discomfort again interrupts her.

Where there are processes, there is variation, and this system is no exception. In the previous section we discussed the variations Judy observed when looking at her two instruments. Here is a partial list of other sources of variation:

- Measurement errors and time lags in the two instruments

- Measurement error in the thermostat and the humidity measurement systems of the humidifier and the air exchanger

- Judy's human error in her feelings of warmth and dampness

- Judy's logical error and memory flaws in her decision-making process

- Judy's human error when setting the dials

- Variations in the many uncontrollable external environmental factors (wind, humidity, atmospheric pressure, temperature)

- Variations in internal generation of heat and humidity (more cooking, showers, and so on)

- Special events (such as a party with 30 people)

- Variation in the heat generated by the furnace at a given setting, and similar variations in the humidifier and heat exchanger

- Slow decline in the humidity generated by a freshly completed plaster wall

Variation falls into two broad categories, *random* and *special cause*. Random variations are the result of a host of independent variables that are impossible to identify. This type of variation has a tendency to be distributed normally, as illustrated in Figures 6.3 and 6.4. Special cause variation takes place, as the name suggests, when a potentially identifiable factor is affecting the variable. These events fall into two categories according to the specific signature they leave on the data. A *drift* is identified by an upward, downward, or cyclical trend in the data triggered by a phenomenon that unfolds gradually. Seasonal drifts in outside temperature, for instance, or even global warming, might well display such patterns. A *shift*, on the other hand, is produced by a discrete event (temporary, recurrent, or permanent) that makes the variable suddenly jump up or down from its normal pattern. The arrival of the meteorological phenomenon known as El Niño, for example, might produce such a shift in temperature. In Table 6.4 we illustrate the notions of shifts, drifts, and control loops further using three examples of simple personal processes: brushing one's teeth, making toast, and planning one's day. Within-cycle controls are actions taken during an instantiation of the process. They are meant to influence the outcome of the process in that instance. Between-cycle controls are actions taken after analyzing the outcome of a cycle and are applied to the next one.

Anyone worried about his weight has a *specification* in mind, that is, an ideal weight or figure he would like to achieve and maintain. Two major processes are involved here: eating and exercising, that is, energy input and output. When it comes to controlling these two processes, weight is the "big Y" (see Chapter 7), and the specification may be set on a continuous scale (such as 160–165 pounds) or on a so-called go/no-go gage: "Do I fit into my black pants or not?" The "small y" for the eating process may be the number of calories consumed in a day, and for the exercising process the number of calories burned while exercising (which many training machines measure). The voice of the customer for each process may then be set as a standard and a tolerance (that is, 1500 calories, ± 50). Failure to meet the standard on either process has a direct impact on the big Y. Controlling these processes requires measuring these data, capturing them, analyzing variations, and taking corrective action when required, that is, process control.

Table 6.4 Illustration of control loops, process shift, and process drift in three personal processes.

	Brushing your teeth	**Making toast**	**Planning your day**
Control loop (within cycle)	"Ouch!" (Action: reduce pressure)	Burnt toast smell! (Action: get it out)	"You'll never do all this—be realistic" (Action: review schedule)
Drift (gradual, between cycles)	Increasing number of cavities (Potential cause: shorter brushing time, brush wear)	Toast increasingly dark (Potential cause: bread increasingly dry because you eat less)	Increasingly falling behind (Potential cause: tired, working more slowly)
Shift (sudden, between cycles)	Gums start bleeding (Potential cause: gum disease)	Toast is now white! (Potential cause: bread is now kept in refrigerator)	Don't follow your plan anymore (Potential cause: sudden change in work habits)

An upward drift in the eating process is a frequent phenomenon, leading to stoutness and the health risk it carries. Upward shifts are also very common, as one suddenly changes some eating habit, such as drinking a beer or two before dinner or eating lunch at a fast-food restaurant twice a week. A downward drift in the exercising process is also very common, as one starts skipping training sessions—always for a good reason, of course! A common cause, such as excessive workload and the pressure and stress it creates, may be at the root of all these phenomena. Without a good control system—because the positive effects associated with eating more (feeling good) and training less (easier, getting more work done) are immediate, and the negative effects on weight and health in general are delayed—many people are easy prey for such phenomena. Unless one is able to detect adverse trends and introduce countermeasures early, correction will have become very hard—often discouragingly so—by the time one feels the need for change (see Chapter 12 for more discussion).

Thus, variation patterns carry a wealth of valuable information about the underlying phenomena that produce the variation. To secure the benefits of such information, one must analyze variation carefully in order to be able to tell its various components apart. This is where statistical analysis comes in. Without it, one is liable to misinterpret the data, seeing a trend where there is none or attributing a significant shift to random variations. This may result in taking actions that will throw a stable process off course or leave a process at the mercy of the forces affecting it. This is discussed further later in the chapter.

The temperature and humidity variations (dependent variable "y") discussed in the previous section are overall results of all these variations (independent variables "x's"). To make the matter of controlling variation more complex, these variations are related in complex ways. This makes it harder for Judy to draw the right conclusions from the information she gets. She may still feel excessive humidity an hour after changing the humidifier setting because the sensor is located in a dryer area of the house, because the outside temperature (which she does not monitor) went up and the sensors have not yet detected the more humid air coming in, or because of the hot coffee pot next to her. If the world would only stand still for a while, she sometimes wished, then we could start changing one variable at a time and find out what happens.

Delays between action and response are another factor that often wreaks havoc in process control. Indeed, between the time a discrete event takes place, such as setting the thermostat higher, and its effects on the system unfold and are eventually felt (by Judy) or detected (by her instruments), 30 minutes may go by. If Judy is not aware of that, she will suffer a serious learning disability as a process controller. Most informal control systems (such as controlling one's weight or home environment) do not adequately factor that delay into control decisions. Oftentimes, this results in attributing a change in the state of the system to a recent occurrence or corrective action while it may in fact be the delayed effect of an earlier one. This results in *overcorrection* (for example, turning the thermostat still higher, even though "the heat is already on its way") and eventually into *overshoot* and *collapse* (also called "boom and bust") cycles.

Judy's basic problem is her lack of understanding of the factors involved and their interrelations. Not being able to understand causes and effects, she tends to look for immediate, obvious changes and thus often draws the wrong conclusion and fails to learn—a common situation for many process owners in organizations.

As one designs a process, one must also ensure that it will be controllable. Designing the control system at the same time is the best way to do this. Deciding how to control a process involves making the following decisions:

- What shall we measure?

- How will we measure it?

- How often will we measure?

- How many units will we measure?

- How will we analyze the data and decide if action is warranted?

- Who will decide what action to take, if any?

- Who will carry out the corrective action?

- Who will be responsible to prevent recurrence?

This is a good time to view Video 6.2.

6.3 PROCESS CONTROL IN PROFESSIONAL SERVICES

In this section we first present an elaborate example of process control in a drugstore, linking strategic, professional, and operational considerations. We then pursue examples started in earlier chapters about youth protection services (Midtown CPS) and consulting services (QKM), this time from the angle of process control.

6.3.1 Positioning and Operations Strategy at Golden Years Drugstore

To transfer the notions discussed earlier to professional services, we use the example of a pharmacy specializing in services for an elderly population (see Box 6.2). Taking a high-level view of GYD's strategic situation, we illustrate the drugstore's positioning in Figure 6.7, based on the model previously discussed in Figure 4.4. GYD's value proposition is radically different from and clearly superior to those of its two competitors for the targeted market segment. The pharmacy services the customers receive blend seamlessly with their daily routine and integrate well with the clinical services they receive from other professionals.

GYD seduces a targeted professional labor segment of clinically oriented pharmacists by creating a stimulating multidisciplinary service and research environment in geriatrics. Professionals are encouraged to get involved with universities (through supervising interns or writing articles) and to spend all the time required with the patients and interacting with other health professionals. They never perform tasks that less qualified (and lower paid) personnel can perform. The pressure for volume, prevalent at competitors, is secondary to professional excellence and quality of relationship. To prevent boredom, the pharmacists alternate between filling prescriptions, visiting the patients, and preparing sterile products. The job concepts offered to the technicians and clerical workers are not shown.

GYD generates profit leverage in a number of ways. The attraction that the job concept presents for the right pharmacist is such that she is willing to accept a

Box 6.2 Customer Service at Golden Years Drugstore

Issue: *Challenges in managing a professional service delivery process*

Golden Years Drugstore (GYD) is one of three drugstores in a small community. The pharmacy's greatest asset is its convenient location in the community's largest mall. Shoppers typically drop off their prescription as they arrive at the mall and pick up the drugs as they leave. Customers are willing to pay a little more to avoid waiting. Discount Drug Mart, on the other hand, targets a more price-sensitive market segment. It draws people to its more remote location by offering lower prices on drugs and on a host of dollar items it sells. GYD opened when a large, upper-end seniors' complex was built on the outskirts of town, next to a private long-term care hospital for elderly who are chronically ill. GYD owner Ida Smith rents the premises next to the medical clinic, at the entrance of the mall. She designed the store with geriatrics in mind from the outset, with comfortable chairs for seniors who need an extended encounter with the pharmacist or a nurse practitioner operating on the premises. With an average age of 85, customers are well-off retirees who are used to getting first-class personalized service. All employees are trained for general and specialized services for the elderly.

Even though prices are high, very few customers would consider going anywhere else. Indeed, they enjoy the personal relationship they have with the pharmacist and that he has all the information required—and immediate access to their doctors and nurses— to give them advice that improves their quality of life. Going to the competition would be expensive (taxi), time-consuming (they would have to provide much information to a pharmacist who is not familiar with them and their problems), and initially risky (it is so easy to miss a critical interaction between two medications, especially for a generalist pharmacist). Far from giving in to complacency, however, Ida realized that it would be relatively easy for either one of her competitors to open an annex store on the other side of the street and copy many of her practices, were customer discontent to build up.

The basic service process for a new prescription (order fulfillment process) at GYD is as follows (see Figure 3.10). The customer hands his prescription to a technician at the reception counter. The technician locates the patient's file in a computer database, checks his identity, enters the new prescription information, prints the vial labels, and places them, together with the prescription itself, in a basket. A second technician takes charge of the basket as soon as she is available, assembles the required medications, places them in the appropriate vials (together with the labels and invoice), and then places the basket on another counter. As soon as the pharmacist is available, he picks up the basket and goes to the computer screen to analyze the patient's record. This involves verifying the dosage, medical interactions, and any possible contraindication. He then does a physical inspection of the medication ("content–container" inspection) and meets the patient at a consultation counter or in an enclosed office, as required, to advise him on how to take the medication, possible side effects, and contingency plans. A third technician takes over from there to process the payment. The processes for renewals and new patients are slightly different.

When the pharmacist detects an interaction or another problem with the prescription, he calls the doctor and they resolve the issue together. Other PSDPs at GYD include a roving pharmacist who visits the patients in a selected location, a back-office pharmacist who prepares sterile products (such as syringes with palliative drugs for terminally ill patients), and a team of three to five back-office technicians preparing medication organizers for patients, their nurse, or the ward masters, under the supervision of a pharmacist. The pickup and delivery service is another important nonprofessional service process.

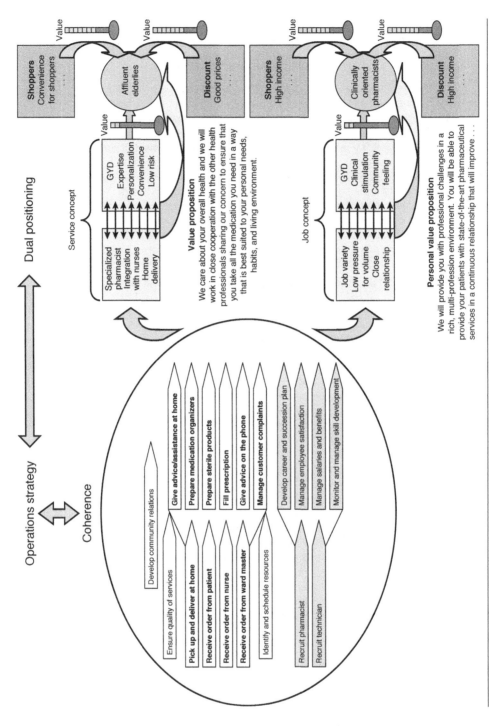

Figure 6.7 The three-way fit (V2P model) between the service concept, the job concept, and processes at GYD.

somewhat lower level of remuneration than that offered by the competition. She is also very loyal, and the turnover is very low. Using a highly leveraged (that is, a high ratio of technicians to pharmacists) assembly line to fill prescriptions allows the professional to focus on activities where she can create the most value (for the patient and for herself): detecting problems and communicating with the patients and other professionals. Doing so reinforces the loyalty of patients and other health providers, thereby bringing in more business and reducing patient attrition. Since a pharmacist costs three to four times as much as a technician, this is achieved at a lower cost than the competition. This is the operations strategy: it increases patients' benefits and reduces costs at the same time.

We show a few selected processes in Figure 6.7. Boldface processes are value-adding processes. Shaded processes are enabling processes critical to the delivery of the job concept (value-adding processes also play a very important role here). The quality assurance and scheduling processes are also important enablers, while maintaining a close relationship with the seniors' community is a strategic marketing and defensive process.

6.3.2 Systems View of GYD

Figure 6.8 presents a systems view of the major clinical and service processes as described summarily in Box 6.2. Figure 6.8 parallels Figure 6.6, with a number of differences. First, we do not show the inputs and outputs of the four processes depicted, for the sake of simplicity (the "fulfill prescription" process was mapped

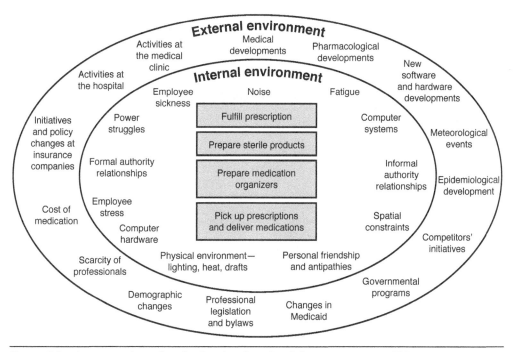

Figure 6.8   A systems view of professional and service delivery processes at GYD.

in Figure 3.10). We also do not show, for lack of space, the process control box itself, but it is very much present, and discussing how it works is a central topic of this section. The reader will also remember that an organization is a system of processes (such as that illustrated by the APQC model in Figure 3.3 or the limited subset shown in Figure 3.5). Processes adjacent to those shown in Figure 6.9, however, are not shown, either, to allow us to focus on feedback and control of a limited subset of processes.

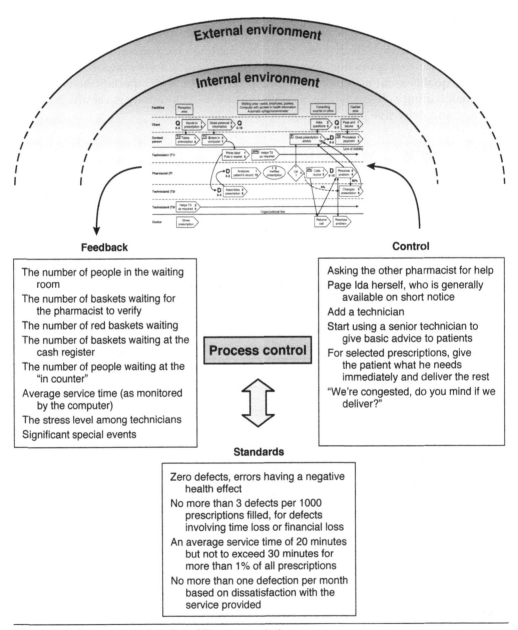

Feedback

The number of people in the waiting room

The number of baskets waiting for the pharmacist to verify

The number of red baskets waiting

The number of baskets waiting at the cash register

The number of people waiting at the "in counter"

Average service time (as monitored by the computer)

The stress level among technicians

Significant special events

Process control

Control

Asking the other pharmacist for help

Page Ida herself, who is generally available on short notice

Add a technician

Start using a senior technician to give basic advice to patients

For selected prescriptions, give the patient what he needs immediately and deliver the rest

"We're congested, do you mind if we deliver?"

Standards

Zero defects, errors having a negative health effect

No more than 3 defects per 1000 prescriptions filled, for defects involving time loss or financial loss

An average service time of 20 minutes but not to exceed 30 minutes for more than 1% of all prescriptions

No more than one defection per month based on dissatisfaction with the service provided

Figure 6.9 Process control at GYD: filling a prescription.

All of the variables shown in Figure 6.8 display variations in one form or another. Pharmacological and medical developments, for instance, may produce shifts and drifts in demand. The sudden withdrawal of a medication (such as Vioxx) from the market or the publication of the results of an important study (such as that on the relationship between hormone replacement therapy and cardiovascular diseases)—through the effect it has on the patients, the doctors, or both—can produce a sudden jump in the number of customers. The slow development of an epidemic, on the other hand, or the gradual aging of the customer base may trigger an upward drift. The introduction of new software may also produce a one-time increase in service time, followed by a downward shift as learning gradually takes place. The arrival of a new employee might have a similar effect. Growing employee fatigue because of a particularly virulent strain of flu may produce a steady increase in the number of errors made by technicians. What makes data interpretation even more challenging is that many of these phenomena are liable to occur simultaneously—a situation quite similar to that faced by Judy in the preceding example, but much more complex.

6.3.3 Managing the Prescription Fulfillment Process at GYD

Most of the time there are two pharmacists on duty (as well as five to seven technicians), and one of them acts as the pharmacist in charge. It is the latter's responsibility to ensure the smooth functioning of all SDPs in such a way that all service standards are consistently met. Figure 3.10 shows a process map of the "fill prescription" process. The standards set by Ida are as follows (see Figure 6.9):

- Zero defects, insofar as professional errors having a negative health effect ("clinical errors") are concerned

- No more than 3 defects per 1000 prescriptions filled, for defects involving time or financial losses ("operational error")

- An average service time of 20 minutes (prescriptions are fairly complex, and some instructions need to be given slowly and repeated several times), but not to exceed 30 minutes for more than 1% of all prescriptions

- No more than one defection per month based on dissatisfaction with the service provided

To determine whether the processes are functioning smoothly, the pharmacist in charge gets feedback from a number of indicators (see Figure 6.9):

- The number of people in the waiting room

- The number of baskets waiting for the pharmacist to verify

- The number of red baskets waiting (red baskets are used for patients waiting on-site)

- The number of baskets waiting at the cash register

- The number of people waiting at the "in counter"

- Average service time (as monitored by the computer)

- The stress level among technicians, as manifested by comments made and other observable behavior

- Significant special events, such as discharge from hospital, special requests, and absenteeism

Each pharmacist (professional autonomy) developed trigger points based on various combinations of these indicators. The levers (means to adjust the process) at the disposal of the pharmacist in charge triggered into taking corrective action include (see Figure 6.9):

- Asking the pharmacist working on sterile products to interrupt her work and help bring the process back under control

- Paging Ida herself, who is generally available on short notice

- Adding a technician working on some other tasks or trying to reach a technician off duty

- Starting to use a senior technician to give basic advice to patients, when indicated

- For selected prescriptions, giving the patient what he needs immediately and delivering the rest later

- Telling technician 1 to inform incoming patients that wait time is longer than usual and that "we will be happy to deliver"

Figure 6.9 illustrates process control for the "fill prescription" process at GYD, in a fashion similar to Figure 6.6. Contrary to Judy's environment control problem or to simpler service processes, such as serving customers in a fast-food restaurant, the triggers cannot be programmed (that is, "when there are five customers waiting, open a second cashier position") and are left to professional judgment. The following questions—all of which affect process control decisions—require professional judgment:

- At what level of pressure or stress does the likelihood of a given pharmacist making a clinical error reach an unacceptable threshold?

- How fast can one really give advice to a patient without taking the risk of being misunderstood?

- What is the consequence to Mr. Jones if he delays taking his heart medication by two hours (until we deliver)?

- How risky is it to ask our senior technician to explain to Mrs. Harper how to take her codeine cough syrup?

- Can I safely give the prescribed medication to Mrs. Stuart, or should I discuss it first with the doctor?

Delays between action and response are omnipresent in this system as well, compounding the challenges involved in process control. Imagine, for instance, that a doctor at the clinic decides to switch from a dermatological ointment available off the shelf (over the counter is different: you have to ask the pharmacist, so they maintain control) to a magisterial preparation, and that the practice gradually spreads to other doctors. For each such prescription, a 15-minute mixing time replaces the old serving time of two minutes. As more and more such prescriptions come in, the average service time, and thus customer waiting time, gradually inches upward. By the time this phenomenon reaches the awareness level of the pharmacists and is traced to the right source, a month or two may have gone by. By the time a solution is found and fully implemented, such as training two technicians to do this and processing these orders in a batch every other day, another two to three months (of low-quality service and higher tension in the team) may have gone by. A glance at Figure 6.8 should make it clear that such an event would be but one occurrence in a dynamically shifting set of variables.

One's professional judgment is initially formed during training and honed through experience. The employer has little control over it. Even in professions where practices are best codified, professional judgment is subject to considerable variation. This additional source of variation compounds the process control challenges in professional services. As much as Ida tries to standardize the process and decision rules, each pharmacist has his way of doing things, to which the technicians must adjust as best they can. Ida's professional competence and reputation, more than her organizational status as owner, are her best sources of leverage on clinical practices and process control. Thus, she regularly holds clinical meetings to review recent events, and explores practice and process improvement.

The process mapped in Figure 3.10 is a manually paced assembly line. It has two inventories (excluding customers, who are not "inventoried" as such but placed in a waiting line—though impatient customers cannot really tell the difference): baskets waiting for inspection by the pharmacist and baskets waiting for payment processing. These inventories fully "uncouple" the pharmacist from the technicians working upstream and downstream from him. This is important because the pharmacist needs to be able to take all the time he requires to do a professional job. With this setup, when the pharmacist takes more time, inventory builds up upstream. If he works fast, inventory builds up downstream. The pharmacist is the scarcest and most expensive resource in the process. He is the bottleneck and sets the pace of the line. If it takes the pharmacist three minutes on average to verify a prescription, then the maximum capacity of the line is 20 prescriptions per hour, provided he is never idle. Adding more technicians beyond the number required to ensure that the pharmacist is never idle is a waste of resources. An hour gained at the bottleneck has a direct impact on productivity, while an hour gained at a non-bottleneck station only adds to idle time. If the pharmacist detects an imbalance between the two inventories, he can reallocate technicians to correct the situation.

6.3.4 Managing Other Processes at GYD

Controlling the prescription fulfillment process, as described earlier, is limited to short-term fixes. The operations planning process is directed at the midterm horizon (one to six months, say). Its mission is to determine the resources required to consistently meet service standards and ensure that they are available where and when they are required. Resources include pharmacists, technicians, support personnel, medication, supplies, and so on. Operations planning consists of forecasting demand levels and patterns, translating them into resource requirements, exploring resource availability and alternate ways to meet demand, and dispatching resources. The performance of this process conditions short-term control (discussed earlier). Through building sufficient safeguards and contingency plans, a good operational plan reduces the risks of imbalances that short-term process control cannot cope with.

Capacity planning is a process taking the long view of capacity needs and solutions. Over the long term (six to eighteen months, typically), it is possible to consider capacity strategies that are not available in the short to medium term. This may include changes in computer hardware or software, recruitment and training of new personnel, changes in layout, or the development of new modus operandi with other health professionals (nurses, doctors, dentists, or ward masters) or suppliers. This process is linked upstream to the strategic planning process, which sends it scenarios to explore and test for operational and financial feasibility.

Figure 6.10 presents a hierarchical view of the various layers of process control just described. Higher-level processes in Figure 6.10 span a longer time horizon, and thus have more leeway. Strategic planning, for instance, may cover a horizon of two to four years. There are very few aspects of the drugstore that Ida cannot consider changing over this period. Once she makes her strategic choices, however, these will limit the options remaining for the capacity planning process. Once a long-term lease is signed, for instance, increasing seating capacity in the waiting room may no longer be an option. In turn, when capacity decisions are made, such as recruiting and training two more technicians, the operations planning process has two more resources to schedule, and so on. Each process in Figure 6.10 feeds useful information about difficulties encountered in functioning within its current operating parameters to the higher-level process for consideration in the next cycle.

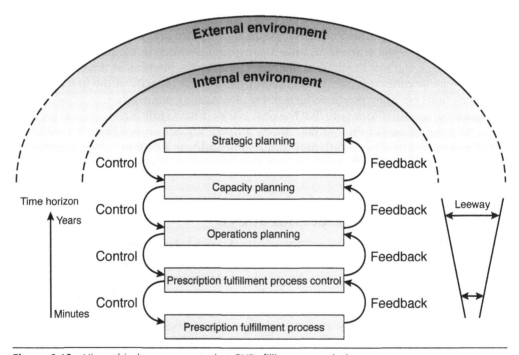

Figure 6.10 Hierarchical process control at GYD: filling a prescription.

Scheduling pharmacists' vacations and setting store hours belong to the capacity planning process. Preparing pharmacists' weekly work schedules is part of the operations planning process. Yet both of these processes have a strong influence on the pharmacists' job concept. While the customers appreciate long store hours (nights and weekends), they ultimately reduce the pharmacists' quality of life. Pharmacists also like regular schedules, but demand patterns sometimes require shuffling the schedule. GYD's positioning somewhat alleviates this problem, however, compared with the predicament of competitors: elderly people are not stuck with a 9–5 work schedule, and many of them live in the complex. Thus, evening and weekend hours are not as important to them as they are for other market segments. In managing these trade-offs between the service concept and the job concept, Ida must always bear in mind the risk that a competitor makes to one of her pharmacists "an offer he cannot refuse" to join him at better conditions. Such a move would greatly facilitate the task of a competitor wanting to take on Ida on her own turf.

We continue this section by discussing various aspects of process management for selected processes within the drugstore.

Feeding the line, that is, ensuring the flow of "things" within the drugstore, is another important process in any assembly line. Any shortage of medication or supplies disrupts the operation and hence has an immediate impact on service time and risks of error. The voice of the customer translates here into standards for the number of shortages, frequency of substitution of medication, or excess inventory. The major challenge involved in this process is that of managing the trade-offs between the cost of shortages and the cost of excess inventory. Indeed, most medications are expensive and have a limited shelf life. They must (imperatively) be discarded past their sell date. Quantity discounts must also be factored into the reordering policy.

Ensuring the quality of pharmaceutical procedures rests primarily with the pharmacist himself, with a risk of stiff professional sanctions in case of malpractice. The role of the owner in that respect is to create a work environment (including processes, technology, and installations) conducive to clinical quality. In the eye of the customer, however, quality goes beyond that and includes, as previously discussed, such factors as convenience, empathy, and speed. Since many processes have an impact on quality (refer to those shown in Figure 6.7, for instance), the process of ensuring quality involves the coordination of the design and operations of these processes so that they perform consistently with GYD's quality standards (such as those shown in Figure 6.9).

Ensuring, for instance, that such processes as preparing sterile products, keeping traceability of every procedure to a specific pharmacist, and never exceeding the prescribed maximum ratio of pharmacists to technicians on the premises are appropriate, understood, implemented, updated, and monitored are all part of the quality assurance system. It is particularly challenging for Ida to manage the many interfaces (and the corresponding potential for friction and conflict) between the clinical responsibilities of the pharmacists and her overall responsibility for quality, productivity, and profitability. In the case of over-the-counter (OTC) medications, for instance (which do not require prescriptions), it is important but difficult for the pharmacist to reach an objective decision to deny a medication to a client who is using too much of it. The fact that denying the medication is clearly not in the pharmacy's immediate financial interest may (consciously or not) distort the professional's judgment.

In a recent incident, the general manager (not a pharmacist) instructed an idle technician to enter the renewals of several expired prescriptions to save time when the (quasi-automatic) prescription renewals came in. A conflict ensued when the pharmacist in charge rescinded the order on the basis that it created a risk of error, that is, serving a medication without a prescription in force.

In concluding this section, four more processes are worth mentioning: recruiting, training, posting, and dispatching technicians. Some technical tasks, such as preparing medication, are very repetitive and can be boring for someone who constantly needs new challenges. Boredom leads to lack of focus on the task, which in turn leads to mistakes, disturbances in the assembly line, conflicts, and stress for all involved. Other tasks involve face-to-face contacts, many of them with disabled, sick, or otherwise impaired persons. Unless Ida recruits technicians with the right disposition, no amount of training or coaching will succeed in avoiding the negative cycle triggered by stress on the part of the technician, generating frustration on the part of the patient, and producing ripple effects all along the assembly line. As much as the pharmacist on duty must be alert and ready to respond to shifts and drifts in the process, he (and the general manager) must be alert to the level of stress of the technicians and ready to respond by bringing in reinforcement, switching technicians around, or taking other appropriate measures. If competitors are indeed on the lookout to win over a pharmacist, they would like nothing better than for him to bring one or two disgruntled technicians with him.

The foregoing discussion illustrates the notion, introduced in Chapter 3, that an organization is a complex web of interconnected and interacting processes. Light but effective feedback and control loops are needed to make these processes, and thus the organization, manageable. Constant awareness of GYD's dual positioning in the market and in the labor market, of GYD's own and competitors' strengths and weaknesses, and of operations strategy is essential to make the right trade-offs. The opportunity to outsource or offshore some processes, as discussed in Chapter 4, must also be regularly revisited, as the parameters that guide this decision are constantly evolving. Does it make sense for the pharmacy to perform home delivery, accounting, data backup, preparation of sterile products, or even recruitment itself? Without this ability to translate global thinking into coherent local action, operations is at best strategically neutral and can never be the strategic weapon that it should be.

6.3.5 Managing the Intake Process in Youth Protection

Viewing Video 6.3 at this point will provide the reader with a better understanding of the notion of supply chain, as it applies to complex services, before reading on. At GYD, a single professional controls a process where all other players are technicians. In many PSOs, however, several professionals, often from different disciplines, interact with one another. Midtown Child Protective Services, discussed in Chapter 4, is a case in point. We first revisit the case in general and the intake process in particular, and then focus on how we could use statistical process control (SPC) in that context.

6.3.5.1 *Understanding the Dynamics of the Process*

Figure 6.11 shows a high-level representation of the intake process for youth protection, of which Midtown CPS (Box 4.2) assumes the front end. A macro map of

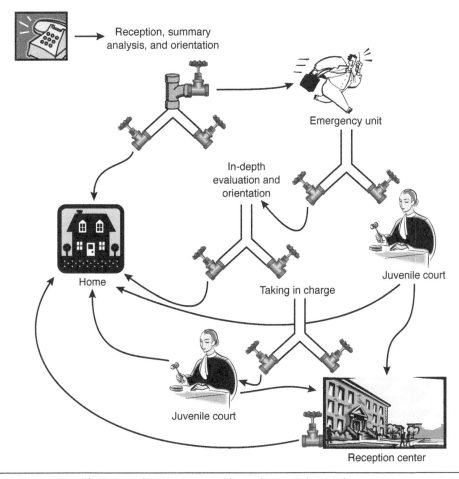

Reception, summary
analysis, and orientation

Emergency unit

In-depth
evaluation and
orientation

Home

Juvenile court

Taking in charge

Juvenile court

Reception center

Figure 6.11 Simplified view of intake process (dispatch process) at Midtown CPS.

that process would show that there are many players involved, belonging to several different organizations, including the Midtown report reception department (described in Box 4.2), Midtown evaluation department, the police department, reception centers, juvenile court, Midtown legal department, and lawyers for the various parties. The process is similar to that shown in Figure 5.4, presenting a generic professional dispatch process. It consists of a series of filters involving various categories of professionals making diagnostic, orientation, and therapeutic decisions. A social worker typically receives the call (as described in Box 4.2). After validating, completing, and assessing the information ("receiving" for short), he may send an emergency team (or the police), refer it to his colleagues for detailed evaluation the next day, or decide that no further action is required. The emergency team may resolve the immediate crisis and refer the child for further evaluation, or they may have to go to court within the next 48 hours should they decide to remove the child from his home. Taking the children in charge may be consensual or may again involve the court.

While receiving involves only two to three hours of work, detailed evaluation requires about five days of work (typically spread over a 30-day period). Going to court involves about the same amount of time for the social worker, plus another five days for a lawyer. Children taken in charge by the system may require years of assistance and are a huge drain on its resources. Since the number of children the reception center can deal with at any given time is limited, its "throughput" depends on the rate at which it can reintegrate them into their family or into the community (foster family or relatives). The mission of the intake process at Midtown CPS is to allocate available protection resources among needy children, through its orientation decisions, to ensure that each of them gets the best short- and long-term protection possible. Accuracy (sound professional judgment), consistency (always using the same criteria, in the same way), and speed of decision are the priorities of that process. As Sam Alonzo at Midtown CPS is in the process of making a decision about the report he just received, he is mentally comparing available data with process standards (accepted guidelines and standards): "Did I probe enough to get all the information I could from the caller, such as history of problems, current state of the children, and options available? In such a case, should I try to check with at least one other source before making a decision? Have I explored all the possibilities?" We refer to what Sam is doing as "within cycle" process control. It can be performed either by process workers themselves or by a process manager.

Controlling this process is quite a challenge from several perspectives. Even though all players agree that the interest of the child is foremost in all decisions, the specific nature of that interest and of the best decision one can make to promote it are the subject of much debate. The practitioners can make two basic errors:

> Type 1 error: intervene in a situation that does not require it, that is, the child is not at risk

> Type 2 error: decide not to intervene in a situation where the child is truly at risk

Understandably, when in doubt, practitioners tend to err on the safe side. This is a major fail point in the process. This type of defensive practice is self-defeating. Because the system is resource bound, an excessively liberal reception process (a wide-tipped filter) means that the downstream process will become congested, resulting in waiting lines, more cursory interventions, or both. If the receiving practitioner, for instance, does not exert her critical professional judgment to the fullest, the reception process fails in its contribution to the mission and becomes redundant. It would be better to do away with the process and replace it with a mere answering service that would pass all the calls on directly to an evaluator ("in-depth evaluation and orientation" in Figure 6.11).

The valves in Figure 6.11 represent some of the control points in that process. Tightening or loosening the orientation criteria at various decision points regulates the flows through the process. The pipeline metaphor ends there, however, as this is obviously much more complex than turning a knob, and the personal consequences on the child and his family can be dramatic, traumatic, and life changing. Merely sending the signal to receiving professionals that the emergency team is overloaded does not guarantee results. Senior professionals are individually "calibrated" through their training and experience. They are very conscious of the professional and personal risks they are taking by turning down a concerned citizen's request to help a child the citizen believes to be in need of protection.

Extensive coaching and support are needed to help practitioners develop risk management strategies, such as asking a relative to take in the child for the night. Adding resources at bottleneck points is an alternative, but even if such resources are available, they may end up merely deferring the problem to the next process (evaluation or taking in charge). Substantial delays may also be involved in implementing any step the manager may select. Thus, by the time the solution comes online, it may be a response to yesterday's problem and only contribute to making today's problem worse.

6.3.5.2 *Controlling and Improving the Process*

The process manager must use data to assess how well the process is functioning and to decide on control measures. If the social emergency center handles an average of 100 reports a week, say, he will want to monitor such indicators as how many times children are removed from their home, how many times police are called in, or how long it takes before any action is taken. He will also check with downstream processes, such as those of the reception center or the police department, to see if they have noticed any significant change, trend, or pattern in the inputs that they have been receiving (their inputs, such as a child to take in for the night, or instructions to investigate a report, are the output of the social emergency process). However, what constitutes a significant shift or drift in the process? Is an increase from 8% to 10% of calls necessitating police intervention "significant"? Is the "feeling" of the specialized educator at the reception center that he is increasingly dealing with "heavy" cases significant? A wrong answer to these questions can be very disruptive.

Concluding that practitioners are increasingly turning to police for support may lead the process manager to take action to bring back the drifting process to a stable state, assuming that it was stable in the first place. Such action may include training or the obligation to obtain the approval of a senior practitioner before calling the police. If the conclusion was unwarranted—that is, based on a misinterpretation of the data, which really showed only a random increase that did not reflect any fundamental change in the process—then the corrective action taken may create instability in a process that was stable. The Hippocratic precept "first do no harm" applies very well to process controllers. Interpreting variations in the light of their statistical as well as their practical significance thus becomes essential to avoid being unduly swayed by the emotions and the pressure of the moment.

To illustrate how variation data can be used in this context, let us focus on the time that elapses between the moment a call is received by the receptionist and the moment a practitioner returns the call (henceforth "response time"). Protecting is about reducing risks. Low risk is critical to customer satisfaction (CTS). Response time is a technical characteristic of the process that correlates directly with risk to the child. Indeed, this initial wait time may be a period of dire vulnerability for a child. Let us assume that following the reception of several complaints, refuted by the practitioners, the process manager decides to get to the bottom of the issue. He first explores the possibility of measuring response time. Since no measurement system is in place, and there is no possibility to automate it in the near future (budget constraints), measurement would have to be manual. Practitioners perceive the request for measurement as an effort on the part of management to control their professional practice, and they resist it. In addition, since they are unionized, they resist the pressure to work harder. A compromise solution is reached whereby one practitioner will randomly (warning bell on the computer) measure the response time to one call per day.

The manager plots the data so gathered on a chart (see the first 50 data points in Figure 6.12). He then calculates the mean (heavy line) and the control limits (UCL, LCL—dotted lines), setting them at 3σ on either side of the observed mean (while setting the minimum at zero, however), and plots them on the graph. Since one observation lies beyond the control limits, he concludes that the process is out of control. He also notices a pattern in the data: every seven days (on Sundays) the response time jumps markedly, only to fall back the next day. The one point that is out of control is also a Sunday. As it turns out, that Sunday was Easter Sunday.

Concluding that the process is out of control means that a special cause (or special causes) is at work, influencing the performance of the process and throwing it off its normal performance. Normal process variation is caused by the joint action of a host of random variables (general causes). Concluding that the process is in control (or stable) means that the process is performing normally (not necessarily to our satisfaction, but as well as it normally does), that is, it does not need fixing, and we should leave it alone unless we mean to launch an improvement drive (see Chapter 9). Thus, the manager finds objective support for his decision to correct the process. Statistics tells us that the odds of making a type I error are very low (probably less than one in a thousand in this case, having observed two phenomena that would be very unlikely to occur in a process under control).

While we defer a detailed discussion of process improvement to Chapter 9, let us assume that the manager concludes that the department is understaffed on Sundays and overstaffed on Mondays. In a staff meeting, he announces new

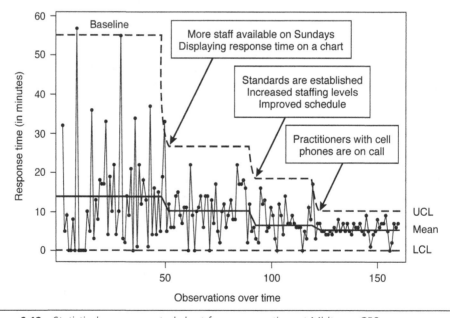

Figure 6.12 Statistical process control chart for response time at Midtown CPS.

scheduling rules and arranges for the daily response time to be posted on a chart the next day, for everyone to see. One can see the effect of these changes in Figure 6.12 (data points 50 to 90). Variation is reduced considerably, as illustrated by a tighter "voice of the process" (the range between UCL and LCL), and the mean response time reduced by three minutes (see the heavy line) to 10 minutes. At the end of this period the manager sets (after long discussions with all stakeholders) the following service standards (there were none before): no call should have to wait more than 30 minutes for a response, and the average service time on any day should not exceed 20 minutes. To meet these new standards, he increases staffing levels and further refines the scheduling system. Data points 90 to 120 show the effect of these new corrective measures. The last data points (120–150) show what happened when a new system was set up whereby additional practitioners were equipped with cell phones and asked to be "on call" (with compensation) during selected "time buckets" during the week. Appendix A provides more specific instructions about building and using SPC charts (see Gruska and Kymal [2006] for examples of practical applications).

Finally, the process manager must take into consideration a number of vulnerabilities and fail points of the process:

- The receiving job is very stressful, very much like that of the doctor in the emergency ward. Whereas the latter can rely on some objective data, the former is always threading shades of gray, interpreting words, tones of voices, and silences from an unknown interlocutor. Managers must be very careful in any attempt to manipulate the intake "valve" not to place additional pressure on the practitioners. It is very important to the job concept that they continually feel supported rather than blamed by management when problems occur.

- As in any profession, there are different philosophies regarding when a withdrawal of children from their home is indicated. One school of thought, for instance, suggests that a family crisis is an opportunity, as long as the intervention is quick thereafter, to understand and resolve problems in dysfunctional families, and that withdrawal at that time may create a chasm that will be very hard, long, and costly to bridge. Social workers work on improving the social dynamics within the family. Special education teachers work to help dysfunctional children (and sometimes families) structure their lives and relearn basic personal, family, and social skills. While the two aforementioned professions are trained to help people, criminologists are clearly oriented toward crime prevention and protection within a legal context. The intake "assembly line" is quite likely to have a criminologist making a decision to withdraw a child from his home and transfer him to a social worker for evaluation, who in turn may transfer him to a special education teacher in a reception center. Since smooth transitions and continuity of interventions are important determinants of success, managing these interfaces, resolving conflicts, and fostering the emergence of a common intervention philosophy are critical roles of the process manager.

- The legal system responds to a completely different logic than the therapeutic and assistance system described earlier. Society, the child protection service, the reception center, the parents, and the children are parties, represented by lawyers, with rights and obligations under the law.

The social workers, medical doctors, psychiatrists, and psychologists are expert witnesses to be cross-examined by lawyers. The judge is a referee whose decisions are enforceable. The reaction of the helping professional when immersed in that system is rather like that of magnesium in water. The consequences for the children, the parents, and the establishment of a productive relationship with the caregivers are very important. Thus, of all the interfaces and fail points to manage, deciding when to go to court and how to do it is a critical one.

To bridge the gaps between the different steps in the process and between the various professions, team-based approaches are very useful. A multistage, multi-profession process team, for instance, including a senior representative from each stage in the process, coordinated by the process manager, can address short- and medium-term process issues and determine the scope of process improvement initiatives. Personalized transfers between process stages, particularly between evaluation and taking in charge, can also be established to ensure a smooth transition. The joint preparation by all involved (during the evaluation stage) of an individualized service plan for the child plays a similar role.

6.3.6 A Job Shop—Capacity Management at QKM

The challenges involved in managing capacity at Quality Knowledge Management (QKM) (refer back to Box 5.1 and Figure 5.2) are quite different, mainly because QKM is a job shop and not an assembly line like GYD or a flow shop (that is, a process involving several paths always flowing in the same direction) like Midtown. A job shop is characterized by jumbled flows. If one were to map the "sell and provide services" process at QKM, using the consultants as players, one would see that depending on the job at hand, consultants may be called on at different points in the proposal or in the execution phase, and that the extent of their involvement would vary considerably from one job to the next. In addition, different consultants can perform the same work, albeit not necessarily with the same quality or within the same time frame. Thus, depending on uncontrollable arrivals of requests for proposals (RFPs) with different scopes and schedules, on the (controllable) way proposals are written, on the (partly controllable) success rate, and on the (partly controllable) rate of progress of the jobs, bottlenecks will appear and move around in complex and unpredictable ways.

Bottlenecks involve delays in the work and quality problems (with the customer complaints that these entail). These create stress on the resources at the bottleneck and slack for the other resources waiting downstream. In other words, bottlenecks are bad for business. The responsibility for managing capacity falls on the managing partner. A FAST diagram of that process would typically include the following functions:

- Determine current capacity utilization and identify bottlenecks

- Forecast future demand (by type of resources)

- Forecast future capacity available (by type of resources)

- Identify imbalances and potential bottlenecks

- Explore options to correct the situation

- Negotiate solutions with all involved (partners, managers, consultants, and clients)

- Implement solutions and follow up

Typical actions that the partner can take include the following:

- Negotiate with clients to accept a delay or a substitute resource (if available)

- Speed up some contracts by adding resources

- Change the criteria used to make bidding decisions (go/no-go, resources involved, markup applied)

- Hire subcontractors (such as freelance consultants or selected "coopetitors")

- Slow down the pace of work, even if client objects

- Advertise, contact old customers, organize free seminars, and find new ways to drum up new business

- Hire additional consultants (longer term) or lay off employees, temporarily or permanently

- Outsourcing to or partnering with another company

- Find ways to increase productivity (longer term)

Appendix A discusses how the managing partner could use SPC to control the process (see Chapter 12 for further illustration of SPC).

6.4 SUMMARY

Variation is the enemy of value but the friend of those who want to improve the process. In the measurement and analysis of variation lies the key to decoding the dynamics of a process (the DNA of the process), and thus to identifying its fail points and its leverage points. Variation analysis is the key to process learning, and hence to organizational learning. Whoever wants to control a process must understand it from a strategic perspective and understand the external and internal environments in which it evolves. By making the process visible, detailed process mapping is an important tool that helps in the identification of the underlying variables.

A control system receives feedback on the important performance variables of the process, compares the values obtained with carefully set standards, decides whether corrective action is required, selects appropriate actions, implements them, and monitors results, thus triggering new control cycles as required. In professional services the professional must be part of the control system. The process managers must pay particular attention to the autonomy of the professionals and to the interfaces between professionals, between professionals and technicians, and between professionals and management.

SPC brings the science of statistics to bear on the analysis of variation and on the decision of whether to intervene. It consists of control charts that make variation visible and decision rules to facilitate and make more objective the decision about whether a special cause of variation is at work.

EXERCISES

6.1 Systems View of Your Business

Refer back to the work you did in the end-of-chapter exercises in Chapter 4, and particularly to the two projects you selected in exercise 4.4c. Prepare a systems view of these processes (similar to that shown in Figure 6.8), specifying the major variables that influence these processes in the internal and external environments.

6.2 Control System

a. Identify potential feedback variables, standards, and corrective action that you could take to control the process mapped in exercise 3.6. Refer to Figure 6.11 for an example.

b. Interview the manager or managers who act as process manager for that process. First ask them how they manage the process. Then show them the diagram you prepared in part (a) of this exercise and discuss the differences (a series of directed "why" and "why not" follow-up questions generally yields useful insight into ways to improve process control).

6.3 Statistical Process Control

a. Review your answer to exercise 6.2 and select a metric (pick a continuous variable, such as elapsed time or cost) from the feedback variables that you feel is particularly important and has not been used (at least not systematically) so far. Review the measurement system used for that variable. If it is inappropriate or if none exists, design and implement one. Gather at least 30 data points, either by using historical data (if valid data are available), measuring the next 30 units, or designing a convenient sampling system.

b. Build a control chart for that process, such as that shown in Figure 6.13 (heavy lines and dotted lines only), following the procedures described in Appendix A and Figure 6.13.

c. Apply the four decision rules presented in Appendix A and Figure 6.14. Draw your conclusions. Share the chart and your conclusions with managers involved in the process and, if appropriate considering the work environment and climate, with the employees.

d. Use this control chart to control the process over a significant period (this may vary depending on the cycle time and the volume), marking the dots on the chart and interpreting the results. Whenever you conclude that the process is out of control, investigate to find the special cause at work. See if you can bring (or keep) the process under control.

e. Set a standard for that metric and draw the line (or lines) in the control chart (such as the heavy dotted line in Figure 6.13). Draw your conclusions on process capability.

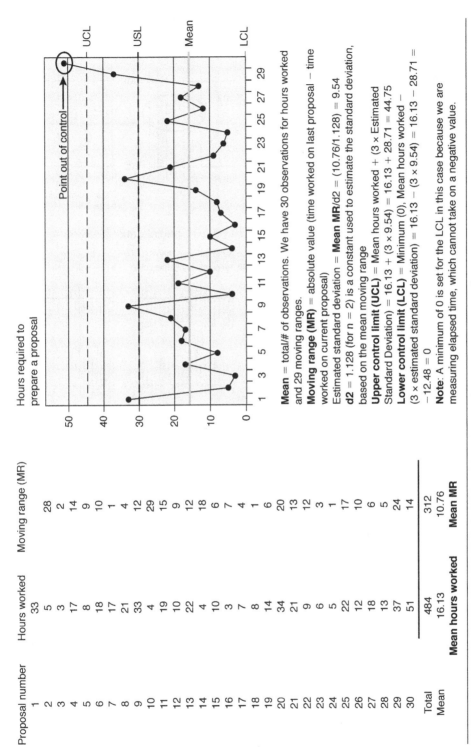

Proposal number	Hours worked	Moving range (MR)
1	33	
2	5	28
3	3	2
4	17	14
5	8	9
6	18	10
7	17	1
8	21	4
9	33	12
10	4	29
11	19	15
12	10	9
13	22	12
14	4	18
15	10	6
16	3	7
17	7	4
18	8	1
19	14	6
20	34	20
21	21	13
22	9	12
23	6	3
24	5	1
25	22	17
26	12	10
27	18	6
28	13	5
29	37	24
30	51	14
Total	484	312
Mean	16.13	10.76
	Mean hours worked	**Mean MR**

Mean = total/# of observations. We have 30 observations for hours worked and 29 moving ranges.

Moving range (MR) = absolute value (time worked on last proposal − time worked on current proposal)

Estimated standard deviation = **Mean MR**/d2 = (10.76/1.128) = 9.54

d2 = 1.128 (for n = 2) is a constant used to estimate the standard deviation, based on the mean moving range

Upper control limit (UCL) = Mean hours worked + (3 × Estimated Standard Deviation) = 16.13 + (3 × 9.54) = 16.13 + 28.71 = 44.75

Lower control limit (LCL) = Minimum (0), Mean hours worked − (3 × estimated standard deviation) = 16.13 − (3 × 9.54) = 16.13 − 28.71 = −12.48 = 0

Note: A minimum of 0 is set for the LCL in this case because we are measuring elapsed time, which cannot take on a negative value.

Figure 6.13 Statistical process control chart at QKM: time required to prepare a proposal.

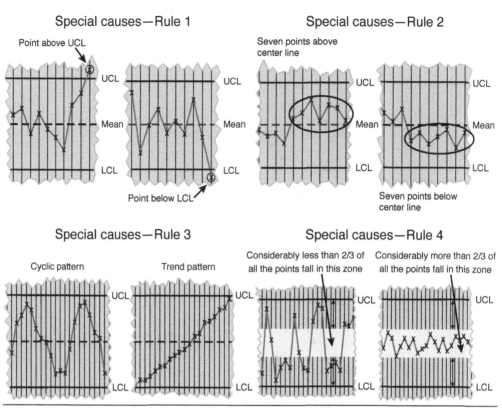

Figure 6.14 Illustration of the use of an SPC chart to decide on the presence of "special causes": four decision rules.

Source: NHS Institute for Innovation and Improvement, posted on the web February 17, 2005.

6.4 Professional Considerations in Process Control

a. Review your answer to exercise 5.2 dealing with the professional service experience. Identify legitimate sources of concern that arise as you try to implement this type of process control in the organization. Make sure you separate the issues that refer to the relationships between various groups of professionals and technicians from those that relate to management–employee relationships.

b. Explore strategies to circumvent these problems, such as team-based approaches, peer groups, and auto control.

NOTE

1. $(45 - 40)/6 = 5/6 = 0.83$. Reading at 0.8 in Table 6.3, we find 0.2118554, or 0.212. We conclude that the probability associated with the range $(40 - 45)$ is 0.288 $(.5 - .212)$, since the curve is symmetrical, and thus that the area associated with the range $(35, 45)$ is twice that value, or 0.576.

7

Connecting Value to Processes: The Techniques

There ain't no right way to do the wrong thing.

—Toby Keith in the country song "Ain't No Right Way"

Deciding on the right thing to do requires the identification of the processes you should focus on to provide superior value and create competitive advantage. Effective change happens in bite-size chunks, but you have to ensure coherence among the pieces. To achieve the proper scope, an organization must determine where a project fits into the global picture and pick the right part of the right process to improve. We present a project scoping methodology to do just that.

In the previous chapters we discussed the notions of value, operations strategy, coherence, and processes. We now turn to methodologies and techniques that can help us connect these elements together. The major technique we use here is adapted from quality function deployment (QFD). It provides a structured approach for translating customer needs into service offerings (or features), translating service features into technical characteristics (metrics), and deploying the latter into processes. It will take us from 10,000 meters to 1000 meters (so to speak); that is, it allows for the identification (at a high level) of the processes on which the organization should focus. Video 7.1 (see Figure 7.1) presents a high-level view of how this should be done.

We then discuss (7.4) the central notion of coherence between operations strategy and operations, and more specifically the pivotal role that process mission plays in that regard. The last section (7.5) presents a detailed 10-step methodology for operationally defining the scope of a process. In Chapter 10, we will take it from 1000 meters to ground level, carrying on with the FPA example started in Chapter 5 and continued in the first part of this chapter.

This material is placed in its logical sequence in the book. However, the methodology presented herein is quite demanding in terms of executives' time. The latter will be willing to make such an investment only if they believe in the approach and are solidly behind it. That is generally not the case unless they have seen it at work and felt its benefits (we discuss this in Chapter 11 in connection with learning maturity level). If your organization is not at this stage, we recommend that you skip the first part of the chapter and go directly to project scoping in section 7.5.

7.1 Scoping process improvement in complex services
This video is a practical and technical extension of the airport video, introducing basic process notions. It shows how these notions can be applied in the more abstract business world of information-based intangible processes. The input here is not a person or a piece of luggage, but a request for proposal, and the output is a legally binding proposal. The scoping phase is critical to the success of any process improvement or process design project. The case of a software developer is used to illustrate the methodology.

Key concepts: Project scoping, problem statement, process mission, efficiency, effectiveness

Techniques: SITOC, FAST, SMART problem statement, Big Y/small y, E&E diagram, influence diagram

Figure 7.1   Video associated with Chapter 7.

7.1 SELECTING THE RIGHT PROCESS

Many trends in management thought and business practice stem from the idea of doing the right thing right (see sections 3.4.3 and 5.3). The "doing" part refers to processes. "Doing the right thing" has to do with focusing on the processes most likely to create strategic advantage. "Doing things right" refers to optimizing the selected process. Studies aimed at demonstrating the long-term benefits of total quality management, business process improvement, reengineering, and other related process-based strategic business initiatives have yielded disappointing results. This may be the fate that awaits more recent initiatives in this field unless the missing link is found. When faced with having to explain this poor showing, few if any authors fault the approaches and tools used for process improvement. Most attribute it to the fact that companies are simply picking the wrong processes for improvement. That is to say, the process improvement drive in many organizations only succeeded in doing the wrong thing right. Whereas the benefits of this may still outweigh its cost, it certainly does not amount to the strategic breakthrough that led them to embrace the initiative. Without a methodology to guide them in the search—particularly in the initial search—for the vital few processes on which they must focus, no process-based strategic initiative will ever be truly strategic, and will thus be short-lived.

Organizations pick the wrong process because they do not know:

- What processes are and why they should bother to find out

- How processes are connected to creating value and beating the competition

- What their processes are and how well they are performing

Let us now turn to a methodology designed to address these problems. It proceeds in six steps:

1. Review and clarify positioning and operations strategy

2. Establish customer needs and wants

3. Define a service package (or verify the coverage of current service package)

4. Identify key metrics

5. Identify processes and evaluate their impact on key metrics

6. Select processes based on salience and performance

It is related to Figure 4.3, which shows the logical connection between processes (supplier's, support, value-enabling, and value-adding), the service package (offerings), the benefit package, positioning, and competitive advantage in the marketplace. In Figure 4.3 value is created and delivered from the left-hand side to the right-hand side. Hence, the methodology used to identify processes for improvement proceeds in the opposite direction, that is, from the customer inward.

The first four steps are already explained and illustrated in section 5.5.3 (with the corresponding box and figures), where we present and discuss the FPA short case. We'll take it from there. The case has not been "engineered" so that everything would fall in place neatly. It is as messy as real life can be. No specialized knowledge of finance and investment is required to understand the analysis that is made of the case.

7.2 IDENTIFY PROCESSES AND EVALUATE THEIR IMPACT ON KEY METRICS

We have not said much so far about what it is that Financial Planning Associates (FPA) actually has to do. That is our next step: identifying the processes and rating them in terms of importance to the customer. Most organizations have an organizational chart, but very few know what their processes are, let alone how they relate to one another. That is the role of a process model, such as that of APQC discussed in Chapter 3. In section 3.4.3 we identified three categories of processes according to the role they play in value creation: value-adding, value-enabling, and support. In Chapter 5 we added the upstream processes of partners and suppliers.

The methodology consists of first prioritizing value-adding processes. We do this below by looking at each process's impact on the metrics identified earlier. We can then assess the importance of upstream processes by looking at their impact on the value-adding processes. We will limit ourselves here to a selection of value-adding and other processes to illustrate the technique.

Value-adding processes include everything FPA does that contributes directly to meeting the goal of being better than its competitors at helping people in the targeted market segment achieve peace of mind about their financial future. How does FPA do that? By getting the right FPs, attracting the right customers, preparing good financial plans, implementing them well, and managing the relationship with its customers. We can break down each of these functions in turn, thus producing a FAST diagram (see Chapter 3), which we show in Figure 7.2. The diagram shows only value-adding processes.

Which of those 22 value-adding processes (level 2 processes in Figure 7.2) are the most important for clients? Those processes that have a strong impact on important metrics. We know from Figure 5.8 what those metrics are, as well as their importance (weights) for clients. That leaves FPA with the task of establishing the impact of each process on each metric, using an impact matrix.

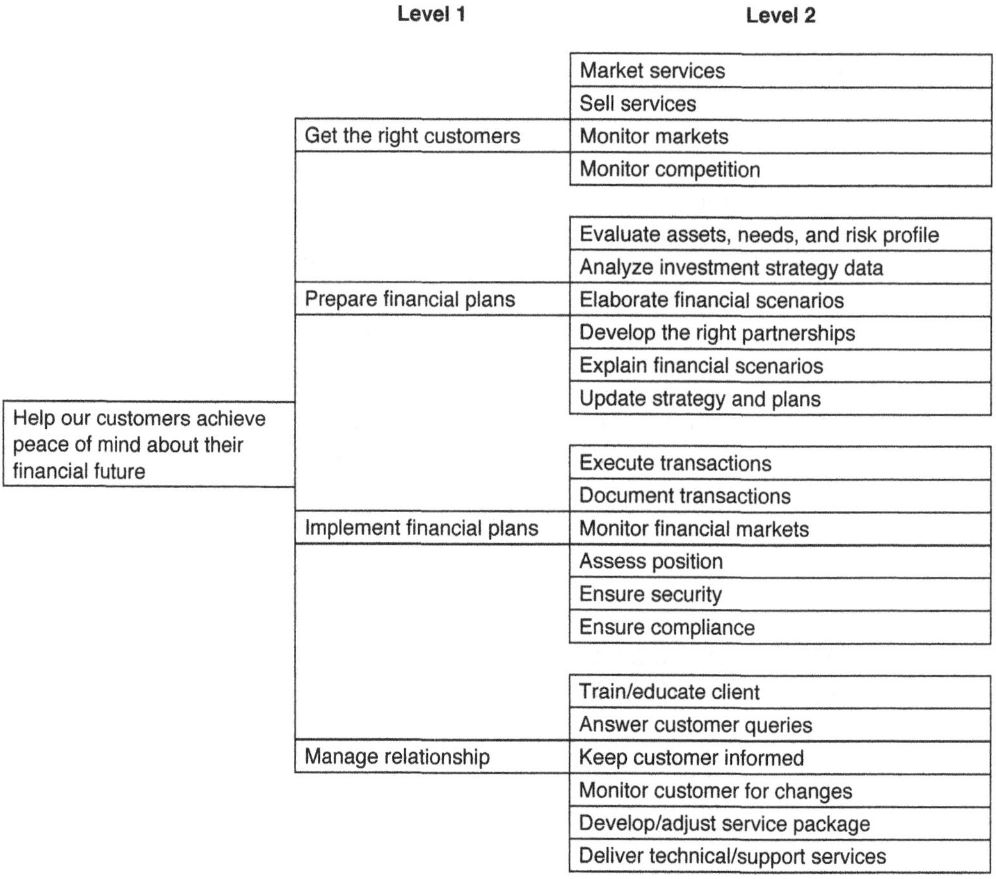

Level 1	Level 2
	Market services
	Sell services
Get the right customers	Monitor markets
	Monitor competition
	Evaluate assets, needs, and risk profile
	Analyze investment strategy data
Prepare financial plans	Elaborate financial scenarios
	Develop the right partnerships
	Explain financial scenarios
	Update strategy and plans
	Execute transactions
	Document transactions
Implement financial plans	Monitor financial markets
	Assess position
	Ensure security
	Ensure compliance
	Train/educate client
	Answer customer queries
Manage relationship	Keep customer informed
	Monitor customer for changes
	Develop/adjust service package
	Deliver technical/support services

(Left-side label spanning: Help our customers achieve peace of mind about their financial future)

Figure 7.2 Partial FAST diagram for FPA.

The technique we use is adapted from quality function deployment (QFD)—the *house of quality,* which is just such a matrix. The top row of the matrix in Figure 7.3 contains the initial list of processes whose importance we want to evaluate (some, the value-adding processes, can be found in Figure 7.2). On the left-hand side are the metrics from Figure 5.8, and their importance rating is shown on the right-hand side. The column of arrows next to the metric indicates whether this is a "more is better" or "less is better" indicator. The "target" sign in that column is a "just enough" indicator: revising the plan too often or not often enough is bad. We use the body of the table to correlate each process with each metric, that is, specifying to what extent each process has an impact on each metric. We use four possible correlation values: blank squares, triangles, circles, and bull's-eyes, standing respectively for zero, weak ("one point"), average ("three point"), and strong ("nine point") correlation between the process and the corresponding metric (no triangles, or weak correlation, are shown in the matrix). *Develop courses,* for instance, has a strong impact on the *time required* by the customer to learn the system but none at all on the *number of golf games* the FP plays with his clients.

The best way to build this matrix is for a team to use sticky notes for column and row headings, and sticky colored dots for correlation ("traffic light" color coding works well: a red dot is a bull's-eye, a yellow dot is a circle, and a green dot is a

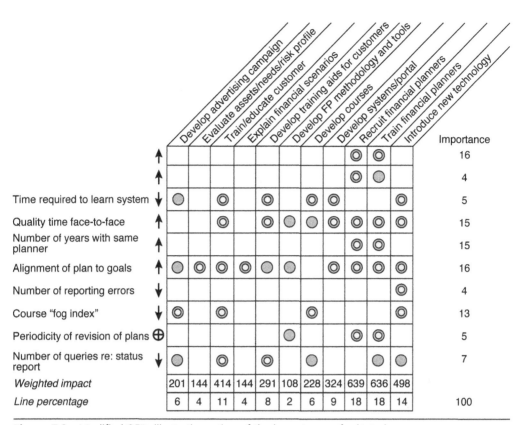

		Develop advertising campaign	Evaluate assets/needs/risk profile	Train/educate customer	Explain financial scenarios	Develop training aids for customers	Develop FP methodology and tools	Develop courses	Develop systems/portal	Recruit financial planners	Train financial planners	Introduce new technology	Importance
	↑								◎	◎			16
	↑								◎	◉			4
Time required to learn system	↓	○		◎		◎		◎	◎			◎	5
Quality time face-to-face	↑		◎		◎	◉	◎	◎	◎	◎	◎		15
Number of years with same planner	↑								◎	◎			15
Alignment of plan to goals	↑	○	◎	◎	◎	◉	◉		◎	◎	◎	◎	16
Number of reporting errors	↓									◎			4
Course "fog index"	↓	◎		◎			◉			◎			13
Periodicity of revision of plans	⊕				◉				◎	◎			5
Number of queries re: status report	↓	○		◎		◎		◉		◉	◎		7
Weighted impact		201	144	414	144	291	108	228	324	639	636	498	
Line percentage		6	4	11	4	8	2	6	9	18	18	14	100

Figure 7.3 Modified QFD: illustrative rating of the importance of selected processes.

triangle). Sticky notes can be moved around, discarded, and replaced—a flexibility that is essential, as reaching consensus is an iterative process.

We can then assess the relative importance of each process. An important process is one that strongly impacts important metrics, that is, having bull's-eye symbols in rows corresponding to important metrics. Thus, we can calculate importance factors (weights) for each process as the vertical cross-product of the correlation with every metric multiplied by the importance weight of that need, using the customary QFD approach of assigning weights of one for a weak correlation, three for an average correlation, and nine for a strong correlation. For example, the weight of *develop advertising campaign* is calculated as (3×5) + (3×16) + (9×13) + (3×7), or 201. We show this weight on the second row from the bottom of the matrix. We show the weight as a percentage of the row total in the last row (6% in this case). This relative weight is easier to interpret than an absolute number. According to Figure 7.3, *recruit financial planners*, for example, is more important than *develop advertising campaign* by a factor of three (18% to 6%).

Figure 7.4 shows the ordered list of processes. The top three processes together represent 50% of the impact. This matrix can be seen as a filter, with a list of processes entering on top, and the most important processes coming out at the bottom (the importance weighting). Some backtracking is in order here to gain better insight into the methodology. The three most important customer needs (Table 5.1) together are assigned 50% of the weight. Thus, they weigh heavily in the determination

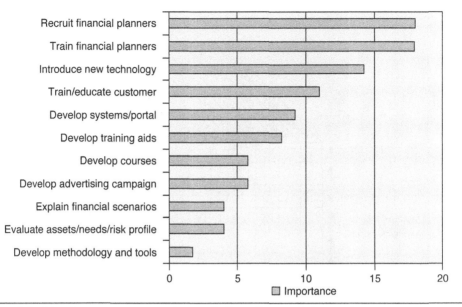

Figure 7.4　Most important processes in sample (from Figure 7.3, last row).

that the three most important features are the ones shown at the top of Figure 5.7, together representing 52% of the overall impact. They in turn guide us toward the top three metrics in Figure 5.8 (46% of impact). The top three processes are thus identified in Figure 7.4 as a result of a customer-in or market-in approach, following the step-by-step deployment from market to needs, to features, to metrics, and to processes.

Note that our results are somewhat biased because of the shortcut we have taken. Indeed, the processes we have selected are a mixture of value-adding and value-enabling processes. They are related to one another: "develop courses" and "develop training aids," for instance, are enablers of the "train customer" process. Hence, they are more important than their weight in Figure 7.4 indicates. In practice, however, if FPA were to select "train customer" for improvement (or design), those two enablers would most certainly be considered to be in scope.

7.3　SELECT PROCESSES ON THE BASIS OF SALIENCE AND PERFORMANCE

Should we conclude from the preceding analysis that we should focus our design and improvement dollar on these processes? Not necessarily. As important as a process may be in meeting customer needs, it is but one criterion in deciding which processes to improve. We must consider two other factors: the strategic impact of the processes and their current performance.

7.3.1　Assessing the Strategic Impact of Processes

Any company has four generic stakeholders: customers, employees, shareholders, and the community. We have focused on customer satisfaction because it is central to the satisfaction of the other stakeholders. However, unless it provides personal value to employees, economic value to shareholders, and social value to the community, the company may not be viable over the long haul. The way to address the specific concerns of these stakeholders is through the company's strategic plan. This is the company's game plan for beating the competition. It typically identifies a small number of (defensive or offensive) key strategic issues. These issues may be related to any or all stakeholders. In the case of FPA, the list of issues identified[1] includes the following:

- Respond to our major competitor's recent introduction of an advanced next-generation web portal

- Exploit an opportunity—recently created by the bankruptcy of a competitor—in a market niche of wealthy retirees less familiar with financial matters

- Reassure a nervous customer base following recent unsettling market events

- Correct the flaws in our professional practices that were harshly criticized following an inspection by regulatory authorities

- Develop our activities in derivatives[2] to exploit upcoming opportunities in financial markets following a change in regulation, and respond to renascent customer interest

The strategic plan specifies as well that the second and fourth of these issues are by far the most important and that the other three issues are on a par with one another. Thus, the partners agree to assign the former an importance weighting of 35 each and the latter 10 each, out of 100. They use a correlation matrix (not shown) similar to that shown in Figure 7.3 to evaluate the impact of the 11 selected processes on each issue. The middle column, under salience, in Table 7.1 shows the resulting weights (the first column shows the customer importance score, taken from Figure 7.4). For example, the process of explaining financial scenarios to customers has to be reviewed to better address a market segment less comfortable with basic financial notions.[3] This process also plays an important role in reassuring customers about the risks associated with their investments. One issue raised by a regulatory authority was that they had found cases where this had not been done properly. Finally, as derivative products are introduced for the first time in the portfolio of some customers, considerable thinking has to go into how to make sure that they understand the intricacies and implications of these investments.

Thus, explaining financial scenarios, developing a financial planning methodology and tools, and developing systems and portals are three processes that are critical to the implementation of the strategic plan. The latter two, being very broad, would benefit from further division into subprocesses to determine which parts of these processes are vital.

The fact that only one of these processes made it into the top five most important in Figure 7.4 clearly shows that this step addresses a different aspect of process salience. Whereas Figure 7.4 ranks the processes based on their effect on meeting customer needs, this step looks at their contribution to the company's game plan to beat the competition.

We define a salient process as one that has a strong impact on both customers and strategy. Thus, we can create a rough index of salience by adding the customer impact value in Table 7.1. Salience data are plotted in Figure 7.5. *Training financial planners* and *developing systems/portal* are the two most salient processes coming out of this exercise.

Table 7.1 Prioritization of processes based on salience and performance.

	Salience			Performance			
	Importance for customers	Importance for strategy	Salience	Efficiency	Effectiveness	Performance	Priority
Develop advertising campaign	6	8	14	3	1	4	
Evaluate assets/needs/risk profile	4	3	7	1	2	3	
Train/educate customers	11	11	22	3	3	6	2
Explain financial scenarios	4	15	19	2	2	4	2
Develop training aids for customers	8	3	11	5	4	9	
Develop FP methodology and tools	2	15	16	2	3	5	5
Develop courses	6	10	16	5	5	10	
Develop systems/portal	9	15	25	2	4	6	1
Recruit financial planners	18	5	23	3	4	7	4
Train financial planners	18	11	28	5	5	10	
Introduce new technology	14	5	19	4	3	7	

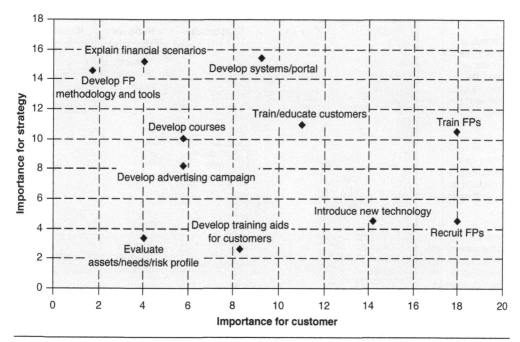

Figure 7.5 Salience diagram: importance of selected processes for the customer and for strategy.

7.3.2 Assessing the Current Performance of Processes

Having identified salient processes, we have yet to answer an important question necessary for us to decide which process we should focus on: How good are the processes currently in place? Clearly, a salient process that is performing at a world-class level should be lower on the priority list than a slightly less prominent process that is in terrible shape. Thus, we must consider both salience and performance.

A high-performance process is one that is both effective and efficient. Effectiveness, as discussed in Chapter 4, consists of producing the desired effect, that is, satisfying or exceeding customer requirements (this is equally true for processes serving internal customers). We can measure this on a five-point scale, ranging from "outputs do not meet any customer requirement" to "outputs exceed most customer requirements" (see scores in Table 7.1). Efficiency is about the best possible use of resources in the pursuit of effectiveness. It too can be measured on a five-point scale, this one ranging from the process being plagued with defects, waste, and long cycle time to being defect-free and having a short cycle time and no waste (see Table 7.1).

We can now construct a diagram (Figure 7.6) using these two dimensions of performance as axes. We can use this diagram to compare and classify processes according to current performance level, from "sick," for any process that scores no higher than a one on either dimension, to "world-class," for a process that scores a five on both dimensions. Categories in between those extremes are labeled fair, satisfactory, and superior. To obtain an overall efficiency and effectiveness (or "performance") score, we simply sum up the effectiveness and efficiency scores. For example, Table 7.1 and Figure 7.6 show that FPA's partners have assigned a score of 10 to the processes for developing courses and training FPs, thereby indicating

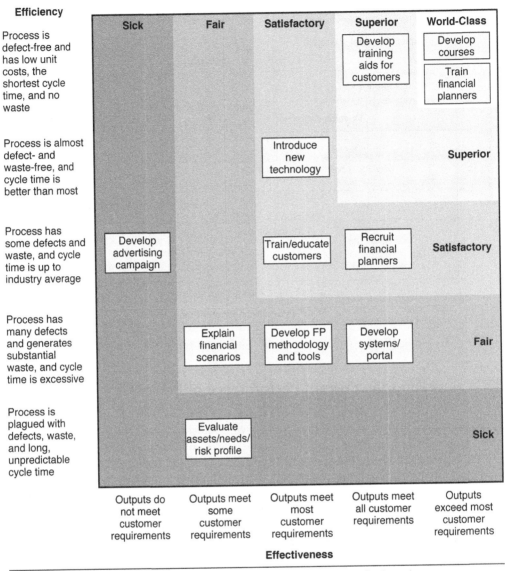

Figure 7.6 Evaluating the performance (efficiency and effectiveness) of selected processes.
Source: Adapted from Tenner and DeToro (1996).

that improving these processes cannot be a priority. On the other hand, evaluating clients' assets/needs/risk profile and developing advertising campaigns are the worst performers and thus badly in need of improvement (or redesign).

One must base process evaluation on data. However, recognizing that few organizations have such data available, they should not wait for them as they set out on their process improvement journey. They should instead direct process owners to plan and launch data-gathering initiatives themselves and perform an initial subjective evaluation. There will be differences of opinion, just as there will be in the preceding exercises. In many ways, bringing these differences to the fore is good for the organization, as it creates a need for data and measurement discipline.

7.3.3 Putting It All Together

Table 7.1 shows the salience score (importance for customer and importance for strategy) and performance score (efficiency and effectiveness) for the 11 selected processes. We plot these data in Figure 7.7. The higher the salience and the lower the performance score, that is, the closer the process is to the lower right-hand corner in Figure 7.7, the higher the process priority. However, FPA can develop its own prioritization rules, such as:

- Eliminate from consideration processes that score below average on both salience criteria

- Eliminate world-class processes (that is, a perfect 10 in the third column)

- Rank remaining processes from the worst performers to the best

- Use common sense and consensus to finalize the ranking

The last column in Table 7.1 shows the top five processes in order of priority, using proximity to the lower right-hand corner of Figure 7.7 as the criterion. The process for developing systems/portal combines strategic importance with a dismal performance. *Explain financial scenarios* and *train/educate customers* display the same pattern, though the latter is more salient, and the former displays lower performance. *Recruit FPs* and *develop FP methodology and tools* thus rank fourth and fifth, respectively.

Figure 7.8 traces the methodological path we have followed so far in this chapter. Starting from FPA's positioning in the market, we deployed FPA's benefit package onto service features, metrics, value-adding processes, and upstream processes using three houses of quality. We identified processes using a FAST diagram. We obtained a rating reflecting the importance of each process for the client.

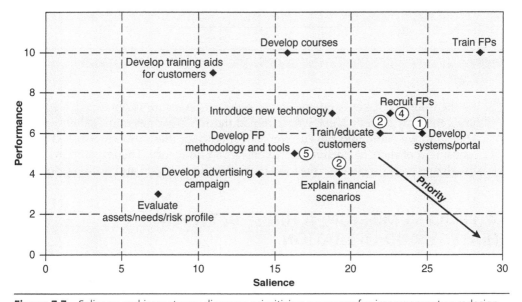

Figure 7.7   Salience and importance diagram: prioritizing processes for improvement or redesign.

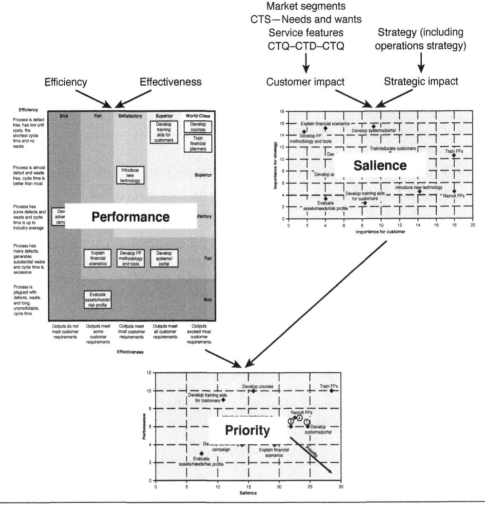

Figure 7.8 Prioritizing processes for improvement: bird's-eye view of the methodology.

We then deployed key strategic issues onto processes, thus obtaining a specific rating for each process. Next, we combined these two ratings into a salience score. After that, we compared the current performance of these processes based on an assessment of their respective effectiveness and efficiency. The last step involved visualizing each process in a performance/salience diagram and setting priorities.

7.4 PROCESS MISSION: A HINGE BETWEEN STRATEGY AND OPERATION

In this journey from a high-level and strategic view to the isolation of specific processes to improve, we need a means to ensure that the reasons for selecting a process are not lost when the time comes to make improvement and design decisions. Further, even though so far in this chapter we have dealt with processes as independent entities, clearly they are not. They receive inputs and provide outputs from and to one another. They must be synchronized and work in harmony. We need a mechanism to make sure that these processes are complementary, do not overlap, and mesh well with one another. In other words, we need a way to promote coherence (see Chapter 4).

The mission statement (see section 3.1.1) is the hinge that ensures the integrity of the "strategy–process design" link and promotes harmony among processes. It is a short statement about why the process exists and what its priorities are. Those who design, modify, and operate the process use it. It helps the process designer make unavoidable trade-offs in process flow, equipment selection, design of facilities, and so on. It ensures that anyone with a mandate to cut costs or otherwise improve the process will not "throw away the baby with the bathwater." Finally, it helps operators in making their own trade-offs as operating problems arise. We obtain it by analyzing its position in the FAST diagram (and process model or process flow diagrams, if available), the metrics it influences, and the key strategic issues to which it relates.

The FAST diagram indicates that *train/educate customers* is part of FPA's way to build a relationship with the client. The QFD matrix (Figure 7.3) shows that a good training process should result in quick learning, quality time between an FP and the client, and better alignment of financial plans to personal goals, and eventually reduce the number of queries made by the client. Table 7.1 shows this process to be an important pillar for strategy as well. It affects the strategic issues of penetrating growing market segments of less knowledgeable investors, reassuring insecure investors following a series of traumas suffered by financial markets, and broadening the market for derivative financial products—an important advantage in an era of reduced yield expectations.

We could thus formulate the mission of the *train/educate customers* process, for example, as follows: "to create for each client a learning environment conducive to personal growth in financial management, and to the parallel evolution (upgrading) of the client's portfolio management system, with FPA as trusted adviser and service provider." Personal growth in financial management means that the client's level of knowledge and comfort with financial matters increases in such a way that he gradually becomes more apt (astute, confident, and mature) to play his role to the fullest in the management of his own financial affairs. The mandate of the team entrusted with the task of designing this process (see Chapter 10) is to find the best way to achieve this mission while respecting any constraint imposed by management (such as deadline, budget, human resources, or technical considerations).

We could formulate the mission of *evaluate assets/needs/risk profile*, for another example, as follows: "to obtain a complete and accurate picture of all the client's assets, his current and future financial needs, and his true attitude toward risk so that FPA can help him formulate an appropriate financial strategy." Thus formulated, the mission does not specify the extent of customer involvement in the process, a decision that would be left with an eventual design team.

As mentioned earlier, we use the *train/educate customers* process as an example to illustrate the process design methodology. The reader who wishes to seize the moment and move on directly to Chapter 10 can do so without loss of continuity, and come back to this point afterward.

7.5 SCOPING A PROCESS FOR IMPROVEMENT OR DESIGN[4]

So far in this chapter, we have presented a rigorous approach to deploying strategy onto processes, that is, to defining the right thing to do. The approach presented requires much rigor. Few organizations are likely to embark on such a journey until they have had firsthand experience with rigor and its benefits. This section presents a methodology to scope a project for an organization that has not explicitly explored the relationships between clients' needs, strategy, and processes. Those organizations that did will find that they still need the methodology to break down selected processes into bite-size projects, fine-tune the scope of the projects, and clarify the boundaries of the processes.

The methodology unfolds in 10 steps. To facilitate generalization, we present it using three examples drawn from very different professional and quasi-professional services: social work, accounting, and software development. After presenting the 10 steps, we discuss the delicate trade-offs involved in delimiting the perimeter of the process.

Think globally, act locally. Strategic options and their implications are not visible unless one takes a global view. However, since trying to change everything at once results in chaos, we must execute change through small, bite-size projects. The same goes for process improvement and process design of a more tactical nature. Unfortunately, a series of beneficial local actions may result in a loss of global coherence (see discussion in Chapter 4) unless we take care to ensure coherence by regularly looking at the big picture.

To get the correct project scope, one needs a good cookie cutter. Too big a scope generates much frustration, and energy is wasted beating around the bush. The greatest risk is that one never reaches the level of detail required to identify and fix the vital variables. By contrast, the greatest risk of too small a scope is to leave these variables out entirely and waste time beating around the wrong bush.

While these issues are well known in manufacturing (see, for instance, Lynch et al. [2003]), mitigating the risks in professional services, where complexity arises from other factors, requires a different approach. The proper methodology in services includes tools designed to force an organization to see where the project fits into the global picture and to help it pick the right part of the right process to improve.

To illustrate this methodology, we will focus on the case of a child protective service (CPS) agency. While the methodology has general applicability, an example drawn from the complex field of human services shows how the approach lends itself to some of our most sensitive social problems. For those readers not familiar with CPS agencies, we will also show how the methodology applies to a software developer and an accounting firm. Here is an overview of the problems each organization faces:

- The CPS agency is concerned about recurring capacity problems, so the general manager hired a process improvement consultant.

- The software developer is not meeting its promised delivery date. Late project start-up was initially thought to be the culprit.

- The accounting firm is experiencing problems in collecting its receivables and thought inefficiencies in the billing department were to blame.

The methodology (see Table 7.2) proceeds from a high-level exploration of related metrics and processes (steps 1–4) through the selection of the specific goal and process to be improved (steps 5–8) to a final delimitation of scope (steps 9 and 10).

Table 7.2 Overview of the methodology.

Step	Purpose	Instructions
1. Pick general problem, select metric (Big Y)	Avoid endless discussions around ill-defined issues.	1. Select a metric that best summarizes the problem you have in mind. 2. Get data to establish the baseline. 3. Find a rationale (benchmarking, market need, or other) to set a target.
2. Investigate adjacent metrics and correlations	Refine choice of metrics, zoom out to a broader view, explore associations, and start thinking about causality.	1. Identify related metrics (think of other metrics closely associated to the one selected in step 1). 2. Identify the relationship among these metrics using arrows and +/− signs.
3. Identify potential processes and explore linkages	Take a first look at what the organization does (processes) that might have to be changed in order to reach the target. Group processes into discrete entities.	1. Starting from the above metrics and their internal dynamics, identify things that you do that have an impact on those metrics. 2. Specify how these things (processes) relate to one another.
4. Explore the impacts of processes on metrics	Raise awareness of process–metric linkages. Promote systemic thinking about the genesis of the problem and potential change levers.	Draw a diagram connecting each of the processes (step 3) to the metrics that they impact. Specify the direction of the impact (+/−). Verify for completeness: If a metric is not touched by any arrow, search for the process that impacts it. If some processes do not impact any metrics, why were they included in the first place?
5. Assess performance of high-level processes	After highlighting salience, it is important to think about performance as a criterion for selecting the process on which to focus.	Perform a summary evaluation of the efficiency and effectiveness of all processes identified in step 3. A five-point scale is used for each axis on an x-y diagram.
6. Perform cursory cause-and-effect analysis	Approaching the problem from a different angle is useful to validate results obtained using the process approach. Cause and effect is more intuitive and less restrictive than step 4—that is, not limited to processes.	Starting from the Big Y (step 1), generate a fishbone diagram, classifying causes into categories.
7. Formulate specific problem and goal (small y)	Having gone through steps 2 through 6 since first stating the problem (step 1), management is in a much better position to be specific about the nature of the problem.	1. Revisit the previous step and pick a metric from the influence diagram (step 2) that you now feel should be the object of the improvement project. Pick one that is at the heart of the problem and that offers a good payoff/risk ratio. 2. Formulate it as was done in step 1.
8. Delimit process perimeter and formulate process mission	Determining what should be considered in-scope and out-of-scope is as difficult as it is critical. All the intermediate outputs of the methodology are now brought to bear on this task. The process mission is the anchor that will ensure continued coherence.	Revisit step 4, focusing now on the metric selected in step 7. Pick the smallest subset of processes that can be the focus of the project, taking into consideration linkages between projects (step 3) and current process performance (step 5). State why this process has to exist (refer to section 6.8).
9. Identify subprocesses	To validate the scope by zooming in to the selected process to see what's in there exactly.	Perform a cursory functional analysis of the process delimited in step 8. Start from the one sentence (action verb–noun) process definition and list functions by answering the question "How?"
10. Assess performance of subprocesses	This is a final validation and represents the finest level of analysis reached in the scoping exercise. The micro-level performance analysis allows management to use a fine-tooth comb to establish final scope.	Repeat step 5, this time using the functions identified in step 9.

7.5.1 Step 1: Identify the "Big *Y*"—What Is the General Goal We Are Pursuing?

The initial problem statement should be formulated to be "SMART" (specific, measurable, achievable, relevant, and time-bound). The CPS agency wants to solve its capacity problems, so its problem statement says, "We want to shorten the time it takes for children in need of protection to be admitted to the reception center from 10 days to 1 day." A diagram such as that shown in Figure 7.9 makes this more vivid. While on the waiting list, these children are at risk, and their situation generally deteriorates. Having recently completed a strategic planning exercise, management had no problem identifying this as its top priority.

This initial problem statement is known as the "big *Y*," referring to the high-level dependent variable. It provides a starting point in an organization's search for the right scope.

The corresponding statement for the software developer says, "We currently meet our deadline on 25% of our contracts, but we should meet our deadline on 90%." The accountant's SMART statement says, "We get paid 85 days after we've performed the work, but we should be paid in 30 days."

This first step of the methodology gives focus to a discussion that is often loose and unstructured. It forces stakeholders to be more rigorous and get data. Benchmarking can be very useful here to help set the target value.

7.5.2 Step 2: Determine Related Metrics—What Other Quantities (or Metrics) Are So Closely Related to the Big *Y* That They Could Potentially Constitute Alternatives to It?

Managers can generally land in the right strategic area, but if left to their own devices, they are quite unreliable when asked to pinpoint the problem. Thus, it is useful to explore the vicinity of the original problem to see whether we can find a more meaningful problem statement. We show the resulting metrics for the CPS agency in Figure 7.10 in the form of a correlation diagram.

Adapted from the field of systems dynamics (see, for instance, Forrester [1969] and Senge [1990]), correlation diagrams illustrate patterns of influence. An arrow

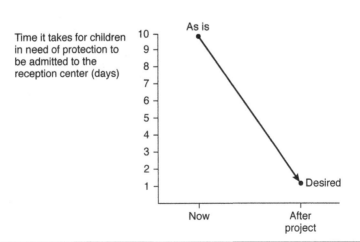

Figure 7.9 SMART problem statement: the big *Y* at CPS.

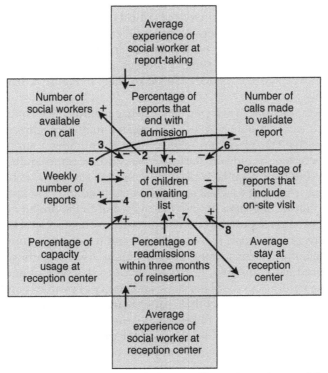

Arrows are correlations, + and − indicate positive and negative correlations,
the direction of the arrow reflects the assumed direction of causality

Figure 7.10 Step 2: Identify related metrics and their interrelationship—CPS.

indicates a correlation, and its direction signifies the assumed underlying causality. Correlation diagrams allow visualization of patterns. Balancing loops, such as the one shown by the correlations numbered 1, 2, and 3 in Figure 7.10, show how a one-time increase in the number of reports when the reception center is near capacity will eventually (that is, with a time lag) lead to an automatic adjustment as management responds to a lengthening of the waiting line by adding resources.

Reinforcement loops, such as the one shown by correlations 1, 2, 3, and 4 in Figure 7.10, are vicious circles. Because of a longer waiting list, children at risk are left in their home environment for a longer period, thus triggering new reports that have to be investigated. This puts added pressure on the social workers who receive and investigate these reports, leading them to cut down on the number of validation calls they make. They tend to deal with this increased professional risk by erring on the side of caution and deciding more frequently to withdraw children from the threatening situation (correlations 5 and 6 in Figure 7.10).

Under the pressure of the longer waiting list, the reception center reinserts children earlier than clinically indicated, thus triggering new family crises and even more reports (correlations 7 and 8 in Figure 7.10). Delays in these reactions (adding more personnel, earlier reinsertion, and so on) typically exacerbate the swings brought about by such situations, as new corrective measures are brought in to try to resolve a situation whose solution is already in the pipeline.

This diagram helps managers understand the dynamics of the situation—a critical asset when the time comes to identify the best leverage point for breaking negative patterns. Though some of the critical correlations can and should be substantiated with data, it is generally impossible and even counterproductive to try to do so systematically. Keeping things simple produces the most benefit for the effort exerted. Assuming that some quantities are exogenous to the model, such as the variable "average experience of social worker" in Figure 7.10, will contribute to the simplicity.

As for the software developer, its influence diagram (see Figure 7.11) identifies metrics such as the number of technical risks initially recognized, the number of staff changes that take place during the project, the number of supplier changes that take place between the bid and start-up stage, and the time required to fully free up designated core team members once the project is started. This brings out a complex dynamic involving a lack of serious risk analysis and planning at the bid stage. Because technical challenges are not discovered until the project is well under way, the developer tends to pull the best resources from other projects to fix the problem, thereby spreading the crisis to these projects and triggering a domino effect.

The accounting firm's diagram (see Figure 7.12) identifies metrics such as delays in producing invoices, errors on invoices, lateness of and errors on time and expense reports, clarity of invoices, and clarity of contracts and customer queries. The firm uncovers the fact that it often starts projects on the wrong foot as the terms and conditions related to billing are often vague or not discussed in detail with the customer. Thus, staff working on the project do not receive clear instructions. This causes delays, ambiguity, or errors on time and expense reports and the

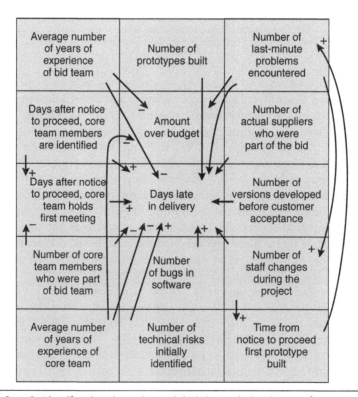

Figure 7.11 Step 2: Identify related metrics and their interrelationship—software developer.

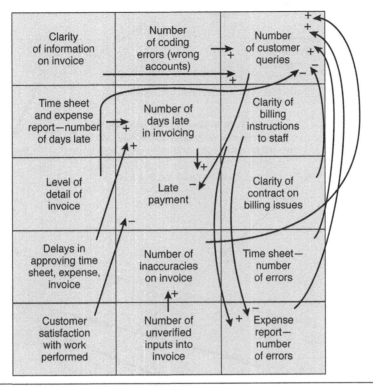

Figure 7.12 Step 2: Identify related metrics and their interrelationship—accounting firm.

invoices. These problems, in turn, trigger customer queries and further delays. The delays eventually build up and generate a backlog that takes months to resolve.

In step 1, the organization is forced to be specific and gather data. In doing so, it realizes it has to exclude related metrics it believes are equally important. Step 2 allows the organization to revisit these metrics to identify and specify the dynamic nature of the relationships among the metrics. This helps focus the project on processes with maximum leverage to resolve the problem.

7.5.3 Step 3: List Potential Processes—What Are We Doing That Has an Impact on These Metrics?

Underlying processes are implicit in steps 1 and 2. Step 3 makes them explicit. We show a potential set of processes relevant to the influence diagram of CPS (Figure 7.10) in Figure 7.13. Managers readily identify these processes, but because no process exists alone, the major links still need to be acknowledged.

We are not looking for correlations here. We are looking for functional linkages that can be found in the answer to this question: If you were to modify this process, which other processes would have to be included in the project and which would have to be tagged up front as related processes to be adjusted to maintain global coherence? The bold arrows in Figure 7.13 represent the former type of link; the regular arrows represent the latter.

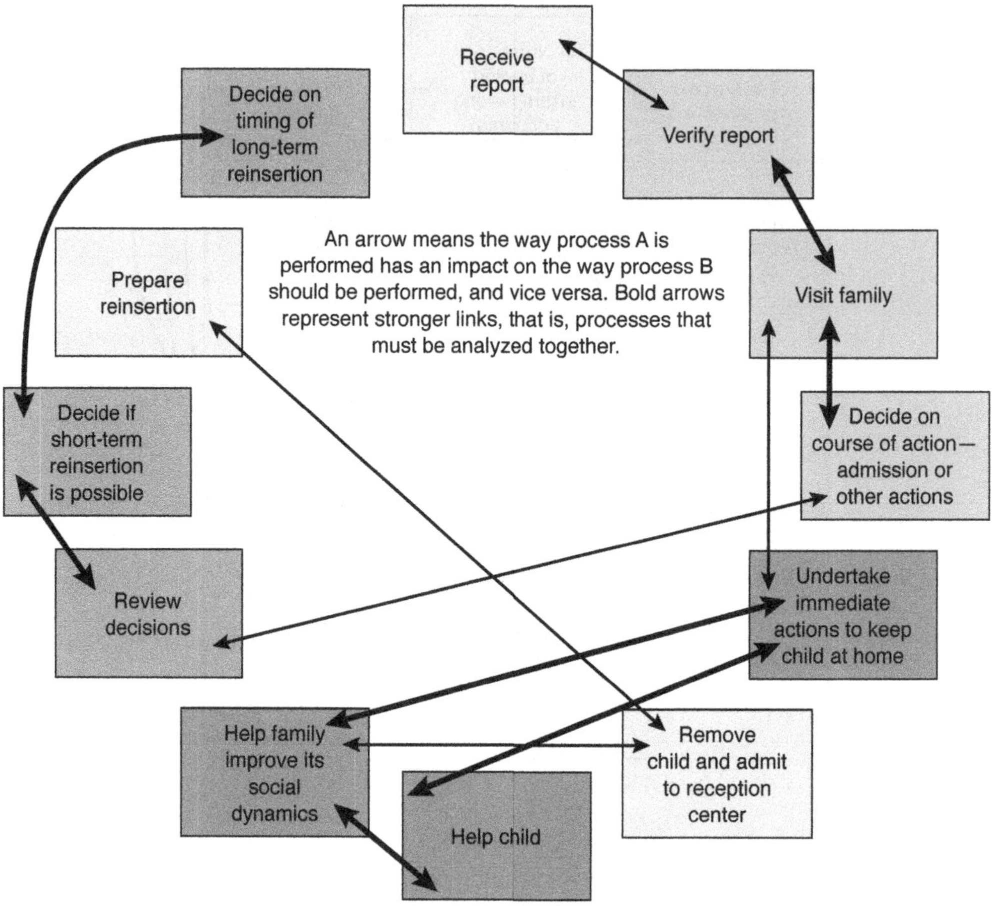

Figure 7.13 Step 3: Identify relevant processes and their functional linkages—CPS.

As the CPS agency managers ponder which process to focus on, they realize that the way short-term reinsertion decisions are made is irremediably linked to the way long-term decisions are made. If criteria are changed for one, they have to be changed for the other. They also realize that they cannot meaningfully separate these decisions from the other decisions that are made when the case is reviewed.

Thus, the three processes linked by bold arrows on the left-hand side of Figure 7.13 form an inseparable whole called the "review initial decisions" process. In a similar fashion, we must consider the three processes linked together in the upper right-hand corner of Figure 7.13. We thus refer to the trio as the "make initial decisions" process.

The managers realize that if they want to change the process through which children are removed from their homes, they must be ready to make corresponding changes in the way families are helped and reinsertion is prepared. While these processes would be out of scope if the "remove child and admit to reception center" process is selected for improvement, they would have to be considered to be adjacent processes, and appropriate experts would have to be included in the project team.

The software developer (see Figure 7.14) ends up linking several processes related to risk management (*assess initial project risk, develop risk management plan,* and *manage risks*) and staffing (*put bid team together, put core project team together, and select project staff*). Several clusters of processes also emerge in the accounting firm (see Figure 7.15), such as those related to the preparation and verification of time and expense reports and those related to the initial billing agreement.

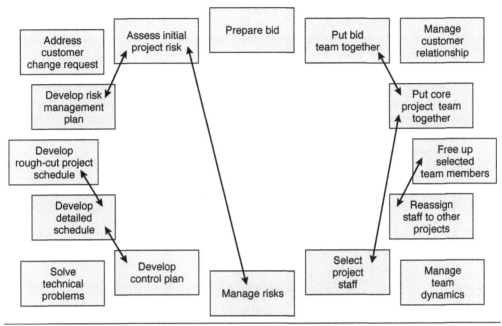

Figure 7.14   Step 3: Identify relevant processes and their functional linkages—software developer.

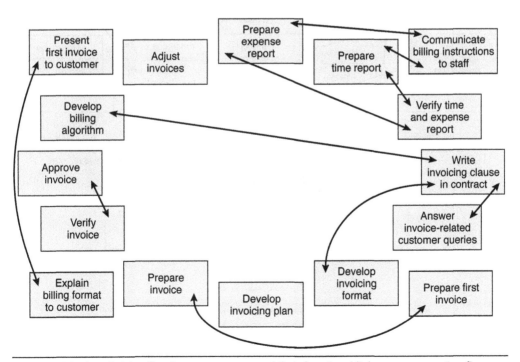

Figure 7.15   Step 3: Identify relevant processes and their functional linkages—accounting firm.

7.5.4 Step 4: Create a Process Metrics Diagram—How Are the Target Metrics and Processes Related?

Figure 7.16 shows the impact of each process on the relevant metrics at CPS. Processes that are inseparable are the same shade. These relationships are especially useful if you look back at Figure 7.10, which highlights patterns of influence between the metrics. The "make initial decisions" process, for example, is at the center of the reinforcement loop mentioned in step 2 due to its impact on the intake valve. The "review initial decisions" process is also a strong factor due to its impact on the outlet valve.

At the software developer (Figure 7.17), the late completion of software projects turns out to be a complex problem with several clusters of processes at its root. Several projects are needed to solve this problem, and each needs to focus on a different aspect of the business, such as team selection, staff movements, prototype development, and risk management.

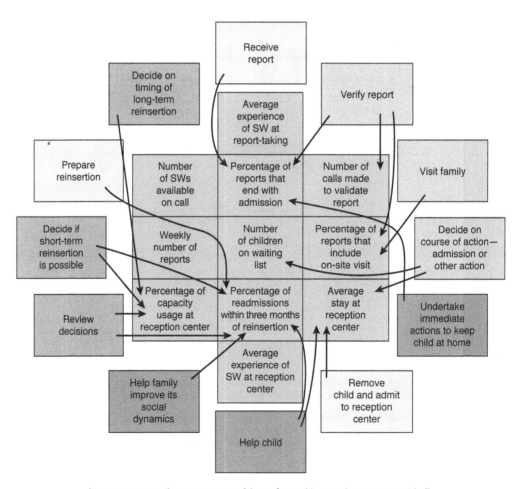

An arrow means the way process A is performed has an impact on metric B.

Figure 7.16 Step 4: Identify the impact of each process on each metric—CPS.

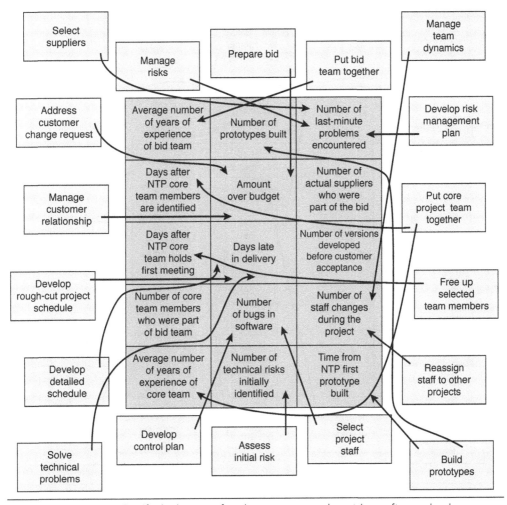

Figure 7.17 Step 4: Identify the impact of each process on each metric—software developer.

This step confirms the accounting firm's suspicion (Figure 7.18) that the initial setup of the invoicing process is an important part of its problem because instructions to staff and customer expectations stem from that process. The firm also found that the preparation and communication of the first invoice are pivotal in detecting and resolving any remaining internal or external issues.

7.5.5 Step 5: Conduct a High-Level Process Performance Evaluation: What Is the Current Performance Level of These Processes?

The answer to what is the current performance level of these processes provides critical input to the scoping decision. Figure 7.19 shows an evaluation of the processes at CPS using an efficiency/effectiveness diagram (see DeToro and McCabe [1996]).

It consists of assessing, on a five-point scale, the performance of each process identified in Figure 7.13 in terms of efficiency and effectiveness (see Chapter 4 for

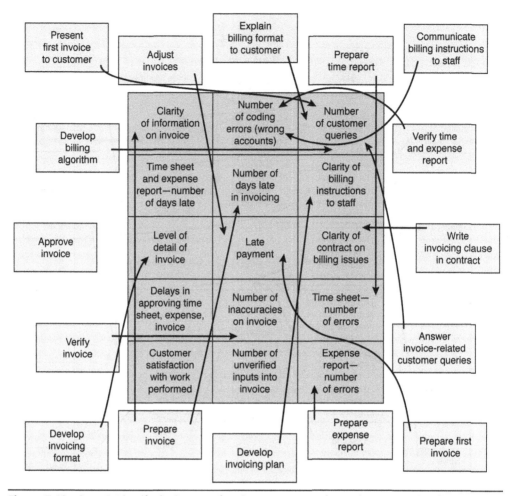

Figure 7.18 Step 4: Identify the impact of each process on each metric—accounting firm.

definitions) and plotting the result on a diagram. Three processes are in dire need of improvement:

- Deciding which course of action to take initially
- Visiting the family
- Removing the child from his or her home environment

Dedicating an improvement project to any of these processes will likely yield a high return. On the other hand, dedicating a project to the decision surrounding the timing of long-term reinsertion will probably not yield important payback.

A similar diagram (not shown) for the software developer shows the risk management and prototype development processes to be sick. Low performers in the accounting firm include verifying time and expense reports, communicating billing procedures, and answering invoice-related queries.

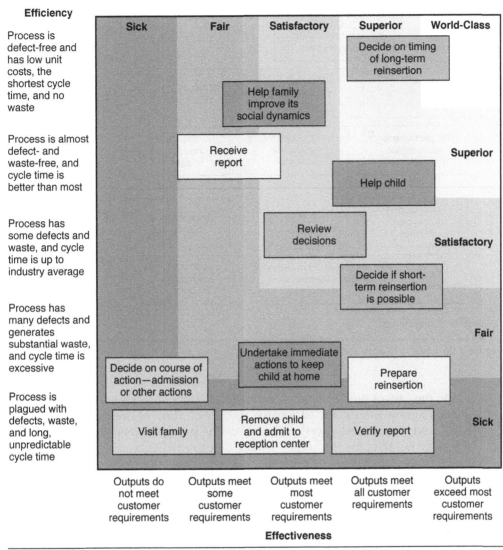

Figure 7.19   Step 5: Assessment of current process performance at CPS.

Source: Adapted from DeToro and McCabe (1996).

7.5.6 Step 6: Create a Cause-and-Effect Diagram: What Are the Causes of the Problem?

We can use a cause-and-effect diagram (also called an Ishikawa diagram) to further validate tentative answers arising from earlier steps—see Figure 7.20. We give detailed instructions on how to prepare such a diagram in Chapter 9. This tool forces an organization to approach the same problem from an angle not restricted by process and metrics.

The organization's earlier conclusions will be reinforced if the most important factors identified by the cause-and-effect diagram point toward the same culprits identified in the preceding steps.

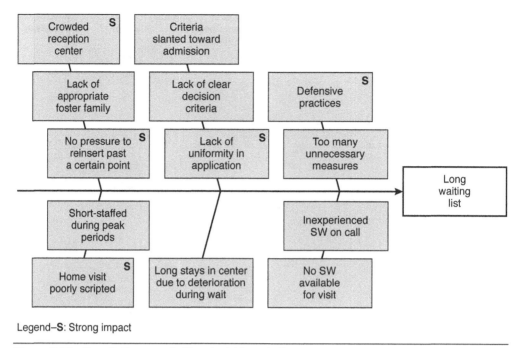

Figure 7.20 Step 6: Cause-and-effect (or Ishikawa) diagram at CPS.

In the case of the CPS agency, correlating earlier analysis with the cause-and-effect diagram singles out "defensive practices," "lack of uniformity in application," and "home visit poorly scripted" as the processes that should be fixed. If that were not the case, the agency would have to revisit earlier results.

Various issues related to risk management come out in the analysis that the software firm conducts, while the accounting firm's analysis reveals that billing procedures are poorly understood.

7.5.7 Step 7: Identify the "Small *y*"—What Is the Specific Goal We Are Pursuing in This Project? What Is the Yardstick That We Will Use to Measure the Project's Success?

From the information obtained in the preceding steps, the percentage of reports that end with the decision to admit a child appears to be at the center of the problem at CPS. It is a bull's-eye type of metric, and there should be a target range within which the processes would be considered within specifications. The SMART statement for the CPS agency (see Figure 7.21) says, "Currently the admission rate varies between 10% and 50%. It should remain within the 15% to 25% range, 99% of the time."

The software developer's SMART statement says, "Our risk management plan currently rates a 3 on our 10-point quality scale. It should rate 8 or higher." The quality scale has to be developed based on a weighted sum of criteria, such as validation of the list of technical issues, the depth of the initial exploration of a

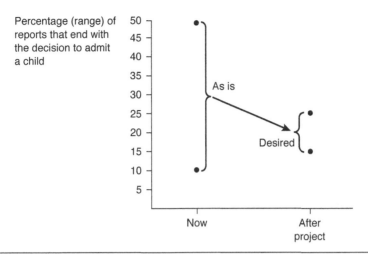

Figure 7.21   SMART problem statement: the small *y* at CPS.

technical solution, the number of risks signed off by experts, and the number of risks with associated contingency plans. It is a common misinterpretation of the measurement imperative (that is, if you cannot measure it, you cannot improve it) that unless a metric is readily available for an objective you would like to reach, it should be dropped in favor of another. On the contrary, it should be kept, and an appropriate metric should be sought or developed.

The accounting firm decides to focus on the errors on the expense reports and time sheets used to prepare the first invoice for a new contract. The error count was eight, and it should have been zero.

7.5.8 Step 8: Delimit the Turf—What Is the Perimeter of the Process to Be Improved or Designed to Reach the Goal Formulated in Step 7?

The process of making initial decisions links directly to the goal (see Figure 7.22). It starts when a report is received and ends with a decision on what action to take, if any. While the process of verifying the report is effective, its low efficiency is likely to have an effect on the waiting list in the resource-bound context of the agency. The process owner is the director of child and youth protection. He formulates a concise mission statement to ensure that the process remains anchored on its reason for existence and that no loss of coherence takes place because of the change.

The process to be improved or designed by the software developer was defined as "develop risk management plan." It starts with receipt of the request for proposal and ends with approval of the plan by the owner of the proposal.

The accounting firm chose "specify and communicate billing procedures to all concerned" as the target process. The process starts with the initial terms of reference (pre-contract) and ends with all concerned parties (internal and external) receiving explicit reporting and billing instructions.

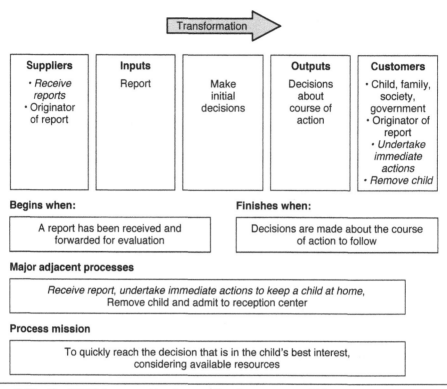

Figure 7.22   The SITOC form used to circumscribe the process at CPS.

7.5.9 Step 9: Check the Scope—Is the Scope Too Broad?

Is management abdicating its responsibility to scope the process down to a manageable size?

If that were the case, the team would feel abandoned because it was forced to use a rigorous analytical methodology to perform a task that required managerial judgment.

A cursory functional analysis such as the FAST diagram (Figure 7.23) can help assess the size of the process. Instructions for preparing such a diagram are presented in Chapter 3. The diagram can be pushed further to the right one level if management still doubts the breadth of the process, or a macro map can be prepared that adds the players involved to another axis. Of course, management will need the counsel of a process improvement expert to make an enlightened decision as to the process's adequate size.

7.5.10 Step 10: Review the Scope—How Can the Scope Be Further Reduced?

A low-level efficiency/effectiveness analysis (see Figure 7.24) can be performed on the functions in Figure 7.23 to determine whether a viable high-leverage (low-performance) subset can be isolated. This may create a loop back to earlier stages of

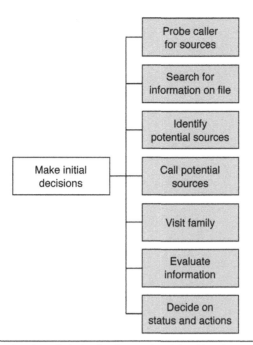

Figure 7.23 Step 9: Functional analysis (FAST diagram) to identify subprocesses at CPS.

the methodology because management may be tempted to leave out subprocesses that display high performance but were previously judged inseparable from the others. Thus, the methodology is iterative, not linear, because early judgment calls may be questioned later and may turn out to be critical to the scoping decisions as things unfold.

7.5.11 A Balancing Act

Determining the scope of a project involves managing a complex trade-off. Scoping must be performed from the top down and should be as scientific as possible, but the top view (management and strategy) deals more with art than science. Establishing the scope of a project means deciding where the boundary between the two realms should lie, at least for the period during which a rigorous analytical framework is to be deployed within the domain of the project. This places managers who must make that decision in the uncomfortable position of spanning the proverbial boundary between art and science. It assumes they will know when to be guided by intuition and good judgment and when to be guided by facts.

Drawing the boundary between art and science is not easy, and doing so requires highly qualified people. They have to be comfortable distilling the experience of the organization one moment and, say, evaluating the normality of a data set the next, accepting a manager's judgment call one moment and rejecting an undocumented assertion the next, taking the broad view one moment and the near view the next.

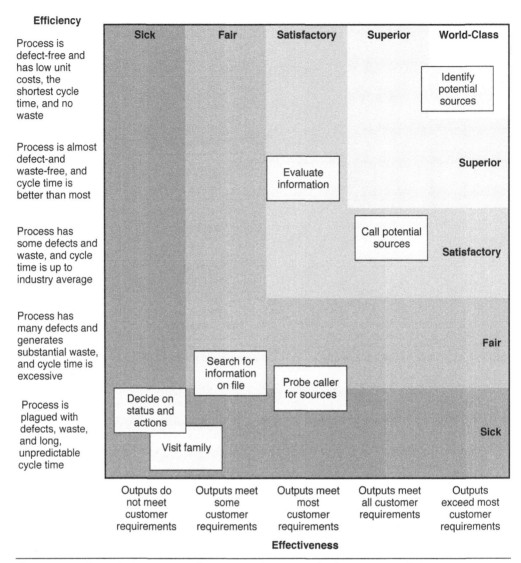

Figure 7.24   Step 10: Assessment of current performance of subprocesses at CPS.

7.6 SUMMARY

Process-oriented improvement philosophies are about doing the right thing right. They are predicated on rigor—rigor in deciding what the right things to do are, and rigor in deciding how we are going to go about ensuring that we do these things the right way. This chapter presented a methodology to do the former. Chapters 9 and 10 present methodologies to do the latter.

The methodology presented here is realistic, rigorous, and in perfect harmony with the "doing things right" methodologies presented later. It deploys strategy and market positioning through a series of matrices, called quality function deployment, or QFD, onto metrics and processes, ultimately allowing the organization to zoom in on important processes to manage and improve. It bridges the gap between strategy and processes, and is thus the missing link that has denied many organizations the breakthrough gains possible through doing things right. The mission statement is an important element connecting processes to strategy and promoting coherence of action across processes, throughout the organization.

To achieve the proper scope, an organization must determine where the project fits into the global picture, pick the right part of the right process to improve, and anchor it well using a clear mission statement. The systems dynamic has been adapted to play a central role in initial exploration of scoping decisions. The methodology and toolkit presented here help bring structure to a complex task and diminish the unavoidable turbulence that occurs at this crucial interface between intuition and rigor. It requires top management to "walk the rigor talk," not to simply ask the rest of the organization to be rigorous in the way they do things. Body language has more impact on employees than spoken language. When management shoots from the hip, so does the rest of the organization.

EXERCISES

7.1 Rating Processes in Terms of Importance for Clients

As in previous chapters, it is best to assemble a team to do this.

a. Review your answers to exercises 2.2, 2.3, and 3.5. Use the list of value-adding processes (about 20) generated through the FAST diagram in exercise 3.5b as input into a QFD analysis. This will be correlated to weighted customer needs generated in exercises 2.2 and 2.3. To keep the matrix to a manageable size, you may limit yourself to the most important needs. If you find that some needs are not affected by any process, revise the FAST diagram accordingly. If some processes do not affect any need, verify whether they would affect some of the metrics left out of the matrix. If some processes do not affect any metric at all, you have an incoherence to resolve: either this is not a process or some service feature or metric is missing.

b. Prepare a Pareto diagram of value-adding processes.

c. Review your answers to exercise 3.5c. Select from this FAST diagram all value-enabling processes. You should get 7–15 processes. Correlate these processes to the most important value-adding processes identified earlier.

d. Prepare a Pareto diagram of value-enabling processes.

7.2 Identifying Salient Processes

a. Review the company's strategic plan and the key strategic issues identified therein. If you do not have such a plan, a brainstorming session should produce a coarse assessment of the major challenges of all types facing the organization. You should have no more than 10 or 12 such issues. Divide 100 points among these issues based on their relative importance for the future of the company. Use these issues in a matrix to correlate with all value-enabling and value-adding processes identified earlier. The matrix should have about 30 columns, but many cells will be blank. Calculate a weighted index reflecting the importance of each process for strategy. If the matrix is too large, limit your assessment to the direct correlates, marking them with a bull's-eye.

b. Prepare a salience diagram such as the one shown in Figure 7.5, plotting each process on the basis of strategic impact and performance.

c. Tabulate the strategic impact and performance scores of each process in a table similar to Table 7.1. Calculate a salience score by summing up both scores.

7.3 Assessing the Performance of the Processes

a. Prepare an efficiency/effectiveness diagram such as that shown in Figure 7.6.

b. Tabulate the scores in the table you started in Exercise 7.2c, including a performance score obtained by summing up the two ratings.

7.4 Prioritizing the Processes

a. Prepare a salience/performance diagram such as the one shown in Figure 7.7. Identify the five priority processes, numbering them one to five. You may use the proximity criteria, the decision rules presented in this chapter, or any other set of sequential decision rules that your organization deems appropriate.

b. Select two processes you would like to use as pilot projects to test the improvement and design methodologies presented later in this book. We suggest that you pick for improvement a process that scores particularly poorly on efficiency. Pick as your design project a process that does not exist or one that is so informal, or whose global performance score is so low, that it is best to start from scratch.

7.5 Formulating the Mission of Priority Processes

Formulate the mission of the five priority processes selected earlier.

7.6 Scoping Two Projects

Follow the 10-step procedure outlined in this chapter to scope two process change projects based on the two processes selected in 7.4b. A well-scoped improvement project is the central input you will need to perform the end-of-chapter exercise in Chapter 9. The same goes for the design project in Chapter 10.

NOTES

1. Discussing strategic planning methodologies lies beyond the scope of this book.
2. Derivatives are products, financial instruments, or securities that are derived from another security, cash market, or index, or another derivative, such as futures, forwards, and options.
3. The firm will have to decide whether to perform the analysis anew, starting from a different set of customer needs, or if it will be sufficient to adjust the results obtained with the original segment based on the differences between the two market segments.
4. This section is largely drawn from Harvey (2004).

8

The Learning Cycle and the Kaizen Event

People don't resist change. They resist being changed.

—Peter Senge

The "learning pump" lies at the heart of the learning organization. But change vehicles are often poorly understood. The kaizen workshop is a very effective vehicle for operational change. It can be difficult to decide which methodology, tools, and change vehicle to use to make the most out of every improvement opportunity, and the impact of mismatches can be fatal to a fledgling improvement program. We present a framework to reduce this risk.[1]

As previously mentioned, organizational learning is vital to long-term competitiveness. At the core of this capability lies the learning cycle, to which we referred as "the learning pump" in Figures 1.2 and 4.7. In this chapter, we explain how the cycle works. It requires a good understanding of the nature of processes (Chapters 1, 3, and 6), of the linkages between strategy and processes (Chapters 2, 4, and 5), and of the cycle anchorage point: project scoping (Chapter 7). After providing an overview, we discuss the major types of process problems and present six different change vehicles. We discuss one of these vehicles, the kaizen event, in much more detail. We conclude with the challenges involved in good matchmaking among these elements.

8.1 THE LEARNING CYCLE: "MOVING" PROCESSES

Processes are at the core of continuous improvement, and improvement is always the result of a process being changed in one way or another. From kaizen events and just-in-time manufacturing (invented in Japan) to Six Sigma projects and reengineering (invented in the United States), philosophies, methodologies, and tools have been developed to make processes more effective and more efficient (see discussion in Chapter 11). These management innovations have originated mostly from management practice, with academics coming in later to interpret and clarify the recipes such innovations embody (Spear and Bowen 1999).

Unfortunately, the abundance of great recipes has created confusion. The "chefs" are prone to promoting their own recipes as the panacea. Since these

241

recipes always involve a considerable investment in time and resources by the organization, picking the wrong one may be very costly. Further, since top management's strong endorsement is always a critical factor in the success of these programs—because it involves a change of culture—backing down and recognizing a mistake when one is made is very difficult. Thus, failures are merely glossed over, and lessons are not learned. This contributes to employee cynicism, which makes it even more difficult to introduce another program at a later date. Yet, failure does not appear to be the exception. Video 8.1 (see Figure 8.1) presents an overview of the challenges involved in process change.

If the history of management thought teaches us anything, it is that there is no panacea. Most improvement approaches that have gained a foothold in management practice are valuable in some circumstances and fail miserably in others. The problem lies in the fact that these circumstances are poorly understood. The purpose of this chapter is to propose a framework that organizations can use to guide them in the selection of the right methodology, tools, and change vehicle for the problem at hand.

The following analogy illustrates the nature of process improvement. Let us say that Jack Jones has to move some belongings from his home on the West Coast to his condominium on the East Coast. To do so effectively, he has to ask himself four specific questions (see Figure 8.2): What is it exactly that has to be moved ("the problem")? What are the major steps I will have to take to move the material ("the methodology")? What tools will I need ("the toolkit")? What type of vehicle will I need ("the vehicle")?

Any organization that wants to improve a process must ask itself these same four questions. It needs to identify the type of process improvement problem it is facing. Next, the organization needs to look at available process change methodologies and process improvement tools. Finally, it needs to take a look at the different process change vehicles available. Only then will it be able to effectively and efficiently undergo process improvement (Anand et al. 2009). As methodologies and tools are discussed in Chapters 9 and 10 in particular, we will not focus on them in this chapter.

8.1 Social and human dynamics

There is a fundamental flaw in the chess metaphor to represent strategy: in real life, the parts only move when they want to, and when they do, it is not always in the direction you had hoped. Different process problems and opportunities present different challenges, and therefore require adapted change "vehicles." A change event needs to be tightly choreographed and managed. Only then can it create the required sequence of moments of truth to generate genuine and durable transformation. These events must be part of an adapted change strategy.

Key concepts: Change vehicle, typology of process problems and opportunities, matching the vehicle to the job, the kaizen event or workshop, moments of truth in the change experience, choreography of change, change management

Figure 8.1   Video associated with Chapter 8.

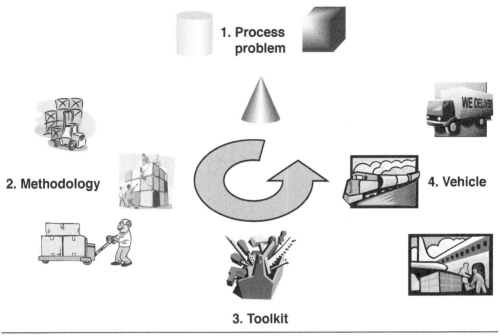

Figure 8.2 The four steps in planning process improvement.

8.2 PROCESS PROBLEMS

Process improvement opportunities are as varied as management itself. Most business problems (and opportunities) are bound to be rooted in processes and can only be solved by changing some process or another. Figure 8.3 presents a typology of process problems and opportunities[2] organized along a tree structure (see Table 8.1 for definitions or examples).

A first category of opportunities stems from the introduction of *new products* (1a) and *new services* (1b). While this may involve modifying existing processes, it generally involves the design of processes that do not exist. For example, when a fast-food chain decides to add a shrimp salad to its product offerings, a whole range of new processes have to be designed. Such processes should be designed from the outside in—that is, first define customer requirements, then specify what is expected of the process, and finally, design a process to meet the specifications. It is very challenging conceptually to start with a customer need—that is often intangible and hard to fathom—and finish with working processes.

Processes that simply do not exist (2) belong to another category. They do not exist in the sense that even though actions are somehow performed, there is no systematic way of performing them. Take risk management as an example. When asked what they do to manage project risk, many organizations will—after a while—list a number of activities that they perform in this regard, such as listing project risks, discussing risk issues at meetings, and taking action to mitigate a risk as their anxiety level rises. Few, however, will be able to show a systematic process that has been designed with the end in mind, that is in current use, and whose performance is systematically monitored with a view to detecting slippage

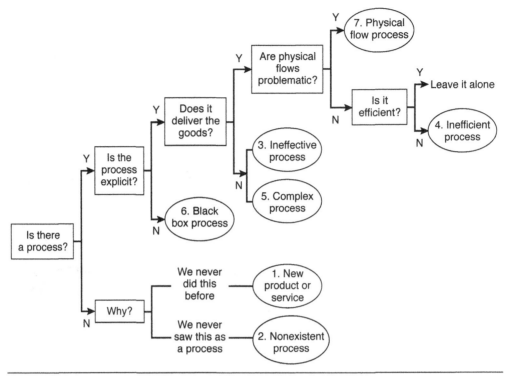

Figure 8.3 Typology of process problems.

and identifying opportunities for improvement. The first need here is for the organization to recognize that this is a process and that investing time and resources in doing it right is worthwhile. The process should then be designed using an outside–in approach, as suggested earlier. The conceptual challenge—the ability to handle and correlate abstract notions with practical aspects of organization of work—is just as important for the change process as it is for new products and services.

Many *processes are ineffective* (3); that is, they do not produce the desired results for the (internal or external) customer. This manifests itself through customer dissatisfaction, defects, low throughput, rework, and a high cost of quality control. As discussed in Chapter 1, the risk-rating process for mortgage-backed securities in the United States has been ineffective. The job was not done right, and the desired outcome never materialized. Fixing such processes may not be quite as challenging conceptually as categories (1) and (2) because a process is already in place. However, using the existing process as a starting point may not lead to the best solution.

Inefficient processes (4) are in a category of their own (see the discussion of process characteristics in Chapter 4). They do deliver the goods, eventually, but long delays and excessively high costs are involved. In other words, these processes generate waste (of time and of money). For example, some organizations have very inefficient processes for controlling office stationery. When an employee needs a writing pad and a couple of pencils, he goes to the clerk in charge. If the clerk happens to be absent, the employee has to come back later. When they finally

Table 8.1 Short definitions or illustrations of problems and change vehicles.

Process Problems	
1a. New product	Designing a new car.
1b. New service	Designing a new vacation package.
2. Nonexistent process	Disjointed activities performed in a haphazard manner.
3. Ineffective process	Process does not meet customer requirements.
4. Inefficient process	Requirements are met, but process is wasteful.
5. The complex process	Results depend on the simultaneous action of a number of intricately related variables.
6. Black box process	Results are produced, but we don't really know how.
7. Physical flow problems	Flow of people, parts, or forms produces congestion, shortages, damage, or other waste.
Change Vehicles	
1a. Project	Small part-time team assembled around a full-time expert. 2–6 months.
1b. Basic tool project	Same, but does not use advanced statistical tools.
2. Kaizen event	One or more full-time teams, fully empowered to transform a process. 1–2 weeks.
3. Workout	Broader and less rigorous effort to bust bureaucracy. 2–3 days.
4. Process management team	Managers assembled around a process owner to design process. Mid to long term.
5. Semiautonomous work team	Process workers organizing to control a process on a day-to-day basis. Ongoing.
6. Just do it	Team involved in implementing a process change. 2–6 months.

connect, the clerk interrupts whatever she is doing, gets the key to the stationery locker, and checks to see whether the items are available. If not, she reaches for a requisition form. "There has to be a better way" is what typically comes to the mind of any outside observer of such a process. Here, the organization has an opportunity to increase profit margins and to free up resources for other tasks. At a deeper level, there is also an opportunity to eliminate employee cynicism about their jobs and about the organization that employs them. The process is easy to fix through identifying activities that add little or no value and finding ways to eliminate them. Benefits are immediate and easy to measure.

Complex processes (5) are a separate class of the ineffective processes described in category (3). The complexity stems from the number of variables involved and their interaction. Whereas improvement opportunities for inefficient processes are quickly made obvious by a structured process analysis, complex processes will not respond to such an analysis. Many machining processes fall into this category, with variables such as pressure, heat, feed speed, and thickness of material interacting in complex ways. There are also complex aspects to professional services processes. A pharmacist evaluating the possible negative interactions in a cocktail of medications prescribed to a specific patient—given the complexities of a human being with a unique medical history—is faced with the same type of problem. Because of this complexity, a very small process must be scoped for improvement—as illustrated by these two examples—lest the number of variables and interactions grows exponentially and the problem becomes intractable. Thus, the involvement of many departments, with the resulting jurisdictional conflicts that this potentially entails, may not be a problem in many cases. Further, the complexity is such that the use of advanced tools (that is, statistical tools such as regression analysis or designed experiments) will be required to solve the problem.

Black box processes (6) can be effective and efficient—for now—but management would be hard-pressed to spell out how and why they work. This situation corresponds to the initial stage (or level 1) in the Capability Maturity Model Integration (Forrester et al. 2009). Motivated, dedicated employees can make things work in spite of "official" processes. Such organizational know-how, however, usually rests with but a few individuals—none of whom will have a holistic, explicit understanding of the process, and the process can thus be fragile. Further, this know-how cannot evolve to meet changing circumstances as it is strictly implicit. In the 1980s and 1990s, for instance, many banks created administrative centers to rationalize clerical tasks performed in branches. What the business cases did not consider, however, was the impact centralization would have on critical roles played by senior clerical personnel in branches. They in fact played a vital—but nondocumented—role in training and supporting the tellers (an entry-level position at the time). The loss of know-how was tremendous and was immediately felt by customers. The business case was perfectly accurate based on what the organization knew at the time. The need here is to make the process *explicit*, find out what is critical to its performance, control it, and ensure that it evolves over time.

Processes where physical flows are the root cause of all the problems (7) have unique vulnerabilities. They are another subcategory of the inefficient processes described earlier. Processes in this category are mostly found among manufacturing processes but may also be found in some transactional processes where the flow of a document, a parcel, or a person is central. Moving parts from the warehouse to the shop floor, producing an insurance policy, delivering a parcel from New York to Hong Kong, or "delivering" passengers to their respective aircraft might fall into this category. Rethinking quantities, lot sizing, setup time, division of work, and physical flows can generate significant gains in these processes.

Of course, reality generally defies categorization, and indeed most process problems are mixed. However, careful diagnostic examination of a process will generally permit identification of a major problem or opportunity.

Consider, for instance, the case of a bank trying to improve two processes involving professionals: renewal of credit lines and dealer audits. The problem with the former is that some 30% of credit lines have not been reviewed at the preestablished date and are automatically extended, exposing the bank to unknown risks. The current process is very long and bureaucratic, involving several forms and three or four departments. Since there is a process and it does not deliver the goods, Figure 8.3 points us toward cases 3 and 5. As the process does not involve complex interactions between variables, it can be classified as an ineffective process.

A division of the bank is involved in financing car dealers' inventories. Since the auditors foresee an imminent economic downturn, they feel that it is urgent to improve their auditing process. There are but a few experienced auditors (all professional accountants) available to audit hundreds of dealers. A first effort at coming to grips with the process results in the process being split into three distinct subprocesses: audit planning (deciding who should be audited), auditing, and follow-up. The team immediately sees that audit planning offers the greatest potential for improvement: unless you knock on the right door at the right time, the audit dollar is wasted. As they start to map that process, it dawns on them that there is no process ("nonexistent process"); that is, whatever activities take place depend on the evolving best judgment of many managers. While the auditing subprocess is formalized, crucial aspects of the process, such as developing the specific audit plan, are poorly understood, resulting in important nonconformities being missed ("complex process"). Finally, the audit follow-up process delivers the goods, eventually. Very bureaucratic, the process involves back-and-forth exchanges between several players (auditors, dealer, and head office) that take forever ("inefficient process").

8.3 CHANGE VEHICLES

Processes can be changed in a number of ways, ranging from sending a memo to all involved to putting together a fully empowered full-time team. We describe six such ways, referring to them as change vehicles because they "load" a process to be designed or improved and "take it to its destination": a fully implemented new way of doing things. Just as vehicles come in different sizes and with different payloads, and have different traction and speed specifications, each change vehicle has its own individual characteristics that enable it to take specific changes to fruition. Figure 8.4 shows the six most common vehicles used by many organizations in the form of a tree structure. Among the many existing variants, we present here the most prevalent form of each.

A *project* (1a) is a two- to six-month endeavor led by an expert in the methodology and tools. A team of employees intimately familiar with the process is built around the expert, all of whom report to a manager (the project owner or champion). The expert has been trained extensively for this task, and manages two or three projects in parallel on an ongoing basis. Team members typically spend two to four hours a week on the project. The project owner gives the mandate to the team, receives their report at the end of each phase, makes decisions about future directions, and is accountable to senior management for the results. Authority to change anything rests with the project owner. A *basic tool project* (1b) is one that does not involve advanced statistical tools and can thus be led by someone with lesser qualifications (for example, by a Green Belt instead of a Black Belt, in Six Sigma terminology).

A *kaizen event* (2) is an intensive drive by dedicated teams of workers to fix broken processes or design new ones. It is arguably the best change vehicle in our organizational change fleet. The team or teams typically spend a week or two, full time, applying a rigorous methodology to a process that has been previously selected and "scoped" by management (see Chapter 7). Kaizen events embody the complex recipe of human, social, cultural, and technical elements required for durable change to take place in shared ways of doing things (that is, in processes). The latter, or hard, elements—such as Six Sigma's DMAIC methodology and its associated toolkit—are discussed in Chapters 9 and 10. Soft elements are difficult to manage and are just as critical as hard elements. Further, those who lead these events are often excessively preoccupied with the technical side. Thus, it is worthwhile to dedicate a complete section (see section 8.4) to why and how the

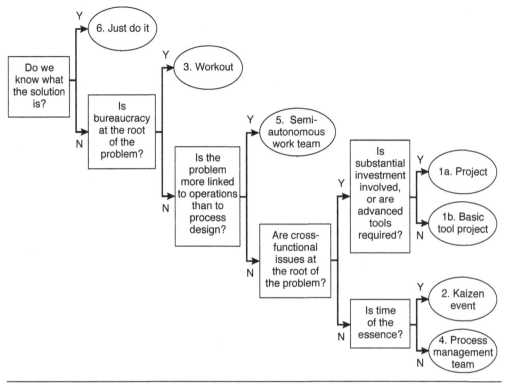

Figure 8.4 Typology of process change vehicles.

ingredients in the kaizen recipe produce the phenomenal success that many organizations have been reporting for years.

The word "workout" (3) was coined by GE to describe an even more intensive—typically lasting two days—vehicle for change. Workouts, which are less rigorous than projects or kaizen events, involve more people, and are not limited to processes, have spread to many other organizations. For Jack Welch, "busting bureaucracy" (Dumaine 1991) involves outside experts (consultants or university professors) coming to a site and organizing a broad-based problem identification session, followed by quick-hit solutions. Management, placed on the hot seat, must decide on the spot and justify any negative answers.

A *process management team* (4) is typically assembled around a process owner to design, improve, and monitor a high-level process. The team is always multifunctional and meets for short but intensive periods—typically two days at a time—first to design or redesign a process, then to monitor and improve it. The time requirement decreases when the process is implemented and capable. Each team member acts as the unique contact point for that process in his department. Process problems are channeled through him to the process team. The process owner is accountable to the management committee for process performance. The team may use other vehicles such as projects and kaizen events to address specific lower-level process issues.

Semiautonomous work teams (5) have been around for a long time. Whereas a process management team owns the design of a process that is generally repeated in many parts of the organization, a semiautonomous work team manages and operates a specific application (or "instantiation") of that process. For example, a process management team may design the process for preparing a service proposal, and a semiautonomous work team may prepare proposals for specific systems or for a specific geographic area. As long as they respect the design parameters set forth by the former, the latter, generally a cross-functional team, disposes of much autonomy in the operation of the process. Semiautonomous work teams may also have a degree of autonomy in some human resource aspects of the work, such as member selection, gain sharing, and interpersonal problem solving, thus the common reference to them as part of a "socio-technical" approach to work.

Sometimes when process problems arise, the organization knows the cause and the solution. All that is needed then is to *just do it* (6). A project is involved, and a team is generally needed to execute it. This, however, is very different from the process improvement and process design teams presented earlier. The team does not have to clarify the problem and look for a solution, but rather clarify the solution and look for the best way to implement it. This is no easy task, however, as the change management challenge can also be daunting. On one occasion, when the author was conducting a project definition session (generally referred to as a "scoping session"), a manager suggested that an improvement project be conducted on the following topic: "We don't do design reviews any more." In the discussion that followed, it quickly became clear that many problems could have been avoided if this manager and his colleagues had kept to that practice. This example would be a typical candidate for a just-do-it project. A word of caution is in order here, however: managers often think that they know what the problem, the causes, and the solution are, but this initial view may not bear detailed analysis for very long.

Adapting these vehicles to suit a particular organizational environment and implementing them are complex undertakings requiring careful attention to the human and technical aspects as well. Each comes with its own organizational requirements, risks, and success factors. They are complementary and can be used individually or in combination. Before discussing the matching between problem, methodology, tools, and change vehicle (section 8.5), we turn to a detailed presentation of a particularly effective vehicle: the kaizen event.

8.4 THE KAIZEN EVENT

There are five different outputs of a well-run kaizen event:

- A new process capable of contributing to the organization's success

- Workers and managers transformed by the experience they have lived

- A team with a shared vision and a sense of ownership of the new way of doing things

- Well-scoped improvement opportunities for future kaizen events that the team's digging has surfaced

- Future leaders who have emerged in the high-pressure human culture medium that is the kaizen event

Changing shared beliefs is the hardest thing to orchestrate in an organization. Speeches and presentation slides won't work. Shared transformational experiences will. When they sit together around the table at the outset of the event, most players believe they know what the problem is and what is required to fix it. The solution they have in mind normally involves vague changes to what some other player or straw man does or does not do. They are promised that if they follow the methodology, they will find the right solution, agree upon it, and be empowered to implement it together. Even though they may not say so out loud, most participants do not believe it. When it does happen, they become different persons, sometimes even fans, and join the forces for change. If it does not, they are reinforced in their superstitious beliefs and become "terrorists," often willing to play an active role in derailing the change initiative. In between these extremes, many participants may leave the kaizen event with either a positive or negative bias toward the initiative, but without any feelings strong enough to trigger them to leave the sidelines and become players. In this section we show how to use the kaizen event to contribute to the critical mass of supporters and movers required to operate a successful turnaround.

8.4.1 Changing Culture by Creating Experiences

The notions of "customer experience" and "customer moment of truth" are now well understood and integrated in customer-focused companies (refer back to Chapter 5). You sell something to a customer by convincing her that the benefits she will get through the use of your product will exceed whatever other benefits she could get by purchasing something else with the money you are asking. That's only a promise, though. She will truly know the benefits, and thus the value (which takes into account the price she paid), when she actually uses the product, service, or combination thereof that you sold her. Those precise moments of use when she realizes what she's bought are called *moments of truth*. All too often, they bring out the lies in the sales pitch. Thus, customers make up their minds and adjust their behavior and word of mouth accordingly.

When top management tells the organization that they know what's wrong with the company and what's required to get it back on track, this is also a sales pitch. At that point, executives are asking employees and managers to trust them and buy into their new way of improving processes. The best sales pitch will only get employees to give it a try. The trial, in time, will generate (employee) moments of truth through which they will make up their mind. The bigger the stretch in belief required of them, the tougher the test to which the new approach will be put, and the deeper and longer lasting the effects of the resulting moments of truth.

Kaizen events are about scripting, choreographing, and orchestrating employee and managerial moments of truth that turn out as planned. The theatrical metaphor is intentional. It takes much perceptive thinking about the effects that various sequences of actions, images, or sound effects will have on viewers to deliver the punch that a movie such as *The Godfather* does (see Box 8.1). This illustrates well the delicate nature of an experience: the line separating success from failure is very tenuous. It also shows that rigor (evidence-based management) is an essential complement to creativity in the creation of a successful experience, and that you should not expect to be perfect at the first trial or throw in the towel when you are not. A slight lag in timing, change of intonation, or glimmer in the eye would produce a different effect that could spoil the moment. It takes a good story (such as Mario Puzo's book), a good screenplay, the right actors and stage props, and above all, masterful directing to make the movie experience come together.

Box 8.1 Lessons from a Master

Issue: *Managing emotions . . . rigorously*

In "The Making of *The Godfather*" Francis Ford Coppola provides a couple of insightful glimpses on the role and challenges facing those who want to create memorable experiences. Since the *Godfather* saga (three movies) spans 18 years, Coppola was asked what he thought was the essence of his role in the making of the series. His answer: "I own the emotions of the Corleone family." The central role of the director is to understand the feelings of the characters, and thus predict how they would react under various circumstances. Ultimately, an experience—any experience—is about emotions. The director must have the sensitivity to get under the skin of the participants and understand what's required to induce the desired reaction. In other words, he must be the CEO of the experience, that is, the Chief Emotion Owner.

In another section of the same piece, Coppola mentions that a few weeks before the premiere of *The Godfather II* they held some preliminary screenings of the movie. It was a failure. That may sound surprising today, since we now know that the movie was a resounding success. One is left to wonder: What could they possibly have done in a few weeks to "fix" a movie that took so many resources and talent to put together over a period of years? Get Robert De Niro to come back and do new takes on a couple of scenes? In fact, Coppola says, they conducted focus groups to understand the reaction of the audience; that is, they obtained data in order to ascertain the facts. In the movie, flashbacks between different life stages of the Godfather (for example, from the five-year-old Vito Andolini in a Sicilian village to the young mobster fighting for turf in Little Italy) are used. Data showed that the audience just did not get it. In fact, Coppola realized that this was due to too much back-and-forth between story lines: people lost track. Once the problem was diagnosed, the solution was easy: reduce the number of flashbacks by staying in time periods longer and alternating less frequently between epochs. So by simply reordering a number of sequences, they transformed a failed movie into a vibrant viewing experience.

We also have a good story to tell: quality culture, together with its supporting elements, really works. The kaizen event is the inspiration for the screenplay. It has also been field-tested and honed through decades of experimentation in a wide variety of environments. The actors are the participating employees and managers. While they do not read lines, they are indeed asked to play a part by performing certain tasks and producing some deliverables at prespecified times. The facilitator acts as the director. We now turn to the sequence of moments of truth that punctuate the experience.

8.4.2 Moments of Truth in the Kaizen Event

A kaizen event consists of four generic stages (see Figure 8.5—top level): (1) project selection, definition, measurement, and planning; (2) the workshop per se (one or more teams, one week, full time); (3) the follow-through on the implementation, involving all the organization; and (4) control and sustenance of the gains realized. Zooming in on the intensive event week (second level in Figure 8.5), we see that it consists of the launch, diagnosis, prescription (solution), and the initial stages of implementation. Ten moments of truth are shown along this timeline. They are given short names here, ranging from trust to vision, and we discuss each in detail later in this section.

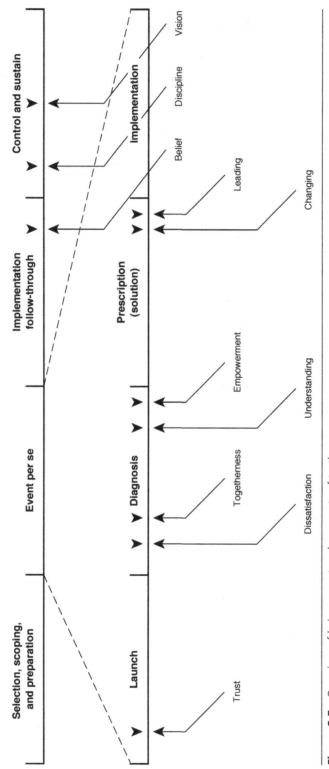

Figure 8.5 Overview of kaizen event and moments of truth.

Figure 8.6 is a flowchart presenting a higher-resolution view of the kaizen event, allowing us to see what the major players do. Executives scope a project to fix, improve, or design a cross-functional process and ensure executive involvement and support. The process owner is selected during the initial phase. She takes over where the executive committee leaves off. She consults with managers in all areas with a stake in the process to ensure that a proper team mandate is produced, to put together a project team, and to define the project.[3] Once the process comes to life during the event, her job is to keep it alive and continuously improving.

If the kaizen event were a play or a movie, she would be the producer, the facilitator would be the director, and the team would be the cast. At first, peers and managers would be the audience, but they would join the cast at the implementation phase as they become active players in the transformation. The cast works mostly backstage under the guidance of the director, with a few key appearances by the producer. They are first explained the play and their role by the producer and the director (see first triangle in Figure 8.6, from left to right). They make three critical stage appearances (the other three triangles) in front of concerned peers and managers to present and discuss the diagnostic, the solution, and the implementation plan. The director facilitates these live and lively encounters, ensuring a level playing field for the exchanges, thereby reinforcing evidence-based management at the expense of hierarchy and bureaucracy.

Figure 8.7 flows from the previous figures. It shows 10 activities of the kaizen team organized around an inner cycle, as each new event goes through the same sequence. A summary description of the associated moments of truth is presented in the outer cycle, formulated in the first person from the team's perspective. Let us explore them in turn: what they are, what role they play, how they could fail, and ways to avoid that fate.

1. *Trust.* "I trust them when they say that it is important, and that we are empowered to fix this and ensure that it stays fixed."

The initiative will never get off the ground unless a minimum threshold of trust is achieved. Does the team trust management's commitment to respect the rules of engagement, or does it have a good basis to fear that it is being manipulated? A company with a long tradition of manipulative management must first take a hard look at its management practices and its fundamental beliefs about employee capabilities and attitudes, at what is expected of them and due to them. Starting on a path that involves empowerment and participative management without doing this will backfire.

What is required: (1) Realism: don't start unless the organization is ready and management is truly committed. If that is not the case, you'd better tackle these issues first. (2) Honesty: be honest and transparent about what you are prepared to do. Body language is what matters; you just can't fake it. Abide scrupulously by the rules you set.

2. *Dissatisfaction.* "Do we really work that way? I would never have thought. We can't carry on like this."

Recognition that something significant is inadequate is a prerequisite for change. When management targets a process for improvement, it recognizes a problem or an opportunity. But it should not assume that the workers involved in the process will, as well. People do not change when you tell them that they

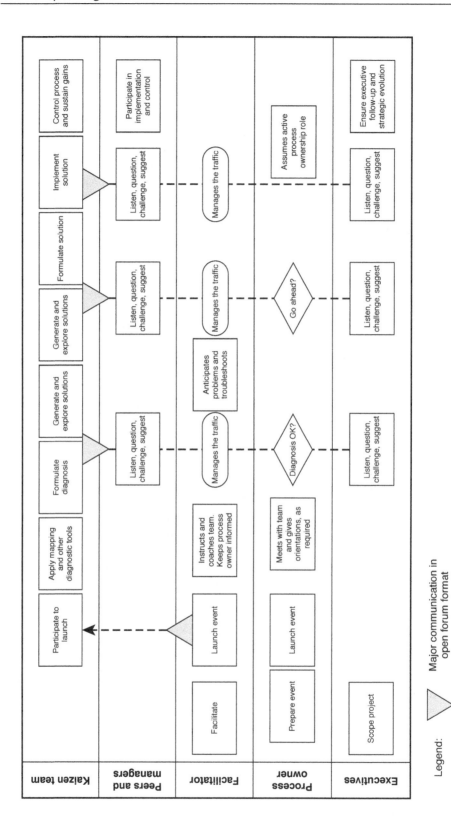

Figure 8.6 Simplified process mapping of a kaizen event.

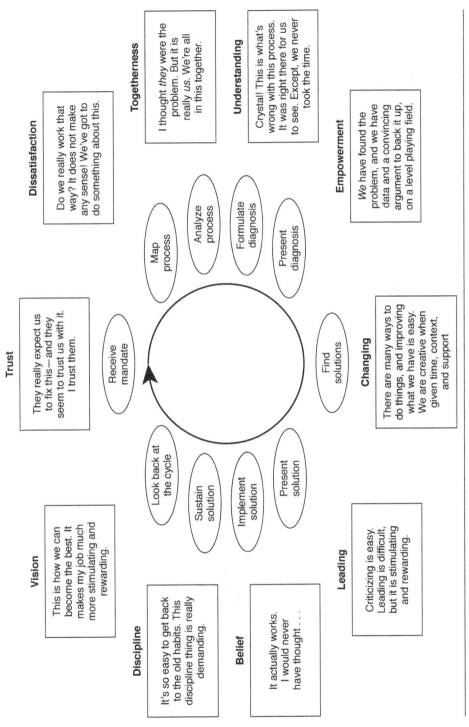

Dissatisfaction

Do we really work that way? It does not make any sense! We've got to do something about this.

Togetherness

I thought *they* were the problem. But it is really *us*. We're all in this together.

Understanding

Crystal! This is what's wrong with this process. It was right there for us to see. Except, we never took the time.

Empowerment

We have found the problem, and we have data and a convincing argument to back it up, on a level playing field.

Trust

They really expect us to fix this—and they seem to trust us with it. I trust them.

Changing

There are many ways to do things, and improving what we have is easy. We are creative when given time, context, and support

Vision

This is how we can become the best. It makes my job much more stimulating and rewarding.

Discipline

It's so easy to get back to the old habits. This discipline thing is really demanding.

Belief

It actually works. I would never have thought . . . .

Leading

Criticizing is easy. Leading is difficult, but it is stimulating and rewarding.

Map process
Analyze process
Formulate diagnosis
Present diagnosis
Find solutions
Present solution
Implement solution
Sustain solution
Look back at the cycle
Receive mandate

Figure 8.7 Ten moments of truth of the kaizen event.

should. They change when they tell themselves, "I must." One of the purposes of many diagnostic tools, such as process mapping, root cause analysis, or failure mode analysis, is to cause dissatisfaction by pointing out the flaws and limitations of the process. These methods are also great at bringing together and building consensus. Because they are simple and visual, they also facilitate sharing with larger groups.

What is required: (1) Make sure that all the stakeholders in the process are represented on the team by "heavyweights." Dissatisfaction with the current state has to be broad-based. (2) Use the right tools right, and give the team sufficient time to make its own determination. Remember: you can lead the horse to the fountain, but you can't force it to drink. Don't try to force it down their throat.

3. *Togetherness.* "I was convinced that it was their entire fault. Now I see that we are not blameless. In fact, we work at cross-purposes most of the time. No one area can solve this on its own."

Only a dedicated cross-functional team using appropriate tools can reach a shared understanding of the totality of a process and the interdependency of its components. Because process workers typically lack such an understanding, they are liable to perform in ways that might appear fine from the area's point of view, but are in fact very detrimental to the overall process. This tends to create frictions and conflicts between areas. Thus, at the outset of the kaizen event players arrive with preconceived ideas as to the causes of the problems, and they generally involve other areas in the role of the villain. It takes about two days, under pressure, to go through the sequence of emotions that form a disparate, even hostile, group of people into a team. The original adversarial relationship slowly gives way to an emerging "we" feeling.

What is required: (1) Leverage the dissatisfaction (previous moment of truth) and skillfully neutralize potential conflicts to allow a common understanding to emerge. (2) Carefully monitor and adjust the pressure being applied on individuals and on the team: pressure from their peers, tensions between team members and emerging "coalitions," pressure to perform in this assignment, and the immediate pressure to be ready on time with the right stuff to present to the audience.

4. *Understanding.* "Crystal! This is what's wrong with this process. It was right there for us to see. Except, we never took the time."

Gradually bringing the diagnosis into focus contributes to the creation of the "we" feeling mentioned earlier. This is where an appropriate methodology with the right set of tools plays a decisive role. Each tool looks at a different aspect of the process or looks at it from a different angle. Just as the image is gradually revealed when you are putting together a puzzle, so a shared diagnosis appears as the team uses a battery of tools. In this writer's experience, it is better to use many tools and limit the time available for each rather than focus on one or two. The team typically gets most of a tool's benefits in the first two hours of use. Sometimes a tool will reveal a fundamental cause that all the others had missed. Sometimes a tool "strikes out." Often, the same cause emerges through different tools. This contributes to reinforcing the team's confidence and creating consensus.

As the team uses the tools, solution ideas emerge, and so do issues that cannot be quickly resolved. It is important not to start discussing solutions at this stage, as this would result in endless and fruitless discussions that would derail the process. Rigor requires problem finding before solving. Until a diagnosis is reached and shared, idea generation should be encouraged, but discussion should be deferred to the "prescription" phase. A good practice consists of identifying an "idea manager," whose role consists of putting two flip-chart pages on the wall, labeling one page "ideas" and the other "issues," capturing emerging ideas and issues on sticky notes, placing the notes under the appropriate heading, and moving on with the discussion.

What is required: (1) Select an appropriate toolkit (see Chapters 9 and 10). (2) Set a time limit for the use of each tool. (3) Closely observe the progress that the team is making with each tool. (4) Adjust allotted time as required. (5) Add or eliminate tools as required by the team's progress. (6) Help the team in formulating a crisp, compelling diagnosis (see Chapter 9 for detailed instructions).

5. *Empowerment.* "We have found the problem, and we have data and a convincing argument to back it up."

The team presents its diagnosis to managers and colleagues on a level playing field. All questions and comments from everyone are welcome. Hard questions are especially welcome as long as they are formulated with respect, are not placing blame, and are supported by facts. Valid points are duly noted by the team, promising (and delivering) follow-up and feedback. The process owner concludes the session: "If anyone has any additional comment to make or fact to bring to the team's attention, speak now or forever hold your peace, for tomorrow we are moving on to the solutions phase." This is empowering, as the team feels supported by the organization. Such sessions, if they deliver on the expectations that they create, are a strong lever for culture change. Many important values are thus demonstrated: it is worthwhile to take the time to improve a process; employees are trusted experts; we are not looking for someone to blame but for a solution; we are guided by facts; problems are best fixed by frank, respectful, and open talk with the right people using a rigorous methodology.

What is required: (1) The rules of engagement must be clear for everyone. (2) The right people have to be present and know what to expect. (3) The facilitator must enforce the rules. (4) The team has to be open to constructive criticism (again, that is the facilitator's job). (5) Make sure that the process owner is trained thoroughly, supported, and kept abreast of the evolution of the workshop.

6. *Changing.* "There are many ways to do things, and improving what we have is easy. We are creative when given time, context, and support."

During the planning, build-up, and analytical phase, the team has not had any impact on the way things are done in the company. Switching from the analytical to the action mind-set is an important transition for the team to make. Making changes affects people, some of whom are likely to resist and complain about the changes. Results are never guaranteed. Some team member may have second thoughts at the time of crossing that line.

What is required: (1) Successful conclusion of the previous steps is vital: if the team does not feel supported, it may come apart at this juncture. (2) Immediately testing some small (safe) changes is often sufficient to give the team the confidence boost it may need. (3) Listen to the concerns of participants who have become gun-shy, and address their legitimate concerns. The "we" feeling among the team is an important asset here. (4) The facilitator and the process owner can leverage the most dynamic and action-oriented members of the team by giving them center stage.

7. *Leading.* "Criticizing is easy. Leading is difficult, but it is also much more stimulating and rewarding."

Once the team completes the prescription phase, they share a vision of a new process that does not yet exist. They become the leaders and champions of the new initiative. As they present this vision, explaining how it is going to work, responding to questions, and explaining what has to take place to make it a reality, they get the same mental image to appear in the minds of all involved. This is a central force for change. Since the team is composed of "heavyweights" from all sectors involved in the process, team members become flag bearers for the new process in their respective departments, identifying problems and incoherence as the implementation unfolds, and resolving them with the team.

What is required: (1) A tight follow-up structure coordinated by a process manager (a team member previously identified for this role) and supported by the process owner. (2) Regular progress meetings to remove roadblocks. (3) A firm deadline to "deliver" a fully implemented process. (4) Supportive behavior by all managers involved.

8. *Belief.* "It actually works. I would never have thought . . ."

Seeing the process performing at the desired level is the proof of the proverbial pudding. It changes beliefs about the nature of processes, the potential for improvement, and how it can be tapped. It affects not only team members but their coworkers and managers as well. In short, it is a cultural experience for the organization.

What is required: (1) Successful implementation. (2) Showcase the new process. (3) Celebrate the team's accomplishment.

9. *Discipline.* "It's so easy to get back to the old habits. This discipline thing is really demanding."

The most difficult part starts when implementation is complete. When the team and the support structures are disbanded, it is back to business. There is a tendency for this to mean business as usual.

What is required: (1) Process control and early detection of shift or drift in the process. (2) Quick corrective action by the process manager. (3) Extended follow-up by the process owner. (4) Punctual team meetings as required. (5) Executive meeting, if required. (6) Measurement of financial impact six months later, with positive consequences for those responsible. (7) Letting the process drift back to where it was before is not an option: it would kill the initiative and generate cynicism.

10. *Vision.* "This is how we can become the best. It makes my job much more stimulating and rewarding."

The organization must leverage the success to make explicit the vision it has of its culture. Without common references, such discussions can become abstract and detached from reality. The kaizen event is now a shared experience to which everyone can relate. It can be used to clarify meaning. As the event unfolds play by play, the organization lives the experience in the "here and now." As much as it might have been explained before, each participant is driven by the instructions and coaching he receives constantly. It is only afterward, given the required time and proper guidance, that fundamental lessons can be isolated and their implications for the future made explicit.

What's required: (1) Use the appropriate forum to let participants at all levels bring out and make explicit the lessons learned. (2) Relate these lessons (appropriate forum) to the cultural narrative envisioned by the leaders of the organization. (3) Translate this vision into a high-level plan of action to make it a reality. (4) Pace yourselves: set a sustainable rhythm for future workshops such that the workload imposed by the follow-through is not excessive, yet ensures that a critical mass of the employees go through the experience within a year (see Box 8.2).

Comparing the development approaches used by Africa and Korea (Box 8.2) provides interesting insights into what works and what does not when it comes to cultural change. Building an elite group is risky business. Training the masses to ensure that we quickly bring on board a critical mass of people in the organization is essential to the survival of a change initiative. This means intensive training[4] starting on day one. For instance, the president of an organization that successfully launched such an initiative decreed that 90% of employees, all levels included, would go through a five-day project-based training session during the first year of the initiative. Half-hearted measures will not allow the program to take off. When you need technical experts, hire consultants, just as the Koreans brought professors from abroad. Just like them, however, do not use them to "catch fish for you" but rather to "teach you how to fish." Make sure that their incentives (fees) are well aligned to this task.

Box 8.2 Comparing the Korean and African Approaches to Development

Issue: *The risk of losing touch with the masses*

In the 1960s and 1970s, African countries picked the best and the brightest among their people and sent them abroad to get higher education—to France, England, and the United States, mostly. In general, they excelled, and often obtained doctorates in a host of different fields. Unfortunately, they grew to be different people in the process and felt that they simply would not fit in anymore in their home environment. Many of them never returned. Those who did were not understood: to local people they sounded like Martians, or worse, like colonizers. They were confined to ivory towers and could never cross the chasm that now separated them from the masses. Many chose exile. Others stayed, creating a disconnected elite that was all too often contemptuous of the masses. They were paid well but did not contribute much. Not only were they not a positive force for change, they became an impediment to it.

Korea, on the contrary, invested massively in basic education and on-the-job, technical, scientific, and engineering training. It initially brought experts and scientists from abroad to assist in the education task. It also sent some of the most gifted to get doctorates abroad. In a very short period (in development terms) it produced masses of well-trained workers sharing a common language, thus setting a new standard to which every Korean youth aspired. In parallel, it created a demand for the services of these workers, promoting the creation of large conglomerates (*chaebols*, such as Hyundai, Daewoo, Samsung, and LG group). Korean universities then developed their own PhD programs. They now had a reception structure for the best and brightest that they sent abroad to get a doctorate.

Thus, without unduly simplifying complex continental development issues, mass diffusion of basic notions and tools and widespread sharing of new experiences beat the creation of a disconnected elite any day.

8.5 THE MATCH

The definition phase of the project is the appropriate moment to match process problem and change vehicle. Because these notions are not well understood, mismatching is common. In the best of cases, the resulting difficulties are puzzling for everyone, as people seek explanations for successes, half-successes, and outright failures. We have witnessed such puzzlement repeatedly. It takes its toll on the improvement program, and it may turn out to be the deciding factor when a new program faces its first challenges and unqualified success is required.

Understanding the ways in which process problems and change vehicles are related is essential to avoiding these problems. Table 8.2 presents a three-way matching of these entities. The "Yes" cells represent a good match. The medium gray cells indicate that this vehicle can contribute to the solution of that problem. The light gray cells are caution beacons, and the dark gray ones indicate a mismatch.

Comparing projects and kaizen events, we see that for new product development and complex processes, projects are clearly superior, while kaizen events are better for dealing with black box processes. Ineffective and inefficient processes are typically best dealt with by projects and kaizen events, respectively. Indeed, the former may require more complex data analysis, and the latter the participation of those who are most familiar with the actual details of execution.

The auditing process for the bank in the earlier example is a complex process. It involves analyzing many financial and operational variables related in complex ways. The way the dealership is operated impacts the financial results of the business. Understanding these results will provide critical clues as to how best to conduct the audit, focusing on the vital few aspects of the operation and not wasting time and money on trivial matters.

Table 8.2 Three-way match between process problems, methodologies, and change vehicles.

Process problem	Vehicle					
	(1) Project	(2) Kaizen event	(3) Workout	(4) Process management	(5) Semi-autonomous work team	(6) Just do it
New product (1a)	Yes			Yes		
New service (1b)	Yes	Yes		Yes		
Nonexistent process (2)	Yes	Yes		Yes		
Ineffective process (3)	Yes			Yes		
Inefficient process (4)		Yes				
Complex process (5)	Yes					
Black box process (6)		Yes		Yes		
Physical flow problems (7)	Yes	Yes				

▮ Will not solve that problem
▮ Will contribute as well, but will not be the primary solution
▮ Might be used in some cases, but be careful

As for new services, nonexistent processes, and physical flow problems, the choice depends on the specific circumstances surrounding the process. A process management team is also a quite versatile change vehicle. However, it will typically not be appropriate for complex processes and will contribute only as a useful complement to projects and kaizen events for inefficient processes and physical flow problems. If the solution is known, a just-do-it project may be in order—but any time spent making sure that it is the right solution is a wise investment.

Kaizen events are very well suited to fixing inefficient processes because basic tools are generally sufficient, and the multifunctional team dynamics thus created go a long way toward bringing solutions to the surface. Projects may be risky in this context, however, because they often lack such dynamics. The strength of projects is that they afford the team enough time to perform the rigorous data gathering and analysis required to optimize the process.

The job required in connection with a black box process is rather fundamental: understand and give some basic structure to a process that is unknown. A process management team followed by kaizen events may be a winning combination in this case.

The best methodology for improving physical flows is *just-in-time* (JIT; see Chapter 11). The optimum implementation of JIT is through a combination of projects, semiautonomous work teams, and kaizen events.

Further examination of Table 8.2 shows that three change vehicles (workouts, semiautonomous work teams, and "just do it") are essentially complements to the three major process change vehicles, with "just do it" always being subject to caution. An initial workout can often be used to look for quick wins, followed by a kaizen event and, if appropriate, by a semiautonomous work team to make the process come alive afterward.

8.6 CONCLUSION

In the beginning of the chapter, we used an analogy to illustrate the nature of process improvement. In considering how he is going to move his belongings, Jones needs to learn quite a bit about the moving business. While he knows his things very well from the static angle of using them every day, he has never looked at them as objects to be moved. Neither has he ever considered moving as a process, being strictly interested in the results. To see them in this new light, he needs to start thinking like a mover, that is, to adopt the dynamic view of objects being prepared for transport, handled, transported, and reinstalled. Similarly, organizations that want to improve processes must learn to view improvement as a process in its own right, to be designed and improved. They must see processes as objects of improvement, each with its specific requirements (Figure 8.3). They must understand that several methodologies and a host of tools are available, each with unique features. Finally, they must be acquainted with the complex characteristics of change vehicles (Figure 8.4), their potential to solve various types of problems (Table 8.2), their limitations, and the associated risks.

The kaizen event plays a central role in mobilizing a critical mass of employees. It enables a culture shift toward rigor and continuous improvement. It involves a complex social recipe and script that must be managed with great care.

The miseries created by the use of an inappropriate methodology or vehicle can be avoided. In order to do so, the process problem being addressed needs to be accurately characterized during the initial definition phase (Chapter 7), and a proper match must be achieved. Clearly, however, not all methodologies and vehicles are available at the outset of an improvement program, as each requires a substantial investment in learning, training, and communication. Thus, some process problems have to be sidetracked initially for lack of an appropriate methodology or change vehicle to address them. It is essential that the reasons for this be explained to all involved and that a time frame be given within which to address each type of process problem. Failure to do so will result in increasing frustration as some types of problems are systematically tossed aside, or worse, as the organization gives in and uses an inappropriate methodology or vehicle, thereby taking the wind out of the sails of a fledgling program.

The learning pump lies at the heart of an organization's learning ability. This in turn is central to long-term competitiveness. Learning to discriminate between the various types of problems, methodologies, tools, and change vehicles is difficult, but essential. Without a good matching capability, the pump will never perform up to its full potential, and learning will proceed at a slower pace.

EXERCISES

8.1 Exploring the Challenges of Matching

Refer back to the work you did in the end-of-chapter exercises in Chapter 7, and particularly to the five projects for which you formulated a mission statement in exercise 7.5.

a. Classify the major problem of each process, using the decision tree provided in Figure 8.3.

b. Using Table 8.2 and the tree structure provided in Figure 8.4, identify the change vehicle that would be most appropriate for each project.

8.2 Kaizen Event

If you are aware of a (noncompeting) company that regularly conducts kaizen events, contact it to explore the possibility of participating in one. Many companies welcome such participation, as the guest is much more than a passive witness: a fresh point of view from someone totally unfamiliar with a process can richly enhance a team's capability. If you do not know of any such company, your local ASQ chapter may help in that regard.

NOTES

1. This chapter is partly drawn from Harvey (2004).
2. The words "problems" and "opportunities" are used interchangeably.
3. If the Six Sigma DMAIC methodology is used, this would correspond to the *define* phase.
4. If you do not know where to start with training, the best place to start is the American Society for Quality at http://www.asq.org.

9

Doing Things Better:
Improving an Existing Process

We become what we behold. We shape our tools and thereafter our tools shape us.

—Marshall McLuhan

It is more effective to act yourself into thinking differently than to think yourself into acting differently.

The DMAIC improvement methodology needs to be adapted to a professional service environment.

Once we have identified important processes and selected the appropriate methodology and change vehicle, the "trip" begins. In this chapter we describe the improvement methodology, and in the next one, the design methodology. After presenting a bird's-eye view of the methodology and some of the principles that underpin it, we illustrate it with a detailed example (QKM). We conclude the chapter with further thought about how and why the methodology works. A five-part video (Video 9.1, see Figure 9.1) is a very useful companion to this chapter. Each part addresses a distinct phase of the methodology presented in this chapter. We suggest that you view the first part now, and then view the other parts as each phase is discussed in the chapter.

9.1 HIGH-LEVEL VIEW OF THE IMPROVEMENT METHODOLOGY

The improvement methodology comprises five stages: define, measure, analyze, improve, and control (DMAIC, for short—see Figure 9.2). The methodology is associated with Six Sigma (to see how it fits into Six Sigma, see Schroeder et al. [2008]). Since the reader is now familiar with processes, it is useful to understand that the methodology itself is a process—a process to improve a process. The five sequential subprocesses, or phases, are each defined by an action verb as listed earlier. The input to the process is an improvement idea, which comes from an idea hopper, such as that discussed in Chapter 7. The output is an improved process that is stable and capable. Each phase or subprocess contributes to that transformation.

263

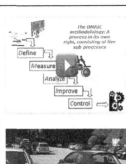

9.1 The DMAIC methodology

Overview of the DMAIC methodology—The process improvement methodology
This five-part series presents the generic DMAIC process improvement methology. Part 1 provides some perspective and gives an overview of the methodology (the "Define" phase is covered in other videos). Parts 2, 3, 4, and 5 cover "M," "A," "I," and "C," respectively.

Measure
If you can't measure it, you do not know anything about it.

Analyze
Primum non nocere: problem finding before problem solving. Share it with all concerned before you even discuss solutions.

Improve
Now you can fix it.

Control
That's the toughest part: woe befalls the organization that cannot stay the course.

Figure 9.1 Videos associated with Chapter 9.

We described the *define* phase in detail in Chapter 7. It starts from the improvement idea and produces a well-scoped project. It uses the tools presented in Chapter 7. The *measure* phase describes the process, the flows involved, the variables, and their measurement systems. The *analyze* phase takes in these variables and separates the "vital few" from the "trivial many" to produce a validated diagnosis. The *improve* phase proceeds from the diagnosis to formulate and validate a prescription. The *control* phase implements the new process and ensures that the improvement will not be lost once the organization moves on to another agenda. We show in Figure 9.2 some of the tools available to effect these transformations, in their respective toolboxes.

Contrast this with the normal way of "resolving problems" in most organizations. We typically discuss the problem during a meeting, and when time is up we consider it defined, and the boss assigns the job of fixing it to an "owner." Often, no data are available. Sometimes we have bad data, measuring the wrong thing, the wrong way. We brainstorm informally for causes, jump on one that sounds

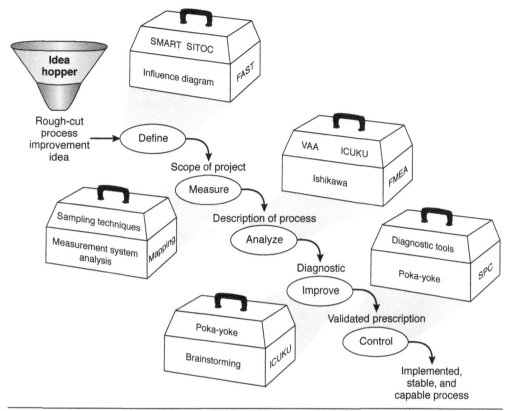

Figure 9.2 The DMAIC improvement methodology: phases, inputs, outputs, and partial toolkits.

right, label it a diagnosis, and start looking for quick fixes. We tinker with the process until we feel that the initial symptoms are gone or attenuated and move on to the next problem without ever looking back. These organizations suffer from "short attention span disorder," a learning disability that condemns them to repeat the same mistakes and face the same situations repeatedly. As discussed in Chapter 11, in such firefighting organizations the culture is perpetuated by promoting the best firefighters, and no one is ever promoted for preventing a fire.

The DMAIC methodology is about rigor. Following are some basic principles that underpin it:

- Any process improvement drive must be based on a well-defined problem statement.

- If one cannot measure it, one does not know much about it, and thus cannot improve it. If ever one improves it, it will be by chance, and we will never know for sure.

- Never trust data unless you know where they came from and how they were gathered.

- Problem finding before problem solving. Get consensus on an explicit diagnosis before moving on to the prescription.

- Formulate hypotheses that are grounded in facts.

- It is fine to work on the basis of an unproven hypothesis. However, the practice (lack of rigor) of accepting such hypotheses as true, called *superstitious learning*, is a fatal cultural trait.

- Prove the solution before implementing it.

- Following up is the most difficult part. Confining rigor to the improvement events, and going back to firefighting mode the day after, will only foster cynicism.

We now turn to a detailed example. The reader is advised to first review Box 5.1, glance anew at Figure 5.2, and read Box 9.1 to understand the company's background and the situation in the following section.

Box 9.1　Quality Knowledge Management: The Action Course

Issue: *A consulting firm wants to improve a hands-on training process*

Among its other services, QKM (see Box 5.1) assists organizations embarking on process-based quality initiatives, such as capability maturity model (CMM), ISO, total quality management (TQM), activity-based costing (ABC), and Six Sigma (see Chapter 11 for a discussion of these approaches). Since competition in this field is fierce—involving several firms that are much larger and better known than QKM—the firm is a niche player. When it considered entering this market, it conducted a survey, which indicated that there was much dissatisfaction. Several organizations felt manipulated by consultants repackaging old programs, re-branding them, and marketing them as novelties. Many organizations also felt that once the consultants had entered the organization, many of them made themselves indispensable and stuck around, charging as much money as they could. QKM felt that much of the industry managed that particular fault line poorly: exploiting one's customers' trust and one's superior knowledge to extract more financial advantage.

Since these perceptions were more widespread in small to medium-size companies, QKM targeted companies with 200 to 2000 employees. Its value proposition went as follows: "We will assist you in the creation of durable and profitable know-how in the field of processes and quality—the tried and true as well as the most recent developments. We will not sell you fish; we will show you how to fish and leave as soon as you have acquired the know-how. We will coach you along as you reach higher levels of capability." As part of its offerings in this program, QKM had developed a training process to jump-start the initiative, produce quick results, and build a critical mass of managers and employees sharing a common understanding and common beliefs in the fundamental notions underpinning the initiative. This was complemented by a parallel offering consisting of coaching top management in the connection of strategy to operations and in the creation of a quality culture. The QKM consultant acting in that capacity also assumes the role of coordinating the PAC.

The PAC consists of five one-day "in-class" sessions and one day of coaching spread over a five-month period. Twenty managers or other high-potential employees are selected and asked, before the sessions start, to select an improvement project on which they will work, together with a team (team members do not take the course), throughout the course. They receive material prior to the start of the course to prepare them and guide them through project selection and initial scoping. Top management is consulted in selecting the trainees and the projects. The PAC typically generates much action in the organization—"teaching it how to fish"—at a relatively low cost for QKM, and thus acts as a major profit lever.

As part of its own continuous improvement efforts, the PAC itself has surfaced as a process that holds substantial improvement potential. The major opportunity lies in improving the success rate of the projects. While the projects are primarily for learning purposes, their success is an important ingredient in the recipe for changing the culture, that is, changing beliefs through a significant personal and organizational experience. Another aspect that needs improvement is the start-up or pre-course phase, which many customers feel is long and cumbersome. QKM recently performed a PAC for a new client: a large national organization that asked QKM to set it up as a pilot, to determine whether it should proceed to national deployment. While the client was impressed overall, it would approve deployment only if QKM agreed to work with them on improving the process beforehand.

9.2 BACKGROUND

Quality Knowledge Management (QKM) agrees with its client that the process action course (PAC) has potential and that they can improve it. Hence, they set up a joint kaizen event. QKM's managing partner is designated as the process owner, and the client's chief learning officer accepts to act as process owner within the client organization. They hold the kaizen as a joint event on the client's premises. The client expects QKM to draw on its experience with the PAC in many organizations since its inception to ensure that the process deployed by the client is world-class. The co-owners ask a senior person from each organization to help them in the scoping exercise.

9.3 DEFINE

The goals of the project are to improve the success rate of training projects undertaken by all participants of the PAC and to streamline the launching of a course. As illustrated in Figure 9.2, the input to the *define* phase is a vague idea, and the output is a well-scoped project, ready to enter the *measure* phase.

The scoping team follows the methodology presented in Chapter 7. The "big Y" reads as follows: "Training projects currently suffer a failure rate of 30%. It should not exceed 10%." This is a SMART statement (specific, measurable, achievable, relevant, and time-bound). "Improving the performance of the process" is not specific or measurable. The goal or goals selected must relate to something important for the organization (relevant). The target must be ambitious and stimulating, yet achievable. A valid measurement system must be available to allow tracing the progress of the project toward the goal. Finally, a date must be set to achieve the target. The team also identifies a secondary problem: "It takes 32 days to start a course. It should not exceed 15 days." While the team realizes that inefficiency is also a problem, it feels that the bulk of the waste occurs in the start-up phase, and that reducing start-up time would simultaneously improve efficiency.

Team members initially start exploring the process "deliver the PAC." They formulate its mission as follows: "To deliver to participants a process improvement experience that will induce a change of belief and transform them into positive change agents toward a quality culture." The FAST diagram shows that there are five subprocesses:

- Plan the course

- Set up the course

- Teach the course

- Support the projects

- Follow up on the projects

The team explores the relative importance of each of these functions using an influence diagram and assesses the current performance of these subprocesses using an efficiency–effectiveness diagram (examples are shown in Figures 7.16 and 7.24, respectively). The team then proceeds to prepare a macro map of the process (see Figure 9.3). It shows that nine generic players are involved, all of whom are at play during the pre-course phase, and that the process is large—too large in fact for a single improvement project. The preceding analysis, much of which we do not show here, reveals that the pre-course (or course setup) subprocess holds the greatest potential to achieve (or contribute to) the "big Y" and other secondary goals. Hence, it is selected for improvement in this project (see the FAST diagram in Figure 9.4). It includes selecting the trainees and their projects, selecting and assembling the material, setting up the logistics, preparing for the class (for the instructor), and supporting the trainees in their preparation for class. Depending on the results achieved at the end of the project, the team feels that it might be worthwhile to tackle the "support projects" subprocess next.

The team then proceeds to formalize the new, narrower scope. It first formulates a SMART problem statement as follows: "The percentage of 'trainee–project' couples that do not meet all selection criteria is currently 70%. It should not exceed 10%." We show this goal in Figure 9.5. This representation makes it clear and visual, thus focusing the project and the team on the goal. The indicator selected (the "small y") is directly related to the "big Y." Selecting the right trainees and pairing them with a project that has the potential to "induce a change of belief" is the key contribution of the process. Counting the number of such pairs that do not meet all criteria (that is, the criteria for selecting the trainees, and those for the project) is one possible metric for this. Counting the number of criteria not met would be another.

We also show the SITOC in Figure 9.5. The process delivers outputs to both the client and internal customers. As in most business-to-business (B2B) service delivery, the process interacts with various players within the organization. Internal customers are generally processes, and, thus, this process supplies inputs to other downstream processes. The inputs to the process are the outputs of other supplier processes—in this case, "plan training" and "plan project selection." The SITOC sets the perimeter of the project and delimits it in time as well. Figure 9.6 completes the scope of the project by specifying relevant customer needs, identifying technical characteristics, and spelling out the mission of the process. In this case, the SMART problem statement is a direct measure of the extent to which the process achieves its mission. This only happens when the purpose of the project is

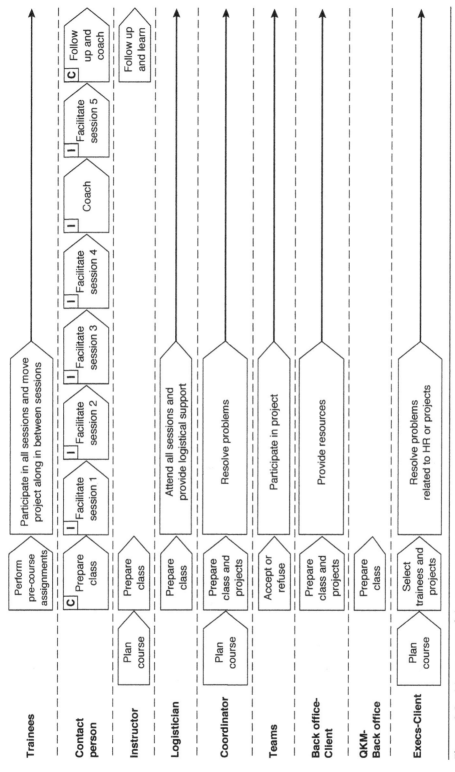

Figure 9.3 Macro map of the PAC at QKM.

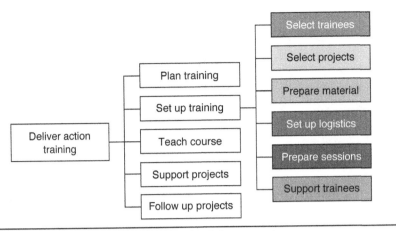

Figure 9.4   FAST diagram of the PAC, with details of the setup phase.

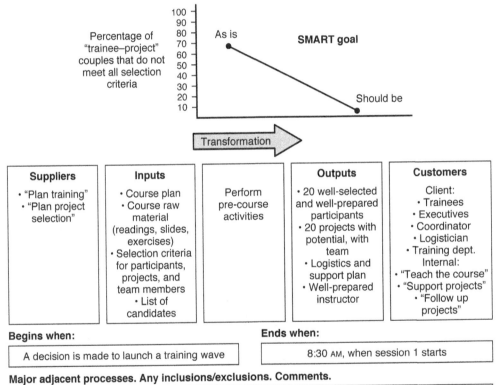

Figure 9.5   Project scope: SMART problem statement, SITOC, boundaries, and comments.

Chain of internal customers connecting the process to the client

> Process is direct to client, and indirect as well to the following processes:
> *teach the course–support projects–follow up projects*

Relevant client needs

> Trainees: hands-on knowledge, a value-changing experience, feeling supported

Relevant needs and priorities of internal customers

> Well-selected and well-prepared participants, well-scoped project (*no surprises*)

Technical characteristics

Quality
Percentage of well-scoped projects
Number of participants meeting selection criteria

Cost
Savings per project
Start-up cost

Time
Number of participants receiving material
with sufficient lead time

Process mission
To deliver, when training begins,
20 well-prepared participants,
with the right profile, the right
mind-set, and a well-scoped project

Figure 9.6 Project scope: customer needs, technical characteristics, and process mission.

to improve effectiveness. When we are dealing with an inefficient process or one that is too slow, the SMART and mission statements are not directly related.

It is important to see the chain of internal customers (or internal processes) that connects the process to the end customer. One must make every effort to identify end customer needs that the process affects, however remotely. We also identify the needs of internal customers, as the process must meet these as well. We finally identify a number of technical characteristics related to quality, cost, and timeliness. Even though the project normally centers on one or two specific goals, it is useful to consider all three dimensions, if only to make sure that what we gain on one front is not lost on another.

The owners then select eight team members as follows:

- A senior QKM partner expert in kaizen events and the DMAIC methodology, but without past involvement in the PAC program and its deployment, to act as team leader

- The coordinator involved in the recently concluded PAC pilot, who is also the person responsible for managing the process on a day-to-day basis, to act as coleader

- Two QKM instructors and a QKM consultant who often acts as coordinator

- Two executives and the person designated to act as logistician for the client

They make sure that all team members are experienced and credible within their respective departments to ensure that they are in a position to exert the leadership role that is expected of them. Considering the size of the process to be improved, they decide that a four-day event should be sufficient. They schedule forums (see Chapter 8) to be held at the end of the second day (diagnosis), at the end of the third day (prescription), and at the closing (fully developed process, with control system). The owners then call a two-hour kickoff session during which they present and discuss the mandate with the team.

9.4 MEASURE

The output of the *measure* phase is a detailed description of the process, allowing for identification of all variables and a validation of relevant measurement systems. At the outset of day one, the team assigns a number of specific roles to various team members: idea manager (to capture ideas, place them in a "parking lot" for future action, and cut short any premature discussion of solutions), a timekeeper, and a scribe.

Process mapping is a key deliverable. Without a good visual representation of the process, no analysis is possible. The SITOC and FAST diagrams serve as guidelines in the preparation of the process map (see Figure 9.7). Remember from Chapter 3 that we use the line of interaction to depict face-to-face contact only. We depict remote contact as bilateral arrows connecting activities on both sides of the line of visibility. The symbols and conventions used are those presented in Chapter 3, with a few exceptions. One difference is that we use average durations instead of ranges, for simplicity's sake. Notice that some tasks take a few hours while others last for days. We mapped the latter, for practical reasons, at a higher level than the former; that is, they are aggregates of many different things. For instance, both the coordinator and the instructor spend five days at the task "answer questions." Obviously, they do not spend five days on the phone. A truly complete mapping of this task would specify, for each call made by a trainee, a decision point (instructor available or not?), a delay (if not available), a callback, another decision point (trainee available or not?), and so on. Since this would be impractical, we use a single symbol. We address this issue in more detail in section 9.5.4, dealing with value-added analysis.

We use color coding to visualize the different functions identified in the FAST diagram (the color schemes used in Figures 9.4 and 9.7 are the same). The process involves nine players, two organizations, and as many as a hundred people, including the trainees, team members, and executives. It involves 17 "handoffs," that is, instances when the flow crosses over from one lane to another. Since several players can act as "contact person" (though, as it turns out, only one does in this case), we place a letter (each player is identified by a bold letter) in the upper-left corner of the task box to specify this role. The instructor, the coordinator, and the back office of QKM ("QKM-BO" in Figure 9.7) are QKM employees; the other players work for the client.

Process mapping is not an exact science. As the team maps the process, it makes many choices. The map shown in Figure 9.7 is still at a high level. We could split "select trainees," for instance, into a much more detailed map, specifying the intricate back-and-forth that takes place between the coordinator, the executives, and potential trainees. The choice the team makes in representing it as it does is to

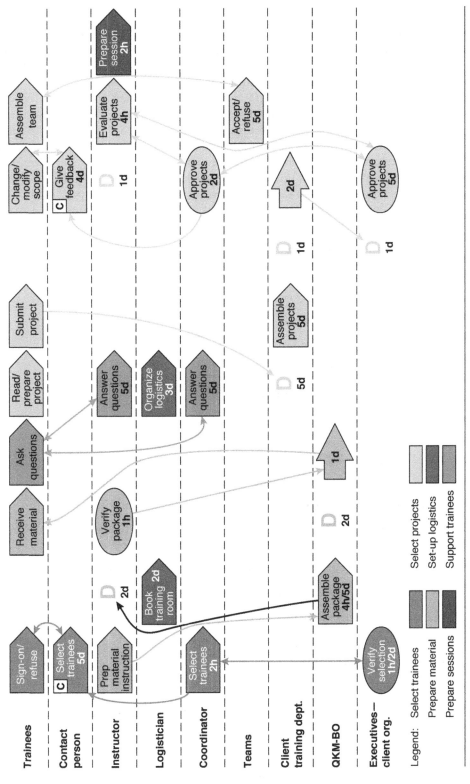

Figure 9.7 Process mapping: pre-course segment.

"dig" selectively into areas where analysis indicates that it may be worthwhile to do so, thus keeping it simple. Further, only the delays that can potentially lie on the critical path (that is, actually make cycle time longer) are mapped. Thus, the team does not map delays in returning phone calls or waiting to receive the material, especially since nobody is idle during these periods.

The process map allows for a first round of identification of variables. We discussed the notion of variables in Chapter 6 and illustrated it with the example of humidity and temperature control in a house. These are continuous variables, such as cycle time in the case at hand. A discrete variable only takes on a limited number of values, generally positive integer values, such as the number of trainees in our case. A categorical or nominal variable is nonnumeric. A mode of contact, for instance, may be face-to-face "tight-spec," face-to-face "loose spec," and so on. Examining Figure 9.7, the team can see that the process really consists of many variables. Here is a partial list:

- Work time and elapsed time of each task

- Number of trainees

- Number and identity of executives involved

- Extent of involvement of executives

- Selection criteria for trainees

- Selection criteria for projects

- Material selection: which and how much?

- Who is involved in the selection processes? Who recommends? Approves? Vetoes?

- In what sequence are they involved?

- Division of work between instructor, logistician, and coordinator

- Who does the clerical work involved in preparing the initial package?

- Deadlines for the various assignments (select a project, turn it in, select team members)

- Degree of support given to the trainee during project selection

- Degree of leeway given to the trainee in project selection

- How are the information and support given: individually or in a group?

- Modes of contact for each contact point

- Criteria for selection of team members

- Number of team members

- Where will the training be conducted? (size of room, breakout rooms, electronic support, meals, and so on)

- Duration of each delay and transport

- How many mistakes are made at each step? How many are caught and corrected in time?

We often refer to these variables as the Xs, or independent variables. The dependent variable ("the small y") is a function of these variables. We can formalize this as follows:

$$y = f(X_1, X_2, X_3, \ldots X_n)$$

In processes where all variables are numerical, this equation can take on a strictly mathematical form. This is seldom the case in professional services, however, though the dependent variable itself must always be numerical. While we selected "the number of projects not meeting criteria" as the "small y," other dependent variables include cycle times (global and for each function) and number of criteria not met. Some independent variables are controllable, some are partly controllable, and others are uncontrollable. Identifying the latter is equally important, though, as one may set the value of controllable variables as a function of uncontrollable variables; that is, while one cannot control these variables, one may consider them in process control.

Once the team has mapped the process and identified its variables, it is ready for data gathering. For numerical variables, the team first evaluates existing measurement systems. In the *define* phase, for instance, the scoping team estimated that 70% of all trainee–project pairs did not meet all the selection criteria. The project team found out that this was based on a guesstimate. This is not good enough. Thus, the team decides to go back to past courses, pull the project and trainee selection sheets from the files, and evaluate the quality of that information. It finds that the sheets, showing tick marks on a five-point scale next to each criterion, are quite usable in general. Some sheets, however, are incomplete, and the team decides on the minimal requirements for a sheet to be usable. Further, after interviewing the people who filled out the sheets, the team decides to consider a score of three or better on any criterion as a "passing grade" (that is, the project or trainee met the criterion).

The coach then proposes a sampling strategy and a sampling plan. Formulating a sampling strategy involves an evaluation of the amount of data available, the quality of the data, and the cost of retrieving the data in light of the use we have for them and the need for validity, reliability, and precision. The strategy strikes the most advantageous balance between these elements, and the sampling plan translates into specific instructions (Who? When? Where? How? How many?) for gathering the data. A detailed discussion of sampling is beyond the scope of this book. A number of simple rules of thumb can be useful, however, for someone who does not have access to competent resources in this field:

- When data gathering is not costly, go for the maximum you can get with the resources at hand and within the time frame available.

- If measurement is ongoing, add a second person to independently measure (in parallel) the phenomenon of interest. To validate the interpretation of "soft" data, that is, data that require much judgment, interview more than one person involved in gathering and interpreting the data. Have them independently interpret a number of observations and compare the results. Unless you have a very good match, do not use the data. It is better to have no data than to have misleading data. Design and validate (using the same approach) a new measurement system and start anew. You will have fewer data, but you will be able to use them safely.

- A guesstimate or ballpark figure can be useful, if you recognize it as such. You can improve such estimates by using variants of the *Delphi method*. In cases where several people are familiar enough with the phenomenon to be assessed (the proportion of trainees that do not meet all criteria, say), the Delphi method consists of asking them independently for their best estimates. These are gathered, plotted on a histogram, and shown to the assessors in a meeting. Those with extreme values explain their reasons to the others, and a general discussion ensues, after which a new round of independent assessment is conducted. The mean result of this second assessment is your best estimate.

- Having 30 observations, whenever possible, allows for confidently producing estimates for the mean and standard deviation, knowing the margins of error. This holds true for any dimension or category for which we need an estimate. For instance, if four modes of contact are used and we would like to know how long a task takes in each case, we will need 30 observations for each mode of contact.

- The preceding rule should not prevent us from using whatever number of observations is available, as long as the measurement system is valid. Any valid data point is vastly superior to guesswork. One must always remain vigilant, however, not to forget that the margin of error grows rapidly as sample size goes down.

Data collection includes categorical variables as well, such as modes of contact. The team finds out that course material has been delivered by mail in 8 out of the last 10 courses, and electronically twice. This is data. It shows variation. This variation will be useful in the *analyze* phase as a potential factor in understanding why some trainees come up with better projects, for instance. The same holds true for other categorical variables listed earlier, such as selection criteria and leeway given to trainees in project selection.

Given the cost and time required, the team only spends time on the variables that have, in its best judgment, a strong probability of being useful in the *analyze* phase. If it misses some important variable that shows up later, it has to validate the measurement system and proceed to data collection at that time.

The team is now ready to analyze the data.

9.5 ANALYZE

The output of the *analyze* phase is a diagnosis. It is a statement of the exact nature of the problem and its causality, together with a summation of the proof.

A lawyer's process to produce his summation or a doctor's process to produce a diagnosis is quite similar to the *analyze* phase. The lawyer uses various techniques (interviews, inquiries, expert assessments, and so on) to understand the facts of the matter and make a convincing case—convincing himself first, so that he can convince other interested parties later. The doctor follows the same logical path. She interviews the patient and proceeds selectively to investigations, such as patient examination, blood analysis, X-ray, and biopsy. When all results are in, she performs a mental process of analysis—that is, using her training and professional judgment to formulate a diagnosis based on the evidence. The team uses various analytical techniques (see Table 9.1) to formulate a diagnosis shared by all team

Table 9.1 The *analyze* toolkit: description, purpose, indication, limitations, and challenges involved with each tool.

Technique	Description	Purpose	Indication	Limitations/Challenges
Influence diagram	Using a systems approach to identify and connect a priori variables to processes.	To assist in scoping the project by projecting the team's original understanding of the set of factors at play.	The more complex the set of problems, the more useful the diagram.	You must be careful to limit the number of variables and processes, lest the tool become unmanageable.
Process map	Detailed description of the sequential flow of the process and the role of each player.	To make the process visible, often for the first time, and provide a starting point for the analysis.	An essential component to any process analysis.	Finding the right level of detail at which to map and maintaining homogeneity.
CTP identification	Singling out three to five activities that play a key role in creating, and thus in solving, the problem.	To isolate the vital few from the trivial many, allowing us to dig in areas where we are more likely to find gold.	Always useful. The discussions it generates help the team move toward a consensus.	Finding data or evidence to support this analysis can be challenging in "soft" professional services.
Ishikawa diagram	Identifying causes of the problem and organizing them in generic categories.	An alternate way to identify causal variables, catching some that our analysis of the mapping might have missed.	Generally useful because it is not based on the process map—thus providing validation through a different route.	May be somewhat redundant at times, when the mapping and influence diagram have been very successful.
ICUKU	Classifying causes or improvement ideas following three binary criteria: impact, controllable/ uncontrollable, known/unknown.	To help the team focus on causes/ ideas that hold the greatest potential.	Whenever a large number of causes or ideas have been generated and the team does not know where to start.	The classification is somewhat arbitrary and may generate considerable debate.
Root cause (why)	Probing some causes, through a series of "why" questions, until the root cause is found.	Some of the causes generated in the Ishikawa diagram are only symptoms. Only through addressing the root cause can a durable solution be found.	Especially useful when the analysis has been superficial and when high-impact, controllable causes with unknown solutions exist.	Sometimes root causes are so philosophical or vague as to offer no viable angle for improvement, at least within the framework of a project.
VAA	Calculating the proportion of the cycle time when value is being added.	Identify the potential for improvement and help focus the effort through identification of "air bubbles."	Particularly useful when the team is working on a process that is inefficient or that has an unduly long cycle time.	If the main problem is that the process is ineffective, the technique may not be helpful.
FMEA	Identifying/rating risks of defects on the basis of three criteria: severity, probability of occurrence, probability of detection.	Focusing on the most important risks to make the process robust. Promote continuous improvement through follow-up or risks.	One of the most powerful tools in the quality toolbox. Can be used in analyze, improve, and control phases.	Must be based on a detailed mapping of the process. May require "exploding" selected activities in more detail.
Diagnostic worksheet	Grouping the major conclusions stemming from each technique used and analyzing to find patterns and formulate diagnostic.	Provide at a glance a summary of all the data points available, thus facilitating analysis and validation.	Whenever more than one diagnostic tool is used.	This does not do away with analytical and synthetic capabilities. The tools facilitate the task but do not by any means provide a recipe.

members. It must first reach a consensus, and then convince other stakeholders. We now turn to a presentation and discussion of each technique.

9.5.1 CTP Identification

An important step toward formulating a diagnosis is being able to weed out the relatively insignificant variables ("the trivial many") in order to concentrate on the most important ones ("the vital few"). The Pareto principle suggests that 20% of the variables are responsible for 80% of the problem. As mentioned in Chapter 3, we refer to these variables as "critical to process" variables, or CTPs. This technique is the team's first effort to identify these variables. At the outset, as he hands out a form similar to Table 9.2, the coach presents the team with the following instructions:

1. Go back to your process map and identify three to five activities you believe to be critical to the achievement of the SMART goal. Base this selection on available data, and be ready to justify your choice. Mark these activities with a diamond.

2. For each of these activities, specify what, exactly, is critical. Be specific. Several things may be critical within each activity. These are the CTPs of your process.

3. For each CTP, identify the mode of control currently used, if any, and explore other possibilities of control that would potentially be more effective or efficient.

Table 9.2 Critical activities, CTP variables, current and alternate controls on activities.

Activity	It is critical that . . .	How do we currently ensure that this is done right?	What are other possible ways to control this?
The coordinator selects trainees	The trainees understand what they are getting into	It is explained in a memo	They meet with the graduates of the last course
	We ascertain that the trainees have the right motivation for the course	They are asked why they want to take the course	They are interviewed by two graduates
	The trainees be able to devote the time required by the course	They are asked if they can fit the course into their daily work	Their superiors are asked to sign a form specifying the time requirement
The instructor and the coordinator answer questions about preparing an initial project scope	The trainees understand what a process is	Nothing	A half-day session is scheduled for that purpose prior to session 1
	The trainees get a clear answer quickly	The instructor and the coordinator do their best	Measure response time and trainee satisfaction (survey)
The coordinator gives feedback to the trainees so that they can adjust the scope of the project	The trainees understand what is wrong with their initial submission and why	The instructor and the coordinator do their best	Ask the trainee to reformulate on the spot, face-to-face

We show the team's work in Table 9.2 (also see the white diamonds in Figure 9.9). Considering the goal of the project, "select trainees" is obviously critical. Team discussion shows that there is considerable variation in the way this is done. The team also pinpoints "answer questions" of trainees, as either the coordinator or the instructor does this, depending on who is available. "Give feedback" to the trainee, to help him change the scope as required, is the last critical activity that the team identifies, as most projects need to be "rescoped," and this is also done in a cursory fashion. The team identifies (see the second column of Table 9.2) three CTPs within the first activity, two in the second, and one in the third. They do this through exploration and comparison of the last few training waves, trying to pinpoint the factors that made a given wave more or less successful than the others. Through heated discussion the team gradually succeeds in reaching consensus. The team initially formulates a dozen potential CTPs but succeeds in "disproving" six of them.

9.5.2 Fishbone (Ishikawa) Diagram and Prioritization Tool (ICUKU)

In the *define* phase, the team used an Ishikawa diagram (not shown here) to assist in scoping the project correctly. Use of Ishikawa diagrams in this context is discussed in Chapter 7. The trigger the team used then was based on the "big Y": "Why is the failure rate of training projects so high?" The team uses the technique again here. However, it uses the "small y" as a trigger this time. The coach thus gives the team the following instructions:

1. Paste together two or three sheets of paper from a flip chart and draw a fishbone diagram with six "bones" on it. Label each with one of the following categories:

   – Methods—activities performed incorrectly

   – Manpower—any human resources–related cause

   – Information systems and information technology (IS/IT)

   – Equipment and installations

   – Measures—any measurement issue

   – Organization and culture—any "soft" cause related to power, formal relationships, and shared values

   You may create different categories, such as "environment" or "suppliers," if you feel this is warranted.

2. Place the following question at the head of the fishbone: "Why is it that so many trainee–candidate pairs do not meet all selection criteria?"

3. In silence, identify all possible answers to this question, write them down on sticky notes, and stick them in the appropriate category. If you start running out of ideas, mentally explore all the categories of the diagram and look at the causes your colleagues are coming up with, as this may trigger other ideas.

4. When everyone has run out of ideas, elect a teammate to facilitate a review and rationalization of the diagram, eliminating duplicates, rewording, and reorganizing as the need arises.

This is a useful tool at this point because it provides a separate route to identify the variables at play, one that is not based on the process map. Using those categories forces the team members to think differently, thus generally bringing out some variables they had not yet identified. However, since the goal of the *analyze* phase is to single out the most important variables, this tool alone is incomplete. The ICUKU (impact, controllable, uncontrollable, known, unknown) classification is a companion tool that serves this purpose. The coach now provides the team with the following additional instructions (see Table 9.3):

1. Split a flip-chart page into three columns, labeling them *major, medium,* and *minor.*

2. Remove the sticky notes from the fishbone one at a time and stick them in one of the three columns according to the team's best judgment about its impact on the problem. The decisions must be consensual and supported by data.

3. Now, split each column in two, separating the causes that the team feels are somehow controllable from those over which it has no control, in the context of the mandate it was given. If the team believes it could have some control, however partial or limited, it should classify the cause as controllable, even though it does not have a specific idea about how it would go about controlling it.

4. Finally, split the first row created in the previous step (the causes classified as "controllable") into those causes for which the team can readily think of a solution ("known") and those for which it cannot ("unknown"). Pulling each cause off the page, the team should ask itself, "Do we know how to fix this?" While the team should not explore solutions in any depth at this time, the team's idea manager should remain on the lookout and keep on filling the parking lot.

In going through these four steps, the team should use the data collected in the earlier phases and bring its experience to bear, supporting its classification with examples and illustrations. These two tools work well together: the first one generates a large number of causes, while the second allows the team to focus on the greatest opportunities, or "low-hanging fruit." Table 9.3 brings out a number of important issues:

- Executive involvement is uneven, both in quality and in timing

- There is a disconnection between the coordinator and the instructor

- Support for trainees takes place through asynchronous and "low bandwidth" modes of contact

- Back offices, both at QKM and at the client, do not consider this task to be a priority

9.5.3 Root Cause Analysis—Five Whys

The five whys tool is closely related to the ones just presented. This technique is particularly useful in—though not limited to—developing a better understanding of the "controllable—unknown" category in the ICUKU classification. Some of

Table 9.3 ICUKU classification of causes according to impact, controllability, and experience (i.e., solution known [experience] or unknown [no experience with this]).

		Impact		
		Major	**Medium**	**Minor**
Controllable	**Known**	Feedback is mostly a one-way street—it does not allow for interaction Some executives do not understand the criteria for project and trainee selection There is no feedback on the revised version of the project before the course The instructor and the coordinator interpret the criteria differently The instructor is not involved in selecting the trainees The coordinator and the instructor do not coordinate with each other Since it is hard to obtain support, trainees do it on their own	Nobody pushes or pulls if things do not happen in the back office Feedback on initial project proposals is often late Nothing happens until all the projects have been received Nobody measures response time There is confusion about who is responsible to answer trainees' questions No reminder of the deadline to turn in the project is sent to the trainees There is no standard response time	The logistician is often late in booking the training room, resulting in the use of inferior facilities Follow-up on those who miss the deadline for turning in the proposals is sporadic The list of candidates is not updated regularly Some candidates are not consulted before their name is put on the list
	Unknown	Some executives are not involved: long response time and poor quality Some candidates are pressured to participate No validation is made of the information provided by the candidates Trainees do not understand what a process actually is	Back-office people at QKM assemble the training material in their spare time It often happens that the wrong version of the material is picked for assembly The client's training department is generally a bottleneck Nobody wants to be on those teams: it takes time and there is no recognition Some candidates are never interviewed (too busy, away on a trip, and so on)	Selection of team members is generally not complete at the outset of training and drags on for days, even weeks The instructor and the coordinator are very busy, and often happy to see the course delayed Some trainees do not care and just go through the motions Some trainees do not understand the importance of what they are doing
Uncontrollable		There is no consequence to the executive for failure to deliver	The material is hard to understand and lacks examples	The coordinator works on several projects in parallel Some trainees do not read the material

the causes originally identified in the Ishikawa diagram are merely symptoms of a deeper problem. While energy devoted to eliminating or mitigating a symptom may produce some effect, unless one fixes the underlying cause, this symptom or other symptoms will soon reappear. Finding and fixing root causes is much more effective. The *five whys*, or *root cause analysis*, is one way to do this.

The technique itself is simple. However, using it may prove very difficult for the team, as it involves soul-searching and may bring out fundamental flaws in the process and the organization. The instructor gives the team the following instructions (see Figure 9.8):

1. Pick a cause from the *major impact—controllable—unknown* pigeonhole in the ICUKU classification. Copy it onto a sticky note and put it at the top of a flip-chart page.

2. Ask yourselves the following question: "Why is this happening?"

3. Each team member writes down answers to that question in silence and sticks them under the first sticky note.

4. When everyone is done, the team leader proceeds to rationalize and structure the sticky notes on the page.

5. The team then decides—again based on the evidence—which one of these causes is the most important determinant of the cause the team originally selected. Mark this cause with an asterisk (see bold outlined boxes in Figure 9.8).

6. Referring now to the cause marked with an asterisk, the team again asks itself: "Why is this happening?" and proceeds to answer this question as it did the previous one.

7. Repeat step 6 as many times as you can, until you are incapable of coming up with any meaningful answer. At that time, you have identified the root cause. Pushing until at least five such "why" questions have been answered is a useful rule of thumb (hence the name of the technique) to avoid the risk of not digging *deep* enough.

8. Looking at the column of causes marked with asterisks, find one that the team feels it can fix. Mark it with an arrow.

Anyone with young, curious children is implicitly familiar with this technique. They drive to the root cause in their quest to understand, and they sometimes drive you mad in the process.

When someone pressed for time faces a problem, he tends to settle for alleviating a symptom instead of taking the time and effort required to understand the origin of the problem. Thus, while the problem appears to be solved, since the bothersome symptom disappears, it surfaces again in one form or another, triggering another short-lived firefighting exercise.

When one starts to dig, one does not know what lies below the surface. Sometimes the root cause is very philosophical, deeply rooted, and thus impossible to eradicate within the time and resource limitations imposed by the team's mandate. This is why the team, when faced with such a situation, is asked to go back up the root until it finds a level of cause at which it can take action (step 8).

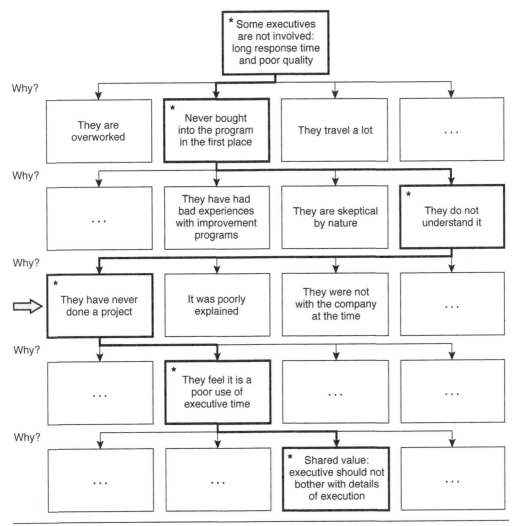

Figure 9.8 Root cause analysis (five whys) for a "major impact—controllable—unknown" cause from the ICUKU diagram (Table 9.3).

At other times, the team discovers a root cause for which it can find a clear-cut solution that lies outside its mandate. This is what happens with our team with the first cause it picks: "some executives are not involved: long response time and poor quality." It finds that training the executives themselves by having them do a project would solve several problems observed in the process (see Figure 9.8).

At that point, the team calls in the process owner and asks her if this solution lies outside her terms of reference. The owner tells them that it does, but that it is an action well worth pursuing in the broader context of improving the process ("big Y") and that they should bring it up at the forum and share their views with all stakeholders. The team thus moves on to apply the tool to other causes selected from Table 9.3 (we do not show their work here). They reach the following conclusions:

- Many executives do not really understand what a project is, since they have never done one themselves

- In some departments, the workload of trainees is not lightened and they are overworked

- The human resource department (at the client's) and the superiors of potential candidates are not consulted in the selection process

- The current support given to trainees is insufficient

9.5.4 Value-Added Analysis (VAA)

The purpose of a process is to add value to the input as it transforms it into an output (that is, the SITOC logic). Value, as discussed in Chapter 2, is in the eye of the beholder. The market ultimately sets the value of an output. When we are dealing with an internal process, we have to rely on the internal customer as a barometer of value creation. We can classify the activities within a process into two categories: those that contribute to value creation and those that do not. Why, might you ask, would we perform any other activities than those that add value? Four major reasons explain why we do:

- The organization must cater to its two other stakeholders: employees and shareholders.

  - Employees are not all the same—they do things differently. They also need to take a break from time to time (delays).

  - Shareholders want to protect assets and minimize risks. They want to make sure that they will not be sued and that they comply with legal and regulatory requirements of all kinds, from environmental to fiscal.

- The business must be managed. Controls are needed. Records must be kept. Work must be divided up between organizational units and coordinated.

- As discussed in Chapter 3, processes take on a life of their own, quite independent from customer needs and their evolution. They evolve as individuals and organizational units evolve, as a function of dynamic interactions of all kinds.

- We are human and we make mistakes. Sometimes we catch them; sometimes we also fix them.

The customer is only willing to pay for the tasks that add value, plus a reasonable markup for overhead and profits. While the four families of non-value-added (NVA) tasks are bound to exist to various degrees, a firm's ability to reduce their relative weight in the process is a clear source of competitive advantage. Indeed, the less NVA there is in a process, the shorter the cycle time, the lower the cost, and the higher the quality. While the first two observations are obvious, the last may be somewhat counterintuitive. One might think that a longer process would leave more time to do a quality job. Remember first that we are not talking about performing value-added tasks faster, but rather about eliminating NVA tasks. By introducing "air pockets" in the process, NVA tasks interrupt, disconnect, and take the focus away from value-added tasks, just as the output of a water pump that sucks in air through a leak decreases drastically. Thus, they create opportunities for defects, make them harder to detect (drowned as they are by the NVA tasks), and make it easier for process workers to unknowingly work at cross-purposes for long periods.

As discussed in Chapter 5, professionals like to protect their autonomy by insulating themselves from managers and other professionals. While this avoids potentially unpleasant discussions, it also deprives the organization of opportunities to surface and resolve issues. A process can be designed either to accommodate problems without too much disruption or to jam completely when a problem occurs, thereby confronting process workers with it and forcing them to address the issue. We call the latter a "lean" process, reflecting the fact that value-added activities are not insulated by "layers of fat" (NVA activities).

Let us revisit the four reasons why we perform activities that do not add value to the customer. The first reason includes activities that are adding value to two other stakeholders, and thus are necessary. These are "business value–adding" activities. In an ideal world, activities performed for the other three reasons would constitute waste to be eliminated or at least minimized. In an ideal world, management would be seamless and effortless because management systems would be perfect, and all employees would be perfectly qualified, trustworthy, motivated, and have access to the right tools. In such a world, no time would be wasted on control, moving things around (the layout would be optimal), filing or retrieving papers, redoing a task poorly done, or simply waiting. Thus, we will label these activities as NVA.

We do not live, nor, unfortunately, will we ever live, in an ideal world. Thus, processes will always include some NVA activities. However, the process with the lowest proportion of NVA is superior. This alone makes it worthwhile to calculate that proportion, benchmark it, and try to reduce it. Distinguishing the NVA tasks, however, is also very useful in the identification of zones of opportunity in the process: the team should try to obliterate the parts of the process that add little value. The instructor thus gives the following instructions to the team, specifying how to identify NVA, calculate the value-added ratio, and prepare the corresponding diagram (see Figure 9.9):

1. Go through your process map, task by task, and mark NVA activities with a red dot. Ask yourselves the question "Is this task essential to meet customers' needs?" Another acid test is the question "If the customer was knowledgeable about our business, and if he was watching as we do this task, would he be comfortable knowing that he is paying for this?" All verifications, controls, rework, delays, and movements are NVA by definition. Leave the customer out of this exercise: we do not want to calculate the value that he adds, but rather the value that we give him.

2. As discussed earlier, some activities may be depicted at a higher level (composite or aggregate activities), and the question formulated in step 1 cannot be answered in one fell swoop. For these, we ask the team to estimate the total value-added time and draw a bicolor bar, proportional in length to span time (three days, if we consider "organize logistics"), with the darker part proportional to value-added time (see Figure 9.9).

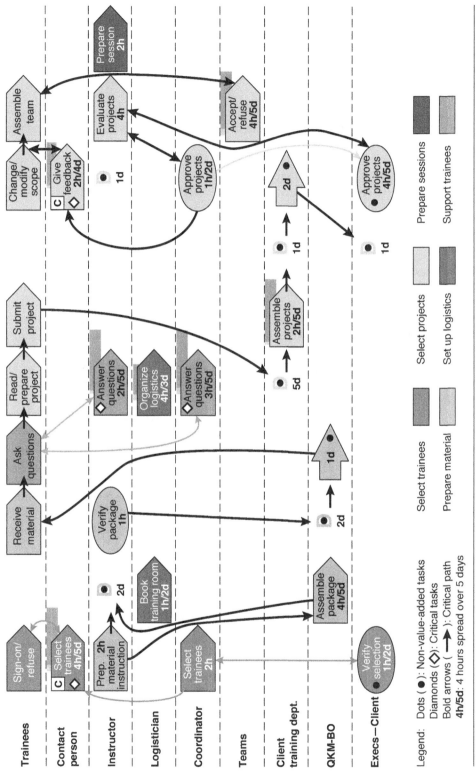

Figure 9.9 Non-value-added activities, CTPs, and critical path.

3. Calculate the value-added ratio of the whole process as the sum of all value-added times (assume an eight-hour workday)[1] divided by the total cycle time.

4. Referring back to the FAST diagram (Figure 9.4), prepare a precedence diagram, that is, visually describe (see Figure 9.10) the precedence constraints that exist between the functions (project selection, for instance, cannot start until trainees have received the material). Calculate the value-added ratio for each function in the FAST diagram and transfer that information onto the precedence diagram. Identify and mark the longest path in the precedence diagram (the "critical path"). Identify and mark the critical path on the process map (see bold arrows in Figure 9.9).

5. Plot the value-added ratios (global and by function) as shown in Figure 9.11, respecting the precedence relationships as you go.

6. Analyze Figures 9.9, 9.10, and 9.11 and draw your conclusions.

Much of this effort is meant to make the analysis visual so that the team can easily relate back to it as it tries to formulate an overall diagnosis and make its case to the rest of the organization. The team draws the following major conclusions from its analysis:

- Executives contribute significantly to cycle time but do not add any value

- Back offices are an important source of NVA

- The back-and-forth between the trainees and support staff for questions and feedback adds much NVA and probably destroys value

- Moving all the paper-based material is long and NVA

The team adds many ideas to the parking lot during this exercise.

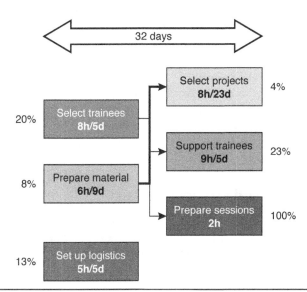

Figure 9.10 Precedence diagram for the six functions, respective value-added ratios, and critical path.

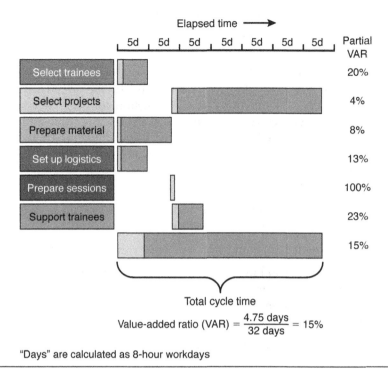

Figure 9.11 Value added: overall and by function.

We must make two important observations at this time. First, putting a red dot on an activity does not mean that you can simply stop performing it. If one has to verify whether someone else's work was performed correctly, it may be because it is often defective. The solution is not to stop checking, but rather to take action to ensure that inspection is no longer required. Second, sticking an NVA dot on a task that one has been performing for a long time is not an emotionally neutral task. It often triggers a deep awareness that the process is flawed and has to be changed. Indeed, this tool often helps the team cross an inner threshold of belief in the necessity and the possibility of change. However, it may also raise doubt in some team members' minds: "Am I shooting myself in the foot if I put a red dot on this task? Am I really sticking a red dot on my forehead?" If this issue is not addressed, it will probably not surface, and fester. Thus, the issue must be raised at the outset of the analysis, and clear "rules of engagement" must be presented and debated.

9.5.5 Failure Mode and Effects Analysis

Quality is about avoiding defects. In order to do this, we must define defects—in the specific process at hand. At a very high level, we already have: any trainee–project pair that does not meet all the selection criteria is a defect. Counting such defects is a good way to track the evolution of the performance of the process over time, but it does not pinpoint improvement opportunities. To that end, identifying specific risks of defects that could occur at various points in the process is more useful. A defect occurs when we do something wrong and thus potentially affect the performance of the process, that is, in the PAC setup, resulting in missing a criterion or increasing cycle time. We define a risk of defect (also called *failure mode*) as a combination of variables (circumstances or events) that could occur and result in a defect. Failure mode and effects analysis (FMEA) is a technique that helps in identifying and ranking risks of defects, thereby focusing the team on finding countermeasures for the most critical ones.

To identify risks, we concentrate on the critical activities identified earlier (see Table 9.2), as we are more likely to find important ones there. The coach gives the team the following instructions regarding how to identify risks:

1. Review the critical activities and the list of critical variables identified earlier (see the first two columns of Table 9.2). For each of these activities, go through a silent idea-generation session, thinking about what could go wrong (failure modes), and writing it down on sticky notes. It helps to consider in turn the six categories used in the fishbone diagram (see section 9.5.2): methods, manpower, IS/IT, measures, equipment and installation, and organization and culture.

2. Review these ideas as a team, clarifying them as you go, eliminating duplicate entries, and brainstorming to generate new ones.

3. Draw a diagram like the one shown in Table 9.4 (consider only the left-hand side of the diagram at this time, as we will discuss the right-hand side later) and paste the result of your work into the first two columns.

The second part of this technique deals with ranking the failure modes just identified in order of importance, that is, in order of priority for the team. A failure mode is more important to the team if its consequences on the customer are severe, if it has a high probability of occurring, and if we have no means of detecting it, when it occurs, until the damage is done. Hence, FMEA attributes to each risk a *risk priority number* (RPN) proportional to the importance of the risk based on these three criteria:

• Severity: How severe are the effects of this defect (should it occur) on the outcome of the process or, more precisely here, on criteria missed and on cycle time?

• Probability of occurrence: How likely is it to occur?

• Probability of non-detection: How likely is it that we will not detect the defect, once it has occurred, until the damage is done?

The team answers each of these questions by assigning a relative numerical value based on a 10-point scale where a value of 1 stands for an insignificant risk and a value of 10 for a critical one, thus obtaining three numerical values (digits from 1 to 10) that we multiply to obtain the RPN. Hence, the RPN scale ranges from 1 to 1000, with the latter representing a risk of the highest possible severity—that

Table 9.4   Partial failure mode and effects analysis (FMEA).

Critical activity	Failure mode	Severity	Occurrence	Non-detection	RPN	Poka-yoke	Severity	Occurrence	Non-detection	RPN
Select trainee	Evaluator misinterprets the meaning of a criterion	10	4	9	360	Provide sheet with examples	10	2	8	160
	The evaluator skips a criterion	4	1	4	16	Require the evaluator to calculate a total	4	1	1	4
	The candidate misunderstands a question (wording problem)	1	5	5	25	Provide the candidate with a sheet containing simple, alternate wording	1	3	3	9
	Candidate's answer is less than candid (wants to be rejected)	6	6	9	324	Use more than one evaluator and make joint assessment	6	2	7	84
	…									
Answer trainees' questions about project scoping	Trainee misunderstands the answer (wording problem)	5	5	4	100	Ask the trainee to repeat his understanding of the answer	5	5	1	25
	Evaluator misunderstands the issue	7	4	6	168	Ask other trainees to be present, and reformulate the issue if needed	5	3	3	45
	Trainee is afraid to ask a question for fear of looking dumb	7	6	10	420	Ask each trainee to write an anonymous question on a piece of paper. Collect, answer, and discuss.	5	2	10	100
	Evaluator does not know the client's business well enough to answer the question	9	10	7	630	Have client executives present when questions are asked	9	1	2	18
	…									
Give feedback to trainee on the project	Evaluator does not know the client's business well enough to provide accurate feedback	9	10	7	630	Have client executives present when feedback is prepared and given	9	1	2	18
	Negative feedback is taken as blame	7	7	9	441	Provide evaluator with standard introductory formulas to use	7	4	9	252
	Feedback is not specific enough for trainee to make required changes	8	6	9	432	Provide feedback and "rescope" immediately with the evaluator in attendance	8	1	2	16
	Trainee cannot reach the evaluator	7	7	1	49	Provide an easily reachable in-house coach	2	7	1	14
	…									

is, highly likely to occur and has a high probability of escaping detection. The instructor gives the team the following instructions to complete this technique:

1. Consider all the failure modes you have listed on the FMEA diagram. Which one do you think has the most severe effect? The least severe? Take the time to reach a consensus. Ties are acceptable. Attribute a value of 10 to the most severe and a value of 1 to the least severe and write them in the appropriate column. Repeat the procedure for the other two criteria.

2. Using a 10-point scale, rate the severity, probability of occurrence, and probability of non-detection of the first five failure modes you have identified, proceeding one risk at a time. Use the ratings you have attributed in step 1 as boundary values, maintaining comparability as you go. Write the values on small sticky notes and place them on your FMEA diagram. Calculate the RPN by multiplying the three values. Place it in the diagram as well.

3. Review and normalize your ratings. In order to do that, compare, one column at a time, the ratings you have attributed with the risks just rated. Adjust the ratings on each of the three criteria as required.

4. Proceed to rate the other risks.

Among the failure modes identified, the most severe is that the evaluator does not understand a criterion. If that happens, many projects or trainees will be defective. The most probable is that the evaluator does not know the client's business well enough to answer the question, as the current process does not include any mechanism through which the coordinator and the instructor can learn the customer's business. A trainee's fear to ask a question is the risk least likely to be detected. Among the 12 failure modes listed in Table 9.4, "evaluator does not know the client's business well enough to provide accurate feedback" and "evaluator does not know the client's business well enough to answer the question" are the most important (RPN = 630).

The full FMEA (not shown) lists 25 failure modes. As the team was working on the diagram, a teammate entered the information in an electronic spreadsheet. Performing a sort operation by RPN allowed reorganizing the risks in the completed Table 9.4 from the most to the least important. The four following failure modes came out on top:

- Evaluators do not know the client's business well enough and their feedback is not specific enough

- Coordinators, evaluators, and executives do not always see eye to eye on what the criteria mean

- Trainees hold back for fear of looking dumb and perceive negative feedback as blame

- Candidates often do not answer evaluators' questions candidly

Three observations about this technique are in order. First, as the team identifies failure modes and assesses their severity, it thinks about what could happen that would affect the outcome of the process. However, the project is focused on two different outcomes: meeting all criteria and having a short cycle time. The failure modes that affect these two outcomes may not be the same. Whenever this is the case, the team must split the original idea-generation session to consider the two outcomes separately, using sticky notes of different colors to capture the risks they identify. The same goes for assessing severity. Hence, it might be worthwhile to prepare two FMEA tables.

Second, sometimes there is an alternate way to use the 10-point scale. Whenever some failure modes may endanger human health or lives, such as may be the case in health services, we can define each value on the scale in absolute rather than relative terms. A value of 7, for instance, could be defined as "a probability of 10% of nonfatal injury." Creating such a scale is an elaborate but essential undertaking when the stakes are so high.

Lastly, we can raise the level of rigor of the exercise considerably, whenever possible, by using numerical data. We can assess severity data through discussion with the customer. We can assess probability of occurrence and detection through calculation of past frequencies.

9.5.6 Formulating a Diagnosis—Diagnostic Worksheet

The team must now formulate a diagnosis. To do so, it must first collate all the partial conclusions it has reached (independently) using eight techniques. It must then analyze this information (comparing, correlating, and cross-validating the elements), synthesize it into an incisive diagnosis, and present it forcefully to convince all the stakeholders (see Figure 9.12).

The coach gives the team the following instructions:

1. Draw a diagnostic worksheet such as that shown in Figure 9.13.

2. Revisit each technique used so far in the *analyze* phase. Write down what the team has learned from each technique that it should consider in the formulation of a diagnosis. In other words, ask the following question: "What do we know about the causes of the problem after using this technique that we did not know before?" Try to summarize your answers into three or four major points and insert them into Figure 9.13. If you end up with five, that is all right. If you end up empty-handed with some techniques, that is all right as well.

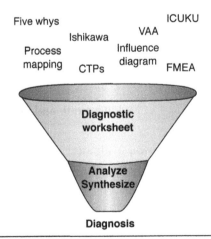

Figure 9.12   Collating and analyzing partial conclusions from eight techniques: synthesizing a diagnosis.

Mapping	CTPs	Ishikawa-ICUKU	Five whys	VAA	FMEA
Many players are involved and much back-and-forth goes on (1)	We do not validate the information used for trainee selection (5)	Executive involvement is very uneven, in both quality and timing (6)	Many executives do not really understand what a project is since they have never done one themselves (6)	Executives contribute significantly to cycle time, but do not add any value (6)	Evaluators do not know the client's business well enough and their feedback is not specific enough (6)
There are six long delays, for a total of 12 days (2)	We do not ensure that trainees understand what a process is (1)	There is a disconnect between the coordinator and the instructor (4)	In some departments the workload of trainees is not lightened and they are overworked (1)	Back offices are an important source of delay (7)	Coordinators, evaluators, and executives do not always see eye to eye on what the criteria mean (4)
Little face-to-face contact takes place with the trainees (3)	Support and feedback in general are deficient (3)	Support for trainee takes place through asynchronous and "low bandwidth" modes of contact (3)	HR and bosses are not consulted in the selection process (5)	The back-and-forth between the trainees and support staff for questions and feedback adds much delay and probably destroys value (2)	Trainees hold back for fear of looking dumb and perceive negative feedback as blame (8)
There are few contact points between the coordinator and the instructor (4)		Back offices, both at QKM and at the client's, do not consider this task to be a priority (4)	The current support given to trainees is insufficient (3)	Moving all the paper-based material is long and non-value-added (3)	Candidates often do not answer evaluator's questions candidly (5)

Figure 9.13 Diagnostic worksheet.

3. Compare and explore relationships between the various elements posted on the worksheet. Some elements are essentially the same. Others are closely related, are complementary, or represent different facets of the same underlying issue. Use color coding to visually relate these elements to one another. If you find apparent contradictions, go back to the source and resolve them.

4. For each factor (that is, color) found in Figure 9.13, write a one-sentence statement that captures its essence. For instance, we could summarize the four elements numbered ③ as follows: "Even though much information is available, we depend solely on the candidates themselves to assess their capability."

5. Considering all the summary factors produced in the previous step, write a short (three lines) overall diagnosis and format it similarly to that shown in Figure 9.14, completing it with a one- or two-line description of each individual factor or problem.

This amounts to distilling the essence of the diagnosis from a loose collection of disjointed elements gathered through a host of different means. For the interested reader, there are more-sophisticated ways to connect some of these tools (ReVelle 2010). This again is quite similar to the critical diagnostic task performed by doctors and the court strategy and summation performed by lawyers. It is professional work at its most complex and most value-added. It requires the judgment, intuition, rigor, and synthetic capabilities that distinguish professional work from any other type of work.

Making the diagnostic so short may result in leaving out some details, but these can be revisited as the team wraps up the *improve* phase later on. However, it also makes it concise, dense, and rich enough for the team to be able to present a vivid image of the situation and focus the discussion with other stakeholders on the fundamentals. By eliminating the "noise" that relatively trivial issues may

Global	
Summary diagnosis	The process involves too many players acting independently, involving delays and interference at each hand-off. Contacts are remote and asynchronous, and lack the richness and "bandwidth" that the nature of the task requires. Too much paper is processed.
Details	
Problem 1	There is confusion between the roles of the instructor and the coordinator throughout the process.
Problem 2	Executives add much delay and little value, yet much of the knowledge of the business and the candidates that exists is not brought to bear on trainee and project selection.
Problem 3	Assembling and transporting course kits in back offices is long and fraught with errors.
Problem 4	There is much "noise" and delay in feedback given to trainees on their projects. Not enough knowledge of the business goes into this, and there is little interaction between those who know and those who want to learn.

Figure 9.14 Process diagnosis.

create at this time, the "signal" is made all the clearer. In complex situations, it is sometimes worthwhile at this point to prepare a new influence diagram to illustrate the dynamics of causes, effects, and relationships and make the diagnosis visual.

That night (end of day two), the team presents its diagnosis to all stakeholders, taking the group on a guided tour of the evidence that supports it. This creates a rich environment, conducive to discussions—on a level playing field, focused on issues and evidence rather than personalities—and thus to consensus.

9.6 IMPROVE

The output of the *improve* phase is a validated "prescription," that is, a new process that meets the goals of the project, ready to roll out.

The general flow of this phase is to first generate more improvement ideas— remember that many ideas generated throughout the *analyze* phase are waiting in the "parking lot"—by revisiting each diagnostic tool, and then select the best ones and design a new process on that basis. The coach gives the team the following instructions:

1. Go back to each diagnostic tool in turn. Looking at the problems (causes, defects, CTP, NVA), ask yourselves, "How can we fix this?" Answer the question as a team, using the idea-generation and brainstorming technique described earlier. The idea parking lot should be filled to capacity by the time you are done.

2. Look for simple solutions. Keep the sweeping, costly, and risky solutions (such as automation) as a last resort. If executives had wanted to do that, they would not have called this event.

3. Clean up the parking lot: eliminate duplicates, dump the ideas you cannot understand, and combine similar ideas. Here is a sample of the ideas left in the team's parking lot at that stage:

   – Include an initial screening of the list of candidates.

   – Only involve executives who have gone through the training.

   – Conduct post-course debriefing with executives, showing the savings produced by well-scoped projects.

   – Perform selection of candidates live in a half-day session. The core team would act as the selection committee.

   – Perform project selection live in a half-day session. The core team would act as the selection committee. Each trainee would bring and pass around copies of her project to each participant. Trainees who miss the session would be barred from the course.

   – Organize a "trainee–instructor–coordinator Q&A" session in a web conference. Schedule it for the end of the trainee selection session.

   – Eliminate approval of trainees and projects by all executives.

- Criteria: give the limited number of places to the most willing and facilitate opting out for the others.

- Invite all executives who want to attend the selection committees.

- Leave it to each trainee to decide with whom he should hold consultations.

- Make the last assignment of the course the sponsoring and coaching of a new trainee.

- Feedback session: all together—live "rescoping."

- E-material only. Hard copies: in-class as needed.

- Make it a part of every employee's goal to participate in two project teams every year.

- Let the instructor herself assemble an electronic package and upload it to the client's intranet.

- Accept that there may be fewer trainees per wave because of the new process—focus on quality. Success will create its own momentum.

- Create a core team at the outset consisting of the instructor, the coordinator, and selected executives.

- The training room must be booked before a date is formally set to launch the session.

- Updating the list of trainees is another process (upstream) delegated to HR.

- Hold a full-day session to do all this.

- Add an assistant from the client to work with the coordinator.

- Standardize and freeze the training package—always have an inventory ready that would be sufficient for any training wave.

4. For each remaining idea, fill out an idea evaluation card (this is the job of the idea manager) such as the one shown in Figure 9.15. The questions are self-explanatory. The first purpose is to help the team build a shared understanding of each idea and to clarify them. Cost estimates can initially be rough, such as high/medium/low, so that no time is wasted evaluating the cost of an idea that will be quickly discarded or for which cost is not a deciding consideration. Do not decide right away whether the idea should be accepted or rejected. You should consider together or group ideas that are strongly linked. Ideas that are mutually exclusive should be tied and considered together.

5. Sort the remaining ideas using the ICUKU classification scheme presented earlier. Use the original sticky notes cross-referenced to the idea cards. The controllable–uncontrollable dimension is now interpreted as, "Is this idea within scope—that is, would it be infringing on some constraints or instructions given to the team with its marching order?" The known–unknown dimension now means, "Do we have experience with whatever is proposed (known) or is this totally new—and thus risky (unknown)?"

Name:	Number:
Description:	
What problem (refer to diagnosis) does it address?	
What proportion of the problem would it eliminate (%)?	
What does it require (constraints, equipment, software, HR changes . . .)?	
Is it linked (complementary, substitute, antagonistic) with any other idea?	
What will it cost?	
How long will it take to implement?	
Pros	**Cons**
Adopted	**Rejected**
For future consideration (out of scope)—Who should follow up on this idea?	

Figure 9.15 Idea evaluation card.

6. Create a new working area on a flip-chart page. Label it "Adopted Ideas." Go through the ideas pasted in the ICUKU classification, starting with the "major impact—controllable—known" category and working your way toward the opposite corner. Discuss the idea and decide whether to accept or reject it. Paste the ideas you accept on the new page. Place a red dot on ideas you reject and leave them in the ICUKU classification. If the team cannot agree after a reasonable amount of time, place a yellow dot on the idea and leave it there as well.

7. When you are done, revisit the yellow-dotted ideas, this time considering them in light of what they would add to the joint effect of all the ideas you have already accepted. The decision is often much easier at this time.

8. Fill out a prescription form similar to that shown in Figure 9.16. The summary has to be short: present the essence in such a way that the reader (or listener) will be able to see how each element fits into the global vision. There may be more than the five elements that you can fit in Figure 9.16. Bring these up in the question-and-answer session that follows the presentation at the prescription forum.

9. Prepare a blueprint (see Figure 9.17—it looks like a mapping except that it does not represent the process as it is, but rather what it will look like once implemented), trying to include all the ideas you have accepted. Incoherencies and gaps may appear as you go since you are creating a new process based on an old one and a set of relatively disjointed ideas. You may have to reformulate or clarify some of the ideas, reconsider earlier decisions,

Global		
Summary prescription		
Much of the interaction that now takes place remotely will be reintegrated in a limited number of face-to-face forums involving all the required players. Only executives capable of contributing will be involved. The role of mentor/coach will be created. Paper kits will replace the binders.		
Details	**Justification**	**Responsible, constraints, timing**
Element 1 Selection will be done face-to-face in real time, in a half-day session involving a core team including the instructor, the coordinator, and selected executives	A core team will have more ownership and cohesion. Face-to-face is required to better assess the candidates.	See Gantt chart (not included)
Element 2 A question-and-answer web meeting will be held by the core team with all trainees attending	It is important that the trainees listen to the questions of their colleagues and to the answers. This eliminates repetition and avoids confusion.	See Gantt chart (not included)
Element 3 A face-to-face half-day feedback session will be held (core team + trainees), and rescoping will be done on the spot	This is a crucial point for both learning and scoping the project right. It is worthwhile to provide the richest forum possible to do this and to maximize interaction and cross-learning among trainees.	See Gantt chart (not included)
Element 4 Before being certified, each trainee will have to act as mentor/coach to a new trainee	This is a win–win–win solution for the trainees, the client organization, and QKM. It solves an important process problem and is effective and rewarding for all involved.	See Gantt chart (not included)
Element 5 The instructor will prepare and send all material electronically	This avoids many non-value-added intermediaries, sources of delays, and defects. Hard copies can be printed selectively by the trainees as required.	See Gantt chart (not included)

Figure 9.16 Prescription: high-level description of the solution and explanation of its major elements.

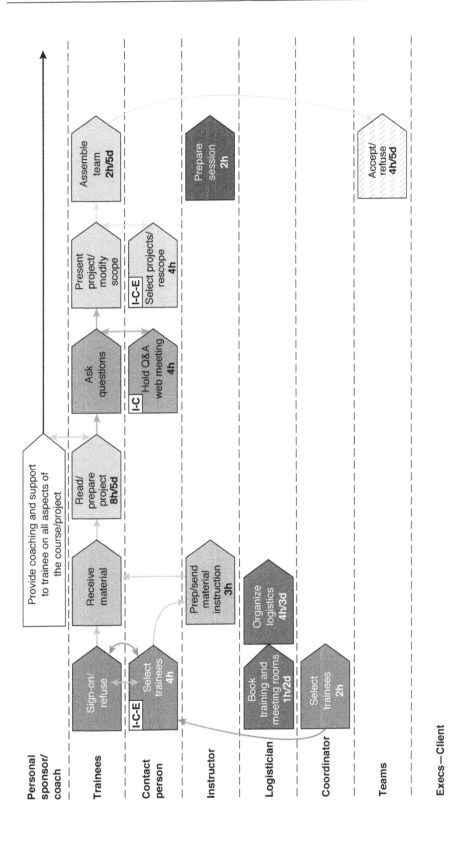

Figure 9.17 Blueprint of new process.

and generate new ideas to fill in the gaps and ensure global coherence. Better yet, prepare an augmented visual blueprint, such as the one shown in Figure 10.18, that includes all important process changes that do not have a direct impact on process flow and thus present a more complete picture of the improved process.

10. Calculate the value-added ratio of the new process, using the technique described earlier. Explore ways to improve it further.

11. Consider in turn each element of the blueprint of the new process as well as the ideas you have accepted. Identify actions of all kinds that will have to take place to make the new process a reality. These will fall into categories similar to those used in the Ishikawa diagram. Write these actions on sticky notes and paste them in a table similar to that shown in Figure 9.18. Notice that it includes a section labeled "implementation plan." Since this is preliminary and subject to review following step 12, you only need to give a general idea

Equipment	Installations	Materials	Suppliers
• Make sure all trainees have easy access to a computer	• Find appropriate meeting rooms for new live sessions	• Prepare a new criteria scoring sheet, including a user guide with examples	• Make sure HR can deliver on its promise to keep up-to-date list of candidates
		• Review course outline to reflect the new process	• Review training plan and recognize that some trainees will drop out before the course starts
HR aspects	**IS/IT**	**Procedures**	**Implementation plan**
• Communicate the new roles to executive	• Make sure all trainees have access to Netmeeting and the latest version of Acrobat reader	• Prepare legal procedure to ensure a binding commitment to confidentiality of material	• See Gantt chart attached (not included)
• Change evaluation procedures to recognize member-ship on a team	• Evaluate new groupware	• Organize scheduling so that the coordinator and the instructor can be available at the same time	
• Mediate the disagree-ment between coordinators and instructors	• Develop security procedure for the uploaded material	• Document new process	
• Valorize the role of executives on the core team	• Create a standardized electronic repository for all training material	. . .	

Figure 9.18 Elements of the new process: choices already made and decisions to be taken (partial).

of what the implementation stage will involve in terms of resources and timing. It may be included on a Gantt chart (a bar diagram with a timeline).

12. Present your work to the prescription forum (end of day three). Do not be dogmatic or defensive. There is not a single, unique solution to a problem. Listen to alternatives that may come up and debate them with an open mind. Considering the work that the team has done, however, and the makeup of the team, it will take considerable evidence to prove that something is fundamentally flawed with your solution. Any comment involving a reconsideration of the diagnosis is not receivable at this point. This debate was closed with the end of the *analyze* phase. Absents are in the wrong.

Process improvement can take many different forms:

- Reintegration of work: eliminating a step in the process, *disintermediation*, that is, avoiding going through an intermediary, combining steps
- Outright elimination of a player from the process
- Changing modes of contact
- Involving the customer
- Changing accountability and incentives
- Training
- Changing or improving tools
- Automating a step or part of the process
- Changing the flow of information
- Adding poka-yokes

Poka-yoke is the Japanese word for a fail-safe device, that is, a simple mechanism to prevent a defect. When one creates a password on a computer, he is asked to enter it again to validate. Since the likelihood of making the same mistake twice is much less than that of making it only once, the risk of a defect is reduced considerably—at a negligible cost. This is poka-yoke. A checklist used in performing a task is a poka-yoke. To identify a poka-yoke, one must have a clear and detailed idea of the genesis of the defect. In the password example, for instance, the risk arises from the interaction of two variables: (1) when one types his password, it does not appear on the screen, and (2) widespread clumsiness in using a keyboard. Understanding this, we see that making the keyword visible on-screen would solve the problem, but it would also create a potentially worse security risk. Repeating it is the best solution since, even though it requires some time and is not absolutely fail-safe, it does not create any other risk. This is the type of analysis that one must perform in evaluating alternate solutions. For a more elaborate discussion on fail-safing, see Chase and Stewart (1994) and Nakajo and Kume (1996).

The right-hand side of Table 9.4 presents a number of poka-yokes for the failure modes appearing on the left-hand side. Providing the evaluators with specific examples of good and bad applications of the criteria is a way to reduce the probability of occurrence of the failure "Evaluator misinterprets the meaning of a criterion." The team thinks that it would reduce it from a 4 to a 2 on the 10-point scale. It would also reduce the probability of non-detection, as the evaluator could refer to the examples to check her work. Thus, the RPN would be reduced from 360 to 160. In searching for a fix, prevention, that is, reducing the probability of occurrence, is always best. Failing that, one should look for a "detection" poka-yoke and a "mitigation" poka-yoke (that is, reducing severity), in that order. The team should first sort the risks (in decreasing order) based on the left-hand side RPN and start from the top.

9.7 CONTROL

The output of the *control* phase is an implemented, stable, and capable process, together with the "owner's manual" necessary to keep it that way. A process is stable or "in control" (see discussion in Chapter 6) if it is functioning within its usual operating parameters; that is, it is not affected by shifts or drifts, and its performance is thus predictable. It is capable if the voice of the process falls well within the voice of the customer, that is, if the number of "defective" trainee–project pairs stays clear of the desired 10% maximum, and the time required to start a training wave never exceeds 15 days.

This is the phase where the team follows up on implementation until it is ready to pass the baton, that is, turn the process over to the process owner and process workers. Minor adjustments to the process and fine-tuning are often necessary to stabilize the process. The team often does this through a pilot project. It develops a control plan (see Figure 9.19) specifying what to measure, how, where, and when. The plan also assigns, after consultations with the process owner, responsibilities for taking corrective actions and for drawing improvement lessons from defects. In this specific case, the coordinator, the instructor, and the executives in attendance are to fill out forms at the end of the selection and rescoping sessions. The instructor will later fill out a form at the end of the course that will be compared with those filled out at the outset. This way the criteria and the way to apply them can be honed through every instantiation of the process.

What must be measured? Number of projects not respecting all criteria. Number of trainees not respecting criteria. Cycle time, from launch decision to the beginning of session 1.

How (measurement system)? Criteria: Two forms have been designed: one for projects, one for trainees. Cycle time will be calculated based on the date of the initial e-mail from the logistician to QKM requesting a new session.

Who must measure and when (sampling plan)? Evaluators will fill out a form together at the end of the trainees' selection session, and another one at the end of the rescoping session. The instructor must decide on the number of trainee projects not meeting all criteria at the end of the course. The logistician will measure cycle time. SPC charts will be gradually built up.

Who is responsible for corrective action and what rules must he/she apply? Coordinator and instructor—jointly.

Who is responsible for learning and disseminating the lessons learned? The process owner, through the dynamic use of FMEA and poka-yokes.

Figure 9.19 Control plan.

At this time the team also documents the process, completing the write-up of the essentials of the process (a procedure is complete when you cannot make it any simpler without losing important content) for future reference and training of new players. The owner will also use the FMEA table (Table 9.4) as a continuous improvement tool. As defects are identified using the tracking system proposed in Figure 9.19, the owner will use the FMEA chart to reassess probabilities of occurrence and probabilities of non-detection for various failure modes, update the chart (calculating new RPNs and re-sorting), and look for new poka-yokes for emerging risks. SPC charts will also be developed (see Chapters 6 and 12) as sufficient numerical data become available.

9.8 UNDERSTANDING THE DMAIC METHODOLOGY

The "idea hopper" (see Figure 9.2), the *analyze* phase, and the *improve* phase share a common principle: first generate a quantity of elements, then distill quality out of the mass of elements generated. In any contest, the higher the number of candidates, the more likely one is to find high-quality ones. The higher the number of project ideas entered into the hopper, the more likely one is to find a high-potential one. The more detailed the mapping, the more likely one is to identify with precision the vital few variables. While the elements generated (activities, causes, risks), the methods used to generate them (brainstorming, process description, risk identification), and the filtering techniques used (search for critical elements, ICUKU classification, risk evaluation) vary, this logic is repeated for all the other techniques: VAA, Ishikawa diagram, FMEA, and improvement ideas.

Rigor is about logical validity and severe accuracy. The inherent logic of each tool discussed in this chapter is obvious even though they all approach the problem from a different perspective. The result of logical reasoning, however, is only as good as the data to which you apply it—garbage in, garbage out. It is in the *measure* phase that we gather most of the data. Data are individual facts or items of information—numerical or qualitative. Statistics is the science that helps us deal rigorously with numerical facts. The statistical tools presented in this book are basic. A host of more advanced tools, lying beyond the scope of this book, are available when the situation warrants it. In professional services, qualitative facts are legion. We describe them with words and sentences, such as those used to describe CTPs, causes, activities, risks, and ideas. Accuracy of wording is therefore of the utmost importance. Seeing eye to eye on the facts is always a challenge, especially when various professions are involved. Indeed, a simple word such as "fact" can give rise to semantic confusion if lawyers, doctors, and engineers are around the table. Thus, for quantitative data, rigor lies in establishing and concisely describing the phenomena that take place and their prevalence. Tight wording avoids semantic confusion.

We have devoted much thought to managing change in the way we have deployed the DMAIC methodology in the kaizen event (the change vehicle). Consider the factors required to succeed in a change initiative, as discussed in Chapter 8. Calculating the value-added ratio and identifying failure modes, for instance, typically brings out dissatisfaction with the current situation and shows that there is room for improvement. The team does all the work on sticky notes and flip charts, using colored markers and dots. This makes the process and the analysis visual and readily accessible by the team throughout the event, as team members leave all the work they do on the wall. This facilitates the emergence of a shared diagnosis and of a vision of the future process. It also facilitates the sharing of these visions with the rest of the organization—a central element in the change leadership role that the team must play.

The simultaneous use of many diagnostic tools serves two purposes:

• Reduces the probability of missing an important causal factor.

• Helps the team isolate the most important factors. Obtaining the same result through different tools constitutes validation and increases the team's feeling of confidence, without which they could not be as convincing to others.

Depending on the problem and the process, some tools are more powerful than others. Unfortunately, there are no set rules for predicting how effective each tool will be in any given situation. Hence, it is better to utilize the limited time available to formulate a diagnosis using many techniques rather than using a single technique to the fullest.

Finally, two additional success factors for change are addressed with this approach. Since the team is mobilized full-time for the event, and since time pressure is present throughout, there is no lack of a sense of urgency. Further, the anxious team is not at risk of going around in circles: it is guided from beginning to end, by means of detailed instructions and coaching, through a rigorous methodology. Thus, the DMAIC kaizen event constitutes a rigorous overall game plan for change. It is a vital piece in any corporate change strategy.

9.9 SUMMARY

The DMAIC methodology provides a detailed road map for process improvement. It consists of five phases: define, measure, analyze, improve, and control. The chapter is built around the example of a consulting process improved by using a kaizen event as a change vehicle. The improvement project starts from a rough-cut improvement idea. The *define* phase determines the precise scope of the project. The *measure* phase describes the process, identifies variables, and validates measurement systems. The *analyze* phase takes the data thus produced and formulates a diagnosis, which becomes the basis for the development of a new process in the *improve* phase. The *control* phase works on incorporating the improved process into the fabric of the organization in such a way that the gains achieved are sustainable.

Each phase uses a number of techniques that we described and illustrated throughout the chapter, together with the instructions required to use them correctly. Each technique approaches the problem and the process from a different angle, applying a different logical grid to different parts of the data set. The use of several techniques in parallel allows for more rigor and helps the team make a more compelling case, thereby reinforcing its leadership role. Taking place as it does here in the context of a kaizen event, the methodology has been molded in such a way that it addresses all the major factors required for successful change: surfacing dissatisfaction with the current situation; creating, projecting, and building support for a vision of the future state; maintaining a sense of urgency; and providing, through a logical methodology and specific instructions, a solid framework for action.

EXERCISE

9.1 Conducting a DMAIC Kaizen Event

Your task (should you choose to accept it . . .) is to apply the tools and methodology presented in this chapter to the improvement project you scoped in exercise 7.6. If your business circumstances make it possible, and if you have had the opportunity to witness a kaizen event, as suggested in exercise 8.2, use the kaizen event as the change vehicle. Otherwise, plan and execute the project in any way that you see fit, while making sure, however, to respect the critical success factors presented in Chapter 8.

NOTE

1. In some circumstances where real time is what matters, we should use 24-hour days. In the case of a patient waiting for heart surgery, for instance, every minute matters.

10

Doing Things Right the First Time: Designing a Process That Works

Just because nobody complains does not mean that parachutes are perfect.

—Benny Hill

The DCDV process design methodology can be adapted to a professional service environment.

In this chapter we present the design methodology. It is a radical departure from the improvement methodology presented in the previous chapter. We illustrate it using the example of FPA that was introduced in Chapter 5 and continued in Chapter 7. The mode of presentation parallels that used in Chapter 9. We conclude the chapter with a retrospective and insights into the methodology, and a comparison with the DMAIC methodology. Figure 10.1 discusses the videos associated with this chapter's content.

10.1 HIGH-LEVEL VIEW OF THE DESIGN METHODOLOGY AND PROJECT SETUP

"Don't automate, obliterate," advocated Michael Hammer (1990) more than 20 years ago. The idea of designing from scratch, starting with the end in mind, gave birth to business process reengineering (BPR). Though the case for reengineering was compelling, there was little nuance and even less methodology behind the advocacy. Many companies added it to their ongoing total quality management (TQM) initiative and seem to have benefited from it (see, among others, Farzaneh [2003]). Now most experts understand that improving and designing are not two distinct quality initiatives, but rather two essential and complementary methodologies belonging to the same global quality initiative.

The purpose of this chapter is to present the design methodology, using a professional service example, and discuss the opportunities and challenges it offers. It flows down from a global to a high-level strategic view, gradually zooming in to more detailed views, until high definition is reached (Smith et al. 2007). Using a format similar to that used in Figure 9.2, Figure 10.2 shows the logical flow of the design methodology as we present it in this chapter: *define, characterize, design,* and *verify* (or DCDV). Each phase consists of two steps. We specify in Table 10.1 the questions addressed at each step and the design principles that underpin the methodology used to provide the answers. Figure 10.2 presents the inputs and outputs of each phase.

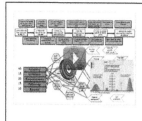

10.1   High-level overview of the DCDV design methodology

Part 1: A simple example—Watching a movie

This is a conceptual lesson. Processes are designed from the market in, or from the customer to the process. From the customer corridor, the critical to satisfaction factors are defined, metrics are generated, the voice of the customer is specified, and process concepts are generated, evaluated, and improved. The video illustrates this general outside-in pattern using different examples. The techniques required to use the methodology are presented in detail in this chapter and are discussed in the next video.

Part 2: A very complex example—Saving a file

This is not as complex as it gets, but getting close. Connected isolated processes, each characterized with irreducible uncertainty, eventually produce an effective value stream.

10.2   DCDV—Characterize and design: A technical note

This is a technical note explaining the inner workings of the QFD matrices (characterize phase), the concept generation technique, and the Pugh matrix (design phase).

Figure 10.1   Videos associated with Chapter 10.

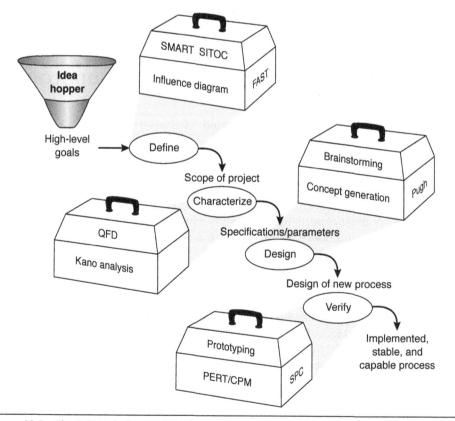

Figure 10.2   The DCDV design methodology: phases, inputs, outputs, and partial toolkits.

Table 10.1 The DCDV design methodology: questions addressed and design principles at each step.

Phase	Step	Questions addressed	Underlying design principle
Define	1. Problem statement	What seems to be the problem? What's the overall goal? Why is this important?	Design outside-in, that is, start with customers and markets, end with the process.
	2. Process scoping	Where does the process start? Where does it end?	Cycle through the problem statement–process scope loop as often as needed to get it right.
Characterize	3. Needs and metrics	What are the needs of various categories of customers? What should we measure in this process? How should we measure it? What are the target values?	Group customers with similar requirements. Design a standard core process, customize at the end.
	4. Critical subprocesses (or functionalities)	What functionalities or subprocesses must be included in the process? Which ones are the most important?	Identify all required functionalities and focus the design efforts on critical ones, that is, the biggest bang for the buck
Design	5. High-level design	How will the new process work in general? (30,000 feet view)	Make sure the best high-level design has been found before committing time and money to details. It is a common and costly mistake for a team to settle too quickly on a design without fully exploiting its creative potential.
	6. Detailed design	How will the new process work, in detail? (ground-level view)	Alternate systematically between creativity and rigor, gradually converging on final design.
Verify	7. Pilot	How will the process perform in a controlled environment?	Perform a pilot project early on, before time and money limitations eliminate any remaining flexibility. Use simulation and prototyping to reduce risks and overall cost.
	8. Implementation and continuous improvement	How will the process perform in the field? How are we going to ensure that it gets better over time?	The project does not end when the rollout starts. It ends when the process is stable and capable.

The questions addressed in the *define* phase are the same as those asked in an improvement project: What is the problem? What is the process that we have to design? The anchor point of the methodology is very different, however: we start from the customer, not from the process. *Characterization* involves a description of customers' needs, metrics, and process functionalities (or subprocesses) involved. The outputs of this phase are the specifications that the new process must meet. The *design* phase turns out a process design that meets these specifications. It involves an alternation between creativity and rigor, and proceeds from a high-level design to a detailed one. We then *verify* that the process performs in the field as expected before proceeding to full-scale deployment. We discuss the underlying design principles in the corresponding sections of the chapter. We show partial toolkits for each phase in Figure 10.2 and present the complete toolbox in Table 10.2.

Table 10.2 The DCDV design methodology: toolbox.

Technique (step)	Description	Purpose	Indication	Limitations/challenges
QFD (3–4)	A matrix-driven technique that takes in a weighted list of items and deploys it onto another one. A connected set of matrices can be used.	To generate a short but complete set of indicators and to identify the most important processes. Also, to verify the adequacy of a service package.	A must for rigorous product, service, and process design.	This is a complex technique, especially when used serially. Beyond a certain size, the matrices become unmanageable. Getting the data is challenging.
Kano (3)	Not really a technique. Classification of service features according to their effect on the client.	To adjust the service package to create maximum competitive advantage in the target market.	A must for service package design/adjustment.	Getting it right requires customer surveys, focus groups, and customer observation.
House 1 (3)	Input: weighted customer needs. Output: weighted metrics.	Identify a short and complete set of metrics. We refer to the most important metrics as CTQs, CTCs, and CTDs. Set target values for the critical metrics. These become specifications for the process to be designed.	Whenever we need to go from intangibles to metrics.	Size limitations.
FAST (4)	Functional analysis to identify required process functionalities.	Identify all functionalities for which processes have to be designed.	Without the FAST, one would not know what it is that must be designed.	It is critical to take a broad view so as not to place unnecessary constraints on the design.
House 2 (4)	Input: weighted metrics. Output: weighted functionalities. If one is looking at a complete business unit, the outputs are weighted value-adding processes.	Identify critical functionalities.	Whenever we want to design anything.	Size limitations.

Table 10.2 The DCDV design methodology: toolbox. (*continued*)

Technique (step)	Description	Purpose	Indication	Limitations/challenges
Concept generation (5)	Idea generation and combination into overall process concepts.	To explore different ways to meet the specifications.	This is the creative part of the methodology. A superior design requires much creativity.	Creating an environment conducive to creativity and getting the right people on the team.
Pugh matrix (5)	A matrix, including weighted criteria. All concepts are compared with a standard.	To compare the process concepts generated earlier and select the best.	Creativity sessions must be combined with "reality checks" to ensure that the final process is feasible.	Getting the right criteria and assigning weights can be a challenge.
Blueprint (6)	A "to be" process map where all players and their respective roles are identified.	Specify the process concept in more detail, including "who does what?"	A must for any new process to be implemented.	Defining the roles of the various players and further specifying the selected concept may be a challenge.
Design table (6)	A table that identifies all the elements required to make the blueprinted process a reality.	To give "design mandates" to various individuals and teams, for all aspects of the process.	Essential to "land" the design and implement it without forgetting anything or creating undue delays.	Challenges: Project management and ensuring that the integrity of the design is not lost.
FMEA/VAA (6)	See Table 9.1	See Table 9.1	See Table 9.1	See Table 9.1
SPC (7–8)	See Chapters 6 and 12	See Chapters 6 and 12	See Chapters 6 and 12	See Chapters 6 and 12

We now turn to a guided tour of the methodology using an example that is a direct carryover from Chapter 7. Viewing Video 10.1 is good preparation for this (see Figure 10.1). Financial Planning Associates (FPA) concluded that training and educating its clients in finance and investment was a critical process to improve. This is the starting point of this example. Few organizations go through the project selection methodology presented in Chapter 7. While doing so greatly increases the odds of selecting "the right thing to do," it is not a prerequisite for using the design methodology. Thus, except for using the general context presented in Chapter 7 as background to the example used here, we do not use any results derived in that chapter. This will ensure that this example has general applicability and constitutes a valid illustration of stand-alone use of the design methodology. To refresh your memory of the FPA case, refer to sections 5.5.3, 7.2, and 7.3, which present a summary of FPA's strategy.

FPA's executive committee decides to do the scoping itself. During the scoping session, it puts together a design team consisting of a mixture of senior partners from the three merged entities and two outside experts, one in the field of adult education and training and another in courseware. Considering the complexity of the tools, they hire a freelance consultant to act as coach. His mandate is to explain the tools, give instructions, facilitate discussions, and manage the human dynamics of the project. The market research firm that conducted the survey agrees to send an expert during the morning of the first session. While an improvement team consists of people who are intimately familiar with the process so that they can perform a detailed analysis of what goes on, such familiarity with any actual process would only result in limiting the team's creativity during a design project. The members of a design team must have a broad understanding of the business, be open to new ideas, and have a background and a mind-set that allow them to generate such ideas. They must not have any interest in preserving the status quo and must be open to radical change. Thus, the presence of outsiders, who have no fear of challenging the organization's sacred cows, is a great asset.

FPA's executive committee chooses a modified kaizen formula as a change vehicle, split into two parts, each consisting of three days. The initial project team is to stay intact until the completion of the first part, that is, when high-level design (step 5) is complete. The executive committee schedules three full days, one week apart, each one ending with a forum with executive committee members. The team will use the time in between sessions to verify hypotheses made during the session and gather whatever data are required to proceed with the next session. At the end of the first part, the team will make recommendations for changes in team composition for the remaining steps. When the organization has agreed on a high-level design and outside experts have served their purpose, it is time to move on to the second part, that is, to think about details and implementation. This is a good time to bring in representatives of the various groups whose daily work will be directly affected by the new process, and who thus care more and can contribute more to the details. Further, the sense of having some control over the change greatly reduces resistance. Original team members whose presence may now be redundant can leave the team as well.

10.2 DEFINE

Inputs to the *define* phase (see Figure 10.2) are a high-level goal and a "rough-cut" project idea. In FPA's case, we can state the idea as follows: "It is critical for our client base and for the execution of our strategy that we design from scratch a process to train and educate our clients in financial and investment matters. The only thing we did in the past—though we did that very well—was to develop public seminars to recruit new clients. Whatever else we did does not constitute a valid starting point for the process we need." This project idea could be the result of a structured approach such as that presented in Chapter 6, of a strategic planning process, or of simple brainstorming by top management.

The output of this phase is a well-scoped project, that is, a SMART problem (or opportunity) statement (this is step 1 in Table 10.1) and the perimeter of the project to design (this is step 2), as presented in a SITOC (refer back to the discussion of these tools in Chapters 3, 7, and 9). The executive committee itself performs the initial scoping using the methodology described in Chapter 7. We show the result in Figure 10.3. The high-level metric that will allow tracking the performance of the new process is the percentage of the customer base involved in the training and education program. A successful training and education process (henceforth "training process") will attract and keep new and existing clients as they embark on a training trajectory, stay the course, and get increasingly involved in managing

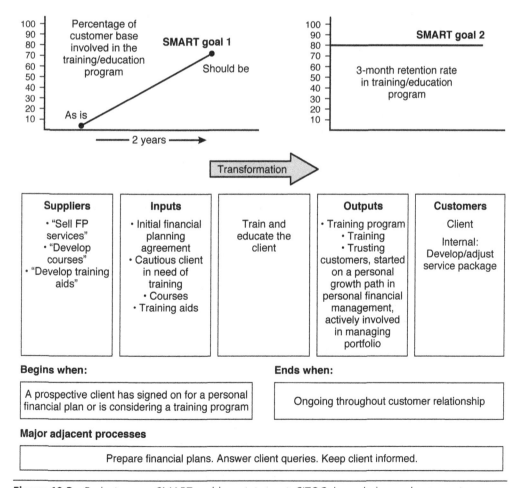

Figure 10.3 Project scope: SMART problem statement, SITOC, boundaries, and comments.

their own portfolio. Analysis of the composition of the client base, coupled with that of data from the market study, leads the executive committee to think that a 70% goal is achievable over a two-year horizon.

The executive committee, however, feels that this goal is not ambitious enough. Indeed, if the program succeeded in attracting many new clients, only to see them drop out of it within a few months, FPA might be misled in thinking that it is on the right track. Hence, it decides to set a target retention rate of 80% based on data obtained from a training and education benchmarking center. The two metrics complement each other well in allowing the executive committee to monitor process performance at a high level.

Turning now to the perimeter of the process (SITOC in Figure 10.3), we see that, besides the client himself, the "develop/adjust service package" process is also a customer (internal) of the process to be developed. Recall that one facet of FPA's strategy is to take advantage of a "fault line" in the services offered by competitors: they have a stake in keeping their clients dependent on their knowledge and services. FPA believes that, given the right pricing structure, making clients as autonomous as they want to be can be a win–win proposition. As clients progress through the training program, they gradually acquire new abilities, allowing them to become more involved in managing their financial affairs. Consequently, FPA must adjust its service package to allow this to take place in a timely fashion.

"Sell financial planning (FP) services" is a supplier process. It delivers a new client of FPA who could potentially embark on the training program. Signing this new client is part of the process to be designed. Developing courses and developing training aids are considered to be supplier processes as well. This is a scoping decision. The processes exist and are performing well. "Train and educate the client" will give specifications to these processes and use courses and training aids as inputs or building blocks to design personalized training programs.

The mission of the process is a short statement of why the process exists, that is, what is its expected (direct or indirect) contribution to value creation and to strategy (this is discussed in section 7.4). The mission of our process, as formulated in section 7.4, is "to create for each client a learning environment conducive to personal growth in financial management, and to the parallel evolution (upgrading) of the client's portfolio management system, with FPA as trusted adviser and service provider." This is the role this process plays in the execution of FPA's strategy. FPA's executive committee formulated the SMART goals for high-level monitoring of the new process to make sure it is on the path to actualizing this mission.

Note, finally, in the SITOC that the process has no ending point. It is meant to be an ongoing process, with training and education goals continually evolving with the client's knowledge and know-how, as well as with the evolving financial and investment environment.

10.3 CHARACTERIZE

Starting with the process scope as just defined, the outputs of the *characterize* phase are the specifications the new process will have to meet as well as the identification of its critical functionalities. (An overview of the methodology is presented in Video 10.2. Viewing it now will make it easier to understand the instructions that follow.) This output is produced in two steps. In step 1 we identify needs and metrics. In step 2 we identify key functionalities of the new process. Customers' needs will guide us to important metrics, and these, in turn, will allow pinpointing of important functionalities. We first identify clients' needs based on market research and prioritize them. We use QFD to first deploy these needs onto technical characteristics (metrics) and then deploy the latter onto functionalities (subprocesses). This is quite similar to the methodology presented in the first part of Chapter 6, with an important difference, however.

In Chapter 7, FPA's objective was not to design a new process (or a new service, which amounts to the same thing—see discussion in Chapter 3) but to identify the processes on which it should focus its priorities. This requires a broad-brush scanning of the complete business. We are now designing a new service delivery process, and thus a new service.

The coach gives the following instructions to the team:

1. Synthesize market data to produce a weighted list of client needs such as the one shown in Table 5.1. Use the customer activity cycle and affinity diagrams such as those used in Chapter 2.

2. For each need, specify whether it holds the potential to develop "basic," "performance," or "delight" service features (refer to Kano model; see Appendix B).[1]

3. Considering each need in turn, generate through brainstorming possible metrics—or measurable technical characteristics (refer back to section 7.2 and Figure 7.3 for the calculations, remembering that row entries are now weighted customer needs, and column entries are metrics)—that correlate closely with it. Look first for indicators that already exist, that are as objective as possible, that can provide quick feedback, and that promote early detection of shift or drift (see Chapter 6). Failing that, look for ordinal scales that could be developed or a metric associated with an upstream process that ultimately affects this need. Follow the procedure set forth in section 7.2 and illustrated in Figure 7.3 to build a house of quality 1 and rationalize it, that is, adding and deleting metrics to obtain the smallest possible complete set.

4. Prepare a Pareto chart of the resulting weighted metrics, as illustrated in Appendix B (this completes step 3 in Table 10.1).

5. Prepare a FAST diagram for the process to be designed. Starting with the transformation shown in Figure 10.3, identify the functionalities that the process requires, that is, break it down logically into subprocesses, as illustrated in previous chapters. Outsiders can play an important role in this task. Insiders, even executives, are often so close to any existing process that they lose their way in details and fail to recognize the functionalities that individual tasks perform. To prepare a good FAST diagram, one does not need to understand the current process. Only logic and general familiarity with the industry are required. Outsiders should go at it first, asking clarification questions to insiders as required.

6. Build house of quality 2 using the weighted metrics generated in house 1 and the subprocesses identified in the FAST diagram. Figure 10.4 illustrates the logical connection between house 1 and house 2.

7. Prepare a Pareto chart of the resulting weighted subprocesses. This completes step 4.

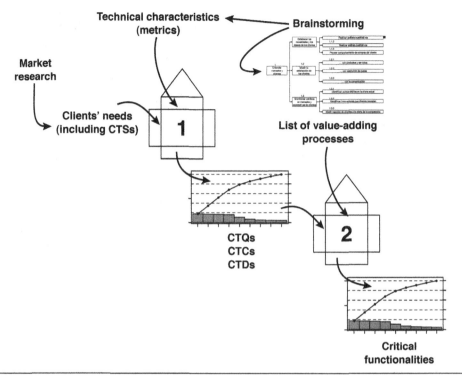

Figure 10.4 Flow of the characterization phase.

Table 10.3 shows the results of the first two tasks. There are 14 needs grouped under seven headings. With 24% of total weight, "insight" represents the client's desire for assistance in better understanding her needs, her preferences, and her evolving emotions vis-à-vis her investments, yield, risks, and retirement needs. Market research shows that competitors are doing a very poor job in that regard and thus that expectations are low. No offerings would be considered basic (see discussion in Appendix B). Offerings that deliver on this need would be meeting a key customer need head-on (performance), with much opportunity for seduction. The situations for trust (18%) and knowledge (12%) are quite similar. As for treatment (14%), convenience (13%), and intelligence (10%), some offerings would be basic, as this segment is used to receiving much from the competition, but focus groups show that when it comes to consideration, ease, and information, for example, more is better (performance), and there still exist ways to surprise them (delight). The only proactivity (9%) to be found at competitors is sales effort. Hence, being proactive in helping the client grow and become more autonomous holds much seductive potential.

Technical characteristics are translations of these needs into measurable process (or service offering) attributes. We are not talking about direct measures of satisfaction, such as those one obtains from customer surveys, which are also needed but do not provide the quick and specific feedback needed to keep processes in control (see Chapter 6). After generating a list of metrics (see Table 10.4), the team members group them into natural categories to check for balance. They then develop a seven-point scale, based on study of the existing client base, to evaluate the gaps between the client's goal and his actual market performance. They have to develop and test several other scales for characteristics that require

Table 10.3 Weighted client needs, with the potential they hold for various categories of service features (Kano model).

Need–high level (importance)	Needs–details	%	Basic	Performance	Delighter
			Potential for service features (Kano model)		
Insight (24)	Help me understand my true needs and attitude toward risk taking	12		X	X
	Help me manage my emotions (greed, fear, panic, etc.) and make rational decisions	12		X	X
Knowledge (12)	Facilitate my understanding of the major choices I am facing and their implications	12		X	X
Intelligence (10)	Give me all the information I need to make enlightened choices, while ensuring that I do not suffer from information overload	6	X	X	X
	Help me assess the implications of events in the environment on my risk/yield levels, and eventually on my financial security	4		X	X
Treatment (14)	Communicate in a language that I can understand and don't make me feel dumb	4		X	X
	Treat me like a VIP	10	X	X	X
Convenience (13)	Help me with the IS/IT required to access the information sources and systems required to be autonomous in the complex world of finance	5		X	X
	Make the process simple and painless	5	X	X	X
	Be reachable at all times through my medium of choice	3	X	X	X
Trust (18)	Assign me a top-notch, personable professional whom I can trust and who will remain my single contact over the long term	12		X	X
	Don't hold anything back and be candid about your own business interest (make me as autonomous as I can and want to be)	6			X
Proactivity (9)	Back me up proactively in areas where you feel I'm not ready to take ownership	5			X
	Monitor my progress and coach me along	4			X

Table 10.4 Generating technical characteristics (metrics).

Category	Technical characteristics
Skill levels	Number of radical shifts in strategy
	Frequency of access to online portfolio (bull's-eye)
	Assessment of client's tactical moves
Learning	Score in finance test
	Number of training program changes within a month
	Number of clients giving up on training
	Number of clients progressing to higher level
	Number of unnecessary calls to FPs
Support	Time to respond to clients' financial queries
	Time to respond to clients' IT queries
	Time to fix IS/IT problem at the client's
	Number of calls for technical support
Relationship	Attendance at FPA events
	Percentage of FP's suggestions that are accepted by client
	Number of people in direct contact with client

professional judgment, such as assessing the number of radical shifts in investment strategy and the quality of the client's self-initiated tactical moves.

They then enter the list into house 1 (see Figure 10.5) and correlate it with clients' needs. Analysis of house 1 shows that indicators 7 and 8 are "colinear"; that is, they correlate in exactly the same way to clients' needs. Indeed, the number of clients giving up on training and the number progressing to higher levels are but two facets of the same question: Is the training program working? While they are not redundant, simplicity requires that we use only one as a guide in the development of the process. The same goes for indicators 11 and 12, both related to response time. To keep house 2 to a workable dimension, the team decides to keep only the metrics that rate 6% or better in the bottom row of Figure 10.5. This leaves the seven metrics highlighted in house 1. The performance gap comes out as the most important indicator, with number of contact points and number of FP suggestions accepted by the client coming close behind.

The team then refines the scale for each of these metrics and obtains some comparative data from an industry benchmarking association, setting aggressive but realistic targets for each that would leave them in the top 1% to 10%, depending on the indicator. Some of the indicators they develop, however, are so personalized as to preclude any valid comparison. In those cases, they use data on the existing client base—digging into historical data and performing retroactive calculations of new indicators—to establish valid baselines and set targets accordingly. If one cannot compare with other organizations, one should at least compare with one's own past performance. These indicators, together with the target values, are the specifications for the new process.

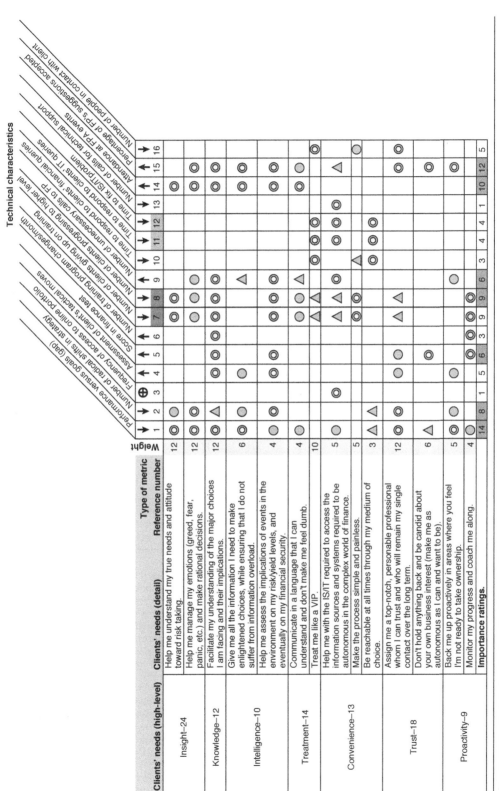

Figure 10.5 Train/educate the client: house 1.

The team thus sets out to identify required process functionalities. We are now in step 4 in Table 10.1. They perform the functional analysis (FAST diagram, see Figure 10.6) and identify seven major functionalities, or subprocesses. The process is triggered when a new client signs on to obtain a financial plan or when an existing client (for other services) is willing to consider embarking on FPA's new program. Someone then assesses the customer's needs, develops a personalized program, and gets the customer to sign on. Next, someone must set up the customer in the required IS/IT configuration, deliver the training and support program, monitor results, adjust the program as required, and adjust other investment services to match the client's evolving level of ability. Upon reviewing its work, the team finds that "deliver training and support program" contains a much larger chunk of the process than the other functions; that is, the subprocesses the team identified are not at the same level. Consequently, it explodes this functionality further by asking the question: how? Five additional functionalities are thus added to the diagram. The team feels comfortable carrying on its design work with these functionalities, that is, the original six plus the five additional subprocesses replacing the seventh one that they just "cracked open."

We use house 2 to identify the most important of those subprocesses and help formulate a mission statement for each of these. Figure 10.4 shows where the inputs into it come from. House 2 (see Figure 10.7) correlates the subprocesses identified in the FAST diagram with the critical metrics coming out of house 1. We obtain

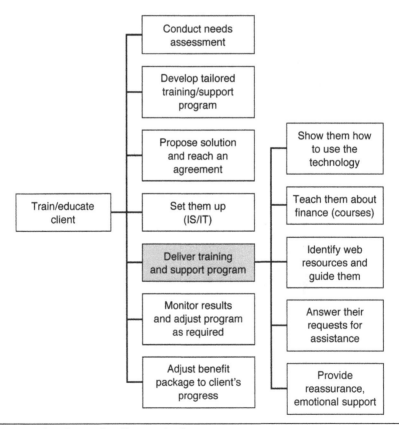

Figure 10.6 Train/educate the client: FAST diagram.

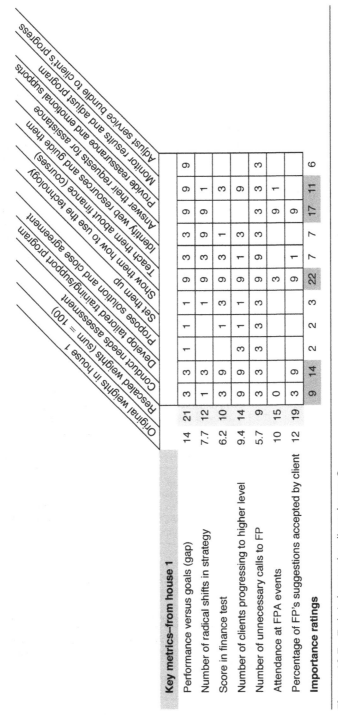

Key metrics—from house 1	Original weights in house 1	Rescaled weights (sum = 100)	Conduct needs assessment	Develop tailored training/support program	Propose solution and close agreement	Set them up	Show them how to use the technology	Teach them about finance (courses)	Identify web resources and guide them	Answer their requests for assistance	Provide reassurance and emotional supports	Monitor results and adjust program	Adjust service bundle to client's progress
Performance versus goals (gap)	14	21	3	3	1	1	1	9	3	3	9	9	9
Number of radical shifts in strategy	7.7	12	3	3		1	3	9	3	9	9	1	
Score in finance test	6.2	10	9	9	1	3	3	9	1	3	3	3	
Number of clients progressing to higher level	9.4	14	9	9	1	1	1	9	1	9	3	9	
Number of unnecessary calls to FP	5.7	9	3	3	3	3	3	9	3	9	3	3	3
Attendance at FPA events	10	15	0					3		3	9	1	
Percentage of FP's suggestions accepted by client	12	19	3	9		3	9	9	1	1	9	1	3
Importance ratings			9	14	2	2	3	22	7	7	17	11	6

Figure 10.7 Train/educate the client: house 2.

correlations by asking, of each process appearing at the top of the matrix and for each critical technical characteristic appearing on the left-hand side: What is the impact of this process on that metric? We obtain importance ratings in the usual fashion. The ratings for each metric appear in the (highlighted) third column. We obtain them by taking the respective ratings in the last row of house 1 (shown in column 2 of house 2) and rescaling them so that they sum up to 100 (for example, the rescaled weight of "performance versus goal [gap]" is $[14/65] \cdot 100 = 21$ [rounded]).

The team singles out the five most important subprocesses (see highlighted numbers in the bottom row of house 2) as the critical ones, as there is a natural cutoff point between the values 9 and 6. These subprocesses are listed in Figure 10.8, together with their ratings. Referring back to the mission of the process it is designing (see section 10.2) and to house 1 and house 2, the team is now in a position to deploy it onto specific mission statements for each functionality (or subprocess). "Conduct needs assessment," for instance, has a direct impact (see house 2, Figure 10.7) on the number of clients progressing to a higher level in the training program. Following that trail in house 1, we see that this technical characteristic correlates strongly (bull's-eye) with:

- "Help me understand my true needs and attitude toward risk taking."

- "Facilitate my understanding of the major choices I am facing and their implications."

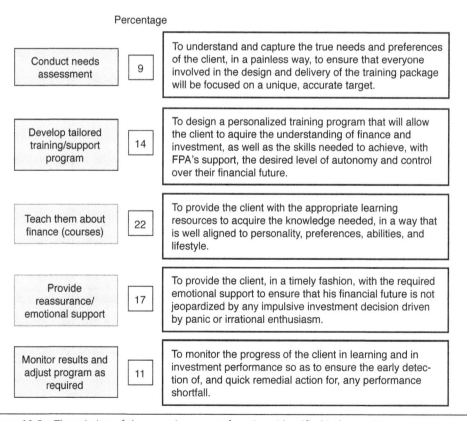

Percentage

| Conduct needs assessment | 9 | To understand and capture the true needs and preferences of the client, in a painless way, to ensure that everyone involved in the design and delivery of the training package will be focused on a unique, accurate target. |

| Develop tailored training/support program | 14 | To design a personalized training program that will allow the client to aquire the understanding of finance and investment, as well as the skills needed to achieve, with FPA's support, the desired level of autonomy and control over their financial future. |

| Teach them about finance (courses) | 22 | To provide the client with the appropriate learning resources to acquire the knowledge needed, in a way that is well aligned to personality, preferences, abilities, and lifestyle. |

| Provide reassurance/ emotional support | 17 | To provide the client, in a timely fashion, with the required emotional support to ensure that his financial future is not jeopardized by any impulsive investment decision driven by panic or irrational enthusiasm. |

| Monitor results and adjust program as required | 11 | To monitor the progress of the client in learning and in investment performance so as to ensure the early detection of, and quick remedial action for, any performance shortfall. |

Figure 10.8 The mission of the most important functions identified in house 2.

- "Help me assess the implications of events in the environment on my risk/yield levels, and eventually on my financial security."

- "Make the process simple and painless."

The team is also aware (see the FAST diagram in Figure 10.6) that this is an upstream functionality that will have an impact on all the others. Armed with this knowledge of the role that this subprocess plays, the team formulates its mission as follows: "To understand and capture the true needs and preferences of the client, in a painless way, to ensure that everyone involved in the design and delivery of the training package will be focused on a unique, accurate target." Applying this approach to the other four critical processes, the team writes the mission statements shown in Figure 10.8. These statements will be very useful in the *design* phase, when the team has to explore and compare different ways to achieve these missions and select the best one.

Having identified critical metrics (and targets to reach) and characterized the critical processes that affect them, the team is now ready to proceed to the *design* phase.

10.4 DESIGN

The output of the *design* phase is a process design capable of meeting the specifications formulated in the *characterize* phase. We produce it in two steps: high-level design, followed by detailed design.

10.4.1 High-Level Design

In high-level design (step 5 in Table 10.1) the team produces a broad-brush description of the new process. In detailed design (step 6), the team "lands it," producing a detailed process design, specifying every aspect necessary to proceed with a pilot project. Having rigorously zeroed in on the critical functionalities to design, it is now time to be creative! High-level design proceeds iteratively from the generation of alternate ways to perform each subprocess to the selection of the best one, ensuring that the process improves with each iteration, eventually converging on a final concept.

The coach gives the following instructions to the team for initial concept generation:

1. Generating ideas. Write down on sticky notes the names of the critical subprocesses identified in the *characterize* phase and place them as a column on the left-hand side of the page (see Figure 10.9). Start with the first one: "conduct needs assessment." Review the mission of that subprocess as spelled out in Figure 10.8. Sitting silently around a table, try to generate as many individual answers as possible to the following question: How can we go about assessing the client's training needs? Each team member writes down the ideas that come to mind on sticky notes, which are placed in the center of the table. When a member runs out of ideas, she can walk around the table and look at what the others have written. This often triggers new ideas. They do this for each of the five

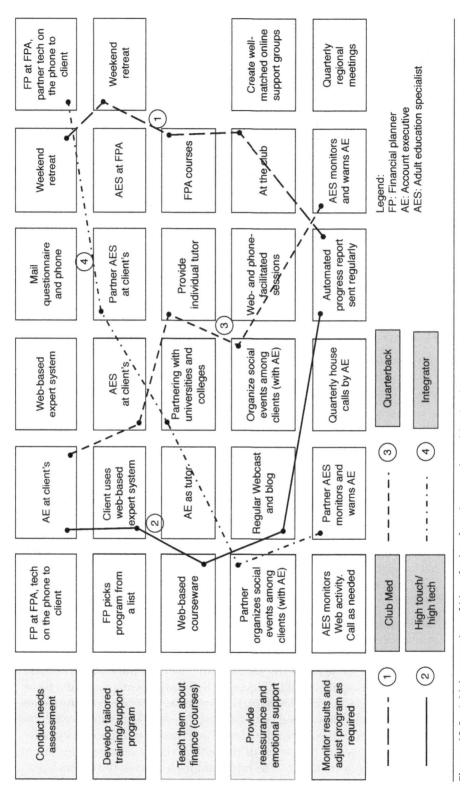

Figure 10.9 Initial generation of ideas for key functions, and combination into process concepts.

critical functions. When they run out of ideas, they analyze their collective work, eliminate duplication, combine similar ideas, and produce the final lineup as shown in Figure 10.9.

2. Combining ideas into process concepts. You must now combine these ideas. A process concept is a high-level description of a possible way to perform the complete process. It is a logical grouping of the ideas generated earlier around a theme. There are 6480 possible combinations of the ideas presented in Figure 10.9 ($6 \cdot 5 \cdot 6 \cdot 6 \cdot 6$), assuming that the ideas formulated for each subprocess are mutually exclusive, which is not always the case. It is impossible to explore each of these, and most do not make sense anyway. Thus, you must now analyze Figure 10.9 and use your intuition and creativity to think of possible themes around which you can organize individual ideas in a cohesive and meaningful way. You should then give each concept a name, the more colorful the better, to make it vivid and allow the team to visualize it and "manipulate it" in the next technique.

3. Describe each process concept in a few short sentences capturing its essence.

Process concepts are alternate visions of what the future process could be. To proceed with the comparative evaluation that follows, the team must share a common (high-resolution) mental image of that process. Much discussion is required to achieve the crispness necessary for this analysis to be meaningful.

The team generates many different types of ideas. For the first subprocess, for instance, the person performing the work may be either an FP (alone or with the help of a technician), a dedicated account executive, or the client himself using an expert system. The technician could be an FPA employee or work for a supplier (or partner) to whom FPA would outsource such work. Whoever does the work could do it on the phone, travel to the client's home, or receive the client at FPA's offices.

In looking for logical combinations, the team first selects a number of ideas involving group activities. They label this concept "Club Med," a name that, in their mind, is associated with group fun and mutual value creation and conveys well the spirit of the concept. The team spends some time exchanging views about how the process would work and is soon comfortable enough with it to write the short description presented in Figure 10.10. The team soon generates three more concepts (depicted in Figure 10.9) and repeats the process, ending with the summary descriptions presented in Figure 10.10. In "high touch/high tech" a strong relationship is centered on the account executive (AE), and technology is used wherever possible. In "quarterback" the AE coordinates a team of FPA specialists. "Integrator" is similar, except that the specialist roles are outsourced. "Cafeteria" involves letting the client choose from a menu of options with different prices. For the subprocess "teach them about finance," for example, the client could choose using web-based courseware, having a personal tutor, or attending a course at FPA. We could not depict this option like the other four in Figure 10.9.

This is a good place for a slight digression. Let us compare two notions: service concept and process concept. The reader should first review the short discussion of service and customer contact in section 3.2.6 and Figure 6.7 presenting an integrated view of the strategy-to-operation connection in the case of a drugstore (GYD).

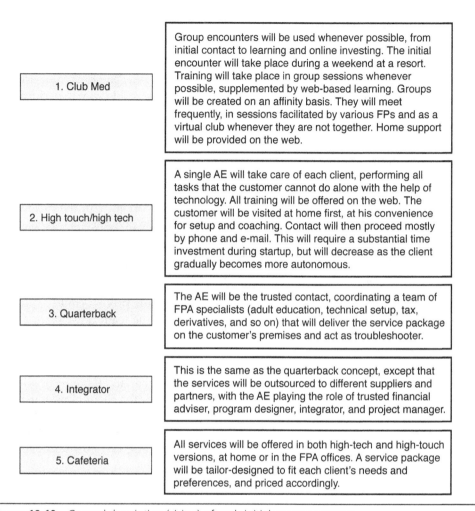

Figure 10.10   General description (vision) of each initial process concept.

In Chapter 2 we defined a service concept as the features–benefits pair. In the case of GYD, benefits include, among others, expertise, personalization, convenience, and low risk. Giving advice to elderly clients at home is one of the service features (or service offerings) that contribute to the "convenience" benefit. Since "giving advice" includes an action verb, it is obviously a process as well. Since it is impossible to separate the "advice" from the "giving," it is impossible to separate the offering from the process. More precisely, it is impossible to separate the customer contact part of the process from the service offerings.

Figure 10.11 illustrates the foregoing discussion. Since the customer contact part of the process is so intimately linked to service features, designing a service concept has direct implications for the part of the process where the organization comes into contact with the customer. We sometimes refer to this as the "coproduction" zone, since both the employee (or system) and the customer work together to produce the desired result. While the client cares much about the work the former performs with the contact person (see section 2.1.2 dealing with the service

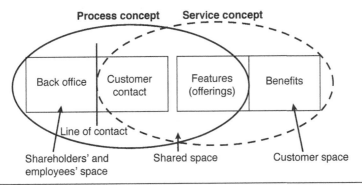

Figure 10.11 Relationship between service concept and process concept: division and sharing of the service space between the three stakeholders.

experience), she does not care about the way work is divided up in the back office, as long as "it works."

On the other hand, for the same reason, designing a service delivery process necessarily affects the service concept. Just as we need a close connection between the front office and service features, we also need coherence between what goes on in the back office and in the front office (see the dotted circle in Figure 10.11). Since the general path of the methodology goes "from the customer in," we start with the customer space in house 1, pinpoint the important processes in house 2, and then move on to generating process concepts that present a global coherence and internal integrity between the back office, the front office, and service features. Comparing the descriptions of the five initial concepts in Figure 10.10, we can see that they imply differences in all three.

Back to our team now. The process concepts the team developed include only the five most important subprocesses. To get a more complete picture, the team must now connect the dots. The coach thus gives team members the following instructions:

1. Expand Figure 10.9 to include all the functions in the FAST diagram.

2. For each concept, "fill in the blanks" by specifying a way to perform each remaining function that is coherent with the theme of the concept while maintaining its integrity.

Figure 10.12 shows the work of the team for concepts 1–4. A fifth concept, "Cafeteria," is an open concept since it would leave the client to choose, and pay for, what she wants, and thus does not appear in Figures 10.9 and 10.12. The theme of three of the concepts is reinforced by this exercise. "Quarterback" and "integrator," for instance, push further their respective themes of coordination of specialists and partners by an account executive. The "Club Med" concept is not reinforced by the exercise, merely completed by a series of ideas the team selects the best way it can.

Thus ends the first truly creative exercise of the methodology. The originality and superiority of the final design depend on the creativity of the team. There are many approaches and techniques available to promote creativity. We do not discuss these approaches here. We refer the reader to the extensive literature dealing with this topic. De Bono (1985), for instance, has many worthwhile suggestions in that regard.

	1. Club Med	2. High touch/ high tech	3. Quarterback	4. Integrator
Conduct needs assessment	Weekend retreat	FP at FPA, tech on the phone to client	AE at client's	FP at FPA, partner tech on the phone to client
Develop tailored training/support program	Weekend retreat	Client uses web-based expert system	AES at client's	Partner AES at client's
Propose solution and close agreement	Weekend retreat	Account exec (AE) at client's	Account exec (AE) at client's	Weekend retreat set up by partner club
Set them up	Sell/install/ support/upgrade IS/IT kit	The client does it with web and phone support	FPA technician	Local technician (partner)
Show them how to use the technology	Central courses (FPA) with access to club	Web-based courseware	FPA technical trainer	Local groups (partner)
Teach them about finance (courses)	FPA courses	Web-based courseware	Provide individual tutor	Partnering with universities and colleges
Identify web resources and guide them	Net meetings	Create resource page in portal	Provide private coach	Partnering with online financial info provider
Answer their requests for assistance	Web meetings	800 line	FP and tech make home calls	800 line
Provide reassurance and emotional support	At the club	Regular webcast and blog	Organize social events among clients (with AE)	Partner organizes social events among clients (with AE)
Monitor results and adjust program as required	Automated progress report sent regularly	Automated progress report sent regularly	AES monitors and warns AE	Partner AES monitors and warns AE
Adjust benefit package to client's progress	AE sets it up with client care rep (CCR)	AE does it for the client on the portal	AE sets it up with client care rep (CCR)	AE sets it up with partner client care rep (CCR)

Figure 10.12 Completed descriptions for four of the five initial process concepts.

The coach's instructions have not placed any limitations on what ideas team members could come up with. Consequently, it is quite possible that some of the resulting concepts lie beyond the realm of the possible, breaching some implicit or explicit constraints that the team or the organization faces. Are the concepts all acceptable from the perspective of clients, employees, and shareholders? Which one is the best? The team now needs to get back to reality, evaluate the feasibility of the concepts, and select the best one. We are now out of the realm of creativity and back in rigorous analysis mode.

The Pugh design matrix is the tool we will use for selecting the best concept. Its inputs are the process concepts just generated and a set of weighted criteria to be used for comparing them. Its output is the best concept. Its general operating principle consists of selecting one of the concepts as a baseline or standard and comparing it with the others on each criterion. Thus, the coach gives the team the following instructions:

1. Draw a matrix such as the one shown in Figure 10.13. Insert the initial process concepts on top and select one as the baseline against which you will compare the others. Select a concept that does not appear, at first glance, to be either the best or the worst (nothing dramatic will ensue if you end up selecting the best or the worst—only a slight delay). Make sure the concept you select is clear in the mind of everyone.

2. Select the most important metrics in house 2 (that is, among the most important metrics already selected from house 1) and copy them to the left-hand side of Figure 10.13, together with their ratings in house 2, under the "client" heading.

3. Since this is a professional service, customer perception of what they are getting may be very different from technical quality of the service (see section 2.1). Clients will assess the value of the service based on their own value equation (see section 2.2). Even if FPA delivers a service with high technical quality, clients will not buy or stay for long unless they perceive the value. Hence, add a criterion (such as perceived value), also under the client heading, and assign a rating to it relative to the other client-related criteria drawn from house 2.

4. Add one or more criteria to take into account the differential effect that the concepts under consideration will have on employees, particularly on the professionals.

5. Add other criteria to reflect the interests of the shareholders.

6. If management has imposed specific constraints on the project (not the case here), such as a deadline for implementation, a budget limit, or a physical ("we do not want to rent more space") or technological ("this has to fit into our integrated operating software") constraint, add these under the heading "management."

7. Consult with management and divide 100 points among the four stakeholders (clients, employees, shareholders, and management) according to how heavily

Stakeholders	Stakeholder weight	Weight in house 2	Criteria	Weight	Club Med	High touch/high tech	Quarterback Integrator	Cafeteria	
									Process concepts
Clients	40	21	Performance versus goals (gap)	10	+	S	+	+	S
		14	Number of clients progressing to higher level	5	+	S	+	+	S
		15	Attendance at FPA events	6	+	S	S	S	S
		19	Percentage of FP's suggestions accepted	9	−	S	−	−	−
Employees	20	21[1]	Perceived value	10	−	S	+	−	+
			Acceptance by FPs	20	−	S	−	−	−
Shareholders	40		Overall risk for FPA	20	+	S	−	+	−
			ROI	9	+	S	−	S	−
			Startup time	5	+	S	−	−	−
			Need to hire	6	S	S	−	+	−
			Weighted sum of "+"		55		25	41	10
			Weighted sum of "S"		6		6	15	21
			Weighted sum of "−"		39		69	44	69

Legend:
  +: Superior
  −: Inferior
  S: Standard or same

[1]This weight does not come from house 1. It was assigned by the team, relative to the weights of the four technical characteristics drawn from house 1.

Figure 10.13 Comparison of the four initial process concepts using the Pugh design matrix.

we want each group of criteria to weigh on the decision. Divide the rating attributed to each customer by the criteria in each category. For those criteria taken from house 2, rescale the house 2 ratings to sum up to the total allocated to the category. We rate "performance versus goals," for instance, as $[21/(21 + 14 + 15 + 19 + 21)] \cdot 40 = 10$ (rounded).

8. Compare each concept on each criterion, line by line, with the standard. First, fill the column under the standard with Ss, for "standard." Use a "+" to reflect a given concept's superiority to the standard on that criterion, a "−" to reflect inferiority, or an "S" to reflect equality ("same"). "Superior" here means "preferable." A lower risk, for example, is preferable to a higher one, and thus rates a "+."

9. If the team cannot agree on a given rating, more work will need to be done to further clarify the concepts or their implications. Identify the specific issues impeding consensus and design an experiment, a benchmarking exercise, a

focus group, or some other analysis to resolve the issue convincingly. Do not reach an artificial consensus or take a majority vote.

10. Calculate the weighted sum of pluses, minuses, and "sames" as shown in Figure 10.13.

11. The concept, if any, with the greatest positive difference between the sum of weighted pluses and the sum of weighted minuses is the best concept of the four. If the weighted sum of minuses is always superior to the weighted sum of pluses, then the standard is the best concept. Review any tie to refine the analysis and break the tie. If you end up with columns full of pluses, it means that the standard is the absolute worst concept. Drop it from consideration, pick a standard from among the other three concepts, and start over.

The team picks the four most important technical characteristics from house 2 and adds "perceived value" as a fifth client-related criterion. This reflects a special concern that management had raised with the new strategy. They wanted to make sure that as FPA made substantial investments in raising its clients' autonomy, thus making them less dependent on professional assistance, they would still perceive the value of FPA's services and remain loyal.

Thus, the team assigns this criterion the same weight as "performance versus goal," the most important metric from house 2. They also identify acceptance of the new process by FPs as an important comparison criterion. Shareholder criteria include risk, return on investment, time required to start up the new process, and need to hire. In a professional service firm where professionals are soon part of a profit sharing plan, hiring and firing are always strategic decisions. Since the new culture arising from the merger has not yet fully consolidated, the firm would rather avoid getting into this at this critical moment in its young life.

The team is looking for the process concept that best meets all these criteria. Clearly, however, they will have to make some trade-offs. Hence, during the first end-of-day forum, after presenting what they have done thus far to the executive committee, the team asks them for guidelines in that respect. The executive committee assigns a 40% weight to client criteria and a 20% weight to employee criteria, and divides the remaining 40% among the four shareholder criteria. The 10 criteria, together with their final ratings, are shown in Figure 10.13.

Team members pick "high touch/high tech" as the standard and proceed with the criterion-by-criterion comparison. After several rounds of discussion and further data gathering and analysis, the team finalizes its evaluation. Quarterback, integrator, and cafeteria are inferior to the standard, presenting more (weighted) drawbacks than advantages. Club Med, however, is superior to "high touch/high tech" and is thus the best concept of the five under consideration. Market research had indeed identified a certain sense of isolation and a clear preference for social and group activities in the target segment. The team concludes that group events are more likely to provide the stimulation and motivation clients needs to keep up their learning efforts, progress to higher levels of knowledge, and make better investment decisions. Further, it is cheaper to train people in groups than in individual tutorial sessions. Thus, the concept would create profit leverage (see section 4.1.2) through the operations strategy formulated by FPA (review section 5.5.3).

The Club Med concept has its drawbacks, however. The team assesses that while the process, in its current form, will forge strong bonds between clients, it may fail to create a strong enough relationship with the FP. Without trust, the required synergism between client and FP may not happen. Since a close professional relationship with clients is critical to FPs' satisfaction (refer back to section 2.4 and to the personal value equation in particular), this concept may generate much resistance to change, and from quarters that hold much power, enough to kill the initiative. Further, the concept would also require FPs to facilitate (real or virtual) group sessions, a role with which many are unfamiliar and that some may find uncomfortable.

A related drawback of that concept is that clients may fail to perceive the full value they receive from FPA. Indeed, they may come to attribute the results they are getting solely to their own efforts and to the new personal relationships that they have created with other investors met at the various FPA forums and events. Without the strong bond with an FP that is part of FPA's operations strategy (see section 5.5.3), FPA may create much value with little profit to show for it.

During the second forum with the executive committee, the team presents its work. This generates much feedback and many other ideas. The executive committee then decides to hold a similar forum for all the available FPs that night, again generating much useful feedback and material.

Club Med may be the best among the initial concepts the team has generated, but it is far from perfect and must be improved. Thus, the team must go back to the drawing board for a second creativity session, this time starting with the Club Med concept as the standard. The coach gives the team the following instructions for how to go about this:

1. Go back to the work done so far in the Pugh matrix and start a new column on the right-hand side. Put the Club Med concept as the heading of that column and fill the column with Ss. This is your new standard and the starting point for the second iteration, as we call this task.

2. Use creative techniques to modify and improve on the Club Med concept. Do not generate new process concepts from scratch. Rather, explore ways to eliminate, minimize, or compensate for the weaknesses of the concept (as pointed out by the three minus signs it rated in the first iteration). You can "borrow" ideas from the other concepts that rated a "+" on those same criteria. You can generate new ideas altogether for these weak aspects of the concept or use the ideas that arose during the forums. As you try to make up for the deficiencies of the concept, avoid weakening its strong point and try to maintain its integrity, that is, the glue or theme that gives it meaning and makes it coherent. Feel free as well to improve on other aspects of the process that rated a "+" in the first iteration. A "+" simply means that it is better than the standard against which you are comparing it, not that it is perfect. As you enter into a creativity session and as the team understands the concept with increasing clarity, such ideas are bound to occur as well. While you must not reinvent the process from scratch, neither should you discard any good idea.

3. Give each new process concept you generate a name that makes it vivid. The name should start with CM, followed by its defining character. Place these names at the top of a subsequent column in the Pugh matrix. When the creativity session concludes, compare these concepts with the original

CM concept and rate them as you did in the first iteration. The differences between the concepts will not be as marked as they were in the first iteration. Hence, your analysis will have to be finer. The concept that comes out on top is your new benchmark.

4. Repeat this procedure several times until you reach a point where the team cannot enhance the process further. Call a forum at that point to validate the results and see if ideas injected by participants can launch a new wave of creativity.

The team thus generates four variants around the CM theme. We show its work in Figure 10.14. At the center of the figure lies the original CM concept, copied from Figure 10.12 and described in Figure 10.10. The boxes under each of the four concepts describe the additions or modifications the team has made to this concept. When the idea or ideas in the box relate to a specific functionality, we use an arrow to show it. Sometimes the idea or ideas have general applicability throughout the process and no arrow is required. We show the results of the team's evaluation of the four variants in Figure 10.15.

The main idea in "CM GO team"[2] is to create teams of three FPs that would share the professional tasks to be performed in the new concept. These tasks include organizing and leading group sessions, one-on-one counseling and coaching, electronic monitoring of individual results, answering phone queries, and developing personalized training programs. Some of these tasks are new and may not be to the liking of every FP. A team approach, where each team has total latitude to allocate the tasks and spread the workload among members, gives FPs some control over what they do and is likely to reduce the stress that the new concept will create and attenuate resistance to change. While for some clients a relationship with three professionals may not be as convenient as a relationship with one FP, it is better than constantly changing contact persons, and some clients may appreciate hearing different views or hearing them in different words and personal styles. This relationship is likely to improve performance and perceived value as well. The only drawback, the team thinks (see Figure 10.15), is that since this is a new approach that touches on culture, work habits, and financial incentives, it is riskier than the original CM concept.

The "CM high tech" concept borrows some of the ideas from the "high touch/high tech" concept as additions to the CM concept, rather than as a substitute. This would improve the performance of the clients and increase perceived value. It would, however, be costly and involve a technological risk, as well as a delay in launching the concept. The main idea behind "CM AE calling" is to add phone support throughout the process, thus increasing perceived value. However, it is costly to do so and would require FPA to hire more personnel. Further, since this is a task that good FPs typically do not like, it would create more resistance to change and would probably not increase performance. The "CM AE face-to-face time" involves adding more face-to-face contact with an AE throughout the process. This would largely eliminate the drawbacks of the original CM concept. It would come at a cost, however, and thus produce inferior financial results and put FPA at risk.

Examination of the second iteration in the Pugh matrix (Figure 10.15) shows that the original CM concept is preferable to "high tech" and "AE calling," both of which involve more drawbacks than advantages. "GO team" and "AE face-to-face time" are superior concepts, but the balance of benefits favors the former. This is

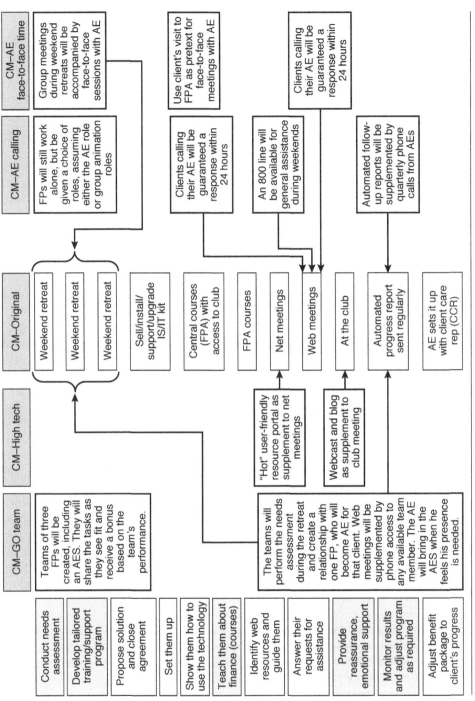

Figure 10.14 Variation on a theme: generating variants of the best concept ("Club Med") selected in the first iteration (Figures 10.11 and 10.12).

Criteria	Weight	First iteration					Second iteration				
		Club Med	High touch/high tech	Quarterback	Integrator	Cafeteria	Club Med	CM-GO team	CM-High tech	CM-AE calling	CM-AE face-to-face
Performance versus goals (gap)	10	+	S	+	+	S	S	+	+	S	S
Number of clients progressing to higher level	5	+	S	+	+	S	S	+	+	S	+
Attendance at FPA events	6	+	S	S	S	S	S	+	S	S	+
Percentage of FP's suggestions accepted	9	−	S	−	−	−	S	+	S	S	+
Perceived value	10	−	S	+	−	+	S	+	+	+	+
Acceptance by FPs	20	−	S	−	−	−	S	+	S	−	+
Overall risk for FPA	20	+	S	−	+	−	S	−	−	S	−
ROI	9	+	S	−	S	−	S	S	−	−	−
Startup time	5	+	S	−	−	−	S	S	−	S	+
Need to hire	6	S	S	−	+	−	S	S	S	−	S
Weighted sum of "+"		55		25	41	10		60	25	10	55
Weighted sum of "S"		6		6	15	21		20	41	55	16
Weighted sum of "−"		39		69	44	69		20	34	35	29

Figure 10.15 Second iteration: comparing the four new concepts (see Figure 10.14) using the Pugh design matrix.

the conclusion of the second iteration. The team could pursue its work by entering a third creativity wave to try to reduce the risk involved with the latest concept. For the purpose of this chapter, however, we will take "GO team" to be the final concept. Thus ends the high-level design step (step 5 in Figure 10.2).

Having gone through this exercise, it is now possible to better understand the rationale behind the Pugh matrix. The "optimization algorithm" proceeds in steps (or iterations) from one solution to another, making sure at every turn that the next solution is better than the previous one. We illustrate this in Figure 10.16. The four initial concepts generated in the first iteration (A-B-C-D) are vastly different from one another, as illustrated by the distance between them. We move from the initial standard (B) to the best of the four concepts (C) (as illustrated by the numbered arrow). We discard the other three concepts, consider C as the new standard, and generate "variants" around it (a-b-c-d-e). The variants are much more similar to each other than A-B-C-D were in the first iteration since they involve only minor modifications of the C concept. Concept "e" now comes out on top, but the gains made in this iteration (arrow number two) are typically smaller than in the previous one. Variants of "e" are then generated, producing an even smaller gain in the third iteration, and so on. While the gains decrease with every iteration, as the process converges, they still represent a huge rate of return on the time invested.

We now turn to detailed design (step 6 in Table 10.1).

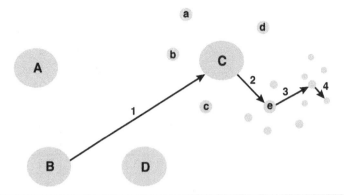

Figure 10.16 Illustration of the optimization algorithm behind the Pugh matrix.

10.4.2 Detailed Design

The input to the detailed design step is the final high-level concept obtained in the previous step (CM GO team). The output is a complete process design, ready for field testing. High-level design started from 30,000 feet (from a clear view of the complete business and its competitive environment) and took us down to 10,000 feet, that is, a broad vision of how the new process will flow. We now have to land it, that is, specify the many operational details that are not visible from the bird's-eye view in the previous step. We also have to use all means at our disposal to make sure that the process is as good as it can be before we release it for field testing. This step marks the start of the second part of the kaizen event, and team composition is thus modified as discussed earlier.

The two major tools we use to specify the design are the blueprint and the design table (see Table 10.2). On the face of it, a process blueprint looks just like a process map. There is a fundamental difference, however. A process map describes the process "as is." A blueprint describes the process "to be." Just as one uses a blueprint to build a house, we use a blueprint to build a process. Starting with the high-level design, the team must first add the organizational layer, which it has not addressed so far, and specify how it will proceed as a series of detailed tasks flowing from one player to another. As it does so, many design issues will arise. The team will capture these and classify them in a design table. Thus, the coach gives the team the following instructions:

1. Study the high-level design in detail and identify the organizational players who will play a role. Write their names on sticky notes and place them on the left-hand side of a flip chart, just as you would if you were building a process map.

2. You will now view the process as a play for which the team is writing the script. Your task is to visualize the customer's experience by simulating it. Since there must be a representative for each player (department) on the design team, assign roles to each team member in such a way that all players, including the client, are represented. The player that initiates the process should then start (speaking in the first person) describing what he does, what inputs he needs to do it, what output he produces, and what other players he triggers into action. As each player is talking in turn, capture the unfolding

action using sticky notes and arrows. Stay at a high level for the first take and avoid getting lost in details. Come back to the beginning when you are done and go through it a second time, adding details and clarifications to improve resolution. Refine the blueprint as much as you can, identifying areas that need further investigation.

3. Walk through the process again, this time asking yourselves at every step: What does the organization need to make this happen? The answers you provide will fall into the following categories: equipment, installations, materials, suppliers, human resources, information systems/information technology (IS/IT), procedures, and implementation plan. Draw a table such as the one shown in Figure 10.17. Capture each required design element in the appropriate category.

4. When the table is complete, revisit each element, specifying—in "design mandates"—decisions or choices to make, additional data to obtain, analyses to perform, or experiments to conduct. Assign all design mandates to team members based on expertise, contacts, affinity, or availability.

5. Prepare a detailed design plan encompassing all design mandates. Specify the support and resources required to make it happen and present it to the executive forum.

Equipment	Installations	Materials	Suppliers
• Equipment to support off-site training • Equipment to upgrade client's installations • Upgrade call center • Furnishing for Club room • Upgrade car fleet	• Revamp training room • Build Club room • Refit the entrance hall	• Review all brochures and forms with advertising agency	• Resort • Social events • Caterer
HR aspects	**IS/IT**	**Procedures**	**Implementation plan**
• Design and validate approach to create FP teams and team-based incentive system • Develop team management system and train FPs • Select and train FPs with the right skill set to become facilitators • Review remuneration policy for off-site work	• Develop net meeting technology • Develop web-meeting technology • Develop automated progress report • Organize to support off-site training • Develop automated client monitoring • Computer setup for Club room • Review online forms	• Procedures to assess and upgrade clients' home installations • Team management procedures • Expense reports procedure • Procedures to calculate all the indicators appearing in House 2 (Figure 10.7), monitor results and use the information for correction and learning purpose.	• See Gantt chart *(not included)*

Figure 10.17 Elements of the new training process to be designed (partial).

Figure 10.18 presents an extract from the macro blueprint the team prepared. Since the process is large, the team had to stick to a broad-brush depiction of it (the macro blueprint is to the blueprint what the macro map is to the process map). The diagram is largely self-explanatory. As the team pushes deeper, it will have to provide many more details, captured in a detailed blueprint, about how such tasks as "set up technological support for weekend" or "analyze customer data and plan weekend," for example, will be performed. More precisely, we shall refer to Figure 10.18 as an augmented visual macro-blueprint, because it not only depicts the high-level flow of the "to be" process, but incorporates as many of the process features as can legibly fit in one diagram. Indeed, not all process features and changes alter the flow of the process, and simple "bubbles" will serve to present a more complete picture of the operations of the process and the changes that it represents for the organization and the workers.

Figure 10.17 gives a partial list of the design elements that will be the object of design mandates. The tasks require a variety of expertise and skills, ranging from human resources to information technology, including procurement, layout, logistics, and ergonomics. Some mandates, such as organizing for catering, are straightforward. Others, such as adapting web-meeting technology to fit FPA's needs, are quite challenging. The human resources category generally includes some of the most difficult challenges, especially in professional services. Creating FP teams, reorganizing the tasks of FPs, and developing team incentives all touch on the job concept of a very powerful group of employees, and thus on FPA's positioning in the labor market. These mandates have clear strategic implications for the organization and must involve the executive committee.

The forum at which the team presents its detailed design plan requires more time. Executives make decisions on the spot about support and resource requirements to produce the detailed design while all key players are present, and the analysis and past deliverables of the team are fresh in everyone's mind. The forum is a level playing field, rich in facts and data to be used to the fullest.

When the plan is adopted, the team does not have to work together all the time anymore. Since team members share a vision of the new process and have agreed on a game plan to make it happen, they can each go their own way to perform their own bits of the detailed design plan. They keep in touch virtually and come together regularly to check progress, identify and resolve interfacing issues between design elements, and make sure that when the parts come together, the end process will function well as a whole.

To improve on the design whose final contours are now taking shape, as the nature of the task suggests, we borrow a tool from the improvement methodology toolkit. The coach instructs the team to perform a process design FMEA (refer back to section 9.5.5). Again, the technique looks very much like the FMEA used in the process improvement methodology. The difference lies in that the team is not trying to fix a broken process, but to identify risk and prevent defects before they occur. While it is relatively easy to identify defects in an existing process, fixing the process can be costly. When the process is still on the design table, it requires more effort to identify the defects that might occur (risks). However, fixing them is much, much cheaper. By filtering the process through a rigorous FMEA, the team is able to introduce many poka-yokes as well as risk reduction and risk management features.

Simulation tools of various kinds, including demos, mock-ups, enactment, or computer simulation software, may be used at this point to obtain previews of the

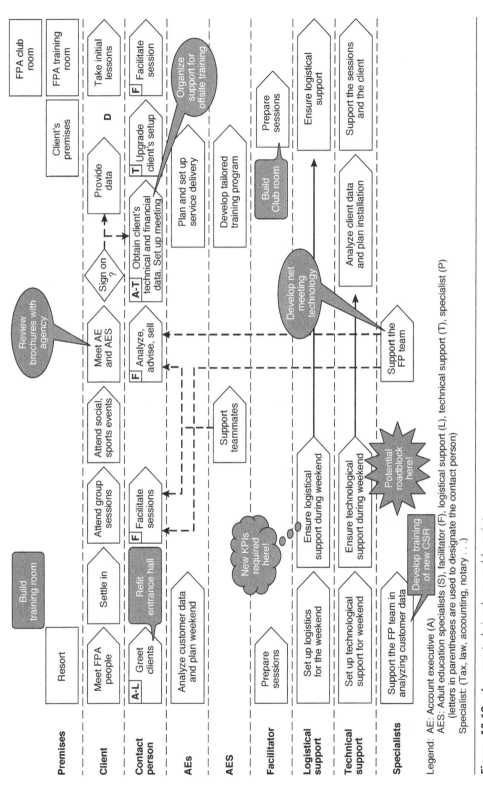

Figure 10.18 Augmented visual macro-blueprint.

"voice of the process" (see Chapter 6) and test it against the specifications (that is, the "voice of the customer") that came out of the *characterize* phase.

The team brings the final design to an executive forum, together with house 1, house 2, and the Pugh matrix that led to it. All participants are then encouraged to probe the design and challenge its capability. This ends the *design* phase. The team is now ready to see how it performs in real life.

10.5 VERIFY

The *verify* phase starts with the detailed blueprint of the process developed in the previous phase. Its output is a process—fully deployed, stable, and capable. It evolves around a pilot project that lies at its core. It is followed by standardization and deployment.

We use a pilot project to create a low-risk yet representative environment that will allow putting the process to the test. Selection of the test site is critical. At this point, the riskiest features of the process are well known. In terms of change management, test results must be, and fence-sitters must see that they are, valid guides to planning full-scale deployment. On the other hand, it would be unduly risky to select the site that provides the harshest testing ground for the project.

The development tools the team used provide useful information about the process's vulnerability. The minus signs in the Pugh matrix provide clues about weak areas. The various iterations through the matrix show the aspects of the process that the team was trying to correct. The FMEA table rates all the risks identified by the team, before and after the fix or poka-yoke the team has found. These elements allow the team to develop a risk management plan for the pilot project.

No matter how rigorous the design methodology, the reality test will yield a wealth of useful information. Thus, the team has to set up a learning system to capture this information and use it to improve its design. Client's agenda, mystery shopping, observation, focus groups, and surveys of all kinds are but a few of the tools available to the team. A dollar invested at this point of the project will yield huge dividends later in terms of field results. The team holds regular progress meetings throughout the pilot project to translate its findings into process improvements.

An essential output that the team must provide is a "user manual." This involves documenting the process, developing a control plan, and providing the process owner with the tools she will need, such as FMEA and SPC, to keep the process at peak performance level. We invite the reader to review section 9.7, discussing the *control* phase of the improvement methodology. The major difference with the improvement methodology, of course, is that the process is completely new and, thus, that everyone who will be involved in it has to be trained from scratch. Thus, having a well-documented and well-instrumented process is critical to a successful deployment.

To deploy the process, the team uses the best process management techniques. The team develops a training program that is respectful of the people's ability to learn. A support team is built to help those who will be affected by the new process, and a help desk is created. The team also builds contingency plans and puts together a strategic team to monitor the deployment phase.

A major mistake is very common at this point. Time gets its revenge on what we do without it. Unrealistic deadlines are always disruptive and often destructive. It may be a great opportunity, and time may well be of the essence. Even more reason to do it well. Launching the new process in a panic, with poorly trained employees, goes directly against the rigor of the approach used thus far, and thus denies its benefits. Further, when a project goes over budget, this is generally the point in the project cycle when the team is most likely to run out of money. The temptation to cut back on training, so that the project will meet its scheduled launch date and budget, may be strong. Resist it. It will only result in incurring huge costs trying to fix it after deployment and an uphill battle to restore a reputation among customers and employees that has been tarnished.

10.6 UNDERSTANDING THE DESIGN METHODOLOGY

The design principles underlying each step of the methodology are presented in Table 10.1. They are self-explanatory. However, a recurring principle of the methodology might have escaped the reader, as it is difficult to understand the logic and the connection when one is focused on the details of each technique. Each technique proceeds by first generating quantity, then distilling quality from the elements generated (see Figure 10.19). A number of approaches are used to generate elements such as customer needs, technical characteristics, process functionalities, process concepts, process variants, or failure modes. Different filtering techniques (various types of rating schemes and matrices) and different criteria are then used to identify the best or the most important elements, on which we should focus.

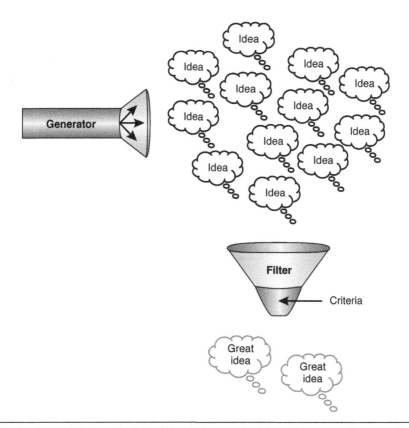

Figure 10.19   An underlying principle of the design methodology: from quantity to quality.

We show the sequence of generators and filters in Figure 10.20. We generate a quantity of the customer's needs and wants by walking in his shoes through the customer activity cycle. We then use an affinity diagram and divide 100 points to identify the critical needs. We use brainstorming to generate an initial list of possible metrics and use a matrix (house 1) to filter them through the weighted needs and distill the most important metrics (CTQs, CTCs, CTDs). We then use a FAST diagram to identify process functionalities and identify the most important ones by filtering them through the critical metrics in house 2.

Concept generation proceeds from these critical functionalities, through brainstorming and combination of ideas, to generating process concepts. We filter these in turn through the Pugh matrix, using criteria reflecting clients' (from house 1), employees', and shareholders' needs to distill the best concept. We then run this concept through several iterations of the cycle of generating variants and selecting the best one. The blueprint of the final process is then screened through an FMEA, allowing designers to isolate and manage the most important risks.

Figure 10.21 provides yet another view of the methodology, outlining how the flow is cut up into four phases. The *define* phase shows the roles of strategy and analysis of existing processes (see Chapter 7) in scoping the process. The arrows

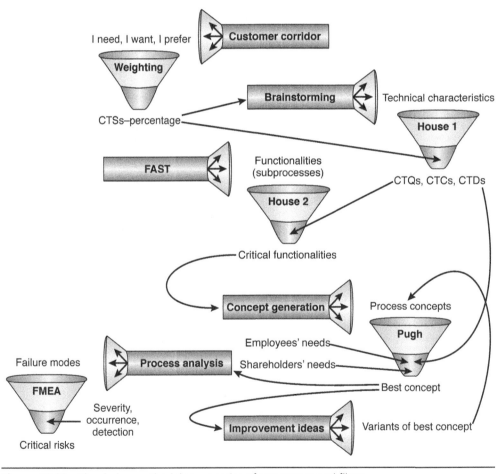

Figure 10.20 The design methodology: a series of generators and filters.

between the SMART statement and the SITOC illustrate the iterations and adjustments involved in scoping a project. The *characterize* phase proceeds from two different points of the SITOC. Analysis of the clients leads to identifying CTSs and then to CTQs, CTCs, and CTDs. Analysis of the transformation, using the FAST diagram, leads to isolating the most important functionalities as the two prongs meet in house 2. Analysis of any existing subprocesses in the organization is also useful at this point. Some critical subprocesses identified in house 2 may already exist and perform well somewhere in the organization (or may be accessible

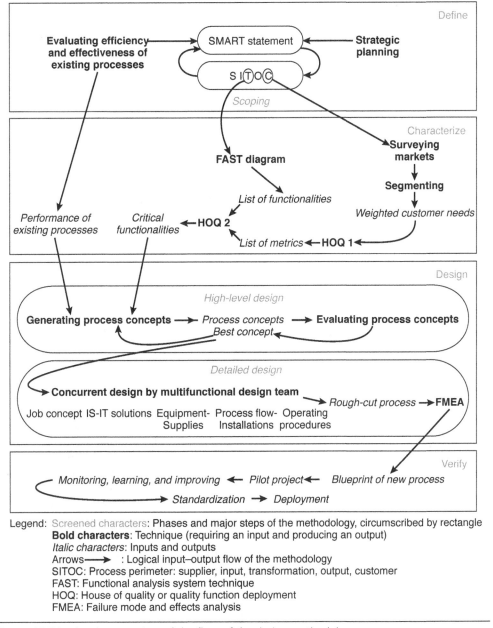

Legend: Screened characters: **Phases and major steps of the methodology**, circumscribed by rectangle
Bold characters: Technique (requiring an input and producing an output)
Italic characters: Inputs and outputs
Arrows───► : Logical input–output flow of the methodology
SITOC: Process perimeter: supplier, input, transformation, output, customer
FAST: Functional analysis system technique
HOQ: House of quality or quality function deployment
FMEA: Failure mode and effects analysis

Figure 10.21   An alternate view of the flow of the design methodology.

through process benchmarking). If that is the case, it is best to focus the design effort on other subprocesses.

We see as well in Figure 10.21 that the *design* phase involves cycling through the "concept generation–Pugh matrix" cycle until it converges on a high-level view of the best process. It is indeed a common mistake when designing a new process to settle too quickly on high-level design decisions before fully exploring alternatives. Iterating through this cycle is fast and cheap, whereas detailed design is costly and time-consuming. By forcing such iterations and involving executives and other players in the forums, one creates much value and makes change management much easier in the implementation phase.

10.7 COMPARING DCDV AND DMAIC

The *design* methodology presents a stark contrast with the *improve* methodology. Its anchor points are the clients and strategy, whereas the latter is anchored on an existing process, as described by the process map. We use the improve methodology when we believe that the process, while currently unsatisfactory, has potential. Thus, we do not have to question whether the process is "the right thing to do." We proceed directly to trying to understand the causes of its poor performance (diagnosis), and proceed from there to fixing it. The approach used for reaching a diagnosis involves several techniques used in parallel, culminating in a synthesis (see Figure 10.17). There lies the biggest intellectual challenge of the methodology.

If one technique in the DMAIC methodology is used poorly and does not yield results, the odds are that the other techniques applied in parallel will make up for it and that the right diagnosis will be reached. This is not the case for the DCDV methodology. Since we use the techniques serially—the output of one becoming the input of the next one—a major mistake at any point is not likely to be corrected downstream by other techniques. The need for rigor is therefore even more important when designing a new process than it is when improving one. This may explain why the latter is much more widespread than the former.

Even an organization that has successfully implemented DMAIC—and thus successfully faced the challenge of rigor in process improvement—is likely to find this new challenge daunting. As previously discussed, considering the nature of the task and its starting point, the composition of a design team has to be very different from that of an improvement team. Designers and improvement experts share a number of attitudes and aptitudes, such as a passion for rigor and leadership and a mastery of statistical tools. They are, however, two different breeds. Designers are very good at dealing with broad, abstract concepts such as (internal or external) customer needs and market segments. Typically, improvement experts are at their best when disentangling intricate interactions between concrete process variables. The best designers tend to have strong conceptual abilities—together with the corresponding tolerance for ambiguity—that allow them to view the global picture. The best improvement experts have a more analytical mind. The former are very good at zooming out, while the latter's comfort zone is limited to zooming in. Since these attitudes are totally incompatible, it is difficult to find them in the same individual, together with the leadership skills required to participate and lead change.

Further, intimate knowledge of the process is an important asset for members of improvement teams, whereas it is a liability for members of design teams, inhibiting their creativity. The latter must be able to keep their distance from any existing process or organizational practice. People who have been exposed to different ways of doing things are best. Finally, process workers are likely to feel threatened by radical change and its implication for their job and those of their friends and coworkers, and thus less likely to come up with or support such changes.

As process improvement skills become more widespread, the battleground to become the best learning organization may well move to excellence in process design. No matter how good an organization is at repairing broken processes, it will not be able to compete with organizations capable of designing a high-performance process on the first attempt.

10.8 SUMMARY

The flow of the *design* methodology is very different from that of the *improve* methodology. The latter starts with what already exists, that is, using the actual process as anchor for the analysis, and will not work if there is no process. The former starts with the customer and proceeds inward to selecting the appropriate metrics, setting standards, and developing a process from scratch. The anchor point is the customer and his or her needs—a much more abstract notion than an existing process. The example used is a direct carryover from Chapter 5, as FPA now develops a process to train and educate clients belonging to a specific market segment.

The methodology involves the development of a set of metrics using quality function deployment. We use the same technique to identify the most important functionalities of the process. These rigorous activities are interspersed with creative ones as the team explores and compares alternate ways of performing the process. The latter steps involve detailed design, field verification, and implementation.

The methodology presents the organization with the challenge of introducing rigor into an area still believed by many to be the sole preserve of intuition and improvisation.

EXERCISE

10.1 Conducting a DCDV Design Workshop

Your task is to apply the tools and methodology presented in this chapter to the design project scoped in exercise 7.6. You might find the two additional forms included as Figures 10.22 and 10.23 useful. After you have completed house 1, use Figure 10.22 to set the target values (the voice of the customer) for the critical metrics and evaluate the respective measurement systems. After completing house 2, use Figure 10.23 to specify the metrics impacted by the key functions and the priorities to consider during design.

Since the methodology is more complex and thus riskier than the previous one, you should manage this additional risk by using an outside resource to help you, or perform the project first in a simulated setting. The latter involves sharing the book with three or four colleagues and performing the project off-line, that is, without involving anyone in the organization. This might give you the added confidence you need to be able to guide an actual team through the methodology.

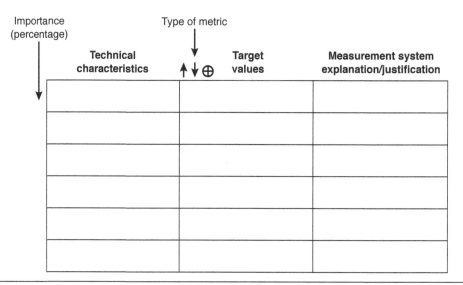

Importance
(percentage)

Type of metric

Technical
characteristics

↑↓⊕

Target
values

Measurement system
explanation/justification

Figure 10.22 Voice of the customer for key metrics and validation of the measurement system.

Functions	Technical characteristics impacted (1–3)	Priorities to consider during design

Figure 10.23 Key functions, metrics impacted, and priorities to consider in design.

NOTES

1. While this step and step 4 are strongly recommended, they can be skipped without loss in the flow of the methodology. To avoid overburdening an already complex chapter, this material was placed in Appendix B.

2. "GO" is short for *Gentil Organisateur* (literally, "kind facilitator"), the term used by a French resort to refer to the young people it uses to animate the "village" and make the customer's vacation an enjoyable experience. It refers to the customers as *Gentils Membres* (kind members). The team wanted to pursue the CM analogy further and include this aspect of the club/brotherhood spirit to capture the distinctive feature of this variant of the CM concept.

Part III
Ingredients and Recipes for Corporate and Personal Change Initiatives

Strategic execution, social cohesion, knowledge, and rigor are four dimensions of the organization that must be harmonized in order to avoid bottlenecks in the drive toward operational excellence. Top management itself, of course, is the fifth element. Several waves of change, from total quality management to Lean-Six Sigma, have swept the business world during the last quarter century, sowing confusion in their wake and often reaping cynicism. The nature of these initiatives and the relationship they bear to the dimensions of the learning organization are the topic of Chapter 11. In Chapter 12, we make a quantum leap: Can an individual, either as a lone professional (the one-person business) or in his or her personal life, benefit from using the approaches promoted in this book, and if so, how? Your life is not a business, but it does have a purpose. Further, you do "operate" many processes in your personal life for various purposes. If you are so inclined, there may be a bonus in this book for you.

11

The Approaches to and Practice of Continuous Improvement

In the firefighting organization, nobody ever gets rewarded for preventing fires. It is the best firefighter that rises to the top. Do not deprive her of opportunities to show her skills.

The world of operations improvement initiatives is confusing. It is difficult to isolate fads from breakthroughs and find what the company needs to move ahead toward the new paradigm: the learning organization. Knowing your learning assets and liabilities and understanding what each initiative can contribute is essential to avoid the "me too" flavor-of-the-month syndrome.

So far in this book we have discussed the notion of value (Chapter 2), the notion of process (Chapter 3), the connection with strategy (Chapters 4 and 5), process management (Chapter 6), the scoping of improvement projects (Chapter 7), change management and learning (Chapter 8), process improvement (Chapter 9), and process design (Chapter 10). The reader is probably wondering at this point, "OK, that makes sense, but what do I do with all this? Where do I start? How do other companies go about it? Which approach offers the greatest chance of success for me?" To address these questions, we first discuss the practice of continuous improvement (11.1) and the most common operations improvement initiatives (11.2). After formulating recommendations about how to deal with these initiatives (11.3), we present what we see as the emerging paradigm (11.4) and give general advice about charting a course toward that priceless but elusive goal of becoming the faster learner. Viewing Video 11.1 (see Figure 11.1) provides a good introduction to these topics.

11.1 THE PRACTICE OF CONTINUOUS IMPROVEMENT

Learning faster than your competitors is a continuing and sustainable source of strategic advantage. This is no big discovery. Every company knows that, at least intellectually. Many companies are doing something about it, more or less formally, with more or less success. When a company, in any industry, achieves breakthrough success, other companies and management consultants, later followed by academics, take notice and try to understand the recipe for its success.

11.1 Toward operational excellence
Beware of management consultants bearing brand new business cards with catchy and intriguing new schemes. In other words, beware of management fads, but don't throw the baby away with the bath water, either. Plot an adapted path toward operational excellence. There are several good reference models out there: select the one that best fits your reality and needs. Give it your brand name. Eclecticism is best.

Key concepts: Operational initiatives, management fads, one size does not fit all, the soft—the hard—the strategic, the dimensions of the learning organization, maturity levels

Figure 11.1   Video associated with Chapter 11.

Whenever they think they do, they try to characterize the approach, brand it, and either use it to polish their corporate image, sell it, or spread it around through conferences, articles, and books. Thus, over the years of the evolution of management thought and action, many such approaches have been born, branded, and promoted, with varying degrees of success. We shall refer to these approaches as operational improvement initiatives, or OIIs, to distinguish them from initiatives that have to do with other management functions, such as competence management in human resources, or relationship marketing.

Because it is difficult and time-consuming to get solid evidence on whether an OII works, it is very hard to state positively what works and what does not. Opinions expressed in this chapter are based on the author's experience and on his interpretation of published evidence, however limited in quantity and quality, and however contradictory. By no means should they be taken to be the final word on the topic. Rather, they should be viewed as an unfinished and tentative map of the complex world of OIIs and of the ongoing search for the path to the elusive land of the learning organization.

Management is prone to fads. For instance, we don't hear much anymore about quality circles, total quality management, or business process reengineering. Not that many ideas and practices promoted by these approaches aren't good or do not work, in some context, but they have largely been discredited by failures due to poor and misguided use. However, many of their best ideas have been incorporated into new initiatives, under a trendy new guise, and appear to have gone the way that bad ideas often do. Quality control and quality assurance certainly have not disappeared. The idea of empowering a group of workers to fix a problem or radically reinvent a process, using technology as an enabler, has not gone away either. The original "package," however, as marketed, hyped, taught, implemented, or debated, has either disappeared or at least faded. Thus, something must have been wrong in the chain of events that transforms an initial concept into a successful implementation.

A fad is something you do because others are doing it and it sounds cool. Mindless adoption of another company's practices ("they are so much better than we are; we can't go wrong copying them") is just as bad as trying to reinvent everything, including the four-hole button, yourself. It is much like taking medication that was prescribed for your neighbor because he is a human being just like you are. This has nothing to do with the quality of the medication. It is just that organizations are different, each with a history, a culture, and challenges that are its own. Let us now explore some common approaches.

11.2 APPROACHES TO CONTINUOUS IMPROVEMENT

11.2.1 ISO 9000 and Industry-Specific Standards— Organizing for Quality

> *Standard:* "something considered by an authority or by general consent as a basis of comparison; an approved model"—*Dictionary.com*

Thus, to standardize: develop such a basis for comparison, together with the measurement system to assess effective performance, and use it to align various instantiations of a process at different times, different parts of the business, or different businesses. ISO stands for the International Organization for Standardization, based in Geneva. The ISO 9000 series of standards deals with quality. An organization can be certified by a third-party auditor that it meets ISO 9001 *Quality management systems—Requirements*. Such certification has to be renewed at regular intervals and is often a requirement to do business with many order-givers. Since its inception in the mid-1980s, the standard has evolved to deal with an increasingly broad array of dimensions of quality management, such as:

- Implemented quality policy, planning, and responsibilities

- Quality control—inspecting output and correcting defective parts

- Quality assurance—making sure that the required systems are in place to avoid defects

- Documentation of quality-related processes, activities, and records

- Customer focus

- Ongoing process management

- Ongoing process improvement

- Demonstrated management commitment to rigorous quality management and improvement

The standard has the potential of bringing order to chaotic or anarchical organizations, and of helping them learn the basics of rigor. If well implemented in an organization that needs it, it stands to generate substantial savings in the cost of non-quality, improve customer satisfaction, and thus make the organization more competitive. Since you cannot improve a process that you do not know, making processes explicit and documenting them may open the path to improvement.

On the other hand, the major critiques of the standard are related to the cost and complexity of developing and maintaining the system. Because of the burden of documenting changes, change may take longer to happen, thus reducing an organization's nimbleness. Depending on how procedures are developed, they can become heavy and bureaucratic, thus making it harder to innovate.

The popularity of the standard is mostly due to the fact that many large organizations have imposed it on their providers as a condition of doing business with them. Thus forced down the suppliers' throats, it was often considered to be a necessary evil. This turned out to be a self-fulfilling prophecy, with these organizations considering it an end in itself, a cost of doing business. Except for the early adopters, who were able to use it as a competitive edge, studies have not shown systematic benefits from ISO 9000 certification. Since the standard has now become widespread, even this advantage proved to be short-lived.

Many industries have developed and continuously evolve a set of standards. There are a variety of motives for this, including government or public pressure, industrial competitiveness, cost reduction, industry image, and smoothing out interfaces between companies or with other industries or other shared interests.

Car manufacturing—national industry group. QS-9000 was developed by American automakers, each contributing a part toward an integrated standard. Because defects can have disastrous consequences, much emphasis is placed on security and supplier requirements (since many suppliers work for several car companies). It is quite similar to ISO 9000 in many ways, with added requirements on several elements. Manufacturing capability requirements and failure mode analysis, for example, are much stricter than ISO 9000 requirements.

Financial disclosure—US government legislation. The Sarbanes–Oxley Act of 2002 ("SOX"), on financial and accounting disclosure information, was adopted to reintroduce some basic accountability following several highly visible public scandals. It meant to reestablish public confidence in capital markets. It centers on independent auditing, financial controls, and governance and applies to US public companies.

Banking—international agreements of central bank governors. The Basel accords define agreed-upon standards through which national banking regulation bodies can set rules to reduce the risks of insolvencies and the catastrophic systemic impact they can have in "too big to fail" banks. When adopted, such regulations force banks to develop, maintain, and demonstrate their ability to manage risks (credit risk, operational risk, and market risk) or face the consequences in the amount of capital they have to keep to protect depositors.

Food processing industry—expert committee advising US government. Hazard analysis and critical control points (HACCP) is another risk management system, this time addressing health hazards (biological, chemical, or physical) in food production, packaging, and distribution. Focusing on the identification and management of risks at critical points in the process, it adapts generally accepted quality management approaches to the specificity of different sectors of the food industry, such as dairy products, juices, seafood, retail, and food service.

Information technology—originally a UK government standard. The Information Technology Infrastructure Library (ITIL) deals with IT service support and delivery. It touches on service strategy, design, operations, and continuous improvement; pays particular attention to security and risks; promotes the use of service level agreements; and promotes the use of the process approach adapted to the IT area.

Systems development—Carnegie Mellon Software Engineering Institute. Originally created for software development, the *capability maturity model* (CMM) has evolved to become CMMI (CMM integration), with general applicability to the design and acquisition of products and services of all types. This is again based on process management, and organizations can be certified for compliance to the standard. A distinctive feature of the approach is its use of a five-level process maturity scale, rather than a 0 or 1 (you're it or you're not).

11.2.2 Total Quality Management and Quality Awards—Tackling Management Culture

Starting with the Second World War and the hitherto unmatched production challenges it raised, the concepts of quality and quality management evolved considerably. From a narrow focus on outgoing inspection and control, the focus moved on to management, and the breadth of the definition followed our growing understanding of that discipline, as conceptualized by a number of gurus. As a result, in the 1980s total quality management (TQM) had taken shape. The Malcolm Baldrige National Quality Award (MBNQA) best captures the essence of TQM (see Figure 11.2). An important asset of this standard is that it is publicly available, publicly funded, and continuously evolving. Self-assessment tools and references are complete, up to date, easy to obtain, and cheap.

According to this model, management excellence involves doing the right thing, doing things right, and getting good results. Following are the criteria, along with their respective weight:

1. Leadership, the development of leaders, having effective and responsible governance (12%)

2. Being able to prepare a good strategic plan and put it into action dynamically (8.5%)

3. Understanding customers and their needs, and letting the voice of the customer guide the organization's actions (8.5%)

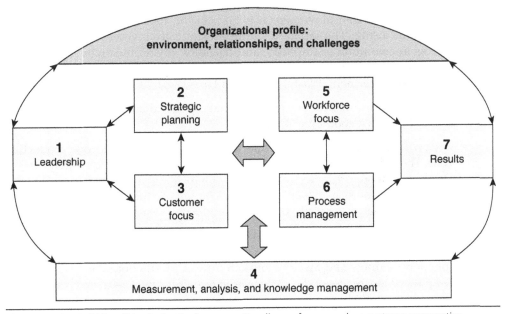

Figure 11.2 Baldrige Criteria for Performance Excellence framework: a systems perspective.

4. Good management information systems and machinery, management of knowledge more broadly, and rigorous and effective measurement of all aspects of performance (9%)

5. Management of employees, their work environment, their commitment, and their performance (8.5%)

6. Design and operation of core processes—of all organization processes—for performance and continuous improvement (8.5%)

7. Documentation of results achieved and trends in all aspects of the organization's performance (45%)

The weighting scheme aims at striking a balance between capable management of the success factors and actually achieving success. This reduces the risk of giving the award to an organization that is going through the motions but never achieves the results, or to one that does not manage all that well but happened to be in the right place at the right time.

Of course, an organization may engage in TQM and never seek the award. In fact, many organizations use the standard to benchmark their performance and progress but never make it a goal to get the highest score or win anything. Prize hunting per se is risky business. Losing can be depressing, especially when expectations have been built up. Somewhat counterintuitively, relentless pursuit of a prize can make the company lose sight that it is not in the business of winning prizes. Winning also has its risks, as it can lead to complacency ("we've got it made").

There is good evidence that TQM works for organizations that take the long view and stick with it. Clearly, however, few organizations have.

11.2.3 Lean Operation—Tackling Waste

What became the lean movement was born in the 1960s in Japan, at Toyota, as lean manufacturing. The Japanese culture historically involves sharing, solving problems in community, simplicity, and frugality. Toyota thus naturally evolved an organizational culture of continuously driving out waste through employee and team empowerment. Waste, or *muda* in Japanese, falls into seven categories:

- *Defects.* Any time and money spent on making sure that things are done right the first time is a good investment.

- *Overproduction.* Economies of scale are often a pretext to generate long production runs. The hidden costs of such practices, including hidden defects and missed improvement opportunities, vastly outweigh their apparent advantages. Using a pull production system, such as Toyota's *kanban* production cards, presents many advantages over traditional push production systems.

- *Inventory.* Poorly located buffer inventory hides problems. Reducing such inventory uncovers hidden process improvement opportunities. It allows for connectedness and favors a smooth flow of production. The resulting heightened awareness of defect causation is an important source of continuous improvement. Reducing setup cost is an important enabler to reducing this and the other wastes.

- *Waiting.* As attention is focused on the cause of idle product, cycle time can be improved, and with it many good things happen: lower cost, increased throughput, faster delivery, and greater flexibility.

- *Transportation.* Similarly, the shorter the distance traveled by a product, the lower its cost through transportation, delay, damage, cycle time, and capital costs.

- *Motion.* Think economy of automation using simple tools, layout, and organization of work.

- *Overprocessing.* Use simple machines and automation wherever appropriate. Complex automation ends up increasing rigidity and generating more of the other wastes described here.

Relentlessly driving out these wastes is the essence of lean manufacturing. Many programs and operational initiatives have been developed to improve different aspects of a company's operations. We discuss some of the best known here.

Five S (5S). While the original Ss are Japanese words, they have been translated in English as *sort, straighten, sweep, standardize,* and *sustain* (a sixth S for *safety* is often added). A disorganized workplace, be it a shop floor, an office, a service outlet, or a home kitchen, is a frustrating place to work. It triggers waste, defects, and accidents. As any family that cooks and eats in the same kitchen knows, making sure that the appropriate tools are available; putting everything in the right place and creating a place for everything that is needed, making it easy to see, find, and return; eliminating things that do not belong; and instigating the discipline in everyone to respect the rules is very challenging. It is, however, very beneficial, and the only way to work for anyone who has experienced it. Systematic change management programs exist to guide an organization through the steps required to achieve this. Because it requires extensive employee participation, touches every employee, and generates visible results quickly, 5S has a strong mobilization impact at the outset of a drive toward becoming a lean organization.

Total preventive maintenance (TPM). Complementary to 5S, making sure that all tools and equipment are always ready to perform up to standards when needed is essential to waste elimination. It involves a clear understanding of the operating requirements of each apparatus; a determination of the type and frequency of maintenance that will make this possible; the setting up of a maintenance process, with the right procedures, tools, gages, and qualified employees; the detailed planning of preventive maintenance; and the setting up of early-warning indicators and correction plans to quickly detect and redress a potentially wasteful occurrence.

Achieving Competitive Excellence (ACE). A United Technologies proprietary program, ACE was developed as a response to GE's (a major competitor in many markets) adoption of Six Sigma. The program includes 5S and TPM, as well as other related initiatives such as setup reduction, continuous improvement workshops, evidence-based problem-solving tools, and mistake-proofing. The distinctive feature, however, is (internal) certification of cells, that is, administrative units grouping a number of related processes. Four certification levels are possible: Qualifying, Bronze, Silver, and Gold. The notion of cells can be generalized to include administrative services, such as the office of the president, for instance.

Criteria are spelled out for each level, including decertification, and independent audits are performed. ACE is a good example of an apparently successful program, with a core focus on the lean philosophy, tailored to the specific needs, history, culture, and competitive circumstances of a company.

While a manufacturing mind-set still permeates much of the lean movement, lean principles extend to service organizations as well. The processing of goods is an important challenge for many of them, such as hospitals or hotels. The principles and tools related to defects, waiting, motion, and transportation very much apply to transaction processing. Wastes of all types exist in services, and there is much to gain by applying the lessons and tools of simplicity, economy, and frugality.

As all organizations that have tried it know, "simple" is hard to achieve and even harder to sustain. The latter involves a cultural change. It took the Western world 20 years to understand the principles and practice of lean. It took globalization and the resulting competitive pressure for companies to resign themselves to try it. For those (mostly manufacturing) companies that have stayed the course, however, the results have been impressive.

11.2.4 Six Sigma—Tackling Variation

Six Sigma (Schroeder et al. 2008) was developed under the leadership of then Motorola president Bob Galvin as a last-ditch response to the inroads made by Japanese competitors into its traditional markets. Though the notion and practice of it are far from standardized, it generally includes the following elements:

• The principle that eliminating defects is the source of all good things to customers and shareholders alike

• A system to count defects (DPMO, or defects per million opportunities), a target (3.4 DPMO, after allowing for normal process shift and drift), and a focus on savings

• A process improvement methodology (DMAIC, see Chapter 9) and a product design methodology (DFSS)

• A data-driven approach using a statistical toolkit consisting of basic and advanced tools

• A project management system and a top-down approach

• The development of dedicated experts (Black Belts) who master the toolkit and facilitate projects

• The independent measurement of the result of each improvement project and the linking of line management bonuses to these results

Motorola's reversal of fortune, largely attributed to Six Sigma, drew the attention of many business leaders and thinkers, including Jack Welch at GE, thus propelling the approach to the stratosphere of improvement initiatives. Despite the many claims found in the literature, most of the data is anecdotal, biased, or dubious in nature, and it is very hard to assess the actual long-term impact of adopting a Six Sigma initiative.

11.2.5 Theory of Constraints (TOC) and Supply Chain Management—Tackling Flows

Productivity can be defined as the volume of good output per unit of resource (see Chapter 4). Once the desired nature and quantity of output have been defined, the task of the production system is to maximize productivity. Throughput, fixed assets, and resource utilization are the key determinants of productivity. Throughput is determined by the capacity of bottleneck resources. These may be related to equipment, employees, policies, and procedures. In the broader context of the supply chain, bottlenecks may be located anywhere upstream (chain of suppliers) or downstream (chain of customers). A number of TOC principles are generally shared by practitioners:

- Any time lost at a bottleneck activity has a direct impact on throughput. Any time lost anywhere else is inconsequential.

- Any extra output at a non-bottleneck activity adds to work-in-process (WIP) inventory and reduces productivity by increasing waste or reducing throughput (congestion and rework).

- The bottleneck activity must dictate the rate of production. In other words, it acts as the drum that gives the beat to the whole system (Goldratt and Cox 1992).

- To avoid overproduction at non-bottleneck activities, production must be "pulled" from the bottleneck activity rather than "pushed" toward it, with the production of each stage tied to each other like hikers climbing a mountain.

- To avoid line stoppage, a buffer must be built at the bottleneck activity in case the flow is interrupted because of a problem somewhere else in the process.

Of course, as you are having success increasing capacity at a bottleneck activity, it eventually becomes a non-bottleneck activity, and a new bottleneck is born. Managing bottlenecks can become quite tricky and require sophisticated tools. Whereas the approach has been developed and applied mostly in manufacturing, the principles have much broader applicability. A sales process, for example, starting from raw market data and ending with a sale, has flows, throughput, WIP, and bottleneck activities. So does the emergency ward in a hospital, for example, or the intake process at the airport (see Video 3.1). Thus, a basic understanding and constant awareness of these principles are essential for any process manager.

11.2.6 IT/IS—Tackling Information Flows

Legacy systems were built around functional groups at a time when the functional mind-set permeated every aspect of corporate life. These systems do not talk to each other. They were designed and evolved largely independently of each other with a view to achieving departmental goals. The language is function-specific and reflects little understanding of a global purpose or the common logic of cross-functional flows. Different words are used to refer to the same things, and there are no mechanisms to reconcile different perspectives of the same reality. The capacity of these systems reaches its limit, and their very design is a major stumbling block to competitiveness. However, the progress of information technology and information systems now makes completely integrated systems technically feasible, but very challenging to implement. Here are some of the new families of systems that have become increasingly popular during the last decade:

- *Enterprise resource planning (ERP) systems.* A comprehensive system including such modules as manufacturing, supply chain management, human resources, financial management, and project management, as well as some basic modules for the other systems described here.

- *Customer relationship management (CRM) systems.* These deal in an integrated manner with all interfaces between the organization and its customers, such as marketing, sales, customer service, and technical support.

- *Supply chain management (SCM) systems.* Systems dealing with inventory management, distribution network management, warehouse management, transportation systems, and cash flows.

- *Product life cycle management (PLM) systems.* This involves managing products from cradle to grave. A complete system includes product design, development, configuration management, evolution, and disposal.

The failure rate in the introduction of these systems was originally very high but is now improving. Many companies conceived of these systems as traditional information systems and implemented them as such without questioning their way of understanding and managing the business. Forced radical change, or *reengineering* as it was called, has generally failed.

These systems typically include so-called best practices. Assuming that there is an absolute best way to do something, and faced with the necessity to make design choices, system designers built these ways into their wares, irrespective of how foreign or strange the practices may seem when implemented blindly and without due consideration for context, adaptation, and training. Poor implementation can and did trigger much resistance to change. On the other hand, tailoring the solution to ensure a better fit with local circumstances is risky, costly, and time-consuming. Further, such adjustments impede the evolution of the system, as it becomes incompatible with new releases.

Business process reengineering was introduced as a (rough-cut) methodology meant to facilitate radical process change in situations where potential gains from new technology had built up in the face of the slow incremental improvement pace set by TQM.

Information gathering, sharing, and interpretation are cornerstones of organizational knowledge and learning. Therefore, replacing legacy systems with state-of-the-art systems lies on the path of any company intent on becoming a learning organization. Without it, the information bottleneck will maintain a stranglehold on the source of companies' ability to quickly adapt to fast-changing environments.

11.2.7 Activity-Based Costing and Management—Tracking Cost Generation

Without valid cost information, process change is likely to result in unpleasant surprises. To be a valid guide to action, a unit cost must truly represent the additional cost that will be generated by one more unit, and the savings that will accrue from a one-unit reduction. In accounting, direct costs are those that can readily be attributed to a product, according to generally accepted accounting principles. Direct labor, for example, is easily allocated using direct manpower time usage and hourly cost. However, according to those principles, all costs must be allocated. Therefore, some arbitrary criterion, which has very little to do with how these costs are generated, such as direct labor hours, is used to allocate indirect or overhead costs. This practice makes it impossible and counterproductive to use these costs for decision making.

Activity-based costing (ABC) is an accounting system designed to address these shortcomings. It seeks to identify the factors, or cost drivers, that are actually responsible for generating these costs, find a way to link them to the productive activities that consume the resources, and link the activities to products and services. This requires serious thinking about and analysis of the nature of the business, its operating model, and its processes. Overhead costs are pooled into meaningful categories, and cost drivers are identified for each and used for cost estimation. A cost pool for which no valid driver is found is simply left unallocated.

The failure rate of ABC appears to be inordinately high. Several factors contribute to this sorry state of affairs. Accountants are trained rigorously in full-cost accounting, and generally accepted accounting principles are drilled into them. They abhor cost estimates and costs that do not add up to full costs. They are not trained to be creative in the search for the right cost drivers. Also, since ABC is generally inappropriate for purposes of public accounting and reporting, the company must maintain a dual accounting system—a costly and unsustainable endeavor.

Further, ABC per se does not result in any savings. Its impact is felt as an enabler of activity-based management (ABM), which generates the savings. Poorly trained or motivated operations managers will not be able to use ABC to its full potential, thus making the organization fail to achieve the desired results. Therefore, despite the obvious need for ABC, the challenges involved in managing the large-scale synchronized change in accounting and operations required for successful implementation make it a risky undertaking.

11.2.8 The Service Warranty—Customer Focus, or Else

Initially proposed by Heskett et al. (1997), the service guarantee is a simple and powerful way to focus an organization on delivering customer results. It consists of specifying to the customer, and thus to the organization and its employees, the specific results promised to the customer and the compensation that will be provided to the customer if this result is not produced as promised. The compensation, of course, has to be significant in view of the consequences suffered by the customer because of the failure, and it must be immediate. It also has to be easy to invoke by the customer.

By doing so, an organization clearly shows its commitment to quality. Immediate apologies and compensation increase the chances of a continued relationship and positive word of mouth, rather than loss of customer and loss of future customers through negative word of mouth. It focuses employees on the task, making it clear what is important and what is not. It clearly shows, as a line in the profit and loss statement, the cost of poor quality, thus making it possible to track its evolution and identify its sources. By making non-quality visible and painful, it also provides an immediate financial motivation to improve service quality, and a direct measurement of progress as well. It is a radical step to take, but may well be the only one consistent with the message—internally and externally—that the company is firmly committed to quality. Unwillingness to offer such a guarantee, or applying it grudgingly, denies the message.

11.3 WHAT TO DO ABOUT THESE INITIATIVES

For many organizations about to embark on a learning initiative, the greatest risk they face is typically hidden in plain sight. It is the muted cynicism accumulated from past initiatives that have resulted in failures—never acknowledged, never understood, merely erased from the "official" company history. They never happened. Thus, they are always present in everyone's mind whenever the rumor of a forthcoming initiative surfaces. As mentioned earlier, a mistake from which you do not learn is one that you are condemned to repeat. A success has no owner. A failure is an orphan. The higher up the true father stands in the organization, the more likely it is to remain an orphan forever.

Therefore, the first demonstration of leadership required for everyone to notice that something serious is afoot is an open diagnosis of past initiatives. This should not be a witch hunt, though humble pie may be on the menu for some people. As Winston Churchill once said, "In the course of my life, I have often had to eat my words, and I must confess that I have always found it a wholesome diet." Failures should be acknowledged. Lessons learned should be shared. Not only will this clear a major obstacle lying on the path to learning, it will also provide essential clues about the culture, identify pitfalls to avoid, and pinpoint areas of opportunity.

The list of OIIs discussed earlier is by no means exhaustive. New ones, modified versions of old ones, and new combinations pop up on the radar every year. According to Miller et al. (2004), fads are characterized by eight common properties: they appear to be simple and straightforward; results are almost ensured; they apply to any organization, under any condition; you can implement them easily; they use all the buzzwords of the day; they amount to repackaging of things that already exist; they are promoted by gurus; and they are packaged in a way that will appeal to businesspeople. Therefore, a fair dose of skepticism is in order when anyone is trumpeting anything that presents most of these characteristics. If it looks like snake oil, tastes like snake oil, smells like snake oil . . . it probably is. Ask questions. Create a climate where anyone with doubts feels free to express them, and take the time to get the facts and analyze them critically. Organizations that adopt a fad sell it internally as a panacea. Then they drop it, typically for a new one. Beyond the obvious waste of resources, this fosters cynicism and makes it increasingly difficult to mobilize employees.

Here are some basic steps to take before committing to any new OII. Make sure that:

- You have a clear and shared understanding of the nature of the problem or the opportunity facing the organization. Put it in writing.

- You have a clear and shared understanding of what the organization has to do to address it. Put that in writing, too.

- The approach will do the job in your organization, at that time. Explore it in depth. Talk to other businesses, and do not confuse hype with straight talk and hard results.

- Whatever initiative you adopt fits well in the big-picture game plan and on the cultural change path of your company. Changing a company culture is a long-term endeavor only achieved using multiple leverage points. Individual initiatives should be consistent with one another. They should push and pull in the same direction.

- While you should give the initiative the time required to work, you should not hesitate to modify it as required by hands-on learning and changing environments.

Different processes have different needs at different points in time (DeToro and McCabe 1997). One size does not fit all (Foster 2006). Eclecticism may work here, as long as there is a well-thought-out master plan and rigorous follow-up.

11.4 EMERGING PARADIGM—THE LEARNING ORGANIZATION

The foregoing discussion may leave the reader confused. This is quite normal, as the world of OIIs is confusing, and no clear pattern emerges. A more detailed discussion of the nature of the learning organization provides a useful framework for a company to better understand where it stands, what it needs most to make progress, and what OII or tailor-made initiative (eclectic) offers the best chance of helping it move forward.

Learning organizations share 15 characteristics (see Figure 11.3) of various natures. The dimensions are defined in Table 11.1. They are not presented in any particular order.

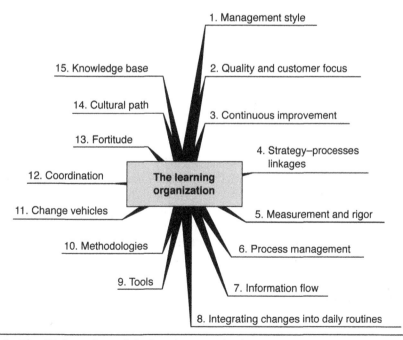

Figure 11.3   The 15 dimensions of the learning organization.

Table 11.1 Defining the dimensions of the learning organization.

1. Management style	Is the business managed with an authoritarian and repressive approach, or in a participative fashion conducive to sharing and learning?
2. Quality and customer focus	Are customers' needs explicit, and do we have systems in place to ensure that we deliver quality services?
3. Continuous improvement	Do we share a philosophy of continuous improvement?
4. Strategy–processes linkages	Do we have a process vision of value creation in this business, and can we connect processes to customer and strategy?
5. Measurement and rigor	How rigorous are we in measurement and decision making? Is the scientific method (by any name) the accepted way to move forward?
6. Process management	Are business processes actively managed?
7. Information flow	Does our information flow along process lines, or does information flow essentially within functional groups?
8. Integrating changes into daily routines	Are process changes systematically integrated into daily operations?
9. Tools	Do we use all the tools available to improve and design processes? Is a critical mass of management and employees acquainted with these tools?
10. Methodologies	Do we use formal methodologies to improve and design processes?
11. Change vehicles	Do we have a fleet of systematic change vehicles and do we use them judiciously?
12. Coordination	Is the learning cycle well understood? Are all change projects the object of global coordination? Are we geared up to evaluate and improve the cycle?
13. Fortitude	Do we stick to our learning drives no matter what, or do we forget everything and change paths when we experience growing pains (internal or external)?
14. Cultural path	Do we manage the evolution of our organizational culture, ensuring that each new initiative is coherent with the culture and contributes to its evolution?
15. Knowledge base	Does the organization's knowledge base rest with a few individuals, or is it explicit, shared, and evolutive?

In Figure 11.4, we have represented them by "proximity" or affinity and grouped them into five broader categories: top management, strategic execution, rigor, knowledge, and social cohesion. We discuss these dimensions in turn in this section, correlating with various chapters of the book and OIIs as we go. The reader can make a quick assessment of where his or her organization stands on these dimensions using the five-point scales presented in Figure 11.5. This is not a statistically validated measurement instrument. It strictly reflects the author's view.

11.4.1 Management Style

As discussed so far in this book, learning is not the sole preserve of the strategic apex of the organization. Unless the organization is managed in such a way that

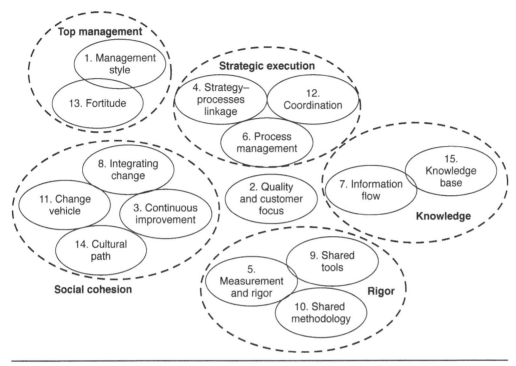

Figure 11.4 Mapping the dimensions of the learning organization by affinity.

every individual has the motivation to learn and is given the means and opportunities to do so, the organization learning rate will remain subpar. It lies beyond the scope of this book to explain how to transform a "command and control" type of organization into a participative one. However, the reader should be aware that much of the potential of the material presented in this book will remain bottled up unless a participative management style permeates the organization. Rate your organization at 5 in Figure 11.5 if this is the case. If an authoritarian and repressive management style is the rule or predominates (1 or 2), or even if the management gives equal place to both styles of management (3), this is a clear hurdle that you have to overcome before embarking on the journey proposed here. Professionals do not grow in such an environment, and given their power, a tug of war often ensues with management.

The author once worked with an organization whose management style rated something between 3 and 4. The official line professed participative management, but the body language often denied this. Despite punctual successes in deploying some of the tools and vehicles presented here, in the end a bottleneck was encountered. As with any bottleneck, it lay at the top of the bottle—in this case, at the very top. It was never really circumvented. Much cynicism on the part of the employees existed at the outset of the initiative, and rightly so. The level of sarcasm had ramped up one notch by the time the initiative was dropped. Better not to start what you will not be able to finish. Better to keep the aircraft on the ground than to take off without a good probability of having a landing strip available when you reach the destination. Among the OIIs discussed earlier, *quality awards* are the best suited to help a company wishing to address this issue.

		1	2	3	4	5
1	Management style	Universal belief in command and control	Command and control dominate	Coexistence of various beliefs	Participative management dominates	Shared belief in participative
2	Quality and customer focus	We rely on professional's diplomas or license	Some quality procedures exist	Most quality procedures exist	Quality certification obtained	Quality system used as learning engine
3	Continuous improvement	Not a clue what you are talking about	Only in crisis mode	Sporadically	Systematically	Shared belief
4	Strategy–processes linkages	None	Within functional silos	Limited to one or two business processes	Some efforts are made, with limited results	Central aspect of governance
5	Measurement and rigor	Firefighting culture, shoot from the hip	Some rigor in accounting and financial data	Some high-level indicators taken seriously	Systematic use of rigorous measures	Generalized use of statistics
6	Process management	Nothing	A committee resolves cross-functional issues	Through service level agreements	Systematic measurement of all processes	This is the way we manage the company
7	Information flow	Antiquated functional systems	Modern functional systems	Some patches and bridges	Several "integrated" systems	Seamless horizontal flows
8	Integrating changes into daily routines	No follow-through	Gains last about one month	Gains last about six months	Some changes stick	Perfect integration achieved
9	Tools	No tools	Some basic tools	Some statistical tools as well	More advanced statistical tools	Full toolbox regularly updated
10	Methodologies	None	Deming wheel (PDCA) used sometimes	DMAIC used	Some elements of DCDV	Judicious use of complete gamut
11	Change vehicles	None	One vehicle, used intuitively	One formal vehicle	Two vehicles	Full fleet—used judiciously
12	Coordination	Projects are totally unrelated	Some projects are linked	Global management of a project portfolio	Regular evaluation of lessons learned	Continuous improvement of the learning pump
13	Fortitude	No initiatives are ever introduced	Flavor of the month	We let go at the first hurdle	We hold on as long as we can, then we let go	Resolve grows during crisis periods
14	Cultural path	No systematic initiative	Disconnected sporadic initiatives	Adoption of every new program	Recognition and learning from failures	Culture kept on a controlled evolutive path
15	Knowledge base	In the head of the boss	In the head of the top management team	Some efforts to capture knowledge	Base exists, but use and update are sporadic	Universal and evolutive
	Legend	Attention deficit disorder	Functional intelligence	Sporadic learning	Sporadic memory blanks	Learning organization

Figure 11.5   Five levels of learning maturity.

11.4.2 Quality and Customer Focus

Understanding evolving customer needs and understanding how we can create more value than competitors for targeted customers is the topic of Chapter 2. Without an explicit understanding of this, the alignment of processes to value creation is impossible. In the professional world (Chapter 5), regulating bodies also specify individual standards required to obtain and maintain certification. Learning organizations not only maintain certification at both an individual and organizational level (level 4 in Figure 11.5), but also use their quality system, whether based on *ISO 9000 or some other industry standard,* as a learning lever (level 5). All organizations that require a certification to operate (such as health organizations) must minimally perform at level 4 on this scale (assuming that the certification process itself is capable). *TQM, lean operation, standards,* and *service guarantees* are the most indicated OIIs in this case. Among the tools presented in this book, QFD is particularly useful.

11.4.3 Continuous Improvement

We discuss the philosophy of continuous improvement at length throughout the book, specifying its dynamic in our discussion of the learning cycle in Chapter 8. The philosophy rests on the belief that it is worthwhile to constantly strive to be the best at what you do, dedicating time and resources to the task. Many organizations never start on that path (levels 1 and 2 in Figure 11.5). When they want to increase output (either quality or quantity), they put more pressure on their professionals. They see the result immediately: output increases. Thus, their belief is reinforced that this is the way to go. What they do not see, however, is that when people simply work harder, they eventually become tired, and when they do, they start cutting corners. Professionals are smart enough to cut where the cutting will not show up, at least not immediately or in ways that are traceable to them. Process improvement, learning, and growth activities fit the bill. The effects of a cut there are diffuse and delayed. When the lost capabilities eventually start to show and output decreases, management believes, incorrectly, that it is because the effect of the original pressure they put on the professionals has waned. Consequently, they go back to putting pressure on the professionals, never waking up to the vicious circle in which they are stuck (Repenning and Sterman 2001).

Indeed, when an organization initially invests in improvement, the short-term result is a decrease in output as an immediate consequence of resource reallocation (that is, from production to improvement). Thus, getting started on the virtuous cycle of continuous improvement is difficult because it requires patience and the fortitude to maintain the course in spite of naysayers. Some organizations make many false starts (level 3) until they get it right (level 4 and eventually level 5). In organizations operating at levels 1 and 2, you often hear the command "I want results, no matter how." In level 5 organizations, "how" matters even more than results, for if you do not know "how" (that is, the process), you cannot repeat it. *TQM, lean operation,* and *service guarantees* are the most appropriate OIIs to use in this case.

11.4.4 Strategy–Processes Linkages

Much of Chapters 4, 5, and 7 is dedicated to the conceptual and technical exploration of the linkage between strategy and processes. The methodology presented in Chapter 7 amounts to deploying customer needs and strategic priorities onto processes, using metrics as a bridge. This is critical to avoid the execution gap discussed in Chapter 1. At levels 1 and 2, such connection is absent. From level 3 to level 5, the linkage grows from being an experiment to being a central aspect of governance. Policy deployment, or *hoshin planning* (not discussed in this book), generally considered to be a component of TQM, can be a strong contributor to moving an organization in that direction.

11.4.5 Measurement and Rigor

The importance of measurement and rigor permeates this book. It may be an overused expression, but many managers are at their best when they fight fires. They love the pressure. They feel that it allows them to show their mettle. They enjoy the feeling of accomplishment when the crisis is resolved. Firefighting organizations value such achievements, reward them, and promote the best firefighters. For these people, the crisis mode is a way of life. It is the only thing that they know. They soon occupy the higher echelons of such organizations and would feel lost if there were no fires to fight. Thus, these organizations do not place much emphasis on prevention and do not reward people for promoting logical validity, precision and accuracy in measurement, and compliance discipline, that is, promoting rigor.

Such organizations would rate a 1 or 2 in Figure 11.5. Organizations at level 3 try to be rigorous when dealing with aggregated data, a pursuit that is much more beneficial if rigor exists at the operating level. Reaching a point where statistics become the shared language to talk about variation and uncertainty (see Chapters 6 and 12) requires a quantum leap that only the best-run organizations are able to make (level 5). Six Sigma is the OII that best focuses on this aspect of the learning organization. SPC is the technique of choice. The balanced scorecard is the management tool most compatible with this orientation.

11.4.6 Process Management

As discussed in Chapter 3, a business process is a logical chain of commitments, from input to output, linking professional, technical, and clerical workers, often spread out over several organizational units. A mechanism is required to bridge the gaps between these units, making the process seamless and agile.

In some organizations, interdepartmental issues are never resolved (level 1). Others set up a committee (ad hoc or standing) to address such issues as they arise (level 2). Yet others have internal customers and suppliers sit together and negotiate service level agreements, which they may or may not enforce seriously (level 3). Adding systematic measurement of end-to-end processes reinforces this approach (level 4). However, making someone accountable for the performance of the process (level 5) is the only way to make it come alive.

Just as in a relay race, where each runner has a personal coach, process workers have their functional bosses (sales, accounting, legal, credit, and so on), whose role it is to foster excellence and coherence in their respective fields. The process owner's job, like that of the coach, is to ensure alignment and cohesion. As long as evaluation and incentives are strictly vertical (that is, functional), efforts exerted to align horizontal flows with processes will go against the grain and remain ineffective. TQM and the ISO (and other) standards can help here. ABC can ensure that the right information is available to manage processes. In some situations, TOC can also have a dramatic impact.

11.4.7 Information Flow

As discussed earlier, legacy systems fall apart when it comes to making people from various functions work together, that is, when it comes to processes and value creation. Many organizations are still stuck in that old paradigm (levels 1 and 2). This creates a bottleneck. It limits any progress the company can make on the other dimensions of the learning organization. Some organizations, understanding their predicament, improve matters by patching together or building bridges between old systems (level 3). Others go for the "integrated system" (level 4), which is never integrated enough and so they have to keep some of the older ones. They end up with a complex web of systems and are still in search of integration. The best organizations have resolved the issue, building a new system from the ground up, mostly through using purchased infrastructural systems. IT/IS systems, the Baldrige award, and ISO and other standards discussed earlier, if well designed and implemented, can eliminate these bottlenecks. Work-flow automation systems can also improve the flow of work and improve control.

11.4.8 Integrating Changes into Daily Routines

Several years ago, the author was hired to assist a service organization getting started on the path to continuous improvement. He conducted three kaizen events, successfully fixing six broken processes. As is his practice, he trained the organization to be able to conduct the event without his assistance. About six months later, the company, invoking growing pains, asked him to come back to help it conduct the next kaizen event. Puzzled, the author accepted. As he was kicking off the event, explaining that the payoffs the organization would get from this initiative were well worth everyone's time, one of the participants raised her hand to ask a question:

"Yes?" said the author.

"Remember when you were here last fall to fix the planning process?" asked a tall woman from one of the two teams.

"Yes, I do. What about it?" replied the author.

"Well, I was there on that Friday afternoon when the team made a demonstration of the new process. I was amazed that a team of our people could come up with so many great ideas and make them work."

"Thank you for pointing that out," said the author, turning away from the participant to carry on with the kickoff.

"There's a problem, however," continued the woman.

"Oh! And what might that be?" asked the author, beginning to worry.

"Well, it's just that we don't do any of this anymore. We gradually dropped most of these ideas, and we are now essentially back where we started. So what's the point of sweating it out for a week if we're going to revert back to our old ways soon afterward anyway?"

This organization was willing to make a one-week investment but was unable to follow through. The kaizen event bypasses regular management and control procedures, and breaks down barriers between departments for one process, one team, one week. The Monday after, we are back to business as usual. Thus, unless we change "business as usual" so that it is able to accept, adjust to, and take care of a new process, there is no point in designing and improving processes. This requires follow-through and good process controls. Rate your organization 1 to 5, from "no follow-through" to "perfect integration achieved." For most organizations, this also requires a cultural shift toward rigor (characteristic 5), continuous improvement (characteristic 3), and information flow (characteristic 7). ISO and other standards, used wisely as continuous improvement approaches, are useful to standardize and integrate new processes.

11.4.9 Tools

This book is loaded with process tools. From SITOC to the Pugh matrix, they range from the simple (FAST, SMART) to the more complex (FMEA, design of experiments, Pugh design matrix, diagnostic worksheet). Proven and honed over the years, they are indispensable companions on the continuous improvement journey. The larger the user base of a tool in an organization, the more potent the tool. While experts in advanced statistics will never be legion in any organization, statistical thinking and the use of basic statistical tools must become widespread.

Some organizations are tool-less (level 1). Others use only the simplest tools (such as Ishikawa diagrams) sporadically (level 2). Yet others use more tools, including the basic statistical ones (such as SPC [level 3]), while at level 4, organizations toy with regression analysis, analysis of variance, and even designed experiments. At level 5, the organization explicitly manages its techniques as a master artisan does his toolbox, dynamically retiring and adding new tools as the organizational challenges evolve. Most OIIs come with their own toolkit.

11.4.10 Methodologies

In Chapters 9 and 10 we presented the improvement and design methodologies as two alternate ways to proceed. They are not as radically opposed to each other as we have made them appear. A number of linkages offer potential bridges between them. As well, improvement and design projects alike can borrow tools from the other methodology's toolkit to resolve specific issues that may arise:

- The improvement methodology assumes that the process has potential, and that if a few vital variables are set right, the process will perform up to expectations. It often turns out, however, that the customer's needs are poorly understood and the metrics used are inappropriate. Building a house 1 in the measure phase can resolve this problem in a structured manner.

- When the process to be improved turns out to be very large, house 2 can help direct the team to the most important subprocesses. It can also give the team the option to design some subprocesses from scratch (using idea generation and the Pugh matrix presented in Chapter 10) and improve the others.

- FMEA (an improvement tool) is already involved in the design methodology presented in Chapter 10. Value-added analysis can also be useful in the detailed design phase to minimize non-value-added activities.

- It often happens in the early stages of an improvement project that one realizes there is no process to speak of. The team may come back from the mapping exercise realizing that there is no set flow to the process and that an infinite number of combinations exist. Under these conditions, switching to the design methodology, without missing a beat, may be the best way to salvage an initiative that could turn sour and leave the team with a bad taste that might constitute a threat to the survival of the whole initiative.

- In the course of a design project, the team may find that the best way to design some subprocesses is to benchmark other (noncompeting) organizations. The improvement methodology (or any combination of tools from it) is then helpful in adapting the "borrowed" process to the organization.

Lean operation (pull systems, TPM, 5S) comes with its own methodologies. So do the HACCP standard and ABC, for instance. Many other variants of these methodologies exist. Prior to the emergence of DMAIC as the dominant improvement methodology, by far the most widespread was the more basic Deming wheel, or PDCA (plan–do–check–act). Many organizations still use it (level 2), while others have "graduated" to DMAIC (level 3). The beliefs of many organizations (level 1) are never strong enough to induce them to make the investment required to learn and deploy a methodology. Businesses at levels 4 and 5 have separated from the pack by investing in a design methodology (DCDV or equivalent), while level 5 organizations are actively engaged in improving the way they use their methodologies.

11.4.11 Change Vehicles

Managing organizational change is a complex and delicate undertaking. When an organization decides to use the learning cycle to create strategic advantage, it must set up to negotiate each turn of the wheel carefully. In Chapter 8, we focused on the kaizen event as change vehicle. We presented it in its standard five-day format. In Chapter 10, FPA modified the format to include two three-day sessions, with a modification of team composition in between the sessions. Further, it held the three days of the first session one week apart to allow for data gathering and validation. *Lean operation initiatives* make extensive use of kaizen events. *Six Sigma* makes heavy use of the four- to six-month project as change vehicle. It is typically led by an expert, with a small part-time team, under the responsibility of a line executive.

When someone is learning to play the piano, he must first learn and practice scales until they become second nature. At that point, he can start introducing variations and combinations into his play. When you start along the path of process management, you should also first experiment with the standard approaches until you reach a comfort zone, that is, you understand how and why they work. When you feel in control, it is safe to start creating your own variants. This will give you more flexibility in tailoring change vehicles suited to any special need that may arise. A three-day kaizen event, for instance, or a four-person improvement team is not anathema and may well be the right way to go in some circumstances.

Organizations that use a change vehicle implicitly (level 2) have an edge over those that improvise every time they face change (level 1). Those that are explicit about it (level 3) have a marked advantage: they waste less energy (efficiency), make fewer mistakes (effectiveness), and can learn with every turn of the wheel, improving the vehicle as they go on improving processes. At level 4, the business has become more sophisticated and uses two vehicles—projects and kaizen events are a common combination. Level 5 organizations have reached a point where they manage a complete "fleet" and are capable of "moving" any process, under any circumstance.

11.4.12 Coordination

At every iteration of the learning cycle, know-how is created. The learning cycle is a repetitive learning process. The organization that manages it best can become the fastest learner: a sustainable source of competitive advantage. We call this "double-loop" learning, that is, learning to be better learners. This is best achieved by treating learning as a process—maybe the organization's most critical one—and putting all our process knowledge to work to make it better. Thus, the process needs an owner, whom we could call the chief learning officer (level 5). Her job, as discussed earlier, is to lead the learning drive (vision, strategy, and communication), ensure alignment and cohesion, set targets, monitor progress, and make the learning process better and faster. This involves, among other things, measuring results, coordinating training (much is required, as this book makes obvious), benchmarking with the best organizations, and ensuring feedback and communication.

At levels 1 and 2, the organization performs improvement or design projects without having a global view of the improvement path or of the effect it is having on the business. At level 3, it is managing a portfolio of projects, ensuring that the brunt of the effect is felt in areas where the business needs it most. At level 4, the organization takes the time to debrief each project to see if anything unusual happened (that is, process variation) that could hide an important lesson to be shared with the rest of the organization.

11.4.13 Fortitude

As discussed earlier, crises put the organization's learning mettle to the test. They often manifest themselves as severe market or profitability setbacks and may be triggered by internal or external occurrences, sudden or gradual. The 9/11 events, technological breakthroughs of all kinds, market shifts, the 2008–2010 global recession, arrival of a new competitor, and currency fluctuations, to name but a few, are potential sources of crises. When the organization finds itself under urgent and intense pressure to increase profits, it takes a hard look at its practices and looks for solutions. That is the time when all the wolves come out of their dens to attack the learning initiative. Unless its roots run deep when the crisis strikes, it stands a good chance of being uprooted.

Because the initiative initially runs on faith, due to the immediacy of the costs and the delayed nature of the benefits, it is vulnerable. In fact, whoever kills it may look like a hero for a while as the fresh influx of resources is immediately felt. Many organizations appear to follow a "me too" strategy, adopting the latest fad and dropping it at the faintest hint of a crisis (levels 1 and 2). Levels 3 and 4 differ in terms of the magnitude of the crisis required for them to drop the ball. Level 5 organizations may put the initiative on a survival regime for a while (that is, put on hold the design of a new fire engine to call all hands to the hoses), they may modify and adapt the initiative to better fit the new reality, but they stay the course (see the discussion in 11.4.14).

11.4.14 Cultural Path

Some organizations do not have a culture to speak of (level 1). Different parts of the organization, often delimited by functional silos, share different values. Professionals do not really have to share much with their colleagues since they work in the professional bubble they create and manage. Other organizations have a culture that has evolved randomly (level 2). Yet other companies adopt all new programs that become fashionable (level 3; see earlier discussion on management fads), sending messages with one that are soon denied by the following one. Organizations at level 4 draw the lessons to be learned from any program they decide to stop or phase out. They use these lessons in the selection of the next initiative. Level 5 organizations nurture their culture as a precious asset. They cater to it. They assess what the organization requires. They investigate any new program that shows up on their watchful radar and adopt only what they find to be of value to them. They never adopt a program wholesale. They always make sure that employees understand the addition and the motivation behind it. Upon entering the premises of such organizations, consultants are typically warned, "Do not mess with my culture."

11.4.15 Knowledge Base

Know-how cannot evolve alone. Knowledge that enables and supports it must evolve as well. Financial institutions need to understand the state of the art in credit algorithms. Drugstores need to know about drug interactions and new ways to administer medications. Law firms must have access to the latest jurisprudence. Consulting and engineering firms must have access to their "recipes" to resolve various professional challenges they face. Clearly, knowledge bases and processes have a symbiotic relationship. Knowledge bases are created and "nourished" (updated and upgraded) by processes, and many processes "feed on" (that is, need input from) them as well.

Knowledge base skills (and associated technologies) are complementary to process skills in the learning organization. When critical knowledge is in the head of the boss (level 1) or the executive teams (level 2), they always have to be "in the loop" for processes to work. They are bottlenecks that limit the output. This role monopolizes executives' time. It is an impediment to their involvement in the learning cycle. Levels 3 to 5 represent three different stages of evolution in an organization's abilities in capturing, upgrading, and disseminating knowledge throughout the organization. IT/IS systems can be a critical enabler in this pursuit.

11.5 CHARTING A COURSE TOWARD BECOMING A LEARNING ORGANIZATION

Learning organizations require many capabilities, ranging from the soft ("culture") to the hard (tools) (Pietenpol 2010). While there is not a unique sequence to their acquisition, you have to stand before you can run. These capabilities are related in complex ways, and imbalances create learning bottlenecks.

In this section, we use the 15 dimensions presented earlier to create a typology of organizations according to the "learning maturity" level they have achieved. Figure 11.5 presents the capabilities associated with each of the five maturity levels. To find out how mature your organization is with respect to its learning capabilities, mark with an X in Figure 11.5 the ratings you established in the previous section and see at what maturity level the majority of marks lie.

At maturity level 1, which we labeled attention deficit disorder, or ADD, organizations do not learn. They repeat the same mistakes, and most steps forward that they take are followed by two steps backward. This is not to say that they are not profitable. Markets are imperfect and often slow to react to inefficiencies. Thus, companies can survive for some time, vegetating in such local pockets or niches of inefficiency. Eventually, however, if there is profit to be made, better companies will be attracted and soon come knocking at the door. Since any competitive asset that they might hold is not sustainable, in time the ADD organization is condemned.

These organizations need shock therapy. The best source for the shock is internal, that is, administered by a new or "born again" (so to speak) CEO. The most likely source, however, is external, and may turn out to be fatal. Adopting an industry quality standard (such as ISO 9000), if appropriate, and setting a (realistic) timeline for certification may be a way to jump-start the change initiative.

At maturity level 2, which we labeled functional intelligence, some learning takes place, mostly in isolated pockets. The good news is that the organization has flirted with continuous improvement. It has used a basic methodology and has an intuitive feel for a change vehicle. However, since learning is not process-wide, there is no knowledge base, and initiatives come and go, there is no synergism. The seeds are there, however, for a learning-friendly environment to emerge. Of course, any dimension for which the organization is rated in the ADD category points out where the bottleneck to its progress lies (this holds true for the "sporadic learning" and "sporadic memory blanks" maturity levels as well). Addressing these dimensions is the best place to start.

Since most of what the organization does is intuitive, what these companies need is to make explicit what is implicit, thus making clear the value of current improvement approaches, their potential, and their limitations. Only then will the organization be in a position to leverage what it does, to put the company in motion, clarifying the vision, charting the course, mobilizing the resources, and strengthening its resolve to stay the course. DMAIC kaizen events may provide the impetus to move ahead and start investing more effort in horizontal management and strategy–process connection.

Balanced scorecards are worth looking into as well at this point. Kaplan and Norton (1992) made a great contribution to rigorous and logical measurement of performance by proposing a "balanced" scorecard for the company. Growing and learning employees drive processes and market share, which in turn drives financial results. Selecting a consistent set of metrics from each of these areas allows the organization to build a dashboard to manage the organization.

Members of organizations that have reached maturity level 3 share strong beliefs about participative management and continuous improvement. They are rigorous and make efforts to connect strategy to operations. They experience problems with horizontal management and follow-through, and they use only part of the fleet and arsenal of the learning organization, thus making their learning sporadic, as we labeled this maturity level.

These organizations should move on to the design methodology and start exploring other change vehicles. The methodology proposed in Chapter 7 would be timely to reinforce the connection between processes and strategy. As well as improving its knowledge base, the company must become more sophisticated about its understanding and management of its culture. The assessment of the impact of past programs, as discussed earlier, would be a good place to start.

The only thing missing for companies that have reached level 4 on the maturity scale is putting it all together. If they could connect all the dots—completing horizontal management, seeing how the mechanisms of the learning pump, knowledge base, and follow-through work together—then everything they still perceive as separate initiatives would blend seamlessly with the way they manage the business, and they would become a mature learning organization (level 5). For these organizations, benchmarking[1] with the best-run companies may be the best way to understand the global vision, complete the journey they have started, and reap its full benefits.

If you are at level 5, you belong to the select category of learning organizations. You should first see if there is any dimension rated less than 5: this is what you should address next. If you are a "straight-5 organization," you may want to pass this book along to a supplier or partner from whose improvement you would stand to gain.

Understanding your current learning assets, the road ahead, and the challenges that lie on the path to becoming a learning organization makes it easier to select improvement initiatives that can assist in building the capabilities required to surmount them. To that effect, Figure 11.6 overlays the main OIIs discussed

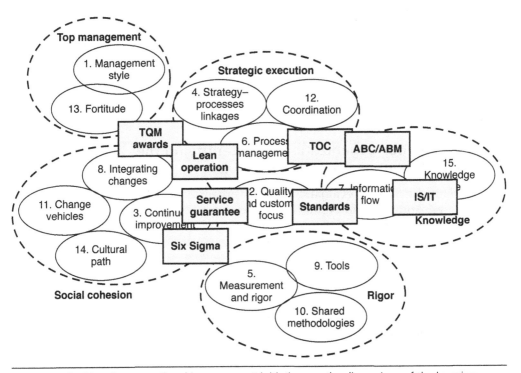

Figure 11.6 Mapping operational improvement initiatives on the dimensions of the learning organization.

here on the dimensions of the learning organizations, as mapped previously in Figure 11.4. OIIs are positioned in the zone where they have the biggest impact. The task is quite ambitious, and the result is of course only indicative. Six Sigma is the closest to the *rigor* dimension. TQM and quality awards are the closest to *top management*. Lean operation touches equally on *strategic execution* and *social cohesion*, and so on.

11.6 SUMMARY

Quality circles led to quality control, which led to total quality assurance and eventually total quality management. Reengineering was then touted as the breakthrough strategy required as a counterweight to the slow pace set by TQM. From Japan, the lean manufacturing philosophy, approach, and methods finally took hold in the West at about that time. Six Sigma then came of age. After incubating at Motorola, it was turbocharged and launched into orbit by the great management thinker and practitioner Jack Welch at GE. Unfortunately, it completely ignored the lean movement, for which mounting evidence of dramatic gains was increasingly compelling. Thus was invented Lean-Six Sigma. In parallel, GE's competitor United Technology was launching its own eclectic mix under ACE.

Many companies adopted these approaches wholesale and were burned. Many more are confused. Thus there is the temptation to discard it all as successive schemes invented by management gurus and consultants to hawk their wares. Both approaches lack in discrimination and are wrongheaded. Much has been learned during the past 30 years, with each wave contributing something new toward the emerging paradigm of the learning organization. A clearheaded and explicit assessment of where the organization stands in this quest, including a distillation of lessons learned from past failures and successes, is the beginning of wisdom. Only then can the company pick the missing ingredients from the rich portfolio of initiatives to help it on this journey.

EXERCISE

11.1 Rating Your Organization and Identifying the Most Potentially Helpful Initiatives

Conduct a cursory evaluation of your organization's learning maturity using the grid provided in Figure 11.5. Referring to Figure 11.6 and the associated discussion, which initiative or combination of initiatives would best contribute to improving your organization's learning ability?

NOTE

1. American Productivity and Quality Center (APQC), at http://www.apqc.org, is a good place to start.

12

Personal Processes: Wellness and the One-Person Business

We are what we repeatedly do. Excellence, then, is not an act but a habit.

—Will Durant, The Story of Philosophy, p. 76

With some adaptation, the philosophy, approaches, and techniques proposed in this book apply to the processes of the autonomous worker or one-person business. They can also be very beneficial in several spheres of our personal lives, if we so choose.

Prologue: An Idea about Dealing with Ideas

Issue: *Anatomy of a dysfunctional process*

For years, when I had what seemed to me like a good idea, I wrote it down on any piece of paper I could find, including a newspaper, a napkin, and even a disposable coffee cup. While it exists only as a collection of activated neurons and synapses, an idea is very short-lived and vulnerable to being superseded by a more pressing thought or feeling requiring immediate attention or action. Thus the importance of capturing it before it joins the millions of others in the burial place of "wonderful ideas that could have changed my life if only I had taken the time to follow through." Please do not tell this to any neuroscientist, or at least where you read it: I have only seen neurons light up on TV documentaries. Whatever the neuropsychology of ideas, I know that if you don't "capture" them somehow when they occur to you, you forget them. So I would write them down. The papers would then accumulate in different places, I would lose them, or I would throw them away in an effort to give my desk some sort of appearance of order.

One day, I finally sat down to design a process for this. Whatever I was doing prior to that certainly did not qualify as a process. It took me all of 10 minutes. I bought a stencil pad and labeled it "Ideas" and placed it on the desk in my home office, out of the way but within easy reach. On the first page I wrote "Short-term: TO DO—ASAP," on the second page "Mid-term," on the third page "Long-term," and on the fourth page "Food for thought." I placed stacks of small yellow sticky notes and pencils in strategic locations: desk, car, gym, bedroom, bathroom, coat pocket, jogging shorts, my wife's purse. I started to jot down, in a few words, all ideas that struck me as important, and stuck the notes on the cover of the pad as soon as I got back to my desk. Whenever I had a minute, I would

(continued)

place the note under the appropriate heading. From time to time, when I was organizing my agenda, I would flip through the pad, select things that I could start, and pencil them into my agenda.

Six months later. For the third time that morning, I glanced at the pad on the corner of the black granite desk, brightly lit by the morning sun coming in through the window, and felt another pang of guilt as I tried to bring my attention back to the computer screen and the list of e-mails that had accumulated throughout the night from other time zones. The green cover of the pad was invisible, pasted over as it was with three layers of haphazardly stuck sticky notes. The originally bright yellow notes were now almost white from the bleaching action of the sun. I had not posted any new ideas for the last two months, and had not tried to classify any idea for even longer. After initial enthusiasm and some success, it had gradually become one more source of demand on my time, not giving back anything in return. Ideas are not like e-mails: if you don't follow up diligently, there is no risk of anyone reminding you of your commitments. This leaves only self-blame. "I don't need that," I thought. I picked up the offending artifact and threw it out, together with the wealth of "potentially life-changing" ideas it contained. "Here's a dumb idea I should have left to its appropriate nanosecond life."

As the prologue illustrates, we are often willing to spend a few minutes to fix a broken process or set up a new one. But we generally do not take the time required to explore several possibilities, to push the exploration far enough to ensure logical validity, and to experiment before settling. In those instances when we do get it right, we also often lack the discipline to follow through, and give up too quickly when problems arise.

In this chapter we first provide an illustration of the strategy-to-process connection in a one-person business. We then suggest ways to improve wellness, including systems thinking, statistical thinking, and evidence-based process management, in a personal context. Video 12.1 presents a personal perspective on processes, in the first person (see Figure 12.1). Before concluding, we move on to a discussion of how to scope improvement projects and manage personal process change. The chapter, and with it the book, closes with an epilogue.

12.1 The pursuit of operational excellence is personal
Excellence is personal. Thus, it means different things to different people. Whatever it means to you, you are more likely to reach your goals with a systems view, rigor, and a process approach. It works just as well for "soft processes" and "hard processes." Since the hard stuff is the soft stuff, this is good news. Because of the nature of the topics, parts of this session are "up close and personal."

Key concepts: Beliefs and values, personal Y, y, and personal processes, health information scanning process, facts and superstition, monitoring, managing time, managing ideas, getting started

Figure 12.1   Video associated with Chapter 12.

12.1 THE ONE-PERSON BUSINESS

As connectivity, access to information, processing capability, and technology have grown, the possibilities for self-employment have followed. The one-person business (OPB) works like a molecule, connecting as required to other molecules and larger ensembles to become part of a value chain. On the upside, this provides the lone professional with the opportunity to specialize in what she does best, and to be free to associate with value-adding units of her choice.

Managing all aspects of the OPB can be challenging, however, especially to a professional who is not really interested in these matters. Managing interfaces with other organizations also requires time and skills, and can be taxing if you are not so inclined. Strategically, the molecular or network organization is very flexible: it can eliminate low-performing units quickly or increase capacity by adding new ones, it does not have to support idle resources and high fixed costs when business is slow, and individual units can reorient themselves and migrate toward other value chains when fundamental changes occur in the market.

Consider Box 12.1, presenting the case of a one-person home design company, and view Video 4.2. This is a high-contact business. The establishment and maintenance of a trusting relationship with her clients is vital to Sandra's long-term success. To ensure the successful conclusion of projects, the establishment of a working relationship with suppliers is also critical, as delighted clients provide the key to new business through referrals.

Box 12.1 The Designer

Issue: *V2P model for an OPB*

Sandra has been an interior designer for about 15 years. Five years ago, she decided she had enough expertise and connections to start her own business. She is an OPB, with many suppliers, partners, and industry acquaintances, and a home office overlooking the beautiful countryside. Even though she has a website and manages her visibility on the web, she gets most of her customers through word of mouth and repeat business.

Tastes in interior design are very personal and vary widely. Assisting a couple in designing the interior of a kitchen, for instance, in which they spend much of their personal time, is a challenging job. The couple's investment may easily exceed $50,000. Following up until the design becomes reality adds much to the value of the service, and to the challenge. Sandra has to build a close rapport with her customers, not only understanding what environment they are likely to enjoy, but also guiding the couple, whose individual needs and tastes are different from each other, through the decision and execution process. Satisfied customers will bring new business; delighted customers, much new business. The converse goes, of course, for disappointed customers.

Market segment and value proposition: You are a well-off, busy couple. You value a quality environment and understand the importance of getting it right, along with the challenges that are involved. I will assist you in clarifying your vision, making sure that your project truly meets your needs. I will also help you in making it a reality, under the best possible conditions, without unpleasant surprises. I will make the experience enjoyable for you and use my industry knowledge and buying power to ensure that you get the best deals and compliant, seamless execution by all contractors.

(continued)

Customer experience: The designer visits the customer's house to chat about their tastes and preferences. They explain what they have in mind—usage, functionalities, ambience, and amenities—as the designer probes to get a better understanding. Incongruence and differences are brought out in the process. As the project clarifies, Sandra starts throwing out ideas to force the couple to clarify and coalesce their visions into one. A sketch is then proposed and discussed. It may go through several iterations until it is finalized into a design plan. The designer then proposes various potential suppliers (furniture, appliances, construction work, cabinetmaker, installer, and so on) and prepares a request for quotes (RFQs). She prepares an implementation plan and assists the customer in signing the contracts. The customers manage the project themselves, calling on Sandra as execution problems of all sorts typically arise. She provides expertise and reassurance throughout and mediates any conflict that arises.

Business model: Key value-creating assets include (1) visualization and anticipation capability; (2) neutral, empathetic, benevolent, and reassuring sounding board; (3) knowledge database of design options; (4) network of competent, trustworthy resources; (5) buying power; and (6) project planning capability. Brought to bear simultaneously on what is only a distant dream, these capabilities turn it into a reality. The designer sells her time, which embodies all these capabilities. The market power she wields over her suppliers comes from her position as the key broker in the value chain. It translates into revenue through the higher fees she can charge for her services, which she bills by the hour.

Personal value proposition: Be your own boss. Spend quality face time with your customers, getting to know them and building a rapport with them. Make projects happen that change the lives of grateful customers. Be a mover in the fascinating and glamorous world of design. Enjoy great variety in your work, from customer contact to computer-aided design and project management. Work out of your home two days a week. Get great deals on the design of your own home and those of your family and friends from dedicated suppliers.

Operations strategy and policies: Sandra uses web-based technologies and telecoms to the fullest and does not require a secretary or business office. She works either on customers' premises or at home. She uses video and laser-based measurement systems. She uses computer-aided design and communicates electronically with her suppliers and other members of her network. She sends images, 3D sketches, and videos to customers and suppliers and receives information the same way. A trusted accountant handles financial reporting obligations and taxes. This mode of operation allows for quick and high-definition responses to customers at the lowest possible variable cost to her. The biggest operational challenge is managing her contacts to maintain a stable workload, as demand is seasonal and there is no backup resource.

Key processes: Answer customer initial query. Conduct initial meeting (needs assessment and exploratory concepts). Produce initial design and sketch. Conduct design meeting (concept selection and high-level design). Produce final design and RFQs. Finalize contracts and build plan. Manage network. Update design software and technology. Scan the design environment for new trends of all kinds and new materials.

Voice of customer: Number of calls per week. Response time. Percentage of calls that translate into contracts. Hours charged per week. Volume generated for network members. Days late per project. Number of serious execution problems encountered. Number of messages from delighted customers. Percentage of repeat business. Number of major issues emerging during execution. Percentage of customers following through to completion.

Since kitchens are her specialty and represent a large part of her income, Sandra has focused on the interface with the cabinetmaker as a critical one. Figure 12.2 shows a macro map of the order-to-delivery process for a kitchen. She has a preferred supplier and a secondary source. The former uses computer-aided design

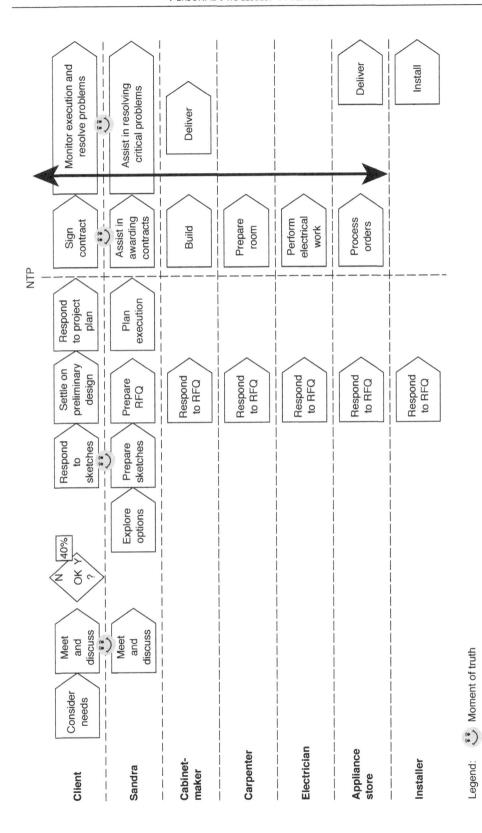

Figure 12.2 Order-to-delivery process macro map for Sandra.

and manufacturing to speed up execution and reduce discrepancies between the drawings and the final results. Because she has the market power, Sandra was able to set and enforce clear ground rules. Responsibilities have been clearly spelled out, as well as a mechanism to ensure quick problem resolution. The cabinetmaker understands very well that if Sandra looks bad as a result of anything he did, she loses future business and his competitor gains a leg up. He is fully committed to deliver. Thus, he does not make promises lightly. He understands that a delighted customer is his best guarantee of a growing and enduring relationship.

Sandra isolated four contact points as moments of truth (see Figures 5.3 and 12.2) in her relationship with a new client: the first encounter, the agreement on a final design, the awarding of the contracts to the various suppliers, and problem resolution. Clients, she understands, gradually resolve four questions they had on their mind at the outset: Can she add value to what we could do on our own? Can I trust her (Is she on my side)? Does she deliver? Can I count on her when a problem arises? Thus, Sandra devotes much time and effort to understanding who her customers are, what makes them tick, and what makes them angry.

In the first encounter, for instance, she displays a genuine interest in understanding her clients. She visits the house and listens intently to their comments. She asks many questions about them and their project, often eliciting different responses when a couple is involved. She also makes it a point to bring up design issues that had been missed and to provide original ideas, treating the client's response respectfully: it is their project. She does not hold back her ideas for fear the client will "steal them" and do business with someone else. If some do, then that's a cost of doing business.

She uses a checklist before and after the meeting. To improve this part of her work, she closely monitors the percentage of these first encounters that translates into contracts and makes every effort to find out the causes when things do not turn out as she hoped.

To the lone professional or OPB, personal and professional processes are inextricably intertwined. Playing tennis with a client, for instance, is taking care of your health, your business, and your social life at the same time. As you plan a visit to a supplier, you have to arrange it so that you can pick up the kids after baseball. You get a great idea about a new business deal when you are gardening, and find a way to build a new closet as you are chatting with a business partner. Thus, since there's only one of you and much demand on your time, you have to think globally about your life. We therefore turn to a discussion of processes in our personal lives.

12.2 WELLNESS[1]

Turning forty can be a wake-up call for someone who has not seriously invested in wellness. "Wellness is a positive, day-to-day approach to a long, healthful, active life. . . . One crucial tenet is that preventing illness is even more important than treating it, especially since many chronic diseases are incurable" (Berkeley Wellness 2010).

As discussed throughout this book, an ounce of prevention is worth a pound of cure. If the approaches presented here can contribute to organizational wellness, they should be helpful in keeping us healthy as well. Such a focus on your health is not egotistical: you will be much more useful to others if you stay healthy. This section aims to open your eyes to the possibilities that such a transfer of approaches, from a business to a personal context, can afford you. Systems and process thinking will make you see your life from a different perspective. This will clarify what processes you should measure and control. A personal illustration will be presented. We conclude with how to deal with the mass of health information and prescription that comes your way.

12.2.1 Systems and Process Thinking

The reader now understands that an organization is a system of processes where the output of one process is input to another. The human body is also such a system, and so are our lives. Figure 12.3 depicts one possible representation of a person's processes. Eating and drinking (1.0 and 2.0) require food, drinks, and time as input. They are processed by the body and the mind for repairs (and growth, in the case of youth) and to produce "energy." It would be reductionist, even in the simplified context of this diagram, to represent the body and the mind as processes. They are complex (as complex as it gets) interrelated systems of processes in their own right. In the respiratory system, for instance, the air we take in (input) is transformed into oxygen and carbon dioxide (output) via respiration. Simultaneously, the brain monitors (feedback loop) whether there is enough oxygen in the bloodstream to keep the body functioning. A change in any of the inputs or output will affect not only the respiratory system but the body as a whole. The flow of oxygen to the brain keeps a complex system of mental processes going, which in turn have a direct impact on our energy level. Box 12.2 provides another illustration with the control of blood sugar level.

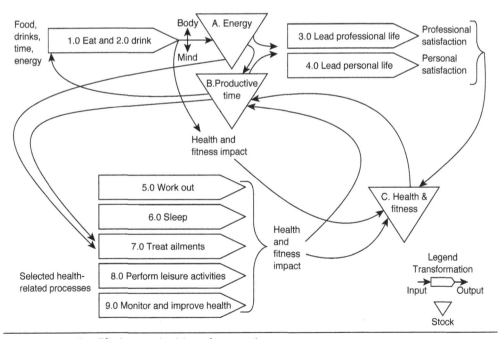

Figure 12.3 Simplified systemic vision of personal processes.

Box 12.2 Diabetes as a Complex Process Control Problem

The body is a system of processes. The eating process, for instance, takes food from our plate, processes it through our hands, mouth, and esophagus, and delivers masticated food to our stomach. The gastrointestinal tract takes this as input, digests it, and delivers various types of nutrients to the blood. Blood transports glucose to various body systems that either store it or burn it as fuel, producing the energy the body needs. For the body to function well, our glycemia level (quantity of glucose in blood) must remain within a given tolerance.

For people suffering from diabetes, keeping this process in control is a permanent challenge. The system produces feedback, which they can use to assist in that pursuit. Excess sugar produces symptoms such as blurred vision, fatigue, and weight loss. Lack of sugar produces different symptoms, such as heavy sweating, shakiness, headache, and trouble with speech. The sufferer must learn to interpret these symptoms and decide if and when corrective action is required. Injecting insulin increases the glucose output from the blood into body cells, thereby reducing glycemia. Drinking orange juice, on the other hand, quickly raises the input of sugar into the blood.

One quality professional working for 3M used statistical thinking to help his spouse control her diabetic condition (Pohlen 1999). Controlling diabetes is a challenging process control problem.

The quality professional measured variation in the glucose level and correlated it with variables that are known to affect it. Variables were both controllable and uncontrollable, such as different foods, exercise, illness, infections, and especially emotional stress. From this he was able to gain a much better understanding of factors affecting his wife's glucose level.

As a result, she was able to achieve better control of her condition. This resulted in less testing, less insulin, better health, and a stronger quality of life. Achieving such results is possible only when you take a rigorous, active, and take-charge approach to your own health.

"The real value of control charts and statistical thinking is to help us learn about our processes," the husband wrote. "Failure to introduce the charts essentially guarantees that one will continue to be ignorant of how to control the process" (p. 235).

Continuing our discussion of Figure 12.3, food and drink, as processed by body and mind, affects our "stock of health and fitness" (C in Figure 12.3), which in turn increases our supply of productive time (B). We can draw on this as needed to lead our personal lives (4.0), work out (5.0), eat (1.0), sleep (6.0), or any other pursuit. High-level processes, such as "lead professional life" (3.0), consist of many lower-level processes, such as "visit supplier" or "prepare budget" (not shown in Figure 12.3). These processes work as a system, since changes in one process can have system-wide impacts through positive and negative feedback loops.

While life goals vary from one person to the next, let us assume for the sake of the ongoing discussion that the goal is to maximize personal and professional satisfaction, and that health and fitness (C in Figure 12.3) are critical means to that end. Also bear in mind that personal satisfaction may very well come from helping others, and thus is not an inherently selfish pursuit.

12.2.2 Measuring and Controlling

How do you know if your wellness system is working well? If you are healthy, feeling good, and full of energy to do what you want, that's a good start. It is not an indication, however, that you are managing the system in a way that will give you the best odds that it stays that way. We inherit our bodies (including our genes, of course), with their inherent potential for a healthy life. We do not know that potential. Whether it will be realized depends on three categories of variables: those that lie totally beyond our control (for example, exposure to chemicals as a baby), those that are partially controllable (for example, car accidents), and those that are controllable (that is, lifestyle related). What we can do is make the best of what we have, acting on what we can control, based on what we know. Measuring this system is thus essential to knowing and, therefore, to improving wellness.

Experts tell us that our cholesterol level is an important health marker. It depends partly on our heredity and partly on processes we can control. However, since it requires a blood analysis, it cannot be used for quick and regular feedback, which is essential to improvement. Blood pressure is another important indicator, and its measurement is quick and easy. Having low levels of LDL cholesterol, high levels of HDL cholesterol, and a blood pressure that does not exceed 115/75 is an indication that you are healthy. However, your cholesterol and blood pressure levels may be all wrong and yet you may feel perfectly healthy. In this situation, you would be slowly inflating a "bubble," as discussed in Chapter 1, with the concomitant risk that it eventually bursts with a bang.

What processes do we control that are known to have a significant influence on these two indicators? The consensus among experts is that processes 1.0, 2.0, and 5.0 in Figure 12.3 have a strong impact. Starting with the former, how can we measure what we eat and drink? Counting calories is possible. It is, however, a time-consuming undertaking and should thus be kept for situations where "lighter" approaches have failed. Since what you eat has a direct impact on your weight, measuring your weight is an easier way to control your eating process.

Of course, while the fact that your weight is under control means that you are not eating too much, it does not mean that you are eating well. Measuring the percentage of fat in your body is an alternative, but again it is more complex and less precise. Measuring your waistline is suggested by some as a better indicator, but consistently getting a correct measurement requires some training, and it is not as sensitive as weight to quickly detect changes in eating patterns. Thus, applying best eating practices (much fruit and vegetables, little red meat) and making sure that your weight stays within a tolerance of your body mass index (BMI) are probably time-efficient ways to proceed for most people.

If your weight is the right thing to measure, it is equally important to measure it right. Several variables related to weight could introduce "noise" or distortion into the data, such as the timing of the reading (related to eating, training, and bodily rhythms), the clothes you wear, and the instrument you use. The author has found that measuring every Thursday morning when he gets up, naked on a medical beam scale, provides a valid data stream. Setting a specific time avoids "choosing," consciously or not, a moment that is more likely to provide a "convenient" reading, thus maintaining objectivity. Beam scales are more precise (less affected by environmental conditions) and avoid the slow drift of other types of balances as parts gradually wear out.

For the workout process, a wristwatch computer connected to a heartbeat monitor, a wireless sensor on the heel of your shoe, or even a GPS can monitor your progress, process the data through an expert system, and provide you with instantaneous state-of-the-art science-based advice. This may be appropriate if you are training for competition but is overkill if you are just trying to stay fit. The time you spend doing aerobic training during any given day is an easy indicator to calculate, as you can simply mark it on your calendar every day and keep track of variations.

12.2.3 Illustration of a Personal Health Dashboard

To illustrate how such process control would work, I will use my own data. The charts that are presented have been explained in Chapter 6. Figure 12.4 shows an "I" control chart[2] for the weight variable, measured weekly as discussed earlier, over a 10-year period (one year of data was lost). The top chart shows the weekly observations for the 10 years, while the bottom one shows the last year only. Visual inspection shows a downward trend. This is confirmed by the numerous outliers that exceed the upper control limit (UCL) during the first two years, and the numerous outliers below the lower control limit (LCL) during the last year.

The one-year diagram is more useful for interpreting weekly variations. Only one point is out of control (below UCL, in observation 38). It resulted from three weeks of traveling abroad and hard work. The last four points show the recuperation effect that coincides with the end-of-year holidays. BMI values of 18.5–25 are considered normal. Using a BMI of 22 as the central value, my "ideal weight" (more on this later) should be 158 pounds. This corresponds to a weight that I have held throughout my 20s, and thus makes sense. Over the years, I have developed a comfort zone within two pounds of this value, that is, 156–160. This zone is shown by the dotted line in Figure 12.4 (bottom part). Thus, I do not wait for the control limits to be reached before introducing some adjustment to the eating or training process. At 160 or so, I am more careful with portion sizes and schedule one or two more outings; below 156, I am a little more indulgent. As the chart indicates, I tend to be more tolerant of lower values, as I know that increasing my weight has

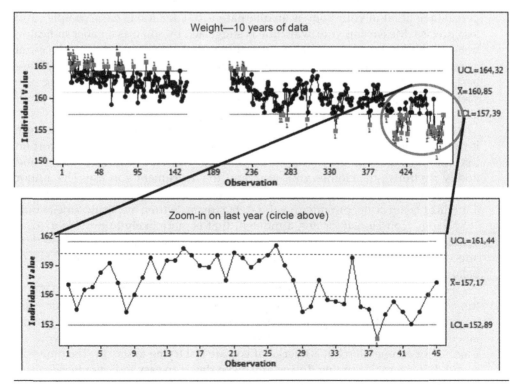

Figure 12.4 Weekly weight over a 10-year period (I chart), with a zoomed-in view of the last year.

never been a problem and I actually find it much more enjoyable than the other way around (go figure).

Figure 12.5 shows a Minitab one-way process capability report for the last year of data. Refer back to Chapter 6 for a discussion of the normal curve. It is beyond the scope of this book to discuss all aspects of such a report and the calculations involved as they appear in Figure 12.5. I have used only the upper specification limit of 160, since in practice I am more concerned with an upward drift. The dotted flat bell curve is based on all data: 45 observations, 7 weeks missing (I cannot take a valid reading when I am away). It shows that my average weight for that year was 157 pounds and that I am capable of respecting the limit 87.98% of the time (1 − .12019391). The solid line and the associated calculations show that if I could control long-term variations in the process, I could do so 97.66% of the time (1 − .02342693). I feel fine as it is, and certainly do not see any necessity to do this.

Examination of the bottom part of Figure 12.4 shows the nature of these long-term variations. From week 10 to week 28 my weight was always above the average. After that, it was mostly below. The explanation for this is very clear to me. From March to June, I was mostly involved in writing, a sedentary activity. Afterward, I was extremely busy with external engagements and traveling and was on my feet most of the day; additionally, I was not eating as much. During the first period, staying below 160 was difficult. This made me aware of the importance of what experts call non-exercise activities that burn many calories (Levine 2002). As a result I changed the layout of my office and set it up so that I could move and engage my muscles much more. I recently verified that it not only works but also is more productive, as physical stimulation somehow triggers mental stimulation (a personal observation, a logical statement, but not a scientific fact).

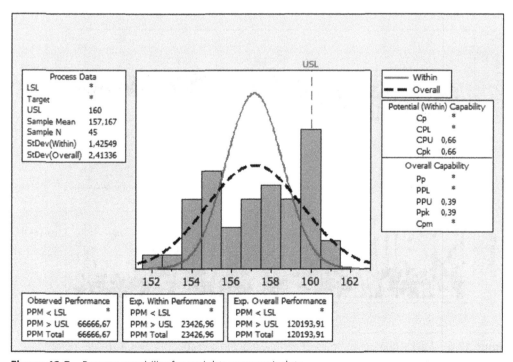

Figure 12.5 Process capability for weight: one year's data.

Figure 12.6 shows an I-MR control chart for the number of hours per week of aerobic training. The MR, or moving range, chart at the bottom shows changes from week to week. With about 1.5 hours average change (1.427), training appears to be variable. Many of the outliers (more than 4.5 hours week-to-week variation) are explained by a previous week with little training. Those are in turn attributable to travel, injury, or illness. Examination of the I chart reveals an upward trend from week 50 to week 300, as training is doubled from about 4 hours to 8 hours. During this period I changed from strictly jogging to cross-training. Biking, for instance, is more time-consuming than jogging. The "standard" I am shooting for is one hour a day, which appears to be a valid target for this intensity of training.

Figure 12.7 shows the two trends mentioned earlier side by side: the increase in aerobic training and the decrease in weight. Both trends were found to be statistically significant, and a line was fitted to estimate the trend using regression analysis. While we will not discuss the statistical techniques involved, it is risky to rely on what appears to be a trend or pattern in the data. They merely suggest hypotheses that need to be tested statistically. If the matter were important, we could correlate the two variables and test the hypothesis that aerobic training in $t-1$ is related to weight in t, which, if inverse correlation is indeed detected, would further strengthen the case for the existence of a causal relationship (precedence being a necessary, but insufficient, condition for causality).

Finally, Figure 12.8 illustrates what a health process control dashboard could look like. It includes the previous data, as well as (actual) data on blood pressure (systole and diastole) and the ratio of total cholesterol to HDL cholesterol. The overall picture is good, with cholesterol, presumably the most important metric,

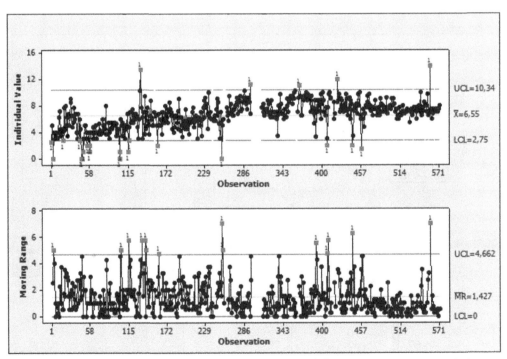

Figure 12.6 Weekly number of hours of aerobic training and changes over a 10-year period (I-MR chart).

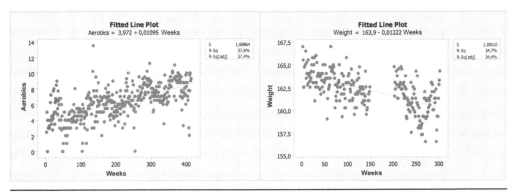

Figure 12.7   Comparing trends: fitted regression line for aerobics and weight over time.

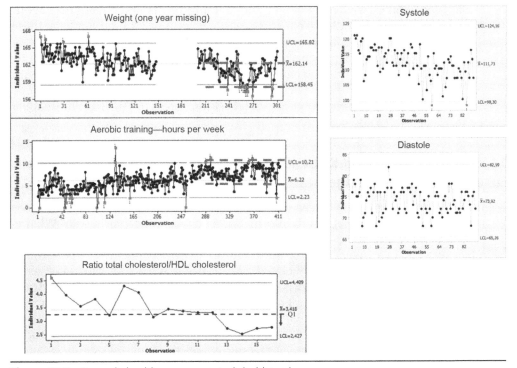

Figure 12.8   Example health process control dashboard.

systolic blood pressure, weight, and aerobic training showing statistically significant improvement. All key parameters are in statistical control and capable, that is, broadly within target ranges.

The reader may have some burning questions at this stage. Do I need to do all this? No. Actually, now that the processes have been improved and have achieved the desired capability, I only capture the data on my calendar (aerobics daily, weight weekly, blood pressure twice a month, and cholesterol whenever I have a test, usually annually). Once a year, during the holidays, I transcribe it in Minitab and prepare the diagrams. Just writing down the information makes me focus on my health and my processes for a few seconds, reinforcing discipline and triggering corrective actions through refreshed awareness of the importance of wellness and of its drivers.

Could I fall victim to a long-term debilitating illness or die tomorrow, and what would it prove if I did? Of course I could, and it would not prove anything, even though it would provide colorful anecdotal evidence that all these efforts dedicated to personal wellness process improvement are a waste of time. I do not control my heredity. I can only try to make the best of it. For all I know, I may have been exposed to viruses or chemicals that, in conjunction with my heredity, have initiated a pathological process that will soon prove fatal. Conversely, if I were to live healthfully until a ripe old age, it would not prove anything either. Witness Winston Churchill, whose lifestyle was somewhat less than exemplary from a fitness point of view, who died at 90 and remained active and productive very long. Epidemiology is a science. Anecdotal evidence only leads to superstition. Meanwhile, I enjoy my eating and training habits and I feel good about my health. Maybe I would be equally healthy or healthier if I did not have these practices. We will never know for sure. The pursuit of wellness involves the adoption of best practices that increase the odds that you will make the best of your potential for a healthy life. You have to think statistically and act consistently with the facts as you know them. Focus on the variables over which you have some control, which have been shown to be critical to process (CTP), and whose ideal settings are well known.

12.2.4 Distilling Useful Knowledge from an Evolving and at Times Fuzzy Health Knowledge Base

Information is power, if you can transform it into knowledge, and from there into know-how. In this sense, health information is power over your health. What is likely to keep you healthy? What keeps us happy? What's likely to cure illness? True and useful answers to these questions are hard to come by. The path to the discovery of truth is often convoluted, sometimes making 180° turns. Just as in business, the search for the truth is done through mining (health) data and extracting useful information. Since missing important new health facts (for example, news that a medication you have been taking has unforeseen side effects) can be very detrimental, the personal process that does this (9.0 in Figure 12.3) is critical. Unfortunately, few people go about this systematically.

For instance, here's a data point: in 2005, a study published in a reputable medical journal (Flegal et al. 2005) concluded that being a little overweight was associated with a somewhat lower death rate. This prompted a *New York Times* editorialist to quickly jump to conclusions, dismissing decades of medical research: "For those of us lacking six-pack abs, this week's report that the overweight live longer is the greatest medical news in history" (Tierney 2005). The study was conducted at the US Centers for Disease Control and was based on epidemiological data spanning some 30 years. Extracting useful information from such data points requires asking questions quality practitioners are quite familiar with, such as:

- *Was the measurement system valid?* The BMI used in the study is not a good indicator of body fat in elderly people: being lean for an adult may mean being muscular, while it probably means being frail in the elderly, as we lose muscle over the years. The ratio of one's waist to one's hips would have been a better indicator of body fat in the elderly, but it is also harder to measure correctly and evenly.

- *Could the correlation be spurious?* Could it be, for example, that smokers and people who are ill (two factors associated with a shorter life span) are also leaner than others? Is their number large enough to explain the correlation observed?

- *What is the underlying rationale that would explain this result?* The study's results fly in the face of everything known in health sciences today, prompting an expert to ask: "What yet-to-be discovered factor is so powerful that it not only counteracts the higher risks of diabetes, cardiovascular disease, and cancer in the overweight, but makes overweight beneficial" (*Nutrition Action*), to which no one could provide a satisfactory answer.

Thus, while the study is too serious to be brushed aside (based on the credibility of its authors and the general soundness of the methodology), a rigorous person concerned about weight would place this issue on a watch list. However, based on the foregoing discussion, she would mark it as doubtful and not take any immediate action.

Jumping to conclusions and disregarding the weight of the evidence can kill you. Yet it is a very human thing to do, driven as we are by emotions, wishes, selective perception, and time pressure. Thus, telling apart the vital few from the trivial many, and rigorously distilling the best theory from available evidence, is a lifesaving skill.

12.3 CHANGING OTHER PERSONAL PROCESSES

John Maynard Keynes once reportedly answered a journalist's pointed question with the quip "When the facts change, I change my mind. What do you do, sir?" Once you conclude that the relevant facts as you know them have changed, it is time to act. This action must first be guided by a SMART statement, such as "My cholesterol level is at 200 mg/dL; it should be less than 130 mg/dL," or "I have a 38-inch waist; it should be 36." Then you have to identify the process or processes you have to change to fix the problem. Processes such as "eat dessert" (a subprocess within 1.0 in Figure 12.3), "drink alcoholic beverages" (part of 2.0), and "work out" (5.0) are all potential candidates, based on what is known about the effect they have on cholesterol and the waistline. The choice depends, of course, on the current functioning of these processes and on an assessment of the (very personal and subjective) level of effort required to modify deeply rooted habits. This is a salience–performance analysis such as the one discussed in Chapter 7 (see Figure 7.7).

As you get into the habit of scoping and fixing personal processes, Figure 12.3 becomes more personalized and gains resolution. As the contours of discrete processes emerge, what at first appears as a jumbled flow of loosely related activities gradually shapes up. Just as each business should evolve its own process model, so should individuals. To make sure yours is real (that is, meaningful to you), it is better to start with a simple, even a simplistic, representation and let the pattern of processes emerge in time. As you learn to recognize different processes and deal with them as distinct units interacting with each other, draw up an explicit model. The drawing itself forces you to recognize incoherence and refine your understanding. As the resolution of your personal process model increases, it becomes easier to pinpoint the right thing to do when unsettling new wellness facts emerge.

Depending on your situation and need, you can decide to either incrementally improve the way you eat or innovate and go for radical change. While the personal context does not require the same degree of formalism as the business context, it does require rigor, of which discipline is a core component. This is particularly challenging to some people, as is well illustrated by the amusing and insightful characters depicted in *Who Moved My Cheese?* (Johnson 2000).

Another author tells the story of how he used a process-based approach to switch from using a minivan to using a bike to get to work, achieving health improvement while securing financial rewards (La Lopa and Marecki 2000). He flowcharted his process in detail and used a process improvement methodology—changing his route and installing new tires—to gradually close all performance gaps between planned and actual output. He concluded, "If this Spartan, yet highly sophisticated, quality management tool was so successful in helping me improve my commute to work, perhaps it will benefit others who desire to make improvements in their business or daily lives as well" (p. 64).

Finally, Box 12.3 shows how a more mundane process was changed. Granted, not all haircuts are that easy to produce or translate into a specification. However, a picture is worth a thousand words, and the odds of getting the result you want are infinitely better if you start with that than if all you have are your own words to help the hairdresser form a mental image of the result she has to produce.

Several barbers have come and gone since that time. Some are talkative. Others are silent and focused. However, they all deliver the core result that I need with only minor variations. Since I own the technical specification and it is a buyers' market, I am a free man. Indeed, what I was locked into with Gerry was more captivity than relationship. I can't help feeling that Gerry knew the power he had over me. However, I am the one who locked himself in and threw away the key by sticking to the superstitious belief that the task was so complex that only Gerry could get it right and that using another barber would result in disaster.

The set of notions we accept and call our "beliefs"—some about fundamental things, others about trivial issues—is a mix of truth, half-truths, and superstitions. We hold ourselves prisoner to the latter two. As pervasive problems of all kinds arise, we should rigorously challenge the premises upon which our current way of doing things is based. This requires (1) taking the time to sit down and think, (2) making the underlying beliefs explicit, (3) challenging them (how do we know this is true?), and (4) asking ourselves if our actions are consistent with the evidence.

Box 12.3 Getting a Haircut

Issue: *Using quality principles to break free of superstition*

For the roughly 20 years I lived in Suburbia, Gerry was my barber. When I first moved there, I began shopping around for a new barber. Mine, like most people's, was essentially a hit and miss process, often involving some personal embarrassment when the miss was particularly bad. My needs are simple. I simply want a "wash and wear" haircut—that is, so short that I do not even have to use a comb when I come out of the shower. Yet, simple is apparently not that easy to explain and perform. I found Gerry on my fourth trial. Since he kept doing the same quality job, and was rather a nice fellow to chat with, I stuck with him. Unfortunately, I was not the only one to spot his qualities. Demand for his services grew over the years. Since this was a first-come, first-served shop, waiting time crept up slowly over the years. While the problem became quite bad, to the point where I kept postponing getting a cut, the force of inertia had become so strong that I could never muster the resolve to start looking for another barber. I was captive.

Then came the move to Smalltown. I briefly considered making the one-hour round trip to Suburbia, but quickly realized that this would be ridiculous. So I resolved to select a new barber, making sure, however, to use quality principles to ensure that the job is done right, fast, and cheap every time.

"Start with the end in mind" struck me as quite relevant to my problem. So, a few weeks before the move, when I arrived home with a fresh haircut, I asked my wife to take a series of close-ups from various angles. The next time I was due for a haircut, I drove to Smalltown and entered the first barbershop I found. Pointing at my head I asked the stylist, "Can you turn this into that?" (pointing now at the photos). I must confess to feeling a bit self-conscious as I did so, much to the amusement of the other customers. To my relief, however, her answer was immediate and straightforward: "Shaver cut, 3 on the side, 4 on top: no problem." "Here's my technical specification," I thought, "my get-out-of-barber-prison-free wild card." The proof of the haircut, of course, is in the cutting: perfect cut, 10 minutes (versus 30 before), by appointment (no wait versus 30 minutes before), $15 (versus $23 before).

12.4 CONCLUSION

Box 12.4 proposes a methodology for getting started on personal process improvement. However, this addresses only the means ("how should I change?") for change. It does not deal with other critical change factors, such as motivation, vision, and sense of urgency. Just as organizations often think of quality approaches as a last resort before going under, all too often dramatic circumstances (such as a heart attack or cancer) provide the motivation and sense of urgency. Better late than never, of course. Quality leadership, however, requires the building and communication of a vision that pulls people into action rather than waiting for catastrophic events to push them into it. A vision of personal excellence performs much the same service for wellness. Prevention and being proactive are central tenets of wellness, since many diseases cannot be cured.

You are not what you think. You are what you eat. You are also what you do. Choosing to see that through the process lens is a natural connection for professionals and managers to make. They should not only be among the most personally rigorous people, but also be advocates of personal rigor. It can be fun and rewarding in a very personal way. Others around you can benefit as well.

I once discussed this with a business acquaintance. He responded that he intentionally refused to introduce any sort of structure into his personal life as a reaction to what he felt was an overstructured professional life. I respect that. I certainly keep many parts of my life spontaneous and intuitive as well. However, systematically disregarding wellness knowledge and know-how comes at a price. Since personal life choices are, well, personal, a reasonable person may decide to forgo these benefits in exchange for immediate freedom from care. It strikes me, however, that most people act out of blatant disregard for inconvenient truths.

Box 12.4 How to Get Started

There is no one correct way to start paying attention to wellness. If you never have, however, there is a rule of thumb about when to get started: the sooner, the better. Here is one way to go about it:

1. Set realistic high-level personal goals (that is, "the big Y"—see Chapter 7). Decide how you will monitor progress toward these goals.

2. View your activities as processes with discrete starting and ending points. Use action verbs to name them.

3. Draw a simple process model, such as that shown in Figure 12.3. There is no right answer. We are all different. Try it. There will be holes and incoherence. Let it be.

4. Design a systematic process for monitoring health news. Keep it simple at first. Make sure it is not excessively time-consuming and fits well in your schedule. Get into the habit of going beyond headlines and exploring the source and validity of the data. When a piece of information draws your attention, look for other sources. Gradually decide what sources you should trust. Build a watch list of health news that you consider relevant (RSS feeds provide a convenient way for doing this).

5. When a worrisome fact emerges, highlighting an important gap between the way you do things and what is required to get closer to your goal, formulate a SMART goal. Do not go for the home run. Nothing succeeds like success. Make sure your first project is a success.

6. Look at your process map and identify the most important culprit or leverage point. Refine your process model as you do so.

7. Start measuring the performance of the process, rigorously and simply. Use variation as a guide to learning about processes. Think statistically. A spreadsheet will come in handy here.

8. Pick one or two simple tools from the process improvement toolkit (such as process mapping, failure mode and effects analysis, or value-added analysis) that are best suited to the job, and get to work on process improvement.

9. When the process is fixed and the goal achieved, think back on the lessons learned about your improvement process. This is called double-loop learning: if every time you improve a process (single-loop learning) you find a way to do it better the next time (double-loop learning), you will soon excel at it. Capture the lessons you learned on a spreadsheet and revisit them every time you are about to embark on a new project.

Epilogue—If You Fail Once . . .

There were about a dozen sticky notes spread out over the desks, as well as stacks of binders and books, when a window suddenly popped up on screen, accompanied by a discreet ding, momentarily interrupting the typing at half sentence. I looked at the clock, surprised. "Wow! 6:30 already. How time flies when you are really focused," I thought to myself. According to what had now become a habit, I finished the sentence, saved the file, and backed up my work of the day. I gathered the sticky notes in a stack and started to read them one at a time. "Buy audio book on Voltaire." "That's something for after work. It goes on the kitchen computer." I gained access to the computer through the network, opened the "weekend notes" spreadsheet to the table of contents tab, clicked on the "buy" hyperlink, typed in the idea, rumpled the note, and put it in the garbage can.

It took about 10 minutes to dispose of the other ideas in a similar fashion, placing them where they would be instantly available when they were likely to be useful: book chapter content, future conferences, client report files, and so on. Most locations were reached directly using hyperlinks in about 20 different spreadsheets. One idea did not strike me as worthwhile, as it apparently had when I took the time to write it down in the morning. I pondered it for a while, and eventually threw the note away. I struggled a while to find the right classification for another one and eventually settled on a category. "I'll never find that one again," I thought to myself. I went to the "find it" hyperlink and copied the idea there, sequentially. That's where I go to do a keyword search for ideas that resist clear classification. When a pattern emerges among elements on the list, I create a new category (another page in the appropriate spreadsheet). A last note was an element to discuss with my wife when I got home: I stuck it on my stack of credit cards. I could not possibly miss it as I emptied my pockets.

That left 15 minutes to clean up. A clean desk policy (see "5S" in Chapter 11) requires that you put everything in its place before you leave. The desk is a workplace, not a place to store work. Sticky notes have a half-life of eight hours. If you leave them longer, they die and become a nuisance. Of the seven "things" that did not belong on my desk, five already had a storage spot from which I had pulled them during the day. Returning them took a couple of minutes. Of the 60 numbered storage spots of various sizes on the shelves around the office wall, some 20 were still available. I picked two appropriate spots and shelved the remaining two elements: a book I had just received and a document I had printed, noting the shelf numbers as I did so. In the "shelves" spreadsheet I entered a short description of the topic, the shelf number, what was supposed to happen to it (outcome), and the next thing I had to do about it. Whenever a deadline is involved, I program an automatic reminder on my time management software. The computer and PDA will see to it that I do not forget: let them worry about it. "6:55. Time to call it quits."

The idea and "things" management system has now been operational for several years. I keep making small changes as the nature of my work evolves and I find better ways. The biggest challenge has been the development of the classification system. If you cannot classify your ideas in terms of when and where they are going to be required, you end up storing them sequentially, and that is a one-way street. As illustrated in the prologue, you keep adding new ideas until you realize that you do not get anything out of it, and the well runs dry. I found classifying the different windows of my life, with sufficient definition, to be a demanding but worthwhile exercise.

Creating the shelf space—with planned overcapacity so that I am never short—was the easy part. Cultivating the discipline to do it every day was the second real challenge. It becomes much easier, however, as you get hooked on the benefits of working with a clean desk: the peace of mind that comes from properly capturing and organizing your ideas, assessing everything on your plate, setting priorities, and being able to focus on one thing at a time.

EXERCISE

12.1 Targeting Personal Processes

Based on the discussion in this chapter, identify three personal processes that you feel could advantageously be the target of improvement projects. Scope one project for each process. Initiate a first project. Make sure you can measure your progress.

NOTES

1. This section is largely based on Harvey (2007).
2. All diagrams have been produced with Minitab, release 14.

Appendix A

Preparing an "I" Chart

To build a control chart, we first use an initial data set as baseline. In Figure 6.12 (page 202), for instance, we used 50 data points for that purpose. Let us suppose that QKM decides to start controlling the process of preparing a proposal, and more precisely its productivity. Since all personnel turn in a time sheet every week, the managing partner sets up a procedure whereby an account number is assigned to each proposal, and the time spent on a proposal is automatically calculated when the proposal is closed (that is, the client accepts or rejects it). The partner decides to build a control chart to analyze the time required for each proposal. Figure 6.13 (page 207) illustrates how he goes about it.

The chart shown in Figure 6.13 is an "I" chart ("I" stands for individual observations) and is normally part of a so-called I-MR tandem control chart (we will not discuss the MR control chart here). The hours worked on the last 30 proposals are displayed in Figure 6.13. After calculating the moving ranges, the partner computes the mean for both variables. The mean hours worked becomes the center of the chart. The standard deviation used in setting the control limits is estimated based on the mean moving range, using a correction factor as shown. The UCL is plotted at three standard deviations above the mean, and the LCL at zero because the calculated value is negative, and thus meaningless when one is dealing with time.

We can use a number of decision rules to interpret a control chart. We will conclude that the process is out of control, that is, that special causes are at work, if any of the following four conditions apply:

- *Rule 1.* There are points (or a single point) lying outside control limits.

- *Rule 2.* A consecutive series of seven points all lying above or below the mean (process shift is likely), or all moving in the same direction (trend, suggesting process drift).

- *Rule 3.* Any unusual pattern in the data, such as a cyclical pattern or systematic alternation above and below the mean.

- *Rule 4.* The proportion of all points lying within a one standard deviation range above and below the mean differs markedly from 2/3 (suggesting a change in the dispersion of the data).

Figure 6.14 (page 208) illustrates all four rules, using material prepared by UK's National Health Service Institute for Innovation and Improvement. Rule 1 applies to the proposal preparation process, meaning that the process is not under control.

Thus, further investigation of the last proposal is likely to yield useful information about the variables that affect the time required to prepare a proposal. Even if the process were in control, it does not mean that we find its performance acceptable. For instance, imagine that the partner feels that spending more than 30 hours on any proposal is unacceptable; then 20% of the proposals do not meet this standard (that is, fall above the upper specification limit [USL—the dotted line] in Figure 6.13).

If the process were in control (not the case here), the partner would conclude that even though the process is functioning normally, its current performance is unacceptable from a normative standpoint. He would then set up an improvement initiative (as discussed in Chapter 9) or design a new process from scratch (as discussed in Chapter 10). Referring back to Figure 5.2, which presents a macro map of the process, a typical improvement would be to include early in the process a "go/no-go" decision to avoid wasting time on proposals that do not meet an a priori set of criteria, and set a specific time limit (as opposed to a unique standard) to spend on each proposal.

There are many different types of control charts, including (for variables) mean and range, and mean and standard deviation, as well as control charts for attributes, including charts for proportions (p chart), number of nonconforming items (np chart), number of nonconformities (c chart), and number of nonconformities per unit (u chart). These are discussed in detail in Mitra (1998). For a general introduction to analysis of variation and SPC, see Wheeler (2000). Minitab is probably the best software available to perform the kind of computations discussed here. (See Chapter 12 for further illustration of SPC and Minitab.)

Appendix B
Specifying the Effect of Each Offering on the Client: The Kano Model

The Kano model classifies the elements of a service package into one of the following categories on the basis of the effect they have on the client:

- *Basic element:* An offering that does not produce any reaction when present but may trigger much dissatisfaction when absent (for example, "the restaurant could not even provide such basics as a clean plate").

- *Performance:* An element directly related to the results sought by the customer in purchasing the service package. A hungry customer might be disappointed by a small portion and pleased by a large one. Performance elements may result in customer satisfaction or dissatisfaction.

- *Delighter:* An unexpected element of the service package that creates a pleasant surprise. The unexpected arrival of a violinist at a dinner table, or being upgraded to business class on a flight, for instance, may delight some customers.

- *Inverse:* An unwanted offering. The customer will be pleased if it is not provided or if he does not get much of it. Some customers at movie theaters, for instance, dislike watching advertisements or previews of other movies before the movie starts.

- *Bull's-eye:*[1] An element that the customer enjoys in limited quantity—too little or too much of it may produce discontent. The service provider's challenge here is to do it just right, that is, provide the right amount of that element. Bringing the check immediately after serving dessert, for instance, may be considered impolite. Having to remind the waiter three times that one requires the check is no better.

- *Indifferent:* An offering that does not correspond to any customer need but that does not irritate him. For example, a bank posting a sign saying that it can provide service in Cantonese will not have any effect on non-Chinese-speaking customers.

Let us consider an example closer to the case of FPA: a one-day seminar on derivatives. Let us also consider two different audiences: a group of undergraduate business students and a group of busy senior executives and senior professionals. Consider the reactions of the two groups to various elements of the service package (see Table B.1). While the executives would consider a personalized greeting as the participants arrive to be basic, it would delight the students. An offering is

Table B.1 Reactions of two market segments to various elements of the service package in a seminar on derivatives.

Offering	Students	Professionals
Personalized greeting	Delight	Basic
Cushioned seats	Delight	Basic
Cocktail with experts after seminar	Delight	Performance
CD to each participant	Wow!	Perfomance
Animated color slides	Delight	Basic
Free coffee at the break	Delight	Basic
China cups	"I'm in the wrong room"	Delight
Filling up the cups at the table during the seminar	"I'm in the wrong room"	Delight
Directed questions to the audience by the speaker	Inverse	"I'm in the wrong room"
Theoretical content	Performance	Bull's-eye
Practical advice	Indifferent	Performance
Speaker's phone number for personal questions	Wow!	Delight
Open bar during seminar	"I'm in the wrong room"	Delight

basic in the eyes of a customer if "it goes without saying." Having attended other such seminars in the past and well aware of their standing as potentially interesting clients, the executives fully expect to be treated as such. Thus, the handshake and greeting "Good evening, Dr. Smith" does not create a "satisfaction" response—merely an unconscious "OK, this is as it should be." A basic service offering goes unnoticed. Clients would, however, definitely notice its absence—in a negative way: "What? Nobody to greet me? What sort of shop is this?" The students, on the other hand, are quite accustomed to entering a seminar room and taking a seat without anyone noticing their arrival. Hence, being greeted at the door by their name would create a positive surprise, and maybe even leave some a bit worried ("What does this guy want from me?"). Finding an open bar in the room, on the other hand, would probably delight many of the executives, whereas it might result in some students squarely turning back and marching out of the room ("I must be in the wrong room").

The students come to the seminar to learn the theory of derivatives: if they get very little, they will be disappointed; if they get much, they will be pleased. Such an offering is alternately labeled performance, linear, or "more is better." Contrary to delighters (which can only produce satisfaction when present) and basic elements (which can only produce dissatisfaction when absent), performance elements have the potential to either please or displease the customer depending on whether they are present or on the degree to which they are present. Since executives come to the seminar to get practical advice, they might consider a one-to-one chat with an expert or a CD with frequently asked questions to be the performance element of the service package.

Theoretical content may be a bull's-eye element for executives, as they require a minimum of theory to understand the topic, but that is not why they came to the seminar: they want practical advice. Directed questions by the speaker to participants are probably a negative for students (inverse). Further, if all they care about is passing an exam and have no money to invest, any practical investment advice may leave them indifferent.

As the foregoing example illustrates, whether a service offering is a delighter, performance, or basic element (or any other category) depends on customers' expectations and needs (as well as the price they pay), and these in turn depend on the market segment (needs, past experience, values, and so on) to which the customer belongs. The effect of an offering on a given customer also evolves over time. While the use of an electronic projector, for instance, may once have been a delighter in executive seminars, it is now basic. One can only delight (that is, surprise) the customer so many times with the same offering until he begins asking for it (performance) and eventually considers it basic. We often refer to this phenomenon as the "ratchet effect," that is, once expectations have been adjusted upward, they do not come back down. Meeting them then merely produces satisfaction, not delight anymore, and may even eventually leave them cold. Notice that competitive offerings also influence the expectations of one's own customer. The minute one bank advertises a no-fee platinum card (thus delighting its own customer base), for instance, all providers of such services are flooded with requests for the same service feature, now considered a performance element rather than a delighter.

The Kano model brings out a limitation of customer surveys: when asked what their expectations are of a given service, customers are liable to respond mostly with performance elements, that is, the explicit result elements they want from the service. One has to probe to find out implicit elements, such as delighters and basics, because the former are "surprises" and the latter "go without saying." Hence, observing the customer in action in a service environment is a useful complement to surveys to fully understand customer needs.

As FPA is designing its service package, it must consider the effect each element will have on clients. Will they consider it basic? Will they be pleasantly surprised? Will they consider it part of the performance they are looking for? The very process of searching for answers to these questions pushes the organization to try to get inside its client's mind, thus countering the natural tendency to look at offerings from the service provider's perspective. It also helps to bring the targeted market segments into sharper focus.

Figure B.1 shows a visual representation of the modified Kano model just discussed, along with a classification of the elements in the initial service package FPA has generated. The horizontal axis shows the extent to which a given element is present, and the vertical axis the client's reaction to the element, with the central line representing the "neutral" point, or absence of reaction. The diagram shows that a delighter ("great courses/conferences") cannot create dissatisfaction, and that a basic element ("courtesy and professionalism") cannot generate satisfaction. Performance ("top gun FP") and inverse elements, on the other hand, can lead to either reaction. To produce satisfaction through a bull's-eye element, one must find just the right dosage of that offering and deliver it with precision.

Note that if "few forms to fill out" had been formulated as "forms to fill out," it would have been classified (more appropriately) as an inverse element.

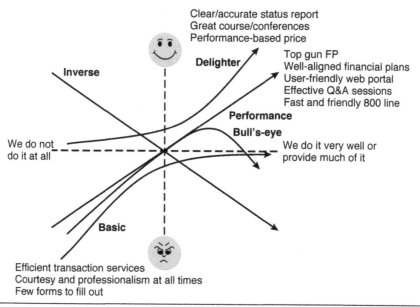

Figure B.1 Classification of some elements of FPA's service package based on their effect on the customer (modified Kano model).

Fees per se would also be an inverse element, even though the fact that they are based on performance per se is a delighter. Other potential inverse elements might include "sales pressure" or "waiting time to reach an FP." The amount of effort required to become better investors might also fall into this category or be labeled a bull's-eye element, as clients may be disappointed and not perceive that they are learning unless they put in some effort.

The Kano model is indispensable for a team charged with the design of a new service package. Without all the basics in place, the client may not even consider the service provider: basics are qualifying elements to enter or stay in the running. Inverse elements often play the same role in clients' decisions. Much competition takes place on performance elements. One or more of these are generally "order-winning" criteria for clients in selecting a service provider from among those they consider qualified. Since delighters are unexpected offerings, they are not part of the client's decision process at the outset. Advertising these elements, however, may induce trial and adoption. They also contribute to transforming merely satisfied (that is, vulnerable to competition) clients into loyal ones.

NOTE

1. Not part of the Kano model.

References

CHAPTER 1

Alexander, C. 2001. *The Endurance: Shackleton's Legendary Antarctic Expedition*. New York: Alfred A. Knopf.

Bossidy, L., and R. Charan. 2002. *Execution: The Discipline of Getting Things Done*. New York: Crown Business.

Collins, J. 2001. *Good to Great: Why Some Companies Make the Leap . . . and Others Don't*. New York: HarperCollins.

———. 2009. *How the Mighty Fall: And Why Some Companies Never Give In*. New York: HarperCollins.

Friedman, T. L. 2006. *The World Is Flat: A Brief History of the Twenty-First Century*. New York: Farrar, Straus and Giroux.

Gawande, A. 2007. *Better: A Surgeon's Notes on Performance*. New York: Henry Holt & Co.

———. 2009. *The Checklist Manifesto: How to Get Things Right*. New York: Henry Holt & Co.

Kling, A. S., and N. Schulz. 2009. *From Poverty to Prosperity: Intangible Assets, Hidden Liabilities and the Lasting Triumph over Scarcity*. New York: Encounter Books.

Main, J. 1994. *Quality Wars: The Triumphs and Defeats of American Business*. New York: The Free Press.

CHAPTER 2

Alvesson, M. 2001. "Knowledge Work: Ambiguity, Image and Identity." *Human Relations* 54 (7): 863–886.

Berry, L. L., A. Parasuraman, and V. A. Zeithaml. 1988. "The Service-Quality Puzzle." *Business Horizons* 31 (5): 33–43.

Bitran, G. R., and J. Hoech. 1992. "The Humanization of Service: Respect at the Moment of Truth." In *Managing Services: Marketing, Operations, and Human Resources*, compiled by C. H. Lovelock, 355–364. Englewood Cliffs, NJ: Prentice-Hall.

Frei, F. X. 2008. "The Four Things a Service Business Must Get Right." *Harvard Business Review* 86 (4): 70–83.

Harvey, J. 1998. "Service Quality: A Tutorial." *Journal of Operations Management* 16: 583–597.

Pine, B. J., and J. H. Gilmore. 1998. "Welcome to the Experience Economy." *Harvard Business Review* 78 (4): 97–105.

Stewart, G. Bennett, III. 1999. *The Quest for Value*. New York: HarperBusiness.

CHAPTER 3

Browning, T. R. 2010. "On the Alignment of the Purposes and Views of Process Models in Project Management." *Journal of Operations Management* 28 (4): 316–332.

TheFreeDictionary.com. 2010. Available at www.thefreedictionary.com. Accessed July 30, 2010.

Mintzberg, H. 1996. "Managing Government, Governing Management." *Harvard Business Review* 74: 75.

Pall, G. A. 1999. *The Process-Centered Enterprise: The Power of Commitments*. Boca Raton: St. Lucie Press.

Van Wyk, R. J. 1988. "Management of Technology: New Frameworks." *Technovation* 7 (4): 341–353.

CHAPTER 4

Garvin, D. A. 2000. *Learning in Action: A Guide to Putting the Learning Organization to Work*. Boston: Harvard Business Press.

Heskett, J. L., W. E. Sasser, and L. A. Schlesinger. 1997. *The Service Profit Chain*. New York: The Free Press.

Yee, R.W.Y., A.C.L. Yeung, and T.C.E. Cheng. 2010. "An Empirical Study of Employee Loyalty, Service Quality and Firm Performance in the Service Industry." *International Journal of Production Economics* 124 (1): 109–120.

CHAPTER 5

Abbott, A. D. 1988. *The System of Professions: An Essay on the Division of Expert Labor*. Chicago: University of Chicago Press.

Christensen, C. M., J. Hwang, and J. H. Grossman. 2009. "Disrupting the Hospital Business Model." Forbes.com. Available at http://www.forbes.com/2009/03/30/hospitals-healthcare-disruption-leadership-clayton-christensen-strategy-innovation.html. Accessed June 15, 2010.

Fisher, C. M., and J. T. Schutta. 2003. *Developing New Services: Incorporating the Voice of the Customer into Strategic Service Development*. Milwaukee, WI: ASQ Quality Press.

Hayes, R. E. 1992. *Measuring Customer Satisfaction*. Milwaukee, WI: ASQC Quality Press.

Meyer, C. M., and A. Schwager. 2007. "Understanding Customer Experience." *Harvard Business Review* 85 (2): 116–26.

Snee, R. D. 2006. "If You're Not Keeping Score, It's Just Practice." ASQ *Quality Progress* 39 (5): 72–74.

Vertosick, F. 2008. *When the Air Hits Your Brain*. New York: W. W. Norton & Co.

CHAPTER 6

Gruska, G., and C. Kymal. 2006. "Use SPC for Everyday Work Processes." ASQ *Quality Progress* 39 (6): 25–32.

Mitra, A. 1998. *Fundamentals of Quality Control and Improvement*. 2nd ed. Upper Saddle River, NJ: Prentice Hall.

Snee, R. D. 2006. "If You're Not Keeping Score, It's Just Practice." *ASQ Quality Progress* 39 (5): 72–74.

Wheeler, D. J. 2000. *Understanding Variation: The Key to Managing Chaos*. 2nd ed. Knoxville, TN: SPC Press.

CHAPTER 7

DeToro, I., and T. McCabe. 1997. "How to Stay Flexible and Elude Fads." ASQ *Quality Progress* 30 (3): 55–60.

Forrester, J. W. 1969. *Urban Dynamics*. Cambridge, MA: MIT Press.

Harvey, J. 2004. "Scoping Improvement Projects in Professional Services—A 10 Step Approach." ASQ *Quality Progress* 37 (8): 64–72.

Lynch, D. P., S. Berolino, and E. Cloutier. 2003. "How to Scope DMAIC Projects." ASQ *Quality Progress* 36 (1): 37–41.

Senge, P. M. 1990. *The Fifth Discipline: The Art and Practice of the Learning Organization*. New York: Doubleday.

Tenner, A. R., and I. J. DeToro. 1996. *Process Redesign: The Implementation Guide for Managers*. Reading, MA: Addison-Wesley.

CHAPTER 8

Anand, G., P. T. Ward, M. V. Tatikonda, and D. A. Schilling. 2009. "Dynamic Capabilities through Continuous Improvement Infrastructure." *Journal of Operations Management* 27 (6): 444–461.

Dumaine, B. 1991. "The Bureaucracy Busters." *Fortune* 123 (13): 36–42.

Forrester, E. C., B. L. Buteau, and S. Shrum. 2009. *CMMI for Services: Guidelines for Superior Service*. Reading, MA: Addison-Wesley.

Harvey, J. 2004. "Process Improvement: Match the Change Vehicle and Method to the Job." ASQ *Quality Progress* 37 (1): 41–48.

Spear, S., and H. K. Bowen. 1999. "Decoding the DNA of the Toyota Production System." *Harvard Business Review* 77 (5): 97–106.

CHAPTER 9

Chase, R. B., and D. M. Stewart. 1994. "Make Your Service Fail-Safe." *Sloan Management Review* 36 (Spring): 35–44.

Nakajo, T., and H. Kume. 1996. "Studies on the Foolproofing of Operation Systems: The Principles of Foolproofing." In *The Best on Quality*, edited by J. D. Hromi, 187–207. Milwaukee, WI: ASQC Quality Press.

ReVelle, J. B. 2010. "Making the Connection." ASQ *Quality Progress* 43 (7): 36–44.

Schroeder, R. G., K. Linderman, C. Liedtke, and A. S. Choo. 2008. "Six Sigma: Definition and Underlying Theory." *Journal of Operations Management* 26 (4): 536–554.

CHAPTER 10

de Bono, E. 1985. *Six Thinking Hats*. Boston: Little, Brown and Co.

Farzaneh, F. 2003. "TQM vs. BPR." ASQ *Quality Progress* 36 (10): 59–62.

Hammer, M. 1990. "Reengineering Work: Don't Automate, Obliterate." *Harvard Business Review* 68 (July–August): 104–112.

Smith, A. M., M. Fishbacher, and F. A. Wilson. 2007. "New Service Development: From Panoramas to Precision." *European Management Journal* 25 (5): 370–383.

CHAPTER 11

DeToro, I., and T. McCabe. 1997. "How to Stay Flexible and Elude Fads." ASQ *Quality Progress* 30 (3): 55–60.

Foster, S. T., Jr. 2006. "One Size Does Not Fit All." ASQ *Quality Progress* 39 (7): 54–61.

Goldratt, E. M., and J. Cox 1992. *The Goal: A Process of Ongoing Improvement*. Great Barrington, MA: North River Press.

Heskett, J. L., W. E. Sasser, and L. A. Schlesinger. 1997. *The Service Profit Chain*. New York: The Free Press.

Kaplan, R. S., and D. P. Norton. 1992. "The Balanced Scorecard: Measures That Drive Performance." *Harvard Business Review* 70 (1): 71–79.

Miller, D., J. Hartwick, and I. Le Breton-Miller. 2004. "How to Detect a Management Fad—and Distinguish It from a Classic." *Business Horizons* 47 (4): 7.

Pietenpol, D. 2010. "Time to Align." ASQ *Quality Progress* 43 (7): 18–23.

Repenning, N. P., and J. D. Sterman. 2001. "Nobody Ever Gets Credit for Fixing Problems That Never Happened: Creating and Sustaining Process Improvement." *California Management Review* 43 (4): 64–88.

Schroeder, R. G., K. Linderman, C. Liedtke, and A. S. Choo. 2008. "Six Sigma: Definition and Underlying Theory." *Journal of Operations Management* 26 (4): 536–554.

CHAPTER 12

Berkeley Wellness. 2010. "About the Wellness Letter." UC Berkeley School of Public Health. http://www.berkeleywellness.com. Accessed June 9, 2015.

Flegal, K. M., B. I. Graubard, D. F. Williamson, and M. H. Gail. 2005. "Excess Deaths Associated with Underweight, Overweight, and Obesity." *Journal of the American Medical Association* 293: 1861–1867.

Harvey, J. 2007. "Exercise a Process Improvement Approach for Your Own Wellness." ASQ *Quality Progress* 40 (11): 18–24.

Johnson, S. 2000. *Who Moved My Cheese?* New York: G. P. Putnam's Sons.

La Lopa, J. M., and R. F. Marecki. 2000. "Quality Management Hits the Road." ASQ *Quality Progress* 33 (4): 59–64.

Levine, J. 2002. "Nonexercise Activity Thermogenesis (NEAT): Environment and Biology." *Best Practice and Research: Clinical Endocrinology and Metabolism* 16 (4): 679–702.

Nutrition Action (Canadian edition), 32 (8): 6.

Pohlen, T. 1999. "Statistical Thinking: A Personal Application." In *53rd Annual Quality Congress Proceedings*, edited by ASQ, 230–36. Milwaukee, WI: American Society for Quality.

Tierney, J. 2005. "Fat and Happy." *New York Times*, April 23.

APPENDIX A

Mitra, A. 1998. *Fundamentals of Quality Control and Improvement*. Upper Saddle River, NJ: Prentice Hall.

Wheeler, D. J. 2000. *Understanding Variation*. Knoxville, TN: SPC Press.

Index

Note: Page numbers followed by *f* refer to figures; those followed by *t* refer to tables.

The Knowledge Center
www.asq.org/knowledge-center

Learn about quality. Apply it. Share it.

ASQ's online Knowledge Center is the place to:

- Stay on top of the latest in quality with Editor's Picks and Hot Topics.

- Search ASQ's collection of articles, books, tools, training, and more.

- Connect with ASQ staff for personalized help hunting down the knowledge you need, the networking opportunities that will keep your career and organization moving forward, and the publishing opportunities that are the best fit for you.

Use the Knowledge Center Search to quickly sort through hundreds of books, articles, and other software-related publications.

www.asq.org/knowledge-center

TRAINING   CERTIFICATION   CONFERENCES   MEMBERSHIP   **PUBLICATIONS**

Ask a Librarian

Did you know?

- The ASQ Quality Information Center contains a wealth of knowledge and information available to ASQ members and non-members

- A librarian is available to answer research requests using ASQ's ever-expanding library of relevant, credible quality resources, including journals, conference proceedings, case studies and Quality Press publications

- ASQ members receive free internal information searches and reduced rates for article purchases

- You can also contact the Quality Information Center to request permission to reuse or reprint ASQ copyrighted material, including journal articles and book excerpts

- For more information or to submit a question, visit **http://asq.org/knowledge-center/ ask-a-librarian-index**

Visit www.asq.org/qic for more information.

ASQ®
The Global Voice of Quality™

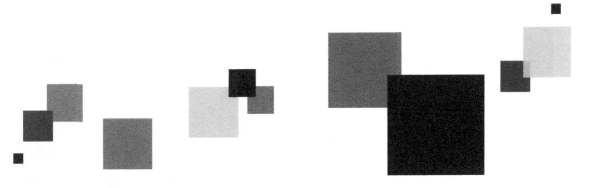

Belong to the Quality Community!

Established in 1946, ASQ is a global community of quality experts in all fields and industries. ASQ is dedicated to the promotion and advancement of quality tools, principles, and practices in the workplace and in the community.

The Society also serves as an advocate for quality. Its members have informed and advised the U.S. Congress, government agencies, state legislatures, and other groups and individuals worldwide on quality-related topics.

Vision

By making quality a global priority, an organizational imperative, and a personal ethic, ASQ becomes the community of choice for everyone who seeks quality technology, concepts, or tools to improve themselves and their world.

ASQ is...

- More than 90,000 individuals and 700 companies in more than 100 countries

- The world's largest organization dedicated to promoting quality

- A community of professionals striving to bring quality to their work and their lives

- The administrator of the Malcolm Baldrige National Quality Award

- A supporter of quality in all sectors including manufacturing, service, healthcare, government, and education

- YOU

Visit www.asq.org for more information.

TRAINING   CERTIFICATION   CONFERENCES   MEMBERSHIP   **PUBLICATIONS**

ASQ Membership

Research shows that people who join associations experience increased job satisfaction, earn more, and are generally happier*. ASQ membership can help you achieve this while providing the tools you need to be successful in your industry and to distinguish yourself from your competition. So why wouldn't you want to be a part of ASQ?

Networking

Have the opportunity to meet, communicate, and collaborate with your peers within the quality community through conferences and local ASQ section meetings, ASQ forums or divisions, ASQ Communities of Quality discussion boards, and more.

Professional Development

Access a wide variety of professional development tools such as books, training, and certifications at a discounted price. Also, ASQ certifications and the ASQ Career Center help enhance your quality knowledge and take your career to the next level.

Solutions

Find answers to all your quality problems, big and small, with ASQ's Knowledge Center, mentoring program, various e-newsletters, *Quality Progress* magazine, and industry-specific products.

Access to Information

Learn classic and current quality principles and theories in ASQ's Quality Information Center (QIC), *ASQ Weekly* e-newsletter, and product offerings.

Advocacy Programs

ASQ helps create a better community, government, and world through initiatives that include social responsibility, Washington advocacy, and Community Good Works.

Visit www.asq.org/membership for more information on ASQ membership.

*2008, The William E. Smith Institute for Association Research

TRAINING   CERTIFICATION   CONFERENCES   **MEMBERSHIP**   **PUBLICATIONS**   The Global Voice of Quality™